Auguste Sabatier, George Gillanders Findlay

The Apostle Paul

A Sketch of the Development of His Doctrine

Auguste Sabatier, George Gillanders Findlay

The Apostle Paul
A Sketch of the Development of His Doctrine

ISBN/EAN: 9783337014186

Printed in Europe, USA, Canada, Australia, Japan

Cover: Foto ©Lupo / pixelio.de

More available books at **www.hansebooks.com**

THE APOSTLE PAUL:

A Sketch of the Development of his Doctrine.

BY

A. SABATIER,

Professor in the Faculty of Protestant Theology in Paris.

TRANSLATED FROM THE FRENCH.

EDITED, WITH AN ADDITIONAL ESSAY ON THE PASTORAL EPISTLES, BY

GEORGE G. FINDLAY, B.A.,

Author of "Galatians" in "The Expositor's Bible."

New York:
JAMES POTT & CO.,
14 & 16, ASTOR PLACE.
1891.

AUTHOR'S PREFACE TO THE ENGLISH EDITION.

TRANSLATION into another tongue is for any book an honourable and a perilous experience. The author of *L'apôtre Paul* is fully conscious both of the honour and the peril. The success of a work which is in any degree original depends not only upon its intrinsic merit, but also, to a great extent, upon a certain instinctive harmony already established between the mind of the author and the requirements of the public to which he addresses himself. No plant is rooted in its native soil by finer and more numerous fibres than is a literary work in the country and society in which it was produced. It is with some anxiety that I inquire whether *L'apôtre Paul*, under the new circumstances in which it is about to appear, will again meet with the inner correspondence and the moral and spiritual sympathy necessary to make it intelligible and to justify its publication.

There are two things, however, which re-assure me. The first is the distinguished patronage under which my work is presented to English readers, the care, learning and judgment of those who are responsible for the translation of my work. My further ground of confidence is derived from the hero of the book himself and the universal interest which he inspires. Where should he be studied, loved and venerated, if not in England? Are not English Christians, in a very special sense, his spiritual children? Do they not owe to him the character of their religion, the form of their doctrine, even their principles of religious liberty and civil right? Is not Anglo-Saxon society his work? Does not his spirit pervade the thousand ramifications of English civilization, extending from individual conduct to the highest scientific activity, from domestic life to the political debates of Parliament? Who is there, we may ask, not among theologians only, but amongst all earnest and cultured men, who is not interested in every attempt made to understand the apostle better, and to explore the inner workings of his mind?

Paul as a missionary and shepherd of souls is great indeed. There is nothing in all antiquity to compare with the record of his travels and his triumphs. Feeble in body, living by his toil like a working-man, this weaver of Tarsus enters the vast world of Paganism, another Alexander, to conquer the faith and the reason of mankind. Merely to form such a resolution was heroic. Darkness covered the earth; the peoples, to use the language of the prophet, were sitting in the valley of the shadow of death. Paul entered, alone at first, into these depths of darkness, with the Gospel torch in his hand ; and wherever he went he left in his track from Damascus to Rome a succession of young expanding Churches, the radiant centres of a new life, the fruitful germs of modern society forming already in the midst of the old world. In all this, I repeat, there is something truly heroic.

There is something greater still in the mind that inspired this mighty work, and of which, in truth, the work itself is only the exhibition and luminous transcription in the visible order of things. Not only did Paul conquer the pagan world for Jesus Christ ; he accomplished a task no less necessary, and perhaps even more difficult, in emancipating at the same time infant Christianity from Judaism, under whose guardianship it was in danger of being stifled. Besides removing the centre of gravity of the new Church, by the advance of his mission, from Jerusalem to Antioch, from Antioch to Ephesus, and from Ephesus to Rome, he also succeeded in disengaging from the swaddling bands of Judaism the spiritual and moral principles which constitute Christianity a progressive and universal religion.

Not that Paul can in any sense claim to be the founder of Christianity, or be compared to Jesus. The apostle gloried, and rightly, in being the servant, and not the master. It is as a servant that he is great. There was nothing creative in Paul's genius. The first impulse came from Jesus. Jesus it is who in our religious life has substituted filial relationship with the Father by means of the Holy Spirit for the legal relationship based upon the Mosaic law and tradition. Jesus established the new covenant; and in doing this planted His cross, if we may so say, between ancient Judaism and the Gospel, in a way that rendered void all attempts at reconciliation. On the other hand, it is equally certain that His first disciples at Jerusalem endeavoured to repair this breach. They wished to keep the new wine in the old bottles. Next to Stephen, the first martyr, it was Paul who broke the Judaistic spell. To his thinking, the Christian principle only took the place of the Jewish principle by destroying it. His conversion was, in effect, the negation of the power of the law as a means of salvation; and his theology, centring entirely in the antithesis of faith and works, law and grace, the old things and the new, the time of bondage and the time of freedom, was but the expression in argument and theory of the moral and religious experiences which began in his conversion. Thus the external revolution had its spring in a psychological regeneration; and it is important to grasp firmly this primary fact, if we would not mistake the meaning of the whole drama.

In reading the epistles of the great apostle, nothing strikes the attentive observer more than this psychological connexion between his doctrinal creed and his inward life. The first is the beautiful fruitage of the second. Of no other doctrine can it be so truly said, that it was lived before it was taught. It may even be affirmed that our minds do not properly apprehend it, unless we have undergone for ourselves, in some measure, the inward experience it implies. An eminent professor of history of the Sorbonne at Paris related one day that he had remained for years without in the least understanding Paul's theology, and that its meaning was made clear to him by a Christian shoemaker at Lyons. The moral crisis of conversion is, indeed, the first and best initiation into the truths of Paulinism.

But if the doctrine of the apostle Paul is always the outgrowth of his experience, it is easy to infer that it must have had a history,—that, in other words, it was developed in the order of these experiences. It is equally plain that from this historical standpoint alone shall we be able to understand it fully, and to account for the various forms it has assumed at different times and under varying circumstances. To regard it in any other way would be inevitably to pervert its character, by making it a system of abstract philosophy, and by separating it from the parent stem whence it still derives its life and truth. This has been done, it seems to me, alike by the orthodoxy of the past and by the rationalistic criticism of the Tübingen School. They both deny the existence of progress and development in Paul's doctrine; they sever the delicate nerves, of which we have spoken, that connected his spiritual thought and his spiritual life.

The former theory assumes that he received his doctrinal system from heaven complete in its dialectical organization and its exegetical demonstrations —a thing absolutely inconceivable, since reasoning always implies effort on the part of the productive intelligence. The second school treats Paul as though, after his conversion, he had lived in solitude like a philosopher, creating by means of speculation and logic the entire doctrinal system that he was afterwards to preach, to expound, and defend before the world. In both instances there is the assumption that his mental and doctrinal development was complete from the outset, and was neither disturbed nor stimulated by new conflicts as they arose,—by the arguments of opponents, and by the experiences of his busy and exciting life.

This is humanly impossible; and it is historically untrue. It must be clearly understood that Paul was no philosopher of the schools. The purpose or wish to construct *a system*, properly so called, was wholly foreign to his mind. He was a missionary, who brought everything to bear upon his work. He learned by teaching. In every crisis of his life he looked for guidance from God. The solution of difficult questions he sought in prayer; and the answer came sometimes like a flash of light, sometimes as the result of profound meditation, but was always regarded by him as a Divine inspiration. He studied events; he reflected upon past experiences; he profited by his travels and his reading. Everything, in short, furnished him with food for thought, and with opportunities for discovering the practical or theoretical issues of the faith that he incessantly preached. Thus his thinking always kept pace with his outward activities; and till the end there was a constant reaction of the one upon the other. Indisputable proofs of this will be found, we believe, in the present work.

It is on this account that we have combined the exposition of Paul's doctrine with the history of his life. The exegesis of the apostle's writings must always start from the latter, and be guided by it. The only means of understanding them, whether as a whole or in detail, is to explain them by the historical circumstances under which they originated. Thus restored to their place in history, they are no longer treatises in abstract theology; they are in reality acts of Paul's apostolic life, weapons of warfare or means of instruction, and living manifestations from time to time of the apostle's heart and will, as well as of his genius. So they acquire for us, together with a singular dramatic interest, a truth and life which are absolutely new.

The historical standpoint has another advantage, and renders us a further and equally important service. It enables us to solve without prejudice or violence the important problem which modern criticism has raised with regard to the authenticity of Paul's epistles. The critics, as is well known, often argue, from the literary or dogmatic differences they have established amongst them, the impossibility of their being the work of one and the same author. They take their stand upon the group known as that of *the great epistles*—Galatians, Corinthians, and Romans; and peremptorily set aside all those which are not exactly of the same type. As if amid changing circumstances Paul's manner of writing were not bound to undergo like changes! As if, to begin with, the epistle to the Romans were not very different from the epistle to the Galatians! It has been forgotten that these four letters all belong to a period of scarcely three years' duration, from 55 to 58 A.D. at latest, and that the apostle's career lasted for nearly thirty years. What a long space of time elapsed, both before and after those momentous years spent at Ephesus and Corinth! How can we infer with any certainty from the four letters of Paul then written what the nature may have been of those he wrote at other periods, relating to other questions? Who would maintain that the apostle, when travelling along with Silvanus and founding the Macedonian or Corinthian Churches, wrote in the same strain to these young communities as subsequently to the Christians of Galatia, at the most exciting stage of his controversy with his Judaizing opponents? Furthermore, is it probable that, after three or four years' imprisonment, he would indite a letter to his beloved Philippians precisely like those he had formerly written from Ephesus to Corinth, or from Corinth to Rome?

The historical doubts accumulated by the criticism of Ferdinand C. Baur and his disciples find their natural answer in the supposition of historical development in the Pauline system. This assumption does

PREFACE. xiii

not ignore, on the contrary it explains, the differences which have been pointed out between the various epistles; nor is it in the least obliged to strain the historical exegesis for the purpose of obtaining an artificial unity and resemblance. By accepting the idea of progress, it makes room for the variations of thought and expression which exist. We perceive, for instance, that in the epistles to the Colossians, Ephesians, and Philippians, the apostle in his moral teaching has happily attained larger views of social and family duties We observe in the same way that from the time of the second letter to the Corinthians, while still anticipating the glorious and speedy coming of Christ, Paul no longer hopes to see it in his lifetime; already, we find, the foreboding of martyrdom shadows his spirit, and has rendered the visible triumph and glory of Christ a prospect more remote. There is the same development in his Christology. But none of these distinctions really affect the authenticity of the letters, so soon as we discover the chain which links them together, and can trace in them a natural and normal development, continuous from point to point.

This is the definite task that the author of this volume has endeavoured to accomplish. How far he has succeeded in reducing to a progressive series the elements previously set in contrast as mutually exclusive, and in supplying their natural explanation, it is not for him, but for his readers impartially to decide. In writing this book, he has striven to open out a path hitherto untrodden in Pauline studies. Others may travel farther along it, and with surer foot; in this he will be the first to rejoice. In theological science as in practical life he sees servants only, working not for themselves but for truth and for the kingdom of God. And in offering his work to those who may read, or even criticize it, he feels that he cannot say to them anything better than that which Paul said to the Corinthians respecting their preachers: πάντα ὑμῶν ἐστίν, εἴτε Παῦλος, εἴτε Ἀπολλώς, εἴτε Κηφᾶς, εἴτε κόσμος, εἴτε ζωή, εἴτε θάνατος, εἴτε ἐνεστῶτα, εἴτε μέλλοντα· πάντα ὑμῶν, ὑμεῖς δὲ Χριστοῦ, Χριστὸς δὲ Θεοῦ (1 Cor. iii. 22, 23).

AUGUSTE SABATIER.

⁂ Besides the Appendix, the English editor has thought fit to insert brief foot-notes, inclosed in square brackets [thus], on some points of controversy. M. Sabatier commands, in the greater part of his exposition, an assent so warm and admiring, that it is with reluctance one records, here and there, a dissent equally decided. He has applied the scientific method of modern historical inquiry to the life and work of the apostle Paul with great skill and penetration, and with a singular charm of treatment, of which the reader will be sensible, even through the medium, necessarily imperfect, of translation. Possibly, through the bias natural to a scholar so versed in historical and psychological criticism, he has leaned too heavily against the older "ecclesiastical theology."

It is unnecessary to bespeak for this gifted representative of French Protestant scholarship a friendly reception upon English soil. We rejoice to claim M. Sabatier, in the words he so aptly quotes from the apostle, amongst the *all things* that are *ours*.

G. G. F.

TABLE OF CONTENTS.

	PAGE
PREFACE	v–xvi
INTRODUCTION	1

Chronology of conversion, epistles &c. 21

BOOK I.

THE SOURCES OF PAUL'S SYSTEM OF THOUGHT . 23–94
   I. The First Christian Community at Jerusalem.—
      Christianity and Judaism 25
  II. Stephen the Precursor of Paul.—Collision between
      the Jewish and the Christian Principle . . 39
 III. Paul's Conversion. — Triumph of the Christian
      over the Jewish Principle 47
 IV. The Genesis of Paul's Gospel 71

BOOK II.

FIRST PERIOD, OR PERIOD OF MISSIONARY ACTIVITY 95–134
   I. The Missionary Discourses in the Acts.—The two
      Epistles to the Thessalonians 98
  II. Primitive Paulinism 112
 III. First Conflicts with the Judaizing Christians.—The
      Time of Crisis and Transition 124

BOOK III.

SECOND PERIOD; OR, THE PERIOD OF THE GREAT
 CONFLICTS 135–211
 I. The Epistle to the Galatians 137
 II. The First Epistle to the Corinthians . . . 156
 III. The Second Epistle to the Corinthians . . . 165
 IV. The Epistle to the Romans 185

BOOK IV.

THIRD PERIOD: THE PAULINISM OF LATER TIMES 213–272
 I. The Address at Miletus.—Appearance of the
  Gnostic Asceticism.—New Evolution in Paul's
  Theological Doctrine 214
 II. The Epistles to Philemon, to the Colossians, and
  to the Ephesians 225
 III. The Epistle to the Philippians 250
 IV. The Three Pastoral Epistles 263

BOOK V.

ORGANIC FORM OF PAUL'S THEOLOGICAL SYSTEM 273–340
 I. The Person of Christ, the Principle of the Christian
  Consciousness 282
 II. The Christian Principle in the Sphere of Psychology
  (Anthropology) 286
 III. The Christian Principle in the Sphere of Society
  and History (The Religious Philosophy of
  History) 307
 IV. The Christian Principle in the Sphere of Meta-
  physics (Theology) 321

ADDITIONAL ESSAY ON THE EPISTLES TO TIMOTHY AND TITUS.

	PAGE
Introduction	. 343
I. The Pastoral Epistles in Modern Criticism	. 344
II. The Vocabulary and Style	. 353
III. The Personal Data	. 362
IV. The Doctrinal Characteristics	. 374
V. The Church System of the Pastorals	. 390

INTRODUCTION.

IT is the tendency of all tradition, and of religious tradition more especially, to resolve into type and symbol the persons of those whom it has once enshrined. It is thus that the figures of Christ's first apostles have generally assumed a sacredness and immutability resembling that of their stone statues as we see them ranged in frigid, symmetrical order on the front of our cathedrals. And yet these daring missionaries of the Christian faith were real men, men of their own race and age, each bringing his peculiar temperament and genius to bear upon the work that it had fallen to their lot to accomplish. It should be the aim of history to discover this original and distinctive physiognomy beneath legend and dogma, the individual life in the traditional type, and, in short, the man in the apostle. And such has been the end, whether consciously or unconsciously pursued, of all the work of Biblical criticism and exegesis accomplished during the last fifty years.

Unfortunately, this kind of historical resurrection is impossible for the majority of the apostles, whose work was, as it were, anonymous, and done in common, leaving no personal trace beyond a bare name, and that often uncertain and surrounded by legend. But with the thirteenth and latest apostle, Paul of

Tarsus, the missionary to the Gentiles, the case is very different. Not only are we in undoubted possession of several of his authentic writings, but his genius and passion have inspired them with an intensity of life which renders them the free and spontaneous revelation of his soul,—one of the most powerful and original that ever came into being. True, the beginning and end of his life are involved in obscurity; but thanks to his epistles to the Thessalonians, Corinthians, Galatians, Romans, and Philippians on the one hand, and the detailed narrative of the second part of Acts on the other, we have a vivid light thrown upon a period of more than twelve years in the very midst of the apostle's career, in which his personality stands out with wonderful distinctness.

Starting from this luminous centre, we are enabled, by means of historical and psychological induction, to trace the main tenor of his life with a fair amount of certainty. For this purpose, dates and places and external things are of minor importance. It has been our aim to write not a general biography of Paul, but a biography of his mind, and the history of his thought.

I. Progressive Character of Paulinism.

The law of development is so inseparable from the idea of life that we always assume its action, even when we cannot trace it. In the life of Paul it is strikingly obvious. The more we study his writings and theology, the more we feel that it was impossible for a mind so ardent and so laborious speedily to reach its limits and to rest in its final conclusions, and that a system of thought so richly and solidly constructed could not be completed at a stroke. The agency of dialectics is equally apparent with that of inspiration. At the same time, we must not think of the apostle as a professed theologian, absorbed in elaborating a speculative system. He was a missionary and a preacher. His mind followed the guidance of circumstances, equally with abstract logic; it developed organically and spontaneously, in response to the demand for new solutions or deductions made upon it by the course of events. His great soul knew no repose; the thinker kept pace with the missionary; mind and will were at equal tension, and within and without were displayed the same ardour and the same energy. The Gospel that he preached to the heathen had to be freed from Judaism, and justified to the Christian understanding by experience and by Old Testament exegesis. The man who spread the name of Jesus from the borders of Palestine to the confines of the West is the same who wrote the epistles to the Romans and Colossians; and the distance between Jerusalem and Rome is but a type of that much longer road the Gospel traversed from the Sermon on the Mount to the Christianity of these great epistles.

The course of development pursued by the apostle's doctrine lies between these two limits. Taking its departure from the first apostolic preaching, it reaches its goal in the theological system to which we have just referred. The internal progress of his thought corresponds exactly with the external progress of his mission; and both were alike stormy and full of conflict. This history has more than a merely personal and psychological interest; it is virtually the history of the revolution which first emancipated Christianity and constituted it an independent religion, beyond the sacred inclosure of the Jewish nation. This revolution, as we know, had various phases. Paul did not in his early days see the full bearing of the liberal and individualistic principle that he was introducing into the traditional faith, nor all the consequences of the work he was doing in the heathen world. They only revealed themselves to his understanding progressively. He walked bravely, but only by one step at a time, in the unknown path at the beginning of which, in spite of himself, the very special character of his conversion had placed him from the outset.

We insist on this point, because it is ignored alike by those whose theory of a mechanical and wholesale theopneustia leaves no room for the workings of the apostle's own mind, and by those who make him out to have been a sort of speculative genius, creating *à priori* and in solitude the system that he was afterwards to preach and defend. Take as an illustration one of the great declarations of Paul: his doctrine of the abolition of the *Mosaic law* as a system and a means of salvation. It is evident that he reached this position by degrees. At first he was able to content himself with having obtained at the famous conference at Jerusalem (Gal. ii.; Acts xv.) a dispensation from circumcision for Christians of heathen origin. A few years later this had ceased to satisfy him. His mind being of an essentially dialectic cast, he rose from the concrete fact to the absolute principle. He had not set out by formulating the latter in its abstract generality, but having found from experience that the law was of no avail in the salvation of the Gentiles, it seemed to him no longer essential to the Jews; and he ended by formulating in his epistle to the Romans his profound and original theory as to its scope: *viz.* that its purpose was not to save sinners, but on the contrary to multiply sin, in order to deliver up the guilty conscience more entirely to the grace of God. Examine this theory more closely; you will soon see traces of the violent conflicts out of which it was evolved. It is not a primitive belief, but a final conclusion—the sum of a long experience, and the end of a fierce controversy.

We might further quote passages from the epistle to the Galatians (Gal. i. 10; v. 11) which seem to imply changes in Paul's conduct with respect to circumcision and the Christians of Palestine. But what is the use of putting forward uncertain inferences, when we have elsewhere a striking proof of the very clear consciousness the apostle had of the successive modifications and constant progress of his Christian views? How many times he laments the incapacity of his efforts to grasp all the riches of the Gospel! "When I was a child," he writes to the Corinthians, "I spoke as a child, I felt as a child, I reasoned as a child (comp. 1 Cor. iii. 1); now that I am become a man (comp. 1 Cor. xvi. 13), I have put away childish thoughts." Reference is here made, as the parallel passages show, to the childhood and maturity of the Christian life. Can it be doubted that the mind of the man who wrote these words obeyed the natural laws of all human knowledge, and that there were elementary conceptions which it had already left behind? In fact, this idea of progress is inherent in Paul's theology, and essential to it. Even his present knowledge, which he regards as that of mature years, does not really satisfy him. In the recollection of progress achieved he only sees a cause and pledge of further progress. The distance separating him from childhood is but an image to him of that which still separates him from the ultimate goal. At no period did his conceptions appear to him either complete or final. "Now we see as in a dim mirror; one day we shall see face to face. My knowledge is but imperfect and partial; one day I shall know as I have been known" (1 Cor. xiii. 11 ff.).

The older the apostle grew, the more this natural feeling strengthened in him. This is how he wrote to the Philippians a few years before his death: "I do not imagine that I have reached the goal, nor obtained perfection; but I am pursuing it. This one thing I do: forgetting the things which are behind me, I strenuously press toward those which are before. I see the goal, and march on to it" (Phil. iii. 12–16). The sequel clearly shows that the progress in question has as least as much reference to his mental development as to his moral perfection. "If you think differently from me in anything," he adds, "God shall make known the truth to you. Meantime, let us walk in unity in the common knowledge which we have already attained."

It would have been astonishing if an idea so natural in itself, and so clearly indicated in the text, had not been pointed out by modern criticism. But we have no such omission to complain of. As soon, in fact, as Paul's life and writings began to be studied from an historical point of view, the idea of a progressive development in his views compelled attention to itself. Usteri clearly suggested the idea, in a work of which the third edition appeared as early as 1831;[1] but at the same time he abandoned it as incapable of de-

---

[1] *Entwickelung des Paulinischen Lehrbegriffes*, p. 7.

monstration, because the historical connexion of the authentic letters was still undefined, and their chronology unsettled, while the great critical epochs of the apostle's life were wholly unrecognised.

The work of reconstruction could not be resumed with any chance of success, until the task of patient and minute analysis had been first performed. The honour of this achievement belongs to Baur.[1] Thanks to his critical studies, abundant light has been thrown upon Paul's epistles; their order of sequence has been recovered, their distinctive features clearly defined, the historical events that occasioned them perfectly established, and their differences marked out not less plainly than their resemblances. In short, the first and essential conditions for tracing out the apostle's mental history were fulfilled.

It is true that Baur's refusal to recognise as authentic anything but the doctrinal type evolved from the great central epistles (Galatians, Corinthians, and Romans) prevented him from completing this task himself. But since then the epistles to the Thessalonians, to Philemon, and to the Philippians have asserted their place by the side of these, not to mention others whose authenticity is now generally admitted, even by the severest critics. Yet the dogmatic differences pointed out by Baur exist all the same. And thus, while maintaining the Pauline origin of these other writings, and recognising at the same time their distinct doctrinal types, modern criticism is shut up more and more to a contradiction, of which the only and inevitable solution is found in the conception of

---

[1] *Paulus der Apostel Jesu Christi*, 2nd ed., 1866 [Eng. trans., 1873].

a progressive development in the apostle's system of thought. This solution was still much disputed when the first edition of this book appeared [1870]. But at the present date, though subject to some modification in detail, it has triumphed completely.

On reviewing, as a whole, those epistles of Paul which have been preserved to us, we see that they fall naturally into three groups: (1) The epistles to the Thessalonians, which appear to be simply an echo of his missionary preaching. (2) The great epistles to the Galatians, Corinthians, and Romans, the outcome of his conflicts with the Judaizers. (3) The epistles of the Captivity. Each of these groups contains a homogeneous and clearly defined type of doctrine equally characteristic in its turn of thought and in the nature of its polemics. It is no less easy to perceive that these three types have a logical sequence, and correspond exactly with the great periods of the apostle's life: the first dominated by his missionary activities and interests; the second by his fierce struggle against Judaism; the third by the appearance of the Gnostic asceticism.

Will the establishment of these three periods enable us, then, to understand how the doctrine of Paul, by virtue of its inner principle and under the outward pressure of events, developed from its elementary into its higher form? And will this conception of a natural and necessary development solve the problems to which the historical exegesis of his epistles has given rise? That is the whole question.

Our answer lies in the reconstruction that we have attempted in this volume, and it will be enough here to explain its historical basis and mode of procedure.

We find our starting-point in the middle group of Paul's writings—the four great epistles to the Galatians, Corinthians, and Romans, which are closely consecutive and intimately related to each other. The system of Paul, eminently dialectic, is here developed in its strong antithesis to the Judaistic tendency. Here, in the midst of the apostle's career, it presents itself in a phase in the highest degree characteristic and indisputably genuine. But however important and glorious, this stage of Paul's doctrine is not the only one, a fact to be carefully borne in mind. These letters written one after another from Ephesus, Macedonia, and Corinth during Paul's last missionary journey, belong only to one period, and that the shortest, of his life, to an interval of three or four years in a career which lasted for nearly thirty. Must we forego all knowledge—all conjecture even—as to the twenty years which preceded, or the six which followed it?

Nay, indeed: we are bold to affirm that Paul the missionary must have thought and spoken differently from the dialectician of these great letters. How could they have been understood, unless those who received them had had previous preparation? On examining them more nearly, we can plainly see that Paul's dialectic expression of thought is due to an external fact, to his conflict with Judaism. The argument of the apostle cannot be understood apart from that of his opponents. In other words, we have here an antithesis, the first member of which is determined and conditioned by the second. We may safely affirm that before the outbreak of Judaistic opposition the teaching of Paul could not possibly have taken the form and development which this opposition alone could give.

Now, we are well informed of the origin and date of this conflict. It could not have arisen before the success of the great missions to the heathen, because their success was the cause of it. Besides, we have on this point the express declaration of the apostle himself in his epistle to the Galatians (chap. i. 18-24). He went, he tells us, three years after his conversion to visit and confer with Peter at Jerusalem. From thence he went to Syria and Cilicia, and the Churches of Judæa rejoiced and gave thanks for his ministry in those regions. The controversy, therefore, did not then exist. It only broke out fourteen years later (Gal. ii. 1), when the Pharisaic Christians came to Antioch and tried to force circumcision upon the heathen converts. Here then is an earlier and prolonged period, during which the doctrine of Paul, developing under other conditions and amid other conflicts, must inevitably have taken a simpler, a more practical and general form. Can we discover the moment at which the crisis that transformed it came about?

At the conference of Jerusalem (Gal. ii.; Acts xv.) new and weighty questions presented themselves to Paul's mind; but they were not at once solved. He contented himself, as we have said already, with having secured for the heathen a dispensation from circumcision. The epistles to the Thessalonians, written a little later, are still without any sign of contention with Judaizers. Evidently the apostle has left Jerusalem and set out on his second missionary journey fully satisfied with his victory, and without any anxiety as to the future. The precise moment of the crisis must therefore have occurred between the epistles to the Thessalonians and the epistle to the

Galatians. What happened in this interval? *The violent dispute between Peter and Paul at Antioch* (Gal. ii. 11-21),[1] and all that the recital of it reveals to us: the arrival of messengers from James in the Gentile Christian community, and the counter-mission organized by the Judaizers to rectify the work of Paul. It was this new situation, suddenly presenting itself to the apostle on his return from his second missionary journey, which by compelling him to enter the contest, led him to formulate in all its rigour his principle of the abrogation of the law (Gal. ii. 16).

While admitting a development in Paul's doctrine during this long and obscure primitive period, some may perhaps consider that it ceased with the epistle to the Galatians. Now, they would say, it has come to realize its essential principle; it cannot make further progress. No doubt this epistle marks an epoch in the apostle's life; but it is a point of departure, rather than a halting place; it inaugurates a new era. Far from being at rest, the mind of Paul was never more active and eager, never more fertile than during this stormy period. Involved from the first in the glaring antithesis of law and faith, his mind strives to get beyond and above it to a loftier point of view, from which he may bring about its *synthesis, by the subordination of the one principle to the other.*

In the epistles to the Corinthians his view had already expanded beyond these limits, and in the epistle to the Romans it is transformed; larger pro-

---

[1] We place this event not at the return of Paul to Antioch after the conference at Jerusalem (Acts xv. 33), but at his return from his second missionary journey (Acts xviii. 23). Thus Neander, Wieseler, Renan, etc.

spects open before it. But there is no more reason for arresting his mental progress at Romans than at Galatians. New events and an altered situation lead to a new expansion of thought.

The last period of his life is of an entirely peculiar character, determined by certain leading facts. To begin with, Paul was in prison. This captivity, in snatching him from the duties and conflicts of his missionary work, afforded him leisure; it sentenced him to solitude and to meditation. Furthermore, there was springing up a tendency at once ascetic and speculative, a sort of early Gnosticism, which invaded Paul's Churches and threatened to ruin them. Naturally, and logically, these errors called forth a fresh development of the apostle's doctrine, more speculative and more theological than the other two. Thus it reached its highest level in the epistles of the Captivity.

The three periods of Paul's life which we have indicated, are as follows:

FIRST PERIOD.—*Primitive Paulinism:* From the conversion of Paul to the epistle to the Galatians. *Documents:* The missionary discourses in the Acts, and the epistles to the Thessalonians. This is the adolescence of the apostle's system of thought.

SECOND PERIOD.—*The Paulinism of the great epistles:* From the epistle to the Galatians to the imprisonment of Paul. *Documents:* the epistles to the Galatians, Corinthians, and Romans. This is the virile and heroic age of his mind.

THIRD PERIOD.—*Paulinism of later days:* From the beginning of his captivity until his death. *Documents:* the epistles to Philemon, Colossians, Ephesians, and Philippians; the parallel record of the Acts of the Apostles (Acts xx. to the end), especially the discourse at Miletus. This is the age of perfect and full maturity.

Such is the course and plan of this history. To these three essential divisions two more must be added: the first, in which the historical and psychological origin of Paul's theology will be set forth; and the last, a necessary conclusion to our history, in which we shall endeavour to explain his theological system in its definitive form, and to sketch its organism.

II. CHRONOLOGY.

Before commencing our narrative, it is important to fix as nearly as possible the chronology of the apostle's life.

Let us admit, to begin with, that the dates of his birth and death are completely lost to us. For us, his historical career ends at the year 63 or 64 A.D. The writer of the Acts leaves him in his prison at Rome two years after he had entered it. From that time we know nothing of him. Did he perish in the burning of the city (July, A.D. 64), or in the persecution which followed? Was he released? Did he go to Spain, as he intended? Did he come back to the East and return to Rome, to die on the same day as Peter in 67 or 68 A.D., according to Catholic tradition? On all these points we have nothing but idle conjecture or legends.

Nor are we any better informed as to the date of his birth. The only two indications of which we can avail ourselves, are the epithet $νεανίας$ applied to him by Luke (Acts vii. 58) at the time of Stephen's stoning, and that of $πρεσβύτης$ which he applies to himself in his epistle to Philemon, written about A.D. 60. These two expressions are very vague; and it is even necessary to strain them a good deal in order to make them agree. The latter and more authentic reference proves that in A.D. 60 Paul had at least passed his fiftieth year. Give him a few years more, and he is almost exactly contemporary with Jesus. This much must be admitted, if we are to give any credit to an indication from the *oratio encomiastica in principes apostolorum Petrum et Paulum*, wrongly ascribed to Chrysostom, but which is found in his works. We read there, in effect, that Paul died in his sixty-eighth year (67 or 68 A.D.), after having served the Lord for thirty-five years. This last figure is exaggerated; but at all events, Paul was born at Tarsus about the beginning of the Christian era.

What is of more importance is to fix the principal dates of his life. To this end we must first seek in his long career for a date, perfectly established, which may serve for our point of departure and a basis of all our calculations. It is not to be found till the close of his history. We may determine beyond dispute, almost to a year, the date of his departure to Rome from the prison at Cæsarea. We know that he was sent thither by Porcius Festus, a few months after the arrival of that governor in Palestine (Acts xxiv. 27). Now the arrival of Festus could not possibly have taken place earlier than 60, nor later than 62 A.D., because he was succeeded in the summer of 63 by Albinus. (Compare the following data: Tacitus, *Ann.* xiv. 65; Josephus, *Ant.* xx. 8. 9, 11; *Bell. Jud.* vi. 5. 3; *De vita* 3.) We can only hesitate therefore between the years 60 and 61. We prefer 60, because even with this date the mission of Festus would only have lasted two years; and one year seems too short a space for all the events narrated by Josephus.

INTRODUCTION.

From the narrative of the Acts we gather that Paul embarked for Rome in the autumn, and that Festus had entered upon office some months before, at the beginning of summer. The apostle had then been in prison for two full years; which fixes the beginning of his captivity at the Pentecost of 58 (or 59) A.D. (Acts xxi. 27–33). Looking backwards from this point, we can trace accurately the course of Paul's life. He had kept the Passover of this same year at Philippi in Macedonia (xx. 6), having arrived there from Corinth, where he had spent the three months of winter (57–8, or 58–9), and written his epistle to the Romans. He had therefore reached Corinth towards the end of 57 (or 8) A.D. How he was occupied during the previous year we know very certainly from his two letters to the Corinthians, the second of which was written in Macedonia in the autumn, and the first at Ephesus about the time of the previous Passover (1 Cor. xvi. 8; v. 7; 2 Cor. ii. 12, 13). The remarkable agreement, during this period of Paul's life, between the data given in his great epistles and those of the Acts gives to this latter record a peculiar authority, and shows that we are standing on firm historical ground.

From the address delivered by Paul at Miletus after the Passover of 58 (or 59) A.D., we learn that he had sojourned three years at Ephesus, or in the province of Asia, so that he must have arrived there in the spring of 55. He came thither from Antioch, where he had spent the winter of 54–55 recruiting after his second missionary journey, the occasion on which, according to all probability, he had his sharp dispute with Peter and Barnabas (Gal. ii. 11–15, and Acts xviii. 22, 23). Paul had then returned, as we have already said, from his great journey through Asia, Macedonia, and Achaia (Acts xvi.–xviii.) This journey cannot have occupied less than two years, or two years and a half, since the stay at Corinth alone consumed more than eighteen months (Acts xviii. 11). This obliges us to place the beginning of the journey in the spring of 52, and the conference at Jerusalem, from which Paul was then returning, in the winter of 51–52 A.D. (xv. 30 ; Gal. ii. 1).

All this chronology of the second half of Paul's life, derived partly from his own epistles and partly from the narrative in Acts given by an eye-witness in the first person, is, so to speak, forced upon us; for it will be readily admitted, however questionable some of the details of our calculation may be, that a period of seven years (51–58) is not too long to embrace all the events of his life and the results of his activity during this period, of which we have such exact and certain knowledge. There is one circumstance connected with Paul's life at Corinth, moreover, that affords us an approximate verification. The apostle on his arrival in that city met with a Jewish couple named Aquila and Priscilla, who had been expelled from Rome by a decree of the Emperor Claudius (Acts xviii. 1–3). If we knew the date of this edict, referred to elsewhere by Suetonius (*Vit. Claud.* 25) and Tacitus (*Ann.* xii. 52, 54), we should have the exact date of the sojourn of Paul at Corinth. From the allusions of the two Roman historians we can only conjecture that the measure belongs to the later years of the reign of Claudius. Orosius, who suggests the seventh year, is not to be relied upon. Now Claudius died in September, 54 A.D. Paul must therefore have reached Corinth, at any rate, before that year. If the edict was issued, as the best critics suppose, in 52, there is obviously a sufficient agreement between this result and that which we had previously reached by an entirely different method. We have yet another, and a more certain datum in the Achaian proconsulate of Gallio, brother of Seneca (Acts xviii. 12). From the life of this personage, which we can easily trace, we find that he did not obtain this appointment to Achaia till the end of Claudius' life (Tacitus, *Ann.* xv. 73 ; Dio Cass., lx. 35 ; Pliny, xxxi. 33, etc.).

It now remains to establish the chronology of the former half of Paul's apostolic career, as we have just determined that of the second. Here our starting point must of necessity be the date of the conference at Jerusalem, to which we have already referred— the winter of 51–52 A.D. It will be observed that it cannot be fixed later than 52, because of the date of Claudius' death, to which we have just alluded ; and this is the important point. Accordingly, the majority of chronologists are divided between the years 51 and 52 (Hug, Eichhorn, Anger, de Wette, etc.). This may content us. Paul has given an account of the conference in his epistle to the Galatians, and we do not think that the parallelism between Galatians ii. and Acts xv. can be seriously called in question. This being the case, we have from the pen of Paul himself all the materials for a precise chronology. We know that at the beginning of his epistle he defines in the clearest manner his relations with the Twelve, and the exact number of his visits to Jerusalem—two in all— up to that time, including the apostolic conference. In such an argument it is plain he could not possibly omit a single visit, for such omission would have laid him open to the charge of falsehood. We must therefore consider the journey mentioned in Acts xi. 30 as apocryphal,[1] it being positively excluded by the declaration of Paul himself (Gal. i. 22). It is plain that the first half of Acts is not of the same historical worth as the second, and that its statements must be tested by the evidence of the authentic epistles. Of this we have further proof. If Luke adds a journey of Paul to Jerusalem, he omits the journey to Arabia (Gal. i. 17). He has no precise idea of the time which elapsed between the conversion of Paul and his first visit to the apostles (Acts ix. 23: $\dot{\eta}\mu\acute{\epsilon}\rho\alpha\iota$ $\iota\kappa\alpha\nu\alpha\grave{\iota}$ = *three years*, according to Gal. i. 18). We cannot therefore depend upon him as before, and must not venture beyond the statement of the apostle himself.

Happily this account is as explicit as it is vigorous and concise. Paul relates that he paid his first visit to Peter and James at Jerusalem three years after his conversion (Gal. i. 18). He only spent fifteen days with them. Then he went to preach the Gospel in Syria and Cilicia. The Churches of Judæa had not even seen his face. It was not till fourteen years afterwards that he made his second journey to Jerusalem, on the occasion of the apostolic conference (Gal. ii. 1). Since this conference, as we have already pointed out, was held in 51–52 A.D., in order to ascertain

---

[[1] But Acts xi. 29, 30; xii. 25 say nothing which implies that on this occasion Paul met the chiefs of the Church at Jerusalem, or made himself "known by face to the Churches of Judæa." The gift was sent "to the elders"; and at a time of severe persecution (Acts xii. 1), therefore probably in a secret and expeditious way. For all that Luke says, Paul himself may not even have set foot in Jerusalem.]

exactly the date of his conversion, we must find out from what point he himself reckons these fourteen years. In our opinion, there is no room for doubt. The adverb πάλιν (Gal. ii. 1), showing that Paul was accounting for his visits to the Holy City; the preposition διὰ which he uses here (instead of μετὰ, which we find in i. 18), indicating the time during which he affirms that he had not set foot in Jerusalem, prove beyond a doubt that the *terminus a quo* of the number fourteen is his first journey, previously mentioned (Gal. i. 18), not the event of his conversion. To obtain the date of the latter, then, we must add the fourteen years spent in Syria and Cilicia to the three years previously spent in Arabia, or at Damascus. Paul, therefore, had been a Christian seventeen years when he came to attend the conference at Jerusalem in 51 or 52; and this carries back the date of his conversion to the year 35 A.D., at the latest.

The only objection that can be made to this date, which is not, we admit, the one generally received (this varies between the years 37 and 42), is that the murder of Stephen must then have occurred before 36 A.D.—that is, before the recall of Pilate. And this, it is argued, is improbable; for Pilate, if still in office, would not have allowed a murder which amounted on the part of the Jews to a usurpation of judicial power. But on what a thread hung Paul's life in the like circumstances (Acts xxi. 31)! The execution of Stephen, occurring in a popular riot, might have happened before the Romans were aware. And it is as easy to assume a temporary absence of Pilate, as a subsequent interregnum; in which latter case, moreover, the authority of Rome would not be left without a representative. The uncertain inference drawn from Luke's narrative could not, in any case, be maintained in face of Paul's definite statements; and we can only overthrow the date of 35 A.D. for his conversion by overthrowing that of 52 for the conference at Jerusalem. This latter once established, the remainder of the calculation is a matter of course.

The history of Damascus, as we find to our regret, is too obscure for us to avail ourselves of the allusion made by Paul in 2 Corinthians xi. 32. At the time of his conversion there was still in that city an ethnarch, representing Aretas the king. The Romans may very well have been able to leave the government of Damascus to a vassal until 36 A.D. But immediately after this time, and before the death of Tiberius, war broke out between king Aretas on the one side, and Herod Antipas and Rome on the other; so that it is impossible to see how the king of Arabia could have retained any later the authority and privileges hitherto allowed him in Damascus. This suggests a further indirect confirmation of 35 A.D. as the date of Paul's conversion, which we had arrived at by another calculation.

It only remains for us, returning to the close of the apostle's life, to put together the slender indications that we have of its date. He embarked for Rome in the autumn of 60 (or 61) A.D.; but was compelled by shipwreck to winter in the island of Malta, and only reached the Eternal City in the spring of 61 (62). Luke adds that he remained there as a prisoner for two years, living in a private house under the guard of a soldier; then his narrative breaks off abruptly, and we are confronted with the unknown (Acts xxviii. 30). Paul is supposed to have perished in the frightful persecution caused by the fire of Rome in July, 64 A.D. At the same time, we would point out that the two years of imprisonment mentioned by Luke at the end of his book, ending, according to our chronology, in the spring of 63—or, extending our calculation by a year, in the spring of 64—must in any case have come to an end before the events of the fire, and the persecution, which cannot have broken out until August or September. All that is certain is that he died a martyr at Rome, under Nero (Clemens Romanus: 1 *Epist. ad Corinth.* v.).

Paul's apostolic career, as known to us, lasted, therefore, twenty-nine or thirty years; and it falls into three distinct periods, which are summarized in the following chronological table:

First Period.—ESSENTIALLY MISSIONARY.

35 A.D. Conversion of Paul. Journey to Arabia.

38. First visit to Jerusalem.

38-49. Mission in Syria and Cilicia. Tarsus and Antioch.

50-51. First missionary journey. Cyprus, Pamphylia, and Galatia (Acts xiii., xiv.).

52. Conference at Jerusalem (Acts xv.; Gal. ii.).

52-55. Second missionary journey. *Epistles to the Thessalonians* (from Corinth).

Second Period.—THE GREAT CONFLICTS, AND THE GREAT EPISTLES.

54. Return to Antioch. Controversy with Peter (Gal. ii. 12–22).

55-57. Mission to Ephesus and Asia.

56. *Epistle to the Galatians.*

57, or 58 (Passover). *First Epistle to the Corinthians* (Ephesus).

57, or 58 (Autumn). *Second Epistle to the Corinthians* (Macedonia).

58 (Winter). *Epistle to the Romans.*

Third Period.—THE CAPTIVITY.

58, or 59 (Pentecost). Paul is arrested at Jerusalem.

58–60, or 59–61. Captivity at Cæsarea. *Epistles to Philemon, Colossians, and Ephesians.*

60, or 61 (Autumn). Departure for Rome.

61, or 62 (Spring). Arrival of Paul in Rome.

62–63. *Epistle to the Philippians.*

63, or 64. End of the narrative of the Acts of the Apostles.

NOTE.—*The Pastoral epistles* (so called) of necessity lie outside the known life of Paul. Their authenticity will be discussed afterwards.

BOOK I.

THE SOURCES OF PAUL'S SYSTEM OF THOUGHT.

THE sources of Paul's system of thought are to be discovered in these three facts: in the Pharisaism which he forsook, the Christian Church which he entered, and the conversion by which he passed from the one to the other.

The first of these facts to be considered is the existence of the Church. It is sometimes forgotten that a Christian community existed before Paul, hitherto its fierce persecutor, came to join its ranks. This conversion, while opening a new era in his life, was at the same time a bond of close connexion with primitive Christianity, and obliges us to look beyond Paul himself for the origin of his Christian belief.

Furthermore, his conversion marked a crisis in the development of the apostolic Church. However unexpected it may have been, this event, we must confess, was wonderfully opportune. At no other time could it have had the same import or the same consequences. We could not have understood its earlier occurrence, before the death of Stephen; nor later, when the missions to the heathen had been already set on foot. But happening just when it did, it seems to us the most weighty fact of this first age.

And it is so closely linked with the past which it crowns, and the future which it inaugurates, that to view it apart from its historical connexion is a thing impossible.

It is indeed in this connexion, and invested with this critical importance, that the conversion of Paul is presented to us in the Acts of the Apostles. If we study the course of this narrative with a little attention, we shall perceive in it three stages, constituting by their logical sequence an internal progress within the primitive Christian community, of which Paul's conversion is the goal and natural conclusion.

I. The first stage is represented by the first five chapters of the Acts. Judaism and Christianity are still closely united and blended in the creed of the first Christians. *Acts* i.-v.: *Union of the spirit of Christianity with Jewish tradition.*

II. The second stage is marked by the episode of Stephen. The conflict between the Jewish and Christian principles, hitherto latent, breaks out in the most violent manner in the speech and the death of the martyr. *Acts* vi., vii.: *Open struggle between the Jewish and Christian principles.*

III. The conversion of Paul is the third stage. The conflict between the two principles, undetermined by brute force, ends within the breast of Saul the Pharisee, by the radical negation of the one and the triumphant affirmation of the other. *Acts* ix.: *Triumph of the Christian over the Jewish principle.*

Such is the progressive course of Luke's narrative; and it is in this historic sequence, and under this light, that we must place and study the great event that made Saul the apostle to the Gentiles.

CHAPTER I.

THE FIRST CHRISTIAN COMMUNITY AT JERUSALEM.
—CHRISTIANITY AND JUDAISM.

THE first beginnings of the Christian Church are involved in obscurity. For the period that elapsed between the death of Jesus and the conversion of Saul, of which we do not even know the length, we have absolutely no information beyond that afforded by the much-disputed record given in the Acts of the Apostles.[1] But this obscure period lies

---

[1] We attach no value to the patristic, or heretical traditions of the second century. They would not, we think, have deserved even the honour of a critical discussion, if the results of Baur's researches had not invested them for a time with some appearance of credit. How is it possible to discuss with any seriousness the historical value of the narratives and descriptions of the Clementine Homilies,—that romance in which the dreams of the Gnostic are mingled with the fastidious scruples of the Pharisee? They are not popular traditions, but the work of fancy; and one cannot think the representation they give of Peter any more lifelike than that of the Apostle Paul. The famous portrait of James furnished by Hegesippus, and preserved for us by Eusebius, has been, it is true, much more insisted on : Οὗτος ἐκ κοιλίας τῆς μητρὸς αὐτοῦ ἅγιος ἦν· οἶνον καὶ σίκερα οὐκ ἔπιεν, οὐδὲ ἔμψυχον ἔφαγεν· ξυρὸν ἐπὶ τὴν κεφαλὴν αὐτοῦ οὐκ ἀνέβη· ἔλαιον οὐκ ἠλείψατο καὶ βαλανείῳ οὐκ ἐχρήσατο· τούτῳ μόνῳ ἐξῆν εἰς τὰ ἅγια εἰσιέναι· οὐδὲ γὰρ ἐρεοῦν

between two other points of history with which we are somewhat better acquainted. On one side is Paul's testimony, which throws light on the course of things previous to his conversion; on the other, from what we know of the life and teaching of Jesus we can infer, with a tolerable degree of certainty, the position of the disciples immediately after His departure. Thus two luminous rays from opposite points focus themselves on this obscure interval, and

---

ἐφόρει ἀλλὰ σίνδονας, καὶ μόνος εἰσήρχετο εἰς τὸν ναὸν, κ.τ.λ., *H. E.* ii. 23. What is there in this tradition or legend but a purely ideal portrait? Its elements are derived, not from popular tradition, but directly from the Old Testament. They are made up of the vows of the Nazarite, the customs of the Pharisees, or perhaps the Essenes, and the prerogatives of the High Priest: comp. Num. vi. 3, etc., and Lev: vi. 3, in the Septuagint. The writer did not himself believe that James had ever been High Priest, or worn a linen robe, or had sole right of entrance to the temple—a fact sufficiently proving that his intention was to draw an ideal portrait. And when, on the other hand, he says that James was sanctified from his mother's womb, and drank neither wine nor strong drink, and that no razor ever touched his head, he was evidently thinking of the birth of John the Baptist (Luke i. 15), or of Samson (Judges xiii. 4). Abstinence from meat, from ointment and the bath, was still a feature of Jewish sanctity, and distinguished the Jewish fast, in the days of Jesus (Matt. vi. 17). To the imagination of the second century, this ascetic and Levitical righteousness seemed the highest ideal of piety; and the writer therefore wished to represent the life of James as that of a Nazarite and perpetual priest. Since James was not High Priest, is it any more certain that he was an ascetic? The epistle which bears his name gives quite a different idea of him. Instead of commending legal sanctity, it rather opposes it (i. 27). In place of the prejudices of the Levite or Nazarite, he gives us reminiscences of the Sermon on the Mount. Moreover, the categorical statement of Paul (1 Cor. ix. 5) authorizes us to believe that James,

they seem to us to set it in a fairly vivid light. Let us first, therefore, gather the testimony of Paul, since this alone can furnish a safe starting point for our inquiry.

The grand controversy maintained by Paul against the Judaizers proves clearly enough the distinctly Jewish character of the primitive Christian community. It does not prove, however, that this community was a mere Jewish sect, hardly distinguished

---

like Peter, was married, which is hardly consistent with the account of Hegesippus.

Nor is James the only one who has been thus idealized. In the second century all the apostles were represented as priests, or ascetics. Thus Clement of Alexandria states that Matthew abstained from meat and lived only upon vegetables (*Pædag.* ii. 1). In the same way Polycrates, in his letter to Victor, bishop of Rome, depicts John with the attributes of the High Priest (ὃς ἐγενήθη ἱερεὺς τὸ πέταλον πεφορηκώς, *H. E.* iii. 31). Finally, about the same period, we find a legend arising which makes Jesus Himself a priest, descended from the tribe of Levi, as well as from that of Judah (*Testament of the Twelve Patriarchs*, Levi 2; Simeon 7). On the origin and specific character of these traditions, see Ritschl, *Die Entstehung der altkatholischen Kirche*, 2nd edition, p. 178. These traditions, while giving us very useful and accurate information about the spirit of the second century, teach us nothing whatever about the rise of the Church; and they are amongst the best proofs which can be adduced to show that the *Acts of the Apostles* was of earlier date than the period at which they originated.

In seeking to ascertain the ideas of the primitive Christians, we should be better warranted in making use of the epistle of James, the Apocalypse, or the Gospel of Matthew, which belong to Judæo-Christian Christianity. But this would bring us to the same result as that already obtained, only by a more uncertain route. The authors of these writings are profoundly Jewish; but no one can deny that they have got beyond Judaism, and that their creed already embraced the specific principle of the new religion.

from that of the Pharisees. On the contrary, Paul himself held, and conveys to us, a very different idea of it. The manner in which he regarded this society, both before and after his conversion, is a decisive proof that he discerned in it an essentially new element. To this his former hatred and his subsequent devotion alike testify.

Let us hear what he says of this Church: "You know," he writes to the Galatians, "how I lived in Judaism. I persecuted *the Church of God* beyond measure, and laid it waste; . . . being full of zeal for the traditions of our fathers" (Gal. i. 13, 14). It is remarkable, to begin with, that Paul never speaks of his past life without associating as cause and effect his zeal for Judaism and his hatred of the Christians: ἐδίωκον τὴν ἐκκλησίαν...ζηλωτὴς ὑπάρχων; comp. Philippians iii. 5, 6, κατὰ νόμον Φαρισαῖος, κατὰ ζῆλος διώκων τὴν ἐκκλησίαν. In the eyes of the jealous Pharisee, it was a merit to persecute this new enemy of the faith of his fathers. His observation, quickened by fanaticism, detected from the first under the Jewish exterior of the Church that which so many modern critics fail to recognise.

In the second place, Paul calls this primitive Christian community the Church of God, τὴν ἐκκλησίαν τοῦ Θεοῦ (Gal. i. 13, and 1 Cor. xv. 9); on another occasion, simply and *par excellence*, τὴν ἐκκλησίαν (Phil. iii. 6) [*the* Church]. He calls the first Christians, of whom he knew a great number, by the new name of ἀδελφοὶ (1 Cor. xv. 6) [the brethren]; or else "the saints," οἱ ἅγιοι (1 Cor. xvi. 1; Rom. xv. 31). He sets them before the Thessalonian Church as models, which he is glad to see them imitate. "You, brethren, became imitators *of the Churches of God which are in*

Judæa, in Christ Jesus: for you have suffered the same evils from your fellow citizens which they did from the Jews, who have killed the Lord Jesus, and persecuted us" (1 Thess. ii. 14, 15). The recollection of having persecuted the Church of God continued throughout Paul's life to be a cause of grief and humiliation to him. He laments for it, as if he had persecuted the Lord Himself. On this account he reckons himself last of the apostles, unworthy even to be called an apostle; he calls himself an abortion, the chief of sinners (1 Cor. xv. 8; 1 Tim. i. 13-15).

It is not the case then that there were *two* gospels, the gospel of the Twelve and the Pauline gospel, each the negation of the other. Paul found himself in fellowship with the primitive Church. His faith rested on the same foundation. The legitimate existence of two *apostleships*, one appointed for the evangelization of the Jew and the other for that of the Gentile, he did indeed admit; but never of two essentially different *gospels*. He acknowledged but one Gospel, which saved equally and in the same way both Jew and Gentile. "If any man preach another, let him be anathema" (Rom. i. 16; Gal. i. 7-9).

Here we are confronted with the passage in Galatians ii. 7-9: "When they saw that I had been intrusted with the gospel of the uncircumcision, as Peter with the gospel of the circumcision (He that wrought in Peter unto the apostleship of the circumcision, having wrought in me also for the evangelization of the Gentiles),—recognising, I say, the grace that has been committed to me, they gave me the right hand of fellowship." Here, it is said, we have the two gospels clearly defined and contrasted with each other: εὐαγγέλιον τῆς ἀκροβυστίας, εὐαγγέλιον τῆς περιτομῆς. But who does not see that by these two genitives Paul meant to indicate, not the dogmatic content, but *the twofold destination* of the Gospel? Besides, these words are clearly explained in the succeeding verse, where the equivalent terms are substituted: τῆς περιτομῆς = εἰς ἀποστολὴν τῆς περιτομῆς; τῆς ἀκροβυστίας = εἰς τὰ ἔθνη. And, what is more, the apostle ascribes these two apostleships and the abundant fruit they bore to one and the same act of God: ὁ γὰρ ἐνεργήσας Πέτρῳ . . . κἀμοί. If two hostile and contradictory gospels are in question, it must be admitted that Paul attributes them equally to God as their supreme Author—a crying absurdity! We have here not a dogmatic definition, but an ethnographical delimitation of two missionary fields. The apostles were able, therefore, without any hypocrisy to give to each other the right hand of fellowship; they felt themselves to be standing on a common basis, which was broad enough to support them all.

What was this common foundation, this identical content of the twofold preaching, which, belonging equally to both fields of labour, for that very reason may be regarded as the primitive Gospel? Paul has stated it for us in the opening verses of the fifteenth chapter of his first epistle to the Corinthians. There he sums up the Gospel that he had preached at Corinth. "I remind you," he says, "of the gospel which I announced unto you, that which also I received, wherein ye abide firmly, by which ye are saved. . . . Among the chief things (ἐν πρώτοις), I taught you that Christ died for our sins, according to the Scriptures; that He was buried; and that He was raised on the third day, according to the Scriptures." Then, after referring to the different appearances of the risen Jesus, he adds: "*This is what we preach, whether it be I or they* (the Twelve); *and this is what you believed.*" These last words apply not only to the appearances recorded above, but to the entire summary of the apostle's preaching as just given.

Another passage in the same epistle, no less interesting to study, shows us how the apostle estimated the work that was being done by others alongside with himself, and that which had been done before him in the Church: "According to the grace of God which was given unto me, I have like a wise architect laid the foundation, and another is building upon it. Let each man take care how he builds upon it. No other foundation can be laid than that which has been already laid,—namely, Jesus Christ" (iii. 10, 11). So far from reproaching Peter with having built on a different foundation, Paul reckons him among the number of those who were labouring at God's building. He neither commends nor blames him, leaving to God the office of appraising the work of each (iii. 22). In the epistle to the Ephesians, Paul calls this primitive foundation θεμέλιον τῶν ἀποστόλων (ii. 20); and, farther on, he adds that the mystery of Christ has been revealed to His *holy apostles* and prophets, as never in former ages (iii. 5).[1]

We see with what absolute sincerity Paul attached himself to the primitive Church. Does not this evidence justify us in inferring the twofold character, both Jewish and Christian, of this original community? Had it not been Jewish in its manner of

---

[1] We are aware that the authenticity of these two last passages is questioned. But we only quote them as confirming the previous citation.

life and its hopes, the struggles and schisms that followed would be inexplicable. But if, on the other hand, it had not in the midst of its Judaism held fast to the new principle of the Gospel, Saul would never have left Pharisaism for a sect which continued so much like it; at all events, he would not after his conversion have remained in communion with it.

Between Jesus and Paul, then, the Church at Jerusalem formed a necessary connecting link. The subsequent course of events can only be satisfactorily explained by the original alliance existing in the faith and life of the first Christians between the Gospel of Jesus Christ and traditional Judaism. It is, in fact, the combination of these two fundamentally hostile principles which gives to this first period of the Church's history its peculiar and primitive character.

In order to understand this unique historical situation, we must carry our thoughts back to the morrow of the death of Jesus. The attitude assumed by the disciples toward Judaism was the consequence and continuation of that in which the Master Himself had stood.

Now, the position of Jesus in regard to the national religion had a twofold aspect. He was emphatically a Jew; He sought to fulfil all righteousness. His life was entirely confined within the limits of Judaism. Nothing is more remarkable than the way in which He has succeeded in bringing about, without any violence, the greatest revolution that has ever taken place. He brought into the world in His own person a new principle of religious life. In presenting *Himself* as the object of faith and love, He instituted a new righteousness, and opened to men a new way of salvation. Thus He supplied another fulcrum in place of that on which the religious consciousness of His disciples previously rested, substituting for their traditional faith an absolute devotion to His person. When He met with a tradition of the elders, or even an article of the law which opposed the application of the new principle, He brushed it aside with a sovereign authority. But His reforms were, nevertheless, as free from violence as His reverence and obedience were from weakness. Jesus never formally abrogated the authority of the law; on the contrary, He vindicated it, sometimes with great solemnity: "I am not come to destroy, but to fulfil." In these words lies the secret of His action. Jesus loved to present His gospel as the realization of the ancient promises, the crown of earlier revelation. So that His disciples, in devoting themselves unreservedly to His person and becoming His messengers, did not in any way feel that they were seceding from the chosen people. On the contrary, they held themselves to belong to Israel now more truly than ever, and with a better claim than their fellow citizens (Acts iii. 23).

But, on the other hand, the revolution not as yet effected in their minds was nevertheless accomplished as an objective fact. Calvary made an irrevocable breach between the religion of the past and of the future. Jesus, in dying, guaranteed His work against any unintelligent or timid reaction. From the outset He planted His cross between Christianity and Judaism; and so often as His disciples are tempted to retrace their steps, they find it placed as an impassable barrier between them and their nation.

The cross, in fact, was the real motive principle of

all the progress which ensued ; it was this which gave impulse and impetus to the primitive Church, and drove it irresistibly beyond the limits of Judaism. In spite of all their attempts at conciliation, the cross was destined to bring the apostles into conflicts, ever renewed, with the Jewish nation (Acts v. 28). Meanwhile it weighed upon their secret thoughts and wrought on them like an inward goad. They have to justify the cross by the declarations of the prophets, to discover the purpose of God in this infamous punishment; in short, to prove its necessity as an essential factor in the plan of salvation prepared by God for mankind (Acts iii. 17, 18 ; viii. 31, etc.). The terminus of this movement of thought is found in the theory of redemption formulated by the apostle Paul. Thus the external development of the Church and the internal progress of the apostolic doctrine equally proceeded from the cross of Jesus. The apostles, to be sure, did not foresee all these consequences. The principle of their faith and their loyalty to their crucified Master were about to lead them whither they would not. For a little while the bark which bears them remains in harbour ; but the last cords are already severed, the anchor is lifted, and from that moment every impulse, every motion of the waves serves to carry it farther from the ancient shore of Judaism, to which it will never more return.

That which seems to us, more than anything else, to characterize the narrative of the Acts is this same latent dualism, this tranquil co-existence of Judaism and Christianity in the primitive Christian life and creed. The union is sincere, because it is complete. It is, in fact, in this very simplicity of hope and this very behaviour that the striking originality of the picture of early Christianity consists. There is no trace of any compromise between hostile tendencies; the two streams are intermingled, and blend in perfect harmony. No one feels it necessary to renounce Moses in order to remain faithful to Jesus. There is actually so little contradiction between the old and new faith, that in some cases conversion to the Gospel awakened a new zeal for Judaism.

We find the early Christians observing the national feasts and holidays (Acts ii. 1 ; xviii. 21 [?] ; xx. 6, 16; Rom. xiv. 5). They take part in the worship of the temple and the synagogue ; they pray at the customary hours (chaps. ii. 46 ; iii. 1 ; v. 42 ; x. 9). They observe the fasts, and undergo voluntary abstinence, binding themselves by special vows like all pious Jews (xiii. 2 ; xviii. 18 ; xxi. 23). They scrupulously avoid unlawful food, and all legal defilement (x. 14). They have their children circumcised (xv. 5 ; xvi. 3 ; Gal. v. 2). In short, they are like the pious Ananias in the eyes of the Jews at Damascus [$ἀνὴρ$ $εὐλαβὴς$ $κατὰ$ $τὸν$ $νόμον$ (Acts xxii. 12). This scrupulous piety won for them the esteem and admiration of the people (chap. v. 13).[1]

The primitive Christians were Jewish alike in their ideas and their hopes. Their creed was still comprised in a single dogma : *Jesus is the Messiah.* This simple proposition, as M. Reuss well observes, was not new in respect to its attribute, but only as regards its subject.[2] Their preaching of the Gospel strictly

---

[1] See Reuss, *Histoire de la théologie chrétienne au siècle apostolique*, vol. i., p. 282, 3rd edition. [Eng. trans., i., 249.]
[2] Reuss, *Histoire*, etc. vol. i., p. 284. [Eng. trans., i., 251.]

followed the lines of Messianic tradition (i. 7 ; ii. 36 ; iii. 20). They awaited, with almost feverish expectation, the approaching advent of their Master, and pictured his return in colours and images wholly borrowed from Pharisaism.

But in reality, all this formed only the outside of their life and creed. The conception of the Messiah, when applied to the historical person of Jesus, could not fail to undergo a transformation. The kingdom of God, which the apostles invited their fellow citizens to enter, was from the first divested of its political and terrestrial character ; it must be entered by repentance and the remission of sins ; and the Saviour of the nation becomes thus, in the nature of the case, the Saviour of the individual. Herein lies the profound significance of the miracle of Pentecost. That day was the birthday of the Church, not because of the marvellous success of Peter's preaching, but because the Christian principle, hitherto only existing objectively and externally in the person of Jesus, passed from that moment into the souls of His disciples and there attained its inward realization. On the day of Pentecost memory became faith.[1]

And thus in the very midst of Judaism we see created and unfolded a form of religious life essentially different from it—*the Christian life.* A new flower blooms on the old stem. In the midst of the national family, the first Christians felt themselves brethren in a peculiar sense ; side by side with the temple ritual, we find the more intimate and

---

[1] See Neander's *History of the Planting and Training of the Christian Church;* De Pressensé's *Early Years of Christianity.*

spiritual worship of the "upper room." Exhortation and prayer, baptism in the name of Jesus, the breaking of bread in commemoration of His death, charity to the poor—here are present already all the essential elements of Christian worship.

At the same time, by the natural effect of discussion, the apostles gained a clearer understanding of the new principle which animated them. Their faith, which at first was nothing more than a powerful sentiment binding them to Jesus, sought day by day to attain a more just and exact definition of its object. Peter at first simply designates Jesus as *a man approved of God* (ii. 22); then, as *the Holy and Righteous One;* as *the Prince and Leader of life* (iii. 14, 15). At last the new faith is revealed in its full import in the courageous declaration of the apostle: " Jesus is the stone which you builders *despised*, and which has become *the headstone of the corner.* In none other is there salvation: for there has not been given to men any other name under heaven by which they can be saved " (iv. 11, 12). To the claim of Judaism to be the sole religion is here opposed the equal claim of the Gospel. Conflict was inevitable.

On both sides, it is true, there seem to have been efforts made to prevent it. The Jewish authorities, alarmed by their too easy triumph over Jesus, hesitated to attack His disciples. They wished to have no more to do with them; they warned, and even implored them. They could not make up their minds to repress them by violence, and yielded readily to the wise counsel of Gamaliel. The apostles, on their side, seemed equally unwilling to precipitate matters. In their naïve expectation of soon seeing their whole nation converted, they avoided giving it offence. If they recall the murder of Jesus, they hasten to excuse it, on the ground of the ignorance of the perpetrators and its Divine necessity (iii. 13-19).

But the logic of principles and events was to prove too strong for this goodwill. The heads of the nation contented themselves at first with forbidding the apostles to speak in the name of Jesus. Unfortunately, this was the one point on which it was impossible for them to obey. The prohibition led to transgression; and the transgression in its turn inevitably provoked violence. These first persecutions stimulated the zeal and enthusiasm of the disciples, and braced them for the struggle (iv. 24; v. 41). "It is better to obey God than man." In this phrase we hear by anticipation the farewell of the apostles to national Judaism.

So, little by little, Christianity and Judaism came to exhibit the hostility latent in their principles. Let a man now arise bold enough to disentangle the two systems and set them in antithesis, and we shall see the great conflict begun by the discourses and the death of Jesus break forth again as fiercely as before. Such a man was Stephen, deacon and martyr.

CHAPTER II.

STEPHEN THE PRECURSOR OF PAUL.—COLLISION BETWEEN THE JEWISH AND THE CHRISTIAN PRINCIPLE (Acts vi., vii.).

THE first verses of the sixth chapter of the Acts indicate a great change in the internal condition of the primitive Church. At the same time, we find ourselves apparently on firmer historical ground. The early days of pure enthusiasm are succeeded by a period of bitter divisions within, and fierce conflicts without.

The growth of the Church destroyed its internal harmony. Opposing tendencies were aroused and displayed themselves in its midst. "In those days, when the number of the disciples was increasing, there arose a loud murmuring of the Hellenists against the Hebrews, because their widows were neglected in the distribution of relief" (vi. 1). Is not this an undeniable proof that the Judaic-spirit, with its prejudice and intolerance, survived in the Christian community? and may we not foresee already something of the more ardent and serious struggles to which this spirit was afterwards to give rise? This dissension was appeased, however, by a triumph of the primitive spirit of charity. The seven deacons who were appointed all bear Greek names. Probably they were selected, by preference, from the aggrieved party, in order to prevent further complaints. Among these deacons, Stephen was designated first, being a man full of faith and of the Holy Ghost, and of favour and influence among the people. He had apprehended the spiritual character of the Gospel better than the apostles themselves, and surrendered himself with absolute faith to the new principle.[1]

He soon found himself in the forefront of the struggle that was beginning against Judaism, carried onwards by the boldness of his views quite as much as by his zeal. To this struggle his intervention gave a new turn. The apostles had remained on the defensive in their preaching of Jesus; Stephen broke through this reserve, and boldly assumed the offensive. In his public discussions he laid bare the materialistic principle of Pharisaic piety; he pointed out with unsparing plainness the secret cause of that invincible obstinacy with which the Jews had always resisted

---

[1] We consider that it was in this faith and holy inspiration—that is, in a clearer comprehension of the gospel of Jesus—rather than in his Hellenism, that the loftiness, courage, and spirituality of Stephen's thought had their source. We believe, contrary to the received opinion, that it is attributing undeserved honour to the Hellenist Jews to regard them as a spiritual and liberally minded party. They were treated somewhat with contempt, because their origin appeared less pure; but it is probable, as in all analogous cases, that they cherished on this account a more bigoted temper and a sterner zeal, in order to atone for their foreign taint and efface the recollection of it. They attached themselves to the Pharisaic party much more than to that of the Sadducees. It was the Hellenists, indeed, who accused and stoned Stephen. Saul was a Hellenist. It was Hellenist Jews, again, who wished to kill Paul after his conversion (ix. 29). And finally, the men who, on recognising Paul in the temple, denounced and sought to slay him were Jews from Asia (xxi. 27).

the word of God. His denunciations of their religious formalism recalled sometimes those accents of the Master which used to excite the Pharisees to fury. This fury again awoke. The capital charge brought against Jesus was renewed against Stephen; false witnesses again repeated the accusation, "We have heard this man speak against the holy place and against the law. We have heard him say that this Jesus of Nazareth will destroy the temple, and change the customs that Moses gave us" (vi. 13, 14).

How far was this charge true or false? What was the real idea of Stephen? We can only learn it through his discourse. This speech is divided into two parts, of very unequal length—one historical, and the other personal. The fifty-first verse forms the somewhat abrupt transition from the one to the other. At first sight, one does not readily perceive the connexion between this long defence and the accusation; and some interpreters, misled by this, have concluded that we have not here Stephen's actual discourse, but a free historical composition which the author of the Acts has substituted for it. That is only a superficial judgment. When we study the address more closely and grasp its main idea, we find it impossible to imagine anything which could have met the accusation more directly or gone more thoroughly to the root of the matter, or any defence, on the whole, more apt and eloquent.

What, then, is its pervading thought? This declares itself in that same fifty-first verse which marks the transition from the first to the second part of the address. "You stiff-necked men," cries Stephen, "uncircumcised in heart and ears, will you always resist the Holy Ghost?" This vehement apostrophe, with which his long historical statement concludes, completely sums it up. Stephen, in fact, endeavours in traversing the course of Israel's history to point out and illustrate the perpetual conflict that existed between the unfailing mercy of God and the stubborn, carnal obstinacy of the people. This tragic antithesis is the one subject of his discourse. He seems, at the first glance, to forget the accusation laid against him; but in reality he does not lose sight of it for a moment. It is the constant goal to which every word is directed. In rehearsing the conflicts of the past he is well aware, and makes it very evident, that he is depicting by anticipation the struggle in which at the present moment he is himself involved. Besides, Stephen had no other means of making himself listened to and understood. To the High Priest's question, Is it true what these men say? he could not answer directly either Yes or No. He could not answer in the affirmative; for in his eyes the Gospel was not the destruction of the law and prophets, but their fulfilment. To answer] No, would have been to deny his cause, and to save himself by means of an equivocation. He must explain, in order to defend himself; and what better explanation can he offer, than to make his case parallel with that of Moses and the prophets? On a similar occasion, Jesus had made much the same reply. Stephen's discourse is the complement and development of the parable of the Vineyard. The orator was obliged to throw his speech into this historical form. By doing so he gave the rage of his opponents time to subside, and meanwhile secured the means of showing clearly the true cause of their hatred. The great epochs in the history of the Jewish people furnish the main divisions of his discourse.

The first extends from Abraham to Moses (vii. 2-19). The nation does not exist as yet; but before its birth it was the object of Divine favour; for to it, in truth, the promises given to the patriarchs were made (vers. 4, 5, 7).

The second epoch lies between Moses and David. In referring to the first period, the orator has extolled the goodness of God; in describing the second, he endeavours to depict with equal force the ingratitude and carnal disposition of the people. This period becomes typical. In Moses the deliverer ($\lambda \upsilon \tau \rho \omega \tau \acute{\eta} \varsigma$), Stephen enables us to recognise the image of a far greater Deliverer. His unworthy reception, the opposition he met with and the incredulity with which his word was received, are set forth in such terms that the history of Moses, by an easy transition, becomes the history of Jesus acted out beforehand (ver. 35).

The third period comprises the times of David and Solomon. Stephen breaks off at the building of the temple. He does not, as some have thought, censure the very idea of such an undertaking; on the contrary, he sees in it a distinct fulfilment of God's original promise made to Abraham: "They shall worship Me in this place" (ver. 7).

He saw fit to confine his historical exposition between these two events—the prophecy, and its fulfilment. In vain the nation displayed its ingratitude. God remained faithful, and the temple was built. But alas! this blessing produced no better result than the rest. The carnal disposition of the people spoilt it, and turned it into a cause of destruction. The very temple where God should have been worshipped in spirit and in truth, became the centre and support of a bigoted and hypocritical piety. Instead of revealing to all mankind the one universal God, who made heaven and earth, it only served to limit and conceal the majesty of Jehovah. This, we take it, is the true interpretation of the passage, the most important in the whole discourse, in which Stephen shows what he really thought about the temple: "David found favour before God, and asked that he might build a tabernacle for the God of Jacob; and Solomon built Him a house. But the Most High dwells not in houses made by human hands, according to the prophet's word: Heaven is My throne, earth the footstool of My feet; what house will you build Me? saith the Lord; or what should be the place of My rest? Is it not My hand that has made all these things?" (vers. 46–50.)

Thus had Stephen advanced slowly, but always in a straight line, to meet the charge laid against him. He now confronts and grapples with it directly and without hesitation. His answer is deduced from this prolonged narrative with overwhelming effect. It is an old contention, this in which he is engaged—the contention between God and His people. Is it surprising that the people to-day show no more intelligence, no better disposition than they had done with regard to Moses, or the prophets, or Jesus? "Which of the prophets did not your fathers persecute? They killed those who foretold of the coming of the Righteous One; and when this Righteous One appeared, you became His betrayers and murderers! You possessed the law, . . . and you did not keep it." In other words, You are just like your fathers: ὡς οἱ πατέρες ὑμῶν καὶ ὑμεῖς (vers. 51–53). At this point the position appears to be changed: the accused has become judge of his accusers. But at the same time he has anticipated, in his reading of the history of the past, the fate which awaits himself and the sentence about to fall upon him.

Stephen, in truth, did not for one moment deceive himself. He knew his adversaries well. He has no hope of either convincing or softening them. This sense of the inevitable is manifest from the first. He does not merely point out a few passing errors or accidental failings; his object was to denounce a congenital vice, inherent in the very character of his people and persisting through their entire history,— a carnal disposition, insensible alike to chastisement and grace, and which had borne the same fruit in every age. Its present obstinacy, therefore, was no matter for surprise. Such a people could not deny its nature. This was a radical condemnation of Judaism, such as the Pharisees had not heard since the days of Jesus. Stephen only discloses this view by degrees. At first, he keeps it back and holds his audience in suspense ; but as he goes on, his purpose grows clearer, and at each new stage of the history he expresses himself more pointedly and plainly. His hearers begin to murmur and grow excited ; Stephen in slow and unrelenting tones unfolds before them this humiliating history, in which all the time they could recognise their own likeness. When at last he has finished, and when, as he perceives, caution could no longer serve him, he launches forth his whole meaning in the apostrophe, "Ye stiff-necked and uncircumcised," etc. Then the rage of his adversaries bursts out in turn, and gnashing their teeth they rush upon him. But they interrupted him too late. Stephen has spoken. He yields himself to their fury; and his martyrdom completes his discourse.

Stephen's heroic death has diverted attention from the depth and force which characterize his mind. He left Peter and the heroes of Pentecost far behind him. He compelled Judaism and Christianity to assume a sharper definition, to affirm their several principles more clearly, and to separate. The negation of Jewish privileges, the right of all men to share in the kingdom of God, the universal and spiritual character of Christianity, are the more immediate deductions following from his discourse. The drama in which he perished seems to have been the sequel and repetition of that which cost the Saviour's life. He continued the work of Jesus, and prepared the way for that of the apostle of the Gentiles. Paul must have heard his address, and in after days would often call it to mind, when experiencing painfully in his turn the invincible unbelief of his people. What has he done more in the ninth and tenth chapters of his epistle to the Romans than formulate dogmatically that decree of reprobation, which we find in Stephen's discourse set forth under the garb of history?

CHAPTER III.

PAUL'S CONVERSION.—TRIUMPH OF THE CHRISTIAN OVER THE JEWISH PRINCIPLE (Acts ix. 4-22).

IT was in the breast of Saul that the violent conflict raised by Stephen was decided, issuing in the triumph of the Christian principle. But the significance of his conversion can only be understood when his Pharisaism has first been clearly defined.

I. SAUL'S ANTECEDENTS.

Saul was a Hellenistic Jew, born at Tarsus in Cilicia. The fact that he was born at this brilliant centre of Greek civilization has often been made too much of. The influence of Greece upon the development of his mind seems to have amounted to nothing. The two or three quotations from Greek poets to be found in his epistles and discourses (Acts xvii. 28; 1 Cor. xv. 33; Tit. i. 12) are lines which had become proverbial, and which Paul may frequently have heard quoted in pagan society. There is a notable resemblance between his style of writing and that of Thucydides; but it only proves the natural affinity of their genius. Paul did not learn his dialectics in the schools of the sophists or rhetoricians; it has much more in common with that of the Talmud and the

rabbis than of Plato or Aristotle. Though he wrote
in Greek, he thought in Aramaic; he seems to have
borrowed from Greece nothing but his vocabulary.
Out of these external elements he has created a
language of his own, vehement and original like
his genius. As for the universalism of his Christian
belief, that was due to anything rather than his
Hellenistic origin. As we shall see afterwards, it is
not the citizen of Tarsus, but the Pharisee of Jerusalem that accounts for the apostle of the Gentiles.

Paul himself has been careful in his epistles to demonstrate the purity of his Hebrew descent, and the strict-
ness of his Judaism. Note the significant gradation he
makes out in Philippians iii. 4–6, when enumerating
his advantages according to the flesh: Circumcised
the eighth day, he belongs to the family of Abraham;
in this family, he belongs specifically to the race of
Israel; within this race, he has sprung from the tribe
of Benjamin—that is, from the tribe which united
with Judah after the separation to form the kingdom
in which the great religious traditions of the Old
Testament were maintained in their purity and
vigour. Finally, among the descendants of these two
Jewish tribes, he belonged to the sect of the Pharisees,
the strictest and most loyal of Jews; and in its
midst he was further distinguished by his remarkable proficiency, and his persecuting zeal (Gal. i. 13).

We have every reason to suppose that, though he
was born at Tarsus, Paul was from tender infancy
brought up at Jerusalem, where he had a married
sister (Acts xxiii. 16). So we may conclude from a
passage in Acts xxii. 3, which we translate as follows:
"I am a Jew, born at Tarsus in Cilicia, but nourished
and brought up in *this city*, at the feet of Gamaliel,

and carefully instructed in the law of my fathers."[1] His parents, intending him to be a rabbi, had no doubt placed him at the school of the illustrious Pharisaic doctor, who is still counted among the highest authorities of the Mishna. There Saul received the scholastic training of a rabbi, and exercised himself for years in the subtle dialectics and the ingenious and refined hermeneutics which characterized the rabbinical teaching. This mode of teaching and discussion had already been determined and formulated by Hillel; and we know what marked traces it has left on Paul's great epistles.[2]

It is, however, the substance rather than the form of Paul's rabbinical teaching which we are most concerned to understand. Paul, on becoming a Christian,

---

[1] In this passage the words ἐν τῇ πόλει ταύτῃ must mean Jerusalem, and not Tarsus. Paul was not only instructed, πεπαιδευμένος, but nourished and brought up from earliest childhood at Jerusalem, ἀνατεθραμμένος. This disposes of all the conjectures that have been made about Paul's Greek education.

[2] On Hillel and Gamaliel, see Derenbourg: *Essai sur l'histoire et la géographie de la Palestine d'après le Talmud*, pp. 178, 187, and 239. Hillel, of whose family, along with the traditions of his school, Gamaliel was the heir, seems to have been, so far as we can judge, the Aristotle of rabbinical theology. He classified and formulated the different rules of its scholastic reasoning. Here is an example of his mode of discussion, quoted by M. Derenbourg. The point in question was whether, if the 15th Nisan, the Passover, fell on a Saturday, it was lawful to sacrifice the Paschal lamb on that day. Hillel answered in the affirmative, and established his assertion by three reasons: (1) by an argument drawn from analogy. The law of the Sabbath does not prevent the daily sacrifice; there is no more reason why the Paschal sacrifice should be forbidden. —(2) By an argument *à fortiori*. If the daily sacrifice was offered notwithstanding the Sabbath, when its omission was

did not abandon all his former convictions; for had not many of his Christian ideas their roots in his early faith? What else, in fact, is his entire system of doctrine but Pharisaism transformed and inverted? Unfortunately, we have only very vague and imperfect information about the doctrines taught in the Pharisaic schools of the period. Nevertheless, it is certain that the apostle's theology owed to Judaism the general basis on which it rests. There is no need of appealing to external documents of doubtful authority, in order to discover the exact nature of this basis. It will be enough to note in his epistles the general ideas which had their origin in Judaism. We shall thus be able to trace the traditional mould in which Paul's system of thought was cast from the beginning. His theology continued to be Jewish to a much greater extent than has been commonly supposed.

From the Old Testament Paul drew the primary and fundamental ideas of his system: the ideas of *God*, of *revelation*, of *righteousness*, and of *holiness*. He is essentially Jewish, in what one might call his mental categories, and in the general point of view

---

not punishable by extermination, how much more should the Passover be, seeing extermination was the punishment for its omission.—(3) By an exegetical argument. It is ordained that the act should be fulfilled at its appointed time; if that means *in spite of the sabbath* in the case of the daily sacrifice, it must have the same meaning respecting the Passover. Is not this the very logic used by Paul in his discussions? Comp. 1 Cor. ix. 8-10; Gal. iii. 15; 2 Cor. iii. 7; Rom. v. 12. Beside these three kinds of argument there were four others, not less exactly defined. There was evidently a complete *organum* taught in these schools and there acquired by Paul, who mastered and wielded it with wonderful effect.

from which he considers the relation of God to the world. The God of Paul is the God of the old covenant; He is the God of Abraham, of Jacob, of Moses and the prophets; He is the One, the jealous God, the absolute Creator of the universe, who manifests in His works the signs of His divinity; He is the one God, living and true (1 Cor. viii. 4-6; x. 26; Rom. i. 20, 23; 1 Thess. i. 9; 1 Tim. vi. 15, 16). This God was the God of Israel in a peculiar sense, because He had entered into a special covenant with them, and had given them the oracles and promises in trust (Rom. iii. 2; ix. 4, 5). On this account, the Old Testament still possesses the authority of a Divine revelation (1 Cor. xv. 4; Gal. iii. 8); it is the revelation of the holy God, with whom we can have no peace without perfect purity of heart. Hence Paul's lofty conception, at once moral and religious, of δικαιοσύνη, and the correlative idea of sin; whose tragic conflict in the apostle's soul was the starting point of his whole spiritual development.

Paul regards the pagan world as did the Pharisees of his day. Paganism is the kingdom of darkness (2 Cor. vi. 14). The heathen know not God; they adore the creature instead of the Creator (1 Thess. iv. 5; Gal. iv. 8). They were at once ἄπιστοι and ἄνομοι (2 Cor. vi. 14; Rom. i. 24-26; 1 Cor. vi. 6). And lastly, as opposed to the Jews, they are essentially ἁμαρτωλοί (Gal. ii. 15).

It was to Pharisaism, again, that Paul was indebted for his notions respecting angels and demons. Ranged in different orders, the angels surround God's throne (Col. i. 16; Rom. viii. 38). They take part in the government of the world, and will accompany Christ at His coming (1 Thess. iv. 16). The idea of the intervention of angels at the giving of the law on Mount Sinai, διαταγεὶς δι' ἀγγέλων (Gal. iii. 19),[1] belongs likewise to the Judaism of that day. To the host of angels is opposed that of the demons, with Satan at their head. It was he who long ago tempted Eve, under the form of a serpent (2 Cor. xi. 3). Since then he has never ceased his endeavours to beguile men into sin (1 Thess. iii. 5; 1 Cor. vii. 5), or to torture them by the infliction of physical pain (1 Cor. v. 5; 2 Cor. xii. 7). His proper domain is heathenism; and he is the real object of the worship of idolaters. He is the god of the present age, as opposed to Christ, the King of the age to come (2 Cor. iv. 4).

For Paul, in fact, as for the Pharisees, the history of humanity had two great divisions: the existing, and the future age (Eph. i. 21). The latter is to be inaugurated by the glorious return of Christ, of which the apostle has the same conception as the other disciples of Jesus (1 Cor. vii. 29; 1 Thess. iv. 16; v. 2; 2 Thess. i. 7; 1 Cor. xv. 51, 52). The first period was one of sin, suffering, and death; the second will be one of holiness and life. Adam is the head of the old humanity; the Messiah is the head of the new.

We know, further, that the doctrine of Predestination, whose roots are found in the prophetic teaching of the Old Testament, had been developed and formulated in the Pharisaic schools. Here, no doubt, lay the origin of the Pauline predestination. The doctrine of the resurrection and of the last judgment are derived from the same source. "The

---

[1] Comp. Acts vii. 53; Josephus, *Ant.* xv. 5, 3; and Deut. xxxiii. 2, according to the LXX.

Pharisees," Josephus tells us, "think that everything which happens has been decreed beforehand by destiny. They do not on that account deny the agency of the human will; for it has pleased God that the decrees of destiny and man's free will should coincide, whether in respect of the practice of virtue or of vice. They believe that souls possess an immortal energy, and that beneath the earth are rewards and punishments for those who in this life have lived virtuously or otherwise; that the souls of the latter shall be imprisoned there for ever, while the rest shall speedily be restored to life."[1]

In the last place, is it not to the rabbinical theology that Paul is indebted for his anthropological views? He did not invent his division of human nature into σάρξ, ψυχή, πνεῦμα; for it can be traced back to the very phraseology of the Old Testament. The idea of original sin hereditary in Adam's race seems likewise to have been formulated by Pharisaism. It was evidently a complete body of doctrine, coherent and systematic, that Paul learned at the feet of Gamaliel. This system he has greatly modified; but for all that, one can easily discern that the new edifice contains much of the material of the old, and follows the main lines of its construction. The mental biography of Paul which we propose to relate is simply the progressive transformation, under the influence of the Christian principle, of that Pharisaic theology which formed the object of his original faith.

The soul of Saul's Pharisaic creed was the hope of the Messiah (2 Cor. v. 16), a hope which fired both

---

[1] We quote this passage as it has been restored and translated by Derenbourg, *op. cit.*, p. 123.

heart and imagination. His convictions were his life; he surrendered himself to them unreservedly. But this ardent piety, these holy ambitions and deep cravings, and the absolute logic which Paul brought into his Pharisaism, supplied the very force which was destined, in driving him forwards, to carry him beyond it.

Let us observe here that dominant feature of Paul's character which enables us to comprehend, if not to account for, the great change that took place in him. We refer to *his passion for the absolute*. Paul's was, in fact, a mind simple and complete—all of a piece—one that must above everything be logical. He sees in a principle all the consequences that it involves; and detects the principle in each of its manifold consequences. It was of no use to speak to him of degrees of truth, of accommodations or compromises; he marches by way of a radical negation to an absolute affirmative. His intellectual temperament was naturally intolerant. To him truth and error, so far from being matters of degree, stand like good and evil in radical contradiction. It is not surprising, therefore, that a mind of this cast failed to acquire the breadth of view and moderation of temper which distinguished his master Gamaliel. He has himself described what he must have been at this period of his life: "You know my past life in Judaism; I excelled in zeal most of my companions in age, showing myself specially zealous for the traditions of my fathers" (Gal. i. 13). The teaching of the rabbis, the prophetic sayings of the Old Testament, the theocratic dreams of his contemporaries—he received them all with eagerness and emphasis; he systematized and formulated them into a complete, coherent whole. It was altogether an ideal world that this

Pharisee contemplated within his soul. But the more he clung to these hopes, the more he had to suffer from the existing state of things. How melancholy was the contrast between his radiant inward vision and the sorrowful state of his people around him! And this contradiction had no possible solution, from the Pharisaic point of view. The future appeared even more threatening than the present. Does not this bitter consciousness, this incongruity endured with so much impatience, explain Saul's furious hatred against the new sect of Christians? For its scandalous progress was hastening the inevitable destruction of Judaism.

In another direction Saul encountered an equally hopeless contradiction. There was in this Pharisee something still more absolute than his intellect, —his *conscience*. In vain would he have sought to satisfy it with a partial righteousness; it demanded nothing less than perfect holiness. This ideal of holiness was set up in the written law; and with this law his conscience entered into an incessant and unequal struggle, in which it was always and inevitably worsted. Every fresh effort resulted, of necessity, in a more humiliating defeat. He has himself described this mournful struggle in the seventh chapter of the epistle to the Romans. "It was through the law that I knew sin, for I had not known coveting, except the law had said, Thou shalt not covet. But sin, taking occasion from the commandment, wrought in me all manner of coveting; for without the law sin is dead. Once on a time, without the law, I was indeed alive; but when the commandment came, sin recovered life, and I died; and the commandment which had been given me to bring life, proved a cause of death"

(Rom. vii. 7–12). Thus Paul found the very power in which he trusted for salvation rise against him and overwhelm him. The situation was without escape; it could end only in despair (Rom. vii. 24).

It was doubtless in the midst of these experiences that Paul encountered Stephen. With our knowledge of his temperament, we may safely assume that he was one of those Jews from Asia and Cilicia who maintained the cause of the temple and the law against the disciple of Jesus (Acts vi. 9). The temptation of breaking a theological lance with Stephen was one he could not resist; he listened to his discourses, and was present at his death. Stephen's arguments and his serene faith could not fail to touch him, and to awaken reflection. Perhaps it was then that he felt in his conscience for the first time the goad of Jesus (Acts xxvi. 14). It was not from this cause, however, that he became a Christian. Not only is it the case that Paul never refers his conversion to Stephen; he forbids, most explicitly, any such explanation by his solemn declaration that he was not taught by any man, and does not hold his gospel in charge from any man.

Between the death of Stephen and Paul's first preaching of Christianity at Damascus, there took place in his life that mysterious event to which he attributes his conversion and apostleship, and of which we must now ascertain the true character.

II. The Appearance of Jesus to Paul.

The Acts of the Apostles contains three accounts of this event—one given directly by Luke (ix. 1–22), the other two taken from the lips of Paul (xxv. 1–21; xxvi. 9–20).

There are some variations in the three narratives. According to the account in the ninth chapter, Paul's companions heard the voice which spoke to him; according to that in the twenty-second, they did not. The ninth chapter states that they saw no one; the two others, that they saw at any rate a dazzling light. In the first account, they remain standing; in the third, they fall to the ground. And, lastly, the words which Jesus is said to have spoken to Paul, vary in all three reports. What the Saviour said to him, according to chap. xxvi. 16, is in the twenty-second chapter put in the mouth of Ananias (ver. 14).

How did these differences arise? Schleiermacher's school tried, for some time, to account for them by the variety of sources from which the author drew his narrative; but even a superficial comparison of the three recitals shows clearly that they were drawn up by the same hand, and had one and the same origin. There is therefore no occasion to inquire, as has sometimes been done, which is the most accurate.

Could these differences have had a dogmatic reason? Did they serve to express in each instance some special aim pursued by the author? So thought Baur. In the first account, he says, the historian, narrating the event from an objective point of view, lays stress upon the external circumstances of the event in order to prove its absolute reality. The two other accounts, put in the mouth of Paul, are from a more subjective point of view.[1] But of what value is this distinction? Was Paul, when speaking before the Jews at Jerusalem, or before Agrippa, less concerned than Luke to prove the substantial reality

---

[1] Baur, *Paulus*, 2nd ed., pp. 72, 73. [Eng. trans., i., 65, 66.]

of this fact? Were this explanation as legitimate as it is arbitrary, it would still in reality explain nothing. The first account, it is said, dwelling on the objective reality of the miracle, makes out that Paul's companions heard the heavenly voice. But why did not Luke add that they saw the light, as appears in the second account? and that instead of standing they fell to the ground, as in the third? Are not these two latter circumstances as appropriate as the first to prove the external reality of the vision? or could it be said that they better accord with the subjective point of view of the later accounts, than with the objective standpoint of the first?

M. Zeller, unable to accept this explanation, offers us another. According to him, the author has been guided by a literary caprice, not by any dogmatic purpose. He is indifferent to historical accuracy and careless of self-contradiction; his discrepancies are such as to show that pious imagination played a leading part in the composition of his narrative. But are we to admit that our author has modified his first account with the sole purpose of variety, or that in order to avoid monotony, he went to the length of contradicting himself?

Can it be correct to assert, in the face of the contrary evidence of his prologue, that the author of the Third Gospel and the Acts of the Apostles cared nothing for historical truth? Do we not find him scrupulously anxious about accuracy, always trying to trace things to their beginning, to get at the original witnesses, and to explain the facts in their true origin and connexion? Supposing he is sometimes in error, has he not succeeded in making certain parts of his work pass for the journal of an actual companion of the apostle Paul? Can we fairly accuse the man who wrote the last chapters of the Acts of indulging an arbitrary fancy?

These divergences are absolutely inexplicable on any hypothesis which assumes that the author was aware of them, and designed them to serve some doctrinal or literary purpose. It is obvious to any unprejudiced mind that they were *undesigned*, and that they entirely escaped the writer's notice. They are discrepancies of precisely the sort that one always finds existing in the most faithful repetitions of the same narrative. Their explanation lies in their very triviality. They cannot in any way affect the reality of the event in question. They arise at certain extreme points belonging to the mere circumference of the narrative. They do not even belong to the circumstances accompanying the miracle, but only to the subjective impressions made by them upon Paul's companions. On this point the record was liable to much more variation, as these impressions could not have been the same in all cases, nor described by all with the same exactitude.

To draw from these discrepancies an argument against the historical character of the narrative seems to us a forced and arbitrary proceeding. If they were perfectly reconcilable, or even if they had never existed, those who will not admit the miracle would just as decisively reject the testimony of the Acts of the Apostles. As Zeller frankly acknowledges, their denial of the miraculous rests on a philosophical theory, the discussion of which lies outside the scope of historical research.[1]

---

[1] Zeller, *Die Apostelgeschichte*, p. 197. [Eng. trans., i., 291.]

For our part, we cannot set aside this triple record quite so easily. We find it repeated at the end of the book, in that fragment which in the judgment of the majority of critics is the authentic testimony of a friend of the apostle. This being so, it is natural to suppose that Luke's narrative was derived from the testimony of Paul himself; and it only remains to ascertain how far it is confirmed by the apostle's statements in his own epistles.

It is a point of the utmost importance to observe that Paul knows absolutely nothing of any progressive stages or gradual process in his conversion to the Gospel. He looked back to it throughout his life as a sudden, overwhelming event, which surprised him in the full tide of his Judaic career and drove him, in spite of himself, into a new channel. He was vanquished and subdued by main force (Phil. iii. 12). He is a conquered rebel, whom God leads in triumph in face of the world (2 Cor. ii. 14). If he preaches the Gospel, he cannot make any boast of doing so; he was *compelled* to preach it, under a higher necessity which he had no power to resist. There he stands, —a slave in chains! (1 Cor. ix. 15–18.)

Independently of this general impression, Paul makes three express statements on the subject, which we must consider with close attention.

The first of these passages, where Paul undoubtedly is referring to his conversion, is Galatians i. 12–17. He only describes it there as an inward experience. One day it pleased God, who had set him apart from his mother's womb, *to reveal His Son in him*, in order that he might go and preach Him to the heathen. Paul here refers his conversion and his apostleship to the same date, and the same cause. His one object being to set forth the Divine origin and absolute independence of his gospel, he contents himself with presenting the inner phase of his conversion (ἀποκαλύψαι τὸν υἱὸν αὐτοῦ ἐν ἐμοί), and makes no reference to the special means employed by God to bring about in him this work of grace. Two remarks will show, however, that the idea of a miraculous and direct revelation from Christ is none the less involved in this passage. In the first place, while attributing his conversion to the grace of God as its prime cause, he at the same time gives as its proximate and effectual cause the personal intervention of Jesus. This comes out clearly in the first verse of the epistle, where the name of Jesus occurs even before the name of God; and it is expressly signified in ver. 12, where Jesus Christ is spoken of, not as the object alone of Divine revelation, but even as its Author.[1]

Secondly, Paul regards his conversion as a sudden occurrence, an event sharply defined and associated with certain external circumstances of time and place. He observes, for instance, that it happened in the midst of the war he was carrying on against Christianity, overtaking him while yet a busy and zealous persecutor. Furthermore, he remembers that it took place in the neighbourhood of Damascus (Gal. i. 17); and that, from this moment, his life followed an entirely different course. Thus in three essential points—the personal intervention of Jesus, and the

---

[1] Δι' ἀποκαλύψεως Ἰησοῦ Χριστοῦ. These two last words form what the grammarians call a subjective genitive. They indicate not the object, but the author, the *subject* of the revelation, as is proved by the words παρ' ἀνθρώπου, to which these are the antithesis.

time and place at which it occurred—the story told us in the Acts is indirectly, but distinctly, confirmed.

While in this passage of Galatians Paul only brings out the inner aspect of his conversion, we find him dwelling quite as exclusively on its exterior and objective nature in the two passages remaining for our consideration. The first is in 1 Corinthians ix. 1: "Am I not an *apostle*? Have I not *seen* the Lord Jesus?" Paul here associates his apostolic call with the manifestation of the Risen One, shared by him with the other apostles; he links them to each other as effect and cause.

The objective reality of this manifestation is still more apparent in the second passage (1 Cor. xv. 8), where Paul puts it on a level with that of which the Twelve were witnesses. "Lastly, and after all the others, Christ appeared to me also, as to an abortion." These last words (ὡσπερεὶ τῷ ἐκτρώματι) should be noted. Only one interpretation is possible: that already given by Grotius, and accepted by Baur. An ἔκτρωμα can only mean a fœtus torn violently and prematurely from the maternal womb; as Grotius has well expressed it, *hoc ideo dicit, quia non longa institutione ad Christianismum perductus fuit, quo esset velut naturalis partus, sed vi subita, quomodo immaturi partus ejici solent.* How could Paul indicate more pointedly than he does in this expression the objective nature of the force exerted over his mind at his conversion?

Whatever the fact may be, no critic will now deny that Paul maintained throughout his life that he had witnessed an external appearance of the risen Christ. Baur contends that the apostle spoke of the matter always with reserve, and with a kind of shame, as though he felt instinctively that he was standing on somewhat unstable ground. But what ground is there for this assertion? Are the two passages in the Corinthian epistle, in which the external side of the occurrence is specially emphasized, of less importance than that in Galatians, which chiefly reveals its internal character? If Paul bases the independence of his gospel on the inward revelation, does he not regard the external reality as the source and proof of his apostleship? Does it seem as though he referred but timidly to this manifestation? We are bold to affirm the contrary. If in his epistle to the Corinthians, he makes no more than a passing reference to the event, it is because the Corinthians already knew about it. The apostle, in the first verses of the fifteenth chapter, is only summing up his previous teaching; and among the leading facts, which he dwelt on before everything else (ἐν πρώτοις), he mentions in its turn this appearance to him of the risen Jesus. Does not this strongly suggest to us that he must have already related the great event in detail, and given an account at Corinth similar to the one we have in the book of the Acts?

Paul's testimony, therefore, is explicit and incontrovertible. But though we may not mistake its import, is it not possible to diminish its weight? The evidence, it is said, proves that Paul believed in the reality of the manifestation,—nothing more. How shall we educe the external reality from this personal and subjective conception? Unquestionably, criticism may push its demands in this way to a point at which of necessity any positive proof becomes impossible. This style of reasoning tends to nothing less than the destruction of all historical certainty; for, in point of fact, history depends on nothing else than subjective and individual testimony. This universal scepticism disarms assailants and defenders alike; on its terms, negation and affirmation are equally unwarrantable. But the evidence of Paul is a fact; as such, it must have had a cause and demands an explanation. To call it inexplicable, as Baur seems to do, is to leave the door open for the supernatural.

This M. Holsten, the boldest and most faithful of his disciples, sees clearly enough. This writer has in his very remarkable work applied all his resources, the closest logic and most penetrating observation, in his attempt to explain the origin and natural formation of this conviction in the apostle's mind. But has his criticism solved the psychological problem thus presented to it? That it has done so, no one, I think, will venture to affirm. M. Holsten himself, after all his endeavours, remains in doubt; he does not mean, he declares, to insist on the truth of his solution, only on its possibility. Practically, it amounts to the well-worn vision-hypothesis. Saul drew from Messianism the principal features of the person of Christ which he claims to have seen. So that all the materials of his vision were ready to hand. Furthermore, he had a natural tendency to ecstasy; his physiological, no less than his spiritual constitution predisposed him to it. He had a nervous disposition easily over-wrought, a sanguino-bilious temperament; and was very delicate, subject probably to epileptic attacks (2 Cor. xii. 7). That he had revelations and visions, both his epistles and the Acts assure us; he spoke with *tongues*, worked miracles, had the gift of prophecy, and often boasts of his spiritual *charismata* (1 Cor. xiv. 18; Gal. ii. 2; 2 Cor. xii. 1–9). What was the appearance of Christ at his conversion but the first of these ecstatic visions, and that which gave rise to all the others?[1]

Much might be said on the details of this argument, which is full of disputable points. The passage in 2 Corinthians xii. 1-9 supplies its nucleus, and is indeed its only ground of support. This text, however, not only fails to establish M. Holsten's theory; properly understood, it even furnishes, to our thinking, a decisive proof against it. It shows that Paul, so far from comparing the manifestation of Christ to him at his conversion with the visions he afterwards enjoyed, laid down an essential difference between them. At the beginning of chapter xii., Paul proposes to give a full account of his visions, and commences with the first, which, far from being confounded with his conversion, is dated at least five years later ($\pi\rho\grave{o}\ \dot{\epsilon}\tau\hat{\omega}\nu\ \delta\epsilon\kappa\alpha\tau\epsilon\sigma\sigma\acute{a}\rho\omega\nu$). He does violence to his feelings in making known this private aspect of his life. At the fifth verse he is checked by this repugnance, this sacred modesty, and suddenly takes quite the opposite course. Instead of glorying in his privileges, he will only glory in his infirmities. The visions referred to in this passage, it would seem, he had never previously related; and just as the insults of his enemies were on the point of compelling him to do so, he checks himself and again drops the veil over these mysteries of his spiritual life. His ecstasies and visions do not belong to his ministry, and are not for others, only for God and himself: $\epsilon\check{\iota}\tau\epsilon\ \gamma\grave{a}\rho\ \dot{\epsilon}\xi\acute{\epsilon}\sigma\tau\eta\mu\epsilon\nu,\ \Theta\epsilon\hat{\omega}\cdot\ \epsilon\check{\iota}\tau\epsilon\ \sigma\omega\phi\rho o\nu o\hat{\upsilon}\mu\epsilon\nu,\ \dot{\upsilon}\mu\hat{\iota}\nu$ (2 Cor. v. 13). But so far from speaking of his conversion in the manner in which

---

[1] Holsten, *Zum Evangelium des Petrus und des Paulus.—Christusvision des Paulus.* Rostock, 1868.

he speaks of his visions, Paul shows neither reluctance nor embarrassment in describing it; it was one of the staple subjects of his preaching. He spoke, in short, of the appearance vouchsafed to him with the same confidence with which the Twelve related those which they had witnessed. This event belonged not to the sphere of Paul's private and personal life (indicated by the words εἴτε ἐξέστημεν), but to that of his apostolic life, aptly characterized in the phrase εἴτε σωφρονοῦμεν, ὑμῖν. Paul therefore perceived an essential distinction between these two orders of facts, corresponding to that which existed between the two different spheres of his life to which they belonged.

To make a second and equally decisive observation, Paul knew that his visions were spiritual *charismata*, effects of the Spirit. He ascribes them to the Spirit's agency as their true cause; whilst he attributes his conversion to a personal and corporeal intervention of the risen Jesus. In the phenomena of his visions he was transported, ravished into ecstasy, carried to the third heaven: at his conversion, Jesus descended to him and appeared before him in the midst of his ordinary life. Moreover, though Paul had several visions, he states that he had seen the risen Lord but *once*, and that this appearance was the last made by Jesus on earth. In the consciousness of the apostle there must therefore have existed a broad line of demarcation between the series of appearances then terminated (ἔσχατον δὲ πάντων, 1 Cor. xv. 8), and the ecstasies and visions which lasted throughout the apostolic age. How could this marked distinction have arisen, except from the conviction that the appearances of the risen Lord had a real and objective character, such as the spiritual visions of ecstasy did not possess.

Finally, if Christ's appearance to Paul had been an inward vision, it must have been not the cause, but the product of his faith. How could the mind of Saul the Pharisee have created such a vision, unless he were a Christian already? and if, on the other hand, he were a Christian already, how could he have attributed his conversion to this cause? Such a transformation makes the enigma still more obscure. M. Holsten's ingenious explanations leave the mystery just where it was.[1]

These considerations, it seems to us, deprive the vision-hypothesis of all exegetical support. And we must not forget that the question of Saul's conversion is not to be explained as a mere isolated fact. It is attached to the question of the resurrection of Jesus Christ, and bound up inseparably with it. The solution we give to the former of these miracles depends upon that of the latter. Any one who accepts the Saviour's resurrection would hardly find it worth while to question His appearance to this apostle. But the critic who, before entering on the question, is absolutely persuaded that there is no God, or that if there is, He never intervenes in human history, will doubtless set aside both facts, and would have recourse to the vision-hypothesis, were it ever so improbable. The problem is thus carried from the field of history into that of metaphysics, whither we must not pursue it.

---

[1] See Beyschlag's excellent criticisms on the vision-hypothesis, in the *Studien und Kritiken* for 1864 and 1870.

III. Paul's Conversion and his Theology.

It only remains to define the dogmatic significance of this conversion. It was the generating fact, not merely of Paul's apostolic career, but of his theology besides. We find in this event—latent in the spiritual experiences and feelings attending it—all the great ideas and the leading antitheses which characterize his doctrinal system. His conversion was the fruit of God's grace, manifesting itself in him as a sovereign power which triumphed over his individual will. Paul rose from the ground the captive of that Divine grace to which henceforth he was to surrender himself without reserve or condition (Gal. i. 16). Here are, in effect, the two terms of that universal antithesis which dominates his thought—God and man, grace and liberty, faith and works.

Embraced within this wide antithesis, we must notice another, which is still more conspicuous,—I mean the radical opposition that displays itself between law and faith, between the Gospel and Judaism.

The other apostles came to Christ through the medium of the Old Testament and the prophecies. For them there was, as one might say, a raised ladder, which they climbed step by step, finding Jesus at the summit. In their eyes, the Law and the Gospel had never been in opposition; they had never felt it necessary to renounce the old covenant in order to enter upon the new. This was the real cause of their hesitation and perplexity, when confronted with the great revolution that was about to take place.

But Paul, from the first, was in a totally different position. The Gospel and Judaism had always seemed to him absolutely and radically opposed (Phil.

iii. 7, etc.). The antithesis existed in his mind before his conversion; and it remained there. His conscience, laid hold of by God's grace, was abruptly and violently forced from one extreme to the other.

His adhesion to the Gospel was, above everything else, the complete negation of his previous life. For this reason it was that his doctrine and his career only attained their full development in the conflict between Judaism and Christianity—the old things and the new. The two terms of this dualism continued to be the poles round which all his theology revolved. This conversion, as we see, exemplifies in the most striking manner the utter impotence of the ancient principle of justification by the works of the law, and the triumph of the new principle of justification through faith and the grace of God (Rom. vii. 24, 25). Here lies the germ of the whole Pauline system. Our task will be to trace its progressive development during the rest of the apostle's life.

To seek the origin of Paul's Christian universalism in his Hellenism is therefore, manifestly, an entire mistake. It is rather to be found in his rigid Pharisaism. We may safely say that if Saul had been less of a Jew, Paul the apostle would have been less bold and independent. His work would have been more superficial, and his mind less unfettered. God did not choose a heathen to be the apostle of the heathen; for he might have been ensnared by the traditions of Judaism, by its priestly hierarchy and the splendours of its worship, as indeed it happened with the Church of the second century. On the contrary, God chose a Pharisee. But this Pharisee had the most complete experience of the emptiness of external ceremonies and the crushing yoke of the law. There was no fear that he would ever look back, that he would be tempted to set up again what the grace of God had justly overthrown (Gal. ii. 18). Judaism was wholly vanquished in his soul, for it was wholly displaced.

CHAPTER IV.

THE GENESIS OF PAUL'S GOSPEL.

WE are now in a position to understand the essential principle of Paul's gospel, and the leading elements which, from the beginning, entered into its working and form the creative factors of his Christian theology.

The origin of his gospel, as we have just seen, is to be found in his conversion. Paul has well defined it in those three words by which he characterizes the essential content of this Divine revelation: *It pleased God to reveal His Son in me*, ἀποκαλύψαι τὸν υἱὸν αὐτοῦ ἐν ἐμοί (Gal. i. 16). The object of this revelation, therefore, was simply the person of Christ. There is, as we have already said, no question here of that external manifestation which accompanied his conversion, but only of a revelation or inward illumination. A veil had concealed from the Pharisee's eyes the Divine glory of the crucified One. The cross was to him a *mystery*, and a *scandal* (1 Cor. i. 18–24; ii. 9, 10). This veil was now removed; and on the instant what seemed luminous before was darkened, and what was dark came into light. Light, the most radiant, burst suddenly out of thickest darkness. We find a very exact and vivid reminiscence of this marvellous phenomenon in a passage which is, in truth, beyond translation: Ὅτι ὁ Θεὸς ὁ εἰπὼν ἐκ σκότους φῶς λάμψαι, ὃς ἔλαμψεν ἐν ταῖς καρδίαις ἡμῶν, πρὸς φωτισμὸν τῆς γνώσεως τῆς δόξης τοῦ Θεοῦ ἐν προσώπῳ Χριστοῦ (2 Cor. iv. 6). At that decisive hour Paul saw shining on the brow of the victim of Calvary the Divine glory of *the Son of God*.

But there is still more in these words, ἀποκαλύψαι τὸν υἱὸν αὐτοῦ ἐν ἐμοί. In the same epistle Paul declares, when wishing to describe his life since his conversion: "*It is no longer I that live, it is Christ that lives in me*" (Gal. ii. 20 ; Phil. i. 21 ; Col. iii. 3, 4). His conversion, therefore, was something beyond a mere illumination. It was a profound crisis of his soul. The old *Ego* had been done away, and a new *Ego* emerged, whose vital principle is Christ Himself. Paul's conversion was nothing less than the spiritual entrance, the birth of Christ in his soul. In this lies the full significance of the phrase, ἀποκαλύψαι ἐν ἐμοί. We find here for the first time that preposition ἐν which occurs so often in the apostle's language, and which always indicates a mystic and indefinable communion.

Such is the mysterious source of his life. Here also lies the root of his whole system of thought. We see what depths it reached, depths from which it drew unceasingly that rich nourishment which kept it always fresh and has given it an undecaying youth. Had Paul's theology been merely an abstract system, it would long ago have disappeared, to be found to-day only in the history of philosophy,—that herbarium of dead and desiccated ideas. But it lives and is still fruitful, because it is the manifestation of the immortal life of Christ Himself.

What is that Christ who thus became the fountain

of the apostle's new consciousness and new life? The words of 2 Corinthians v. 14–17 come to our aid, completing and defining, in the clearest manner possible, the sense of the Galatian passage which we have just been studying. "We are possessed by the love of Christ, judging that if *one* died for all, all died with Him; and He died for all, in order that the living should no longer live unto themselves, but unto Him who for their sakes died and rose again. Henceforth we know no man after the flesh. And even though we *have known Christ after the flesh, yet now we know Him so no more.* If any one is in Christ, he is a new creature. The old things are passed away; all things are become new."

Now what is it to have known Christ after the flesh, and to cease to know Him in that character? In the apostle's life, these words can only refer to the period preceding his conversion. What then is the Christ whom Paul knew previous to that event? It was not the human and historical person of Jesus of Nazareth, whom most certainly he did not know as Christ.[1] The only Christ whom he knew before his conversion was the Jewish Messiah, a national, exclusive Messiah, who should win his triumph by carnal means. This Christ he knows no longer. By His death and resurrection Jesus destroyed this carnal notion of the Messiah; and these events presented Him as a new Christ, a Christ κατὰ πνεῦμα. But all Christians had

---

[1] This does not imply that Saul, brought up in Jerusalem from his childhood, studying at the feet of Gamaliel, and having a married sister in Jerusalem, might not have met Jesus, and heard Him preach in the temple. On the contrary, we consider that this is probable, and that his conversion, independently of human agency, cannot be very well explained otherwise.

not reached this point; a great number of them, forgetting the cross, hid the true character of Jesus behind the carnal glory of the Jewish Messiah, and doing so, knew nothing but a Christ according to the flesh,—that is, Christ without His death and resurrection. It was quite another Jesus ('Ἰησοῦν ἄλλον) whom Paul's adversaries preached at Corinth (2 Cor. xi. 4). For Paul, in fact, there was an old and a new Christ, just as there was the old man, the man after the flesh, and the new man, the man after the spirit (τὰ ἀρχαῖα, τὰ καινά: v. 17). Christ had died, and by His death abolished the flesh and all the relationships designated by this word. The men who are in Christ died and are raised with Him, and appear in Him as new men; so that we may truly say that we no longer know any one after the flesh, since through this great crisis of death and resurrection everything has been transformed, both with regard to the Head and the members; the old things are passed away, and everything made new. The Christ who entered the soul of Paul and dwelt there, was the Christ who had died and risen again; for this reason He has effected so radical a change. It is not enough to say that the death of Christ disturbed Saul's early conceptions; it has slain the Pharisee in him. By learning to know this new Christ, Saul is raised from the dead to a new life.

Thus, from the very beginning, the whole Christian life of Paul depended on the death and resurrection of Jesus. These two great events first made for themselves in his heart the place that they were subsequently to occupy in his theology. How could it be otherwise? The death of Jesus, which had been to him the great scandal, must needs, in the very nature of things, become the great mystery. In proportion as Saul had been revolted by it, Paul was to devote himself to it. The object of his repugnance became his boast and the mainstay of his faith. The point where human wisdom stumbled, became that in which the wisdom of God was triumphantly displayed. This logical reversal of his views was so radical and so complete, that henceforward, in his eyes, the whole life of Jesus and the entire Gospel are summed up in the cross. His preaching is nothing more than a λόγος τοῦ σταυροῦ; he would fain know nothing but Jesus Christ, and Jesus Christ crucified (1 Cor. i. 18, 23, 24; ii. 2).

To this object all Paul's thoughts were linked, as to their organic centre; this was their starting point, from which we shall find them advancing in all directions under the vigorous impulse of his dialectic. The resurrection of Jesus was the triumphant proof that this crucified man was the Messiah, the Son of God; but such a death as that of the Son of God could in no wise be an accident, occurring without cause or consequences. If it has taken place, it must have been necessary; and it has served to carry out God's own plan. What then is the meaning of this death? Death is the wages of sin; Christ not having known sin, did not die for Himself, but for humanity. His death could be nothing else than a sacrifice, through which, in the view of faith, the justifying grace of God is realized (δικαιοσύνη Θεοῦ). We will not push this deduction further at present. The great theory of redemption was certainly not formed in the apostle's mind in a single day, and we do not wish to anticipate; but we have here its outline very clearly indicated.

Such is the essential content and the creative principle of that gospel which Paul justly claimed to have received as a direct revelation from Jesus Christ. He was on this matter, to use one of his own expressions, emphatically *God-taught*. He might well call this gospel *my gospel*,—that which had been given him by God, and made his own by close assimilation. On it he has stamped ineffaceably the mark of his original genius.

I. Paul and the Historical Christ.

But the fact that this inner revelation of Christ is independent of all human tradition makes it the more important to determine the relation in which it stood to the actual life and teaching of Jesus, and the nature of the link which united Paul's new consciousness to the historical personality of the Saviour. The question amounts to this: To what extent was Paul acquainted with Christ's earthly life? and what influence did this knowledge exert on the formation of his views?

We consider that the Tübingen school has dismissed this question altogether too lightly. According to that school, Paul was either very imperfectly acquainted with the life and historical teaching of Jesus, or else he despised its traditions as being a knowledge of Christ according to the flesh, such as would have made his gospel dependent on the teaching of the first apostles. But these two explanations are equally baseless. The first is only supported by 2 Cor. v. 16, a passage which we have already discussed. The distinction Paul makes there between Christ after the flesh and Christ after the spirit, as we have seen, is not a distinction between the historical

Christ and the Christ dwelling in himself. Besides, we cannot see how the traditional knowledge of the doings and sufferings and teaching of Jesus could possibly interfere with the independence of his apostleship or the originality of his gospel. It is very clear that this external knowledge, however minute and exact it may have been, could not of itself make him an apostle, nor even convert him. Before his conversion, he had no doubt heard many particulars respecting Jesus of Nazareth; but they remained in his memory as so much foreign and dead matter, altogether beyond his understanding. The inward revelation, while it irradiated his soul, lighted up at the same time the historical life of the Crucified. So far from being contradictory, this revelation and that external knowledge of Christ lent mutual confirmation; each was necessary to the other. Without the former, the historical tradition is mere worthless and inert matter; without the second, the inward revelation could have produced only an idealistic theology, having no root in the realities of history. The two are related to each other as the soul is to the body, and form in combination an indissoluble organic unity.

At first sight, Paul's knowledge of the historical Christ seems to have been very limited; and we are surprised, on first examining his epistles for this purpose, to find so few allusions to the events of the life of Jesus and so few quotations from His discourses. But we should be mistaken in yielding to this first impression; and it may very readily be explained.

Modern criticism, which detects so many subtleties and such delicate shades of meaning, sometimes fails to perceive the simplest and most obvious things. It has forgotten, for instance, that Paul was a missionary before he was a theologian, and that he preached the Gospel in places where neither Jesus nor the Messiah had ever been heard of. Must he not then, of necessity, have described this strange Person and explained His title? Must he not have given in the synagogues of Asia such a conception and impression of Jesus—His life, miracles, death, and resurrection—that candid minds were naturally led to declare, This Jesus was the Christ? Can we imagine the apostle's missionary preaching apart from these conditions?

But all this early preaching and historical instruction about the life of Jesus necessarily belonged to a period of Paul's life antecedent to that which gave birth to his great epistles; and these letters, therefore, though not containing many Gospel narratives, assume in their believing readers a previous and fairly detailed acquaintance with the history of Jesus. Let us try to gather up the passing allusions and brief indications which are found scattered throughout them; when collected, they will be found, as a whole, more definite and substantial than at first sight one could have ventured to hope.[1]

The first epistle to the Corinthians shows us what place Christian tradition held in Paul's preaching (1 Cor. xi. 23, xv. 1–9). The death and resurrection of Jesus no doubt formed the centre of his earlier ministry. But the importance of the theological ideas which he attached to these great facts only made his care in relating them the more signal. He did this

---

[1] See Parch, *Jahrbücher für deutsche Theol.*, 1858, pp. 1–85, *Paulus und Jesus;* and Keim, *Geschichte Jesu von Nazara*, vol. i., p. 35 (*Zeugniss des Paulus*). [Eng. trans., i., 54–64.]

with such exact and vivid detail, that after his description of the great scenes of the passion, his listeners felt as if they had seen them with their own eyes : οἷς κατ' ὀφθαλμοὺς Ἰησοῦς Χριστὸς προεγράφη ἐν ὑμῖν ἐσταυρωμένος (Gal. iii. 1). What Paul had done in Galatia, he had certainly done at Corinth, and in all the Churches of Asia (1 Cor. xi. 23, xv. 1-9).

Among these historical details we may note several preserved in his letters, which are identical with those found in the Gospels. They were the rulers of the people (οἱ ἄρχοντες) who condemned Jesus (1 Cor. ii. 8; Acts xiii. 27; comp. Matt. xxvi. 3). It was through an act of treachery, perpetrated at night (νυκτὶ παρεδίδετο), that He fell into their hands. In the course of this night, and before His betrayal, Jesus, during His last repast with His disciples, instituted the holy supper. The account that Paul gives of this in 1 Corinthians xi. 23 corresponds literally with that in Luke's Gospel.

Paul knows that the Saviour's passion was the time of His weakness, and of His entire desertion; and that He was overwhelmed with afflictions and outrages,—accepted without a murmur (2 Cor. xiii. 4; Rom. xv. 3-6). Many other passages assume previous descriptions of His sufferings and death (τὴν νέκρωσιν τοῦ Ἰησοῦ περιφέροντες, 2 Cor. iv. 10; comp. Gal. vi. 17; Col. i. 24). According to Paul, Jesus was fastened to the cross with nails, and His blood poured forth (Col. ii. 14; comp. John xx. 25). The comparison he makes between this death and the sacrifice of the Paschal lamb tells us the exact time of its occurrence (1 Cor. v. 7).

With no less precision Paul had related the burial and resurrection of Jesus. The words of 1 Corinthians

xv. 1-9 are nothing else than a summary of his preaching on this point. This resurrection occurred on "the third day." That we have here an historical statement, and not the application of a saying of prophecy, is proved by the substitution in the Pauline Churches of the first day of the week for the Sabbath (1 Cor. xvi. 2). Finally, Paul seems, in this same chapter, to have arranged the different appearances of the risen Lord in chronological order; and everything that follows leads us to infer that he had moreover insisted on the external and corporeal nature of this resurrection.

The apostle, therefore, was perfectly familiar with the last scenes of the life of Jesus, and told the story of them with great exactness. The passion and resurrection of Christ were not to him, as to the Gnostics, a pair of abstract notions,—the passion and triumph of an ideal Christ resembling the *Sophia* of Valentinus; they were historical and concrete facts, preserved in their actual character, and with all their accompanying circumstances. He sets before us the veritable cross on which Jesus of Nazareth had hung but a few years ago; the tomb where His body was buried, and from whence He rose in triumph. Even had it been impossible to prove that Paul knew anything else of the historical life of Jesus, the manner in which he has examined and estimated these two great events sufficiently proves the connexion of his faith with the historical Christ, and forbids our reducing his theology to mere idealism.

When he has related these last events in such detail, can we believe that the apostle ignored all that belonged to the previous life of Jesus? Is it a very hazardous conjecture to suppose that during his fifteen days' visit to Peter at Jerusalem after his conversion, he questioned him minutely about the life of their common Master? Surely the term which Paul employs in Galatians i. 18, ἱστορῆσαι Κηφᾶν, allows us to think so. Besides, how could this eager follower of Jesus Christ do other than seize upon and master all that wealth of Gospel tradition so piously preserved by the early Christian communities, and reproduced in our first three Gospels?

If he never appeals to the Saviour's words to establish or defend his doctrines, this fact, however strange it may appear to us, encumbered as we are with scholastic methods, has nevertheless a cause and an explanation other than that of ignorance or contempt. The apostle was far from regarding the teaching of Jesus as a collection of sayings, an external law or written letter (γράμμα), which he had nothing more to do than to quote at every turn. Christ was to him, above all things, a *life-giving spirit*, an immanent and fertile principle, producing new fruit at each new season. There was such a perfect identity in his eyes between the historical and the indwelling Christ, that he never separates nor distinguishes them, and even attributes to the former that with which the latter had inspired him, and to the latter that which unquestionably he owed to the former. We find a remarkable example of this identification in 1 Corinthians xi. 23.

But was this a purely subjective idea? When Paul expresses his certainty that his apostolic teaching is indeed the faithful interpretation of the Master's, is he the victim of an illusion? Or is it not more natural to suppose that he had studied the discourses of Jesus, and knew them well enough to feel sure that no one could seriously bring any of Christ's words in argument against him? If, after all, we still feel surprise at not meeting with more frequent quotations in his epistles, we must remember that the epistle of Peter, the Apocalypse, the Acts of the Apostles, and the first epistle of John contain still fewer. From the beginning, Christ was not so much the herald or preacher of the Gospel, as Himself the object of the apostles' faith and teaching. To know what Christ had said or done seemed less important than to love Him, to receive Him, and to give oneself to Him.

There certainly existed for Paul, as for the other apostles, an objective, traditional teaching of Jesus. It is enough to recall the care and exactness with which he has preserved and transmitted to the believers at Corinth the very words used in instituting the Lord's supper (1 Cor. xi. 23). The whole discussion on marriage and celibacy, which occupies the seventh chapter of the same epistle, furnishes a proof yet more decisive. The apostle distinguishes with perfect clearness between the Saviour's express command and his own inspiration, and repeatedly sets them in contrast: οὐκ ἐγὼ ἀλλὰ ὁ Κύριος—ἐγὼ οὐχ ὁ Κύριος (1 Cor. vii. 10, 12, 25). The commandment Paul refers to is found in the Gospels; and on the points concerning which he declares he has received nothing from the Lord we find, as a matter of fact, that Jesus was silent. Should any one, notwithstanding this remarkable coincidence, refer this commandment to an inspiration from the indwelling Christ, he must in that case admit that when Paul gives his personal opinion in the 25th verse (γνώμην δίδωμι), he is speaking independently of his apostolic inspiration. But this is to come into collision with the 40th verse, where he appeals to his inspiration for the very purpose of justifying this opinion : " I believe that I also have the Spirit of God."

In chapter ix. 14 there occurs another quotation, introduced in a still more remarkable manner. The apostle wishes to establish the right of evangelists to live by the Gospel. He first gives a rational argument, drawn from the nature of things; then an exegetical argument taken from a passage in the Law : " Thou shalt not muzzle the ox that treadeth the corn "; and finally he completes his proof by quoting a positive command of the Lord : ὁ Κύριος διέταξεν (comp. Matt. x. 10 ; Luke x. 7). Evidently the word of Jesus comes in at the last, as the supreme and decisive authority. Observe further, throughout this passage, the images Paul employs to describe the work of the Gospel ; they are the same that Jesus loved to use : φυτεύειν ἀμπελῶνα, ποιμαίνειν ποίμνην, σπείρειν, θερίζειν, ἀροτριᾶν. Reminiscences like these are scattered through all the epistles :

Comp. Rom. xii. 14, 17, 20 with Matt. v. 44, etc.
„ 1 Thess. v. 1, etc. „ Matt. xxiv. 36, 44.
„ 1 Cor. xiii. 2 „ Matt. xvii. 20.
„ Acts xx. 35.

Paul does not relate the events of the life of Jesus to any larger extent than he quotes His discourses ; but he assumes that they are known to his readers. To people who had never heard the principal Gospel narratives, his epistles would present insoluble enigmas at every line. I need no further proof of this than the manner in which the apostle of the Gentiles speaks of the Twelve, and of the brethren of Jesus and His relations with them.

There is one thing, however, calculated to impress

us more powerfully than all these isolated facts. It is the general picture Paul draws of the Saviour's life, so exactly answering to the impression left on us by the Gospel narratives as a whole. Jesus was essentially man; nothing at first sight distinguished Him from other men (Rom. v. 15; Phil. ii. 7). He was born a Jew; he lived under the law (Gal. iv. 4); He confined His ministry to the people of Israel, and continued till the end the *minister of the circumcision* (Rom. xv. 8). The apostle speaks of Jesus as Jesus Himself speaks of the Son of man: He was poor, despised humble, obedient; He did not come to be ministered unto, but to minister; He took the rank and the form of a servant; His whole life was service and obedience (διακονία, ὑπακοή). It is perfectly true, as Baur observes, that Paul views the Saviour's life throughout in the light of His death, and sees in this death the climax of His ministry and the consummation of His obedience. But was it not from the same point of view that Christ Himself regarded His life and work? See Matt. xx. 28; Luke xxii. 27; Mark x. 38; John xii. 27.

The Christ who lived in the apostle's newly awakened consciousness was, therefore, by no means a mere ideal and subjective image. This indwelling Christ remained at the same time an external type— One whom Paul cherished in his memory and strove daily to know and imitate more perfectly. Indeed, the imitation of Christ is, as we know, an essential principle of the Pauline ethics; and does not this principle imply of necessity an objective and historical model, which every believer keeps before his eyes (1 Cor. xi. 1; Phil. ii. 5)? In this way, Jesus is at once the immanent principle of sanctification in the man, and the ideal of holiness realized before his eyes. It is impossible to detect any contradiction or breach between the indwelling and the historical Christ. The latter was essentially *spirit* ($\pi\nu\epsilon\hat{\upsilon}\mu\alpha$). During His earthly life this Divine force was localized; it was inclosed in the limits of the flesh. But when the flesh was destroyed by death, this Divine force, which was the very soul of Jesus, displayed all its expansive power. Poured into the heart of believers, it made not only Christ's memory live again there, but His actual holiness. Christ Himself became the believer's interior life.

Thus we see how the two Christs continued one, and how the apostle passed from the one to the other. Instead of being opposed in his ideas, they could not exist apart from each other; they are mutually dependent and confirmatory. From this intimate blending of history and faith, of the subjective and objective in his mind, the Pauline theology resulted; and in this combination lies its distinguishing feature. In brief, the apostle was so fully inspired by Jesus of Nazareth and understood Him so well, that his apostolic teaching, with all its originality and independence, was, notwithstanding appearances, an entirely faithful interpretation of the Master's views.

II. Paul's Use of the Old Testament.

Besides this primary external factor in the genesis of Paul's system of thought we must notice a second, which, though much less important, was equally essential. I refer to the Old Testament, and the use which the apostle continued to make of it after his conversion.

The faith in the Son of God, which had seized him

in his strict Pharisaism, had destroyed the unity of his religious consciousness. He found himself placed between the ancient and venerated revelation which he could not possibly renounce, and the new revelation which had been forced upon him. So soon as the contending emotions of the first few days were passed, Paul must at once have set to work to re-establish the unity of his belief, and recover peace of mind. Nothing furthered the development of his views more than this long internal struggle.

The first result of the revolution which had been wrought in him was to subordinate the old revelation to the new. The Christian faith served as a principle of criticism to direct him in his study of the Old Testament, sifting out its different elements and enabling him to estimate the worth of each. By this means he soon came to distinguish and contrast the *Law* and the *Promise*, and to proclaim the abolition of the one and the perfect realization of the other. But the Divine authority of the sacred writings in no wise suffered from these distinctions. If the old covenant ceased to exist as an economy of salvation, it became all the more important as a *preparation* and a *prophecy*. The typological method was the result of this situation, its function being to clear away contradiction and re-establish harmony between the old and the new oracles. This method, which was no more than the inevitable result of the relationship that the new faith wished to maintain with the the old, was employed by all the New Testament writers. But Paul's rabbinical education gave him in this respect an immense advantage over the other apostles. He may be said to have read the Old Testament books with the eyes of a Christian, and the penetration of a rabbi. Everything in this long history of God's people became prophecy; its personages and events equally so with its discourses. Its language became transfigured; the spiritual meaning shone forth through the veil of the literal sense. Thus a rich typology was created and evolved, which served to support and illustrate all the apostle's demonstrations. Only a few examples of this teaching are preserved in the epistles; but this method must have held a much larger place in Paul's missionary teaching.

It will not do to regard this typology as a mere formal accommodation to the Jewish mode of thinking, or as a style of literary illustration. It is inherent in the matter of Paul's doctrine, and forms an integral part of it. At the same time, Baur goes much too far when he says that the Old Testament was to Paul the sole objective source of truth, the only external ground of his religious belief. As we have seen, he found a fuller and higher revelation in the person of Jesus. No; it was not from the Old Testament, not by way of exegesis, that the apostle attained the ground on which his doctrine rests. If his faith depends on his exegesis, his exegesis depends still more on his faith. His convictions are not the result of his bold method of interpretation; that method can only be explained by the new convictions, which of necessity gave rise to it. Paul borrowed little from the Old Testament beyond its forms; it was an ancient mould into which he poured a new material.

But we can understand how greatly his ideas must have been influenced by this constant effort to trace them in the old covenant. Nothing is better calculated than allegory to develop an idea to its fullest extent. The famous allegory of Hagar and Sarah should be studied from this point of view (Gal. iv. 21-31). It is evident in this case, that if the idea created the image, the image in its turn was a wonderful help in defining the idea and developing its fulness.

We now perceive how the different elements of the Pauline system were constituted. The inner revelation of Christ is its central and generating principle, to which the other two are related as the body is to the soul. Historical knowledge concerning Jesus, and the institutions and prophecies of the Old Testament, were in themselves nothing more than inert matter which the Pauline principle permeated and vivified, finding in them its constant nourishment, the means for its expression and realization. But that is not all. We must further ask, where the power lay that created the system, that united these different elements and gave to Paul's theology its eminently original character. This power consisted, and could consist in nothing else than the apostle's strong individuality. His spiritual individuality explains his doctrine, for it has produced it. Let us endeavour, in conclusion, to indicate its essential features.

III. Paul's Idiosyncrasy.

The lofty character of Paul has not always been properly apprehended, because it has too often been considered from a narrow point of view. Its striking originality seems to be due to the fruitful combination in it of two spiritual forces,—two orders of faculty which are seldom found united in this degree in one personality, and which in the case of Jesus alone present themselves more perfectly blended and carried even to a further height than in the apostle.

I mean *dialectic power* and *religious inspiration*, the rational and the mystical element; or, to borrow Paul's own language, the activity of νοῦς and that of πνεῦμα.

The rational or dialectic nature of the great apostle's doctrine has been very forcibly exhibited by Baur. Paul evidently belongs to the family of powerful dialecticians; he ranks with Plato, with Augustine and Calvin, with Schleiermacher, Spinoza, Hegel. An imperious necessity compelled him to give his belief full *dialectic* expression, and to raise it above its contradictories. Having affirmed it, he confronts it at once with its opposite; and his faith is incomplete till it has triumphed over this antithesis and reached a point of higher unity.

It is interesting to study, in this aspect, the progress of ideas and the unfolding of the apostle's argument in his great epistles. From the particular question Paul's mind rises at one bound to the general principle governing the whole discussion. Having lighted up the subject from this height, he descends again with irresistible power to the level of fact. It is this dialectical procedure which imparts such crushing force to his logic. This method is apparent in the two epistles to the Corinthians, and still more in the epistle to the Romans. At the very outset Paul ascends to the general idea of *righteousness* (δικαιοσύνη), which he at once divides into a negative and a positive conception. The first eight chapters are only the dialectical development of these two opposing ideas. The apostle follows each to its ultimate consequences. He shows—with what power of logic we know—how the former notion, that of justification by works, soon disproves itself, and inevitably ends in the despairing cry, "Oh, wretch that I am! who shall deliver me from this body of death?" But at the same time he follows the development of the latter conception in all its fruitful consequences, till we hear the final song of triumph: "Who shall separate us from the love of God?" (Rom. vii. 25; comp. viii. 35, 39.) His dialectic power is certainly the mainspring of Paul's thought. It is this which impelled it forward, which gave it organic form and created the rich and powerful system in which it has embodied itself.

However important this rational element may be, those who look no further only see the surface of the Pauline thought. Beneath this reflective force of reason there is that which we have called, for lack of another name, the *pneumatical* life, taking its rise at the point of contact between the human soul and the invisible world. Paul's habitual state is, in fact, not that of a mind which reasons, but of a soul which contemplates and adores. Beyond the reasoning faculty there lay in him the realm of intuition,—truth palpable to the soul, deep feeling which nourished and gave birth to thought, and which thought was never quite able to express. It was in this region that he felt those ineffable things which it is not possible for man to utter (ἄρρητα ῥήματα, ἃ οὐκ ἐξὸν ἀνθρώπῳ λαλῆσαι, 2 Cor. xii. 4). There we have a mysterious life at once active and passive, an inexplicable intercourse between the spirit of man and of God, which the psychical man with his ordinary common sense regards as foolishness (1 Cor. ii. 14); but in which lay, nevertheless, the apostle's chief wealth and power, and his supreme consolation.

This condition of soul cannot be analysed, because the soul on entering it ceases, to some extent, to belong to and observe itself. It is the sphere of ecstasy, of vision, and of all the phenomena that we describe as inspiration. It is a permeation of the individual soul by mysterious forces. In it, strangely enough, we find our personal life expand, while at the same time our dependence increases. To condemn such a state as morbid is, in my opinion, a proof of great levity of mind and rashness of judgment. No doubt this mystical tendency may be perverted and corrupted, like all other faculties. But it is not in itself a disease, any more than they, for it is natural to every human soul. I am perfectly aware that ordinary psychology gives it no place in its traditional categories; but these categories are far from including the whole of life. Where could we find a more wholesome mental constitution than belonged to Socrates, or to Luther; where a more true and delicate conscience than that of Joan of Arc? And yet we know that their spiritual life had its source far beyond the sphere of pure reason. If this faculty of mystical exaltation is a disease, we should have to acknowledge that Jesus, despite the harmony of His nature, possessed an unsound mind; for He had His moments of ecstasy—sacred moments, which a coarse, vulgar understanding profanes by calling them hallucinations (Mark i. 12; iii. 21; Luke ix. 29; x. 18). No; this is not the sign of a morbid disposition. In truth, he is much rather the sick man who has never known any state but that of dry, cold reason. What else is religion, what is prayer and adoration, but an exaltation of spirit—to employ again Paul's own language, an ἐν πνεύματι εἶναι?

We recognise this mysterious life underlying all

the reasonings of the apostle. It constitutes the foundation of his being; and we feel the throb of its mighty pulsations through all his dialectic machinery. This dialectic is, in fact, a mere instrument which of itself creates nothing. The life of the Spirit, an ever gushing spring, throws out the material which his logic interprets, elaborates, and organizes. This inner life had been created in Paul by the first revelation of Christ in his soul. Christ living in him continued to reveal Himself in and through him. This abiding and inward revelation forms the basis of apostolic inspiration. It supplies to him an absolute assurance, springing from his conviction of being in immediate possession of the truth; it is an unerring instinct that guides the apostle alike in thought and action. From that hour this *pneumatical* life remained in him, and was ever growing and increasing. It manifested itself not only in the joy, the strength and authority that it gave him, but in extraordinary phenomena and exceptional *charismata*, in his *gift of healing*, his *speaking with tongues*, his *ecstasies, visions and revelations* (2 Cor. xii. 12; 1 Cor. xiv. 13; 2 Cor. xii. 1).

In this mysterious sphere great problems were solved, and great resolutions taken. Whenever the apostle reaches a critical stage of his career, we find one of these inner revelations occurring, to show him what course to pursue and to put an end to his hesitations. Just when his anxiety is keenest and his excitement most intense, there comes to him a sudden illumination. We find this phenomenon occurring in all the great crises of his life. Thus on his first encounter with the Judaizers at Antioch, it was a revelation that pointed out to him the way to Jerusalem (Gal. ii. 2). When on the point of leaving that city to begin his great mission to the heathen, he had a vision in the temple (Acts xxii. 18). It was a vision again that directed his course to Europe (Acts xvi. 9). On another, less familiar occasion, when, buffeted and beaten by Satan's messenger, he despaired of his apostleship, there resounded in his ears the comforting words : " My grace is sufficient for thee" (2 Cor. xii. 9). Lastly, during that frightful tempest which drove the vessel bearing him to Rome upon the shores of Malta, a vision came to assure Paul that he should see Rome and Cæsar (Acts xxvii. 24).

We recognise therefore that Paul's apostolic inspiration bore the chief part in the genesis and development of his belief. But we must understand its working differently from the way in which it has been understood hitherto. Faith without criticism, and criticism without faith seem to me to result equally in a moral impossibility. The first assumes that this theological system—so human, rational, and individual in its traits—fell straight from heaven into Paul's mind; the latter makes Paul out an enthusiast, a sort of Swedenborg, who mistook his own ideas for a revelation from God. Let us take the gospel of Paul for what it was—not a series of scholastic formulæ, but the positive and immanent revelation of Christ, which while it continued to unfold itself in the hidden depths of his consciousness, displayed its ethical product in the fruits of righteousness, and its intellectual result in his theories and his ideas. Thus we find it render a priceless aid to our faith, without imposing a burdensome yoke upon our understanding.

Being now in possession of all the elements which combined to form the Pauline system, we might endeavour to reconstruct it *à priori*, by way of logical deduction. But we shall resist this temptation. To construct it in this way would only be to cramp and petrify it. Paul's theology was not developed after this fashion; it was not wrought out in solitude. Its development was logical, no doubt, but slow and laborious notwithstanding. The apostle's circumstances, his external conflicts and practical necessities, have left their impression deeply marked upon his doctrine. The course of this historical development we must now proceed to recover and describe.

BOOK II.

FIRST PERIOD, OR PERIOD OF MISSIONARY ACTIVITY.

From 35 to 53 A.D.

PAUL'S missionary preaching was, unquestionably, the earliest historical outcome of his system of belief. It occupied a period of nineteen or twenty years—the longest in his life, but also that in which he wrote the least; and it therefore remains comparatively in the shadow.

During these long years the greater part of Paul's apostolic work was accomplished. It was the period of his great journeys, of his fairest hopes and his early successes. Then it was that, in Asia and Greece, he conquered for himself the wide sphere of which his great epistles show him in possession. It is not surprising that during this time he wrote but little. There was no occasion for it. Oral preaching of necessity everywhere preceded written preaching; and the work of founding Churches had to be undergone, before the labours of their edification or of doctrinal controversy were possible.

The missionary character of this first period naturally determined the special form in which the apostle's doctrine was cast. It cannot be doubted that when preaching to Jews or Pagans for the first time, he presented his gospel to them in a fashion essentially different from the learned and logical exposition of his great epistles.

Those who refuse to recognise the true Paul except in the abstruse dialectician of the great epistles, forget that he was a missionary, and must have addressed himself in the first instance to women, to working men, to the ignorant, to little children—indeed, to all sorts of low people (1 Cor. i. 28). If he had spoken to them as he afterwards wrote, he would not even have been understood. But when we find this man, meagre and feeble in appearance as he was, exercising such an irresistible ascendency over every one who came near him, and from Damascus to Rome, wherever he sets his foot, becoming a cause of disturbance and popular excitement, can we doubt that beside his powers of abstract thought and logic, Paul had a striking, impressive utterance, and set forth his faith, in the first instance, under a very concrete and palpable form? It was then that he laid the historical basis upon which the laborious edifice of his religious thought was afterwards to be reared.

His doctrine, therefore, could not have at this time the dialectic character that conflict was to impart to it. It is, as it were, wrapped up in itself, taking shape only in the general and oratorical form of preaching. Yet it does not remain stationary; it advances all the while, stimulated in its progress by success and fructified by experience. These years were a long, obscure period of gestation. It is certainly to be regretted that, for the purpose of tracing this inner progress, we have not more numerous, and especially more positive, documents belonging to the period. But is not that an additional reason for trying to turn those that remain to us to better account?

After the fact of Paul's conversion, which is here our secure starting point, we have his first missionary discourses in the Acts, an indirect echo of his preaching no doubt, but far from being unfaithful. With these discourses the two letters to the Thessalonians are in close connexion and sequence, resuming and carrying forward their teaching. Finally, at the close of this first period, we have the discourse at Antioch addressed to Peter and the Judaizers, which has been preserved in the epistle to the Galatians (chap. ii. 15–21).

These, I frankly admit, are but scant, uncertain way-marks on a very long road. But do they not form a progressive and ascending series, and indicate unmistakably the general direction that the apostle's doctrine naturally followed, under the pressure of logic and of circumstances?

CHAPTER I.

THE MISSIONARY DISCOURSES IN THE ACTS.—THE TWO EPISTLES TO THE THESSALONIANS.

I. PAUL'S DISCOURSES IN THE ACTS.

THE missionary discourses preserved in the Acts are three in number, delivered at Antioch in Pisidia (xiii. 16-41, 46, 47), at Lystra (xiv. 15-17), and at Athens (xvii. 23-31). The first was addressed to Jews; the other two to Gentiles. Do these discourses furnish us with material for delineating the apostle's preaching?

This question has been answered in different, but for the most part in equally arbitrary fashions. Before replying to it, we must endeavour to gain a definite conception of the preaching itself and its contents. We can do so, I think, by combining certain scattered indications in the later epistles, which hitherto have been neglected. These indications will furnish us with a sure starting point, and moreover with an excellent standard of appreciation.

Paul himself has given us a summary of his apostolic preaching in his first epistle to the Corinthians: "I call to your mind, brethren, the gospel that I have preached unto you, which ye have received, and in which ye stand fast. . . . I delivered unto you that which also I received: above all, that Christ died for our sins *according to the Scriptures*; that He was buried; that He was raised again *according to the Scriptures*. . . . This is what *I and the other apostles* preach, and what you have believed" (1 Cor. xv. 1-11). To this passage should be added the following: 1 Cor. xi. 23; Gal. iii. 1; Rom. ix. 4, 5; 1 Thess. i. 10. It is manifest that the apostle's preaching consisted, above everything else, in a recital of the passion, death and resurrection of Jesus, with scriptural arguments designed to prove that Jesus was the Christ, and that in Him there was remission of sins. Affirmation predominates here over reflection, historical facts over theological ideas. Paul's preaching, in its general character, did not differ essentially from that of the Twelve. Prophecy, it appears, was from the first Paul's grand argument in debate with the Jews (Rom. i. 2; iii. 21; iv.; Gal. iii.); and the author of the Acts is perfectly correct when he says that the apostle in the synagogue of Thessalonica reasoned with the Jews from the Scriptures (ἀπὸ τῶν γραφῶν), showing from them that Christ must needs suffer and rise again from the dead (Acts xvii. 2, 3). There could not be a better summary of Paul's preaching in the synagogues.

How did he address his pagan hearers? The epistles leave no doubt on this point either. According to Romans i. 18-23, the Gentiles' chief offence lay in allowing the idea of the true God to become obscured and lost. With their religious consciousness, their moral conscience became darkened; still, there remained in their nature some gleams of light. Their conscience was inwardly disturbed, accusing and defending itself by turns, unable to find rest (Rom. ii. 15). Here it was that Paul evidently found the basis and starting point of his appeals. To restore the primitive idea of the one invisible God by showing the vanity of worshipping idols ; to awaken the moral consciousness, by giving it a foresight of *the wrath of God* ready to punish all iniquity ; to renew it by preaching repentance, and faith in Jesus the Saviour and the Judge,—such must have been the apostle's first and constant endeavour when in the midst of heathenism (1 Thess. i. 9 ; 2 Cor. vi. 16, etc.; Eph. iv. 17, 18 ; Rom. i. 19 ; ii. 16).

When we compare with this twofold result the missionary discourses put into Paul's mouth in the Acts, we find a correspondence sufficiently exact, at least in regard to their fundamental ideas. These discourses are not literal reproductions of the apostle's words ; they are a little blunted and indistinct, and too much resemble those of the other preachers of the Gospel. In drawing up the discourse at Antioch in Pisidia, for example, the writer has evidently Stephen's address and Peter's Pentecostal sermon in his recollection. But to infer from these resemblances that the addresses in question are merely free compositions and have no historical value, is, in my opinion, going too far. Although their tenor is very general, original features and bold and novel ideas are not altogether wanting ; and there are passages in which we distinctly catch the inimitable accents of Paul's voice. It will be well to analyse them more closely.

The discourse delivered in the synagogue of Antioch in Pisidia has three essential divisions. The first, relating the history of the Jewish people up to the time of David, recalls the beginning of Stephen's address (xiii. 16–23). It must, however, be acknowledged that if it presents the same history, this passage exhibits it from a new point of view. It is no longer the people's ingratitude, but the idea of the promise which guides Paul as he proceeds in his course across the wide field of the history of Israel. And is not the summing up of the history under the idea of the promise an essentially Pauline conception? Besides, we find that Paul makes David the terminus of his historical exposition, instead of descending, like Stephen, to the time of Solomon and the temple. For it was from the family of David that the Messiah was to come.

ACTS xiii. 23.	ROMANS i. 2, 3.
Τούτου ὁ Θεὸς ἀπὸ τοῦ σπέρματος κατ' ἐπαγγελίαν ἤγαγε τῷ Ἰσραὴλ σωτῆρα Ἰησοῦν.	Ὃ προεπηγγείλατο διὰ τῶν προφητῶν αὐτοῦ, . . . περὶ τοῦ υἱοῦ αὐτοῦ τοῦ γενομένου ἐκ σπέρματος Δαβὶδ κατὰ σάρκα.

A more novel and characteristic Pauline trait is the profound distinction made in regard to the Old Testament between *the law* and *the promise*,—the one being pronounced impotent (ver. 39), and the other realized in Christ (ver. 32).

The second part of the discourse (vers. 24-37) shows the fulfilment of the promise in the death of Jesus. Its details might very well have been taken from the Third Gospel; though it will be observed that Paul says nothing about the Saviour's public labours. He dwells solely on three points: the sufferings and death, the burial, and the resurrection of Jesus,—that is, on the very points which are emphasized in 1 Corinthians xv. 3, 4. Notice above all the reference, so remarkable in this place, to the intermediate event of the burial, which has no importance in the preaching of the other apostles, but which had an essential bearing on Paul's ethical conception of faith and baptism (Rom. vi. 3, 4).

The Pauline cast of thought is still more obvious in the third and *subjective* part of the discourse (vers. 38-41). Certainly we do not find here as yet the theory of expiation, nor that of justification by faith; they are equally wanting, as we shall see, in the two epistles to the Thessalonians. The germ of these doctrines, however, is present: διὰ τούτου ὑμῖν ἄφεσις ἁμαρτιῶν καταγγέλλεται. The words διὰ τούτου do not relate to καταγγέλλεται, which would not make sense, but to ἄφεσις ἁμαρτιῶν. Peter had said at Pentecost: "Repent, and be baptized every one of you in the name of Jesus, for the remission of your sins." There is much more implied in Paul's phrase. The remission of sins, instead of being connected with baptism, is associated here with the death and resurrection of Jesus, in and through which redemption is objectively realized. It is also at the same time, a complete and absolute justification: καὶ ἀπὸ πάντων ὧν οὐκ ἠδυνήθητε ἐν νόμῳ Μωυσέως δικαιωθῆναι, ἐν τούτῳ πᾶς ὁ πιστεύων δικαιοῦται. Justification by faith is here presented in its negative form. But, as M. Reuss has remarked, it is under this form that the idea must have first originated in Paul's mind. The passage is a perfectly just expression of the experience which Paul himself had made of the ineffectiveness of the law. Add to this, that it would be difficult to imagine a phrase more true to Paul's peculiar style. In the first place, the very singular grammatical form of the sentence is Pauline (comp. Rom. xv. 18). Secondly, its terms are all found amongst those most characteristic of the epistles: ἠδυνήθητε ἐν νόμῳ (comp. Rom. viii. 3 : τὸ ἀδύνατον τοῦ νόμου); δικαιωθῆναι construed with ἀπό (comp. Rom. vi. 7); and the general and comprehensive phrase πᾶς ὁ πιστεύων (comp. Rom. i. 16 ; iii. 22). Lastly, in the whole proposition, ἐν τούτῳ πᾶς ὁ πιστεύων δικαιοῦται, the words ἐν τούτῳ cannot be grammatically related to πιστεύων—which, however, would still express a Pauline idea (Gal. iii. 26)—but must be attached to δικαιοῦται, conveying a meaning far more original and profound (comp. Gal. ii. 17 : δικαιωθῆναι ἐν Χριστῷ).

Verses 46 and 47 mark the transition by which the Gospel passed the Jews to address itself to the Gentiles: "It was necessary that the word of God should first be spoken to you (ὑμῖν ἦν ἀναγκαῖον πρῶτον; comp. Rom. i. 16: Ἰουδαίῳ πρῶτον). But since you reject it, and judge yourselves unworthy of eternal life, behold, we turn to the Gentiles." This double experience, often repeated, of the obstinate unbelief of the one people, and the receptiveness of the other, gradually created in the apostle's mind the conviction that the kingdom of God was about to be transferred from the Jewish to the Gentile nations,— a conviction entirely opposed to the hope to which the apostles of the circumcision who remained in Palestine fondly clung. Paul was the instrument of a new and radical evolution of God's plan. His experience, as it widened into a general principle, naturally took in his eyes the shape of that Divine law which he was afterward to interpret and formulate in the ninth, tenth, and eleventh chapters of the epistle to the Romans. At the same time, he gained a clearer understanding of his special vocation as *apostle to the Gentiles.*

A vast horizon was now opening before his eyes.

As the heathen world, with its history and its destinies, entered more and more into his thoughts, they could not fail to gain a greatly wider scope. This epoch is marked by the two discourses of Lystra and Athens. They are naturally associated together; for indeed they express the same idea.

These two addresses being more original than that of Antioch, have excited critical suspicions to a less degree. In the Athenian discourse especially, so exquisite in rhetorical style and so admirable in its profundity of thought, one can scarcely refuse to recognise the master's touch. It is, in fact, a piece of apologetics of a new order; and there is nothing to compare with it either in preceding or in following discourses.

Paul's preaching no longer finds its starting point in the Old Testament, but in the moral and religious consciousness of humanity (comp. Rom. i. 19).

ACTS xiv. 15.   1 THESS. i. 9.

. . . εὐαγγελιζόμενοι ὑμᾶς ἀπὸ τούτων τῶν ματαίων ἐπιστρέφειν ἐπὶ Θεὸν ζῶντα.

. . . πῶς ἐπεστρέψατε πρὸς τὸν Θεὸν ἀπὸ τῶν εἰδώλων δουλεύειν Θεῷ ζῶντι καὶ ἀληθινῷ.

But in these two discourses there is something beyond the general notion of God, which belonged properly to Jewish theology much more than to Christian teaching. They are an attempt to comprehend paganism and its history from the standpoint of the new revelation; they are a sketch of that philosophy of history which the apostle was destined afterward to complete. Notice, to begin with, his new and profound conception of paganism. "I find you, O Athenians, devout to excess. Passing through your city, and looking at your temples and altars, I have found one with this inscription, To the unknown God! What you worship in ignorance, I come to make known to you" (Acts xvii. 22, 23). In polytheism thus understood Paul could have no difficulty in finding a point of attachment for the worship of the true God. That paganism which the Jews, and Paul himself, were accustomed to regard as a pure negation of piety, has here a positive value assigned to it; and is in this way brought into the plan of salvation prepared by God for all humanity. The difference between Jews and Gentiles is reduced to its minimum. God has made all nations of one blood. He is not the God of the Jews alone, but also of the Gentiles (Rom. iii. 29). His providence has regulated the destiny not only of Israel, but of the Gentile nations as well, determining the place, the time, and the boundaries of their earthly habitation. They have walked in darkness, it is true, groping their way; but they have been moving towards a goal fixed by God Himself. In the Divine plan, the history of paganism unfolds itself in a line parallel with that of Israel, and both meet at the cross of Jesus Christ. Thus the universalism of the new Gospel found expression; and thus was formed in the mind of Paul that great historical plan which he will expound in the epistle to the Romans.

The Athenian address was interrupted, and its specifically Christian portion remained undeveloped. But on comparing 1 Thessalonians i. 9, 10 and Acts xvii. 30, 31, it is easy to see that Paul would have confined himself to the assertion of a few very simple ideas and essential facts: the necessity of repentance, the imminence of the last judgment, the death and resurrection of Jesus, and deliverance from the wrath to come.

Such was Paul's early missionary preaching. If the discourses of the Acts do not give us his whole theology, yet they mark the first stage in the development of his system. The experiences of this epoch were so many fertile germs out of which, under the influence of the apostle's intense meditation, a rich harvest of profound views and great thoughts would shortly be produced.

II.

THE TWO EPISTLES TO THE THESSALONIANS.

These two epistles are connected with the discourses we have just analysed, alike in their chronological order and in the nature of their ideas.

It will be noticed, in the first place, how readily the two letters adjust themselves to the setting furnished by the account of Paul's second missionary journey in the Acts, and what constant harmony exists between them and it. In the address of both letters we read the names of the three missionaries who appear in the narrative: *Paul, Silas,* and *Timothy* (1 Thess. i. 1; 2 Thess. i. 1). Silas, moreover, is mentioned before Timothy; his name ranks second in the epistles as it does in the Acts —a fact all the more surprising, inasmuch as Silas' name only occurs once besides in the rest of Paul's epistles. This circumstance is inexplicable on the hypothesis of a pseudo-apostolic authorship of the two letters; but it is fully confirmed by a phrase in the second epistle to the Corinthians, where also the second place is assigned to Silas (chap. i. 19).

Furthermore, we gather from the two epistles that

Paul arrived at Thessalonica from Philippi, and that from Thessalonica he passed on to Athens (1 Thess. ii. 2 and iii. 1 ; comp. Acts xvii. 1 and 16). We find reference made in very precise terms to the ill-treatment that he and his friends had been subject to at Philippi : προπαθόντες καὶ ὑβρισθέντες, καθὼς οἴδατε, ἐν Φιλίπποις, ἐπαρρησιασάμεθα λαλῆσαι πρὸς ὑμᾶς τὸ εὐαγγέλιον τοῦ Θεοῦ ἐν πολλῷ ἀγῶνι (1 Thess. ii. 2). This *boldness* and *great contention* answer very well to the account of the Acts (xvii. 1-9). Again, it appears from the two epistles that the majority of Christians at Thessalonica were of heathen origin ; and this is just what is said in Acts xvii. 4 : τῶν τε σεβομένων Ἑλλήνων πλῆθος πολύ, γυναικῶν τε τῶν πρώτων οὐκ ὀλίγαι. The Jews, on the contrary, had violently opposed the preaching of the Gospel, and having rejected it themselves, did their utmost to prejudice the heathen against it and to make Paul's ministry in Thessalonica impossible (Acts xvii. 5 ; comp. 1 Thess. ii. 15, 16). These statements remind us at every point of the narrative of the Acts : nay, the phraseology of this last passage recalls its very style (ἐκδιώκειν, κωλύειν ἡμᾶς τοῖς ἔθνεσιν λαλῆσαι ἵνα σωθῶσιν). It was amid affliction and persecution that the Christians at Thessalonica received the Gospel (Acts xvii. 5 ; comp. 1 Thess. i. 6; ii. 14). Finally, these persecutions compelled Paul to remove from Thessalonica prematurely and to leave unfinished the work so full of promise which he had begun there (Acts xvii. 10 ; 1 Thess. iii. 1-5 and 10: καταρτίσαι τὰ ὑστερήματα τῆς πίστεως ὑμῶν).[1]

---

[1] This very striking agreement has been fully brought out by Baur in his *Paulus*, vol. ii., p. 97 [Eng. trans., ii., 85 ff.]. He

On the other hand, the whole character of the two letters is such that they can only be under-

makes use of it as an "unmistakable" proof that the author of the two epistles borrowed their historical setting from the Acts, and at the same time imitated the style of that narrative. But it is surprising that a writer who so scrupulously copies the Acts in the first chapters of his epistle should contradict its statements in the third chapter, making Paul and Timothy meet first at Athens, when, according to the Acts, they only joined each other at Corinth (Acts xviii. 5); though here, according to Baur, the writer no longer wished to imitate the Acts, but the epistles to the Corinthians, making Timothy go backwards and forwards between Athens and Thessalonica, just as Titus between Corinth and Ephesus !

More than this, in the second edition of Baur's *Paulus* we find two opinions respecting the epistles to the Thessalonians which present a flagrant contradiction,—one which neither Baur nor M. Zeller, his editor, appears to have noticed. In the body of his work [vol. ii., pp. 85-88], Baur demonstrates that the author of the two epistles was acquainted with the Acts and imitated its style, and that the passage in 1 Thess. ii. 14-16 had no other source ; whence it is easy to conclude that since the Acts, according to Baur, cannot have been written before 120 or 130 A.D., these two epistles date at the earliest from 130 or 135 A.D. But at the end of this second volume is a dissertation in which Baur adopts Kern's idea, that the Antichrist can be no other than Nero; and hence, according to him, one of the two epistles was written in the reign of Vespasian—Vespasian being the κατέχων who delays Nero's return—and the other after the fall of Jerusalem ! We must, however, make our choice between these two dates, and this double series of arguments. One might perhaps say, in order to reconcile them, that the author of the two epistles had before his eyes the very journal of travels which the writer of the Acts afterwards inserted in his narrative, and which might be known in 67 or 68 A.D. Even this would not remove the difficulty, so far as Baur's exposition is concerned ; for beside his unwillingness to accept the idea of a journal of travel, he asserts that the style of our two epistles is strictly moulded upon the general style of the Acts.

stood in this historical setting, and in connexion with this period. They contain nothing either of the keen and profound polemics of the great epistles, nor of the lofty speculation belonging to those of the Captivity. They are as distinct from each of these groups as they are allied both in form and substance to the discourses of the Acts. In them Paul is in truth only preaching from a distance; he continues and completes by letter his oral instruction. Their originality consists just in this practical character. They were written without premeditation, and we must not expect to find in them skilful construction or logical divisions.

The traditional division of Paul's epistles into the dogmatic and the hortatory is here entirely inapplicable. Dogmatic pre-occupations are altogether wanting. The doctrines which seem most insisted on, those of the *parousia* and of Antichrist, are no exception to this, for even on these two points the apostle does not enter into any theoretical discussion; it is a practical end which he has in view (1 Thess. iv. 13). This is why some have been led to speak of the dogmatic *indifference*, or *neutrality*, of these letters,—terms which are both alike inappropriate, and give an utterly misleading impression of the specific character of these brief pages. There is nothing tame about them, nothing vague or indefinite; on the contrary, they breathe a spirit of strong faith and overflowing life, and above all, an ardour of hope destined before long to be extinguished.[1] They give a first sketch of Paul's doctrine,

---

[1] [*Subdued*, or *chastened*, we admit; but not "extinguished." On p. 111 this hope is spoken of as "transformed." Paul never

corresponding with that primitive period when it possessed all its vigour without having as yet attained its fulness. Let us note some of its special features:

1. The anti-Judaistic controversy which characterizes the great epistles has not broken out, or at any rate has not as yet absorbed the apostle's attention. It is entirely absent from these two letters. The contention which they bespeak is of a general character; it is the warfare that the great missionary waged against both Jews and pagans, the same that is found in his discourses in the Acts (1 Thess. ii. 14-16). The ἄτοποι καὶ πονηροὶ ἄνθρωποι spoken of in 2 Thessalonians iii. 2 are not Judæo-Christians, but Jews who are impeding Paul's work at Corinth. Again, it is to the calumnies of the Jews of Thesssalonica, or elsewhere, that the personal defence in the second chapter of the first epistle refers. There is no need for us to see in this an artificial imitation of passages in 1 and 2 Corinthians, such as Baur discovers. The apostle is not so much endeavouring to defend himself, as to present his own laborious and disinterested life for an example to the Church at Thessalonica (chap. ii. 9-12).

2. The great Pauline antithesis between the law and faith, having no existence as yet in these two epistles, we are not surprised to find that the doctrine of Justification remains undeveloped and is presented there under a very general form. It is

ceased to look forward ardently to the *parousia*; though at a later time the event seemed less imminent, and death came between him and this glorious prospect. See Rom. viii. 18, 19 (comp. 1 Cor. i. 7); Col. iii. 4; Phil. iii. 20, 21,—to say nothing of the letters to Timothy and Titus. See further, on this point, p. 379.]

the same with the doctrine of Redemption, which is unquestionably connected with the death of Jesus (1 Thess. v. 10), but in a decidedly external fashion, not otherwise than in the missionary discourses. The death and resurrection of Christ are placed side by side, but their inner logical connexion, their redemptive and moral significance are not brought to light.

3. While the apostle's Soteriology is scarcely developed, his Messianic Eschatology, on the contrary, holds an important place in these letters. This is in fact their characteristic element, and gives them their peculiar originality. In the following epistles it will be gradually transformed, yielding to Soteriology the place of honour which it occupies here. At the same time it furnishes another essential and notable feature of resemblance between these two earliest epistles and the discourses of the Acts (chap. xvii. 7, 31). Paul as yet had not advanced far beyond the general type of apostolic preaching.

The epistles to the Thessalonians, it is evident, resemble the missionary discourses in what they leave out, as well as in the special points on which they dwell. Certainly there is a wide distance between these vivid pages and the pale reproduction given us in the Acts; but nevertheless we stand, here and there, on the same ground. At the basis of the two epistles and of the discourses analysed above there lies one and the same type of doctrine, which gives its character to this first stage of Paul's theology. This we must endeavour to extract and define more clearly.

CHAPTER II.

PRIMITIVE PAULINISM.

PAUL'S doctrine in its primitive type is quite simple, and was organized in an elementary fashion. Its ideas are still general, and their logical connexion is not always apparent. They may be completely summed up under these two heads: *the Gospel message*, and *the parousia*.

I.

THE GOSPEL (εὐαγγέλιον τοῦ Θεοῦ).

In common with Jesus and the Twelve, Paul designates by the name of *the gospel* the message of salvation that he bears to Jews and Gentiles. It is the gospel of God, because it is God who sends it and who is the Author of it (1 Thess. ii. 2, 8, 9); or again, the word of God, λόγος τοῦ Θεοῦ (1 Thess. ii. 13; Acts xiii. 46). It is the gospel of Christ, because Christ is its essential content (1 Thess. iii. 2; 2 Thess. i. 8). Again, Paul calls it *our gospel* (διὰ τοῦ εὐαγγελίου ἡμῶν, 2 Thess. ii. 14). This expression, however, has not as yet the particular shade of meaning that it afterwards acquired in the discussion with the Judaizers (τὸ εὐαγγέλιόν μου, Rom. ii. 16). Lastly, salvation being the end of this

Gospel, it is further called ὁ λόγος τῆς σωτηρίας (Acts xiii. 26 and 1 Thess. ii. 16).

There can be no question of the Messianic character of the apostle's early preaching. This constituted for those times precisely what we should now call the religious point of view. The apostle of the Gentiles began, like the rest, by preaching the near approach of the judgment of God and describing "the wrath to come," in the fashion of John the Baptist (ὀργὴν ἐρχομένην, 1 Thess. i. 10; 2 Thess. i. 8, 9; Acts xvii. 31). He called men to repentance, and to faith in Jesus, by whom the world was to be judged, and by whom they might be saved: "God, overlooking the times of ignorance, now requires that repentance be proclaimed to all men; for He has fixed a day for judging the world in righteousness by the man Jesus, whom He has chosen, having raised Him from the dead" (comp. Rom. ii. 16).

At the same time, Paul proved that the promises were realized and the prophecies fulfilled in Jesus the *Messiah* (ὁ Χριστός). This Messiah is far more than the heir of David; He is *the Son of God,—the Lord* (ὁ Κύριος). This last name, as we know, is the one by which the apostle preferred to designate Jesus. It even became in his epistles the proper name of Christ (comp. 1 Cor. viii. 6). It implies an absolute sovereignty over man's conscience, over the Church, and the historical development of the world. In the Septuagint, ὁ Κύριος is specially applied to Jehovah. This name, when given to Jesus, is in itself an intimation that He has become to the Christian consciousness that which Jehovah was to the prophetical consciousness. So *the day of Jehovah* becomes the day of the Lord Jesus (1 Thess. v. 2; 2 Thess. ii. 2).

8

In some few passages it is difficult to see whether Κύριος designates God or Christ. On the other hand, it is in Jesus the *Son of God* that the *Fatherhood* of God with regard to men is revealed and realized. Hence the formulæ, ἐν Θεῷ πατρὶ καὶ Κυρίῳ Ἰησοῦ Χριστῷ, Θεὸς πατὴρ ἡμῶν καὶ Κυρίου Ἰησοῦ Χριστοῦ (1 Thess. i. 1 ; 2 Thess. i. 2), which continue to be characteristic of all Paul's letters.

But so far we have only touched on the more external aspect of the apostle's doctrine, and that which least distinguished it from the preaching of the Twelve. Underneath these general forms an intense spiritual life, singularly original in its nature, was all the while developing itself, which had been called into being on the very day of Paul's conversion, and was speedily in its turn to give birth to a rich and unique system of dogmatics. We must never forget that with Paul, in truth, experience preceded system and feeling theory. What is really Pauline in these two epistles is the spiritual inspiration which pervades them. If we do not find here the same kind of reasoning as in the epistle to the Romans, we have the same modes of thought and sentiment, the same moral experience, and the same specific type of Christian life, which has indeed attained already in the soul of the apostle a richness and sublimity that compel our admiration. We find in every phrase that full-charged feeling and moral weight, and that profound intuition of spiritual things which characterize the style of his great epistles.

The fruitful source of this new life is the great idea of *grace* (χάρις τοῦ Θεοῦ, 2 Thess. i. 12). This grace, actuated by the Father's eternal love, is historically manifested and fulfilled in Christ, and is also called the grace of the Lord Jesus Christ (1 Thess. v. 28). It is the fundamental principle of the vocation (κλῆσις) and election (ἐκλογή) of believers (1 Thess. ii. 12, i. 4). Through it we are not only called, but also predestinated to salvation and to life, οὐκ ἔθετο ἡμᾶς ὁ Θεὸς εἰς ὀργὴν ἀλλὰ εἰς περιποίησιν σωτηρίας (1 Thess. v. 9; comp. Acts xiii. 48). These are the earliest traces of the doctrine of predestination. The effect produced on men's minds by the apostle's preaching did not seem to him fortuitous. In the unbelief of some, and the faith of others, he saw from the first the consequence of a fixed determination of God (2 Thess. ii. 13, 14; comp. Rom. viii. 30).

But we must not conceive of this grace as external to man, as though it were an arbitrary gift, a *donum superadditum*. It is an active force (δύναμις), whose immanence is its essential characteristic,—a regenerative power working by faith from within outwardly. Hence the Gospel preaching proves to be no mere succession of empty words, but a *Divine energy* taking possession of the soul of the believer in order to renew it (λόγος Θεοῦ, ὃς καὶ ἐνεργεῖται ἐν ὑμῖν τοῖς πιστεύουσιν, 1 Thess. ii. 13; i. 5). The essential medium of this power of salvation is Jesus Christ, in whom we live and who lives in us through faith. The Christian life is thus an organic creation, having its root in the virtue of Jesus Himself, and attaining its development and completion in the glory of the Saviour (1 Thess. v. 9, 10; 2 Thess. ii. 13, 14). Those who are dead in Christ (οἱ νεκροὶ ἐν Χριστῷ) are not lost; Christ, in whom they have their principle of life, will raise them up. Let us mark well this *moral dynamic*; it will gradually transform the Jewish eschatology which Paul inherited, and which so far he has done little more than reproduce.

Lastly, this whole Christian life, in its essential principle, its permanent character, and glorious end, has already found expression in the three virtues which gather up and exhaust it: *faith, love, hope* (μνημονεύοντες ὑμῶν τοῦ ἔργου τῆς πίστεως καὶ τοῦ κόπου τῆς ἀγάπης καὶ τῆς ὑπομονῆς τῆς ἐλπίδος, 1 Thess. i. 3; comp. v. 8; 2 Thess. i. 3, 4, 11; ii. 13, 16; iii. 5). The work of faith is that profound change by which the Thessalonians turned from the vain worship of idols to serve the living God, and were consecrated to Jesus Christ (ἐν ἁγιασμῷ Πνεύματος καὶ πίστει ἀληθείας, 2 Thess. ii. 13). By this consecration they were separated from heathenism and snatched from all its defilements; and they must carry it out in their whole life and being, by the entire sanctification of spirit, soul, and body (ἁγιάσαι ὑμᾶς ὁλοτελεῖς, 1 Thess. v. 23). But this destruction of the old nature is the consequence of the new life in them, the essence and strength of which is love. The first duty of Christians is mutual love among themselves (2 Thess. i. 3). This mutual love is the love of brethren, for all Christians form one family (1 Thess. iv. 9). It should further extend itself to all men (εἰς ἀλλήλους καὶ εἰς πάντας, 1 Thess. iii. 12). Christians must not return evil for evil; according to God's example of love, they must seek the good of all (1 Thess. v. 15; 2 Thess. iii. 5). It is this holy labour of love, which spends and wearies itself in service and self-sacrifice, that Paul describes in the energetic phrase κόπος τῆς ἀγάπης. After faith and love comes *hope*, a constant source of joy and consolation, even in the midst of the darkest and severest trials. Hope begets patience. Rooted in Jesus Christ, Christians are enabled to stand firm in Him, awaiting His speedy coming (στήκητε ἐν Κυρίῳ, 1 Thess. iii. 8).

Thus the apostle's thought, starting from eschatology, returns to it and there reaches its goal. The Messianic ideas, in short, here come both first and last; they supply not indeed the vital principle, but the external framework of this early Paulinism. We must now examine them more directly.

II. Eschatology.

It is an apocalypse in brief which these two epistles set before us. The *great apostasy*, the appearance of the man of sin, or Antichrist, the *advent* and *victory* of the Lord, the *resurrection* and the *judgment*—such are the successive scenes of this great drama. Underneath the differences of detail we feel the profound analogy of this eschatology to that of John. Fundamentally, Christian eschatology in the apostolic times followed a regular course of development. It is not so richly unfolded here as in the Apocalypse, but much more definitely than in the discourses of Jesus; it is at an intermediate stage between these two extreme points of its history.

The apostle Paul has referred no part of his teaching to that of Jesus more expressly than his eschatological doctrine. What he says on this point is taught, he assures us, ἐν λόγῳ Κυρίου (1 Thess. iv. 15). Indeed, we may certainly recognise in the first verses of the fifth chapter a faithful reproduction of some of the Master's words. Jesus Himself had also spoken of the outburst of evil in the last days, of the apostasy of a great number of believers, and of the appearance of false Christs and false prophets. He had, in like manner, maintained a very sober reserve respecting the time and hour of the Parousia, simply comparing its sudden coming to that of a thief in the night. He too had spoken of the resurrection, of the assembling of all the faithful with the Son of man, and of the final judgment which will render unto every man according to his works. Only, in the teaching of Jesus there is found, under the most material images borrowed from Jewish apocalyptics, an indefinable inner spirituality, which gives them breadth and freedom, and invests these pictures with a symbolical import. In the apostolic preaching, on the contrary, these ideas become set and rigid, and they fall into a systematic order and scheme. It could not be otherwise. The work of systematization was carried on under the constant influence of the Book of Daniel, traces of which are easily to be discerned in the Gospel of Matthew, the epistles to the Thessalonians, and the Apocalypse of John (2 Thess. ii. 4; comp. Dan. xi. 36).

The end of the world will be brought about by God's direct intervention. But the moment of this intervention has not been arbitrarily chosen. It depends upon the historical development of the forces at work in the world. And for that reason this time may, to some extent, be foreseen and calculated. Such is the fundamental idea of the Jewish Apocalypse. The first catastrophe is to be a judgment, a condemnation of the power of evil. That which precedes and prepares for it, therefore, is the growth of this power to its culmination and full maturity. The world, in fact, must become *ripe* for destruction, the sins of the fathers and children uniting to fill up their measure (Matt. xxiii. 32; 1 Thess. ii. 16). That is what Jesus taught, and His disciples also. In like manner, Paul expressly declares that the end cannot come until evil has attained its final manifestation (ἡ ἀποστασία πρῶτον, 2 Thess. ii. 3).

This power of evil at work in the world is as yet in a state of secret ferment, of *mystery* (τὸ μυστήριον τῆς ἀνομίας, 2 Thess. ii. 7). But it will break forth violently, incarnated in a personality who will serve as its medium,—*the man of sin, the son of perdition* (ὁ ἄνθρωπος τῆς ἁμαρτίας, ὁ υἱὸς τῆς ἀπωλείας). This personage will be in the order of evil what the person of Christ is in the order of good. He is, therefore, the evil and anti-divine principle in its ultimate revelation. As God came into the world in the person of the Messiah, Antichrist will appear as the radical and absolute negation not only of Christ, but of God Himself. He will set Himself above everything Divine, and will make His throne in the temple and cause Himself to be worshipped as God (2 Thess. ii. 4).

Whence will this head of the powers of evil arise? The general answer is, From the midst of heathenism; so the epithet ἄνομος (ver. 8) might lead us to think. But this adjective is used here in an absolute sense; it is not the man without law, but the man who knowingly tramples on the law, who is the conscious negation of the law, because he is the negation of good. The two epistles to the Thessalonians, as a whole, lead us to suppose that in Paul's view the Antichrist who will enthrone himself as God in the temple of Jerusalem itself in place of the true Messiah, is to arise out of Judaism. Did not the Jewish people already embody for him the fiercest possible opposition to the Gospel? Those ἄνθρωποι ἄτοποι καὶ πονηροὶ of whom the apostle complains, were they not Jews (2 Thess. iii. 2)? And, finally, is it not the Jews whom Paul describes as hostile to the human race, constantly multiplying their sins, filling up the measure of their iniquities, and ready for destruction by the Divine wrath (1 Thess. ii. 15, 16)? Antichrist, therefore, is not Nero, nor any other Roman Emperor; he is the representative of the Jewish revolution, which was already at work. The power that represses it and prevents its outburst, the κατέχων, is the Roman government which maintains order. Was it not this which saved Paul at Corinth, and which had everywhere saved him from the machinations of the Jews? When this barrier is removed and the ideal power of evil, already active in Judaism, shall have triumphed and in its transgressions far surpassed heathen idolatry (2 Thess. ii. 4)—when the king of evil has come—then the world will be ripe for judgment.[1]

---

[1] A renewed examination of these passages now renders us less confident of the Jewish character of the Antichrist spoken of in this much controverted passage. The apostasy in question seems to extend far beyond the limits of Judaism, and to be the outcome of a general and hopeless revolt of the whole world against God and the order established by Him. In Daniel xi. 36, the passage alluded to by Paul, the king who blasphemes and sets himself above every god, becoming the symbol of Antichrist, is a heathen king; it is Antiochus Epiphanes. But that is no reason why, in Paul's belief, the ἀντικείμενος of 2 Thess. ii. 4 should be a Roman emperor. In assuming a deeper moral and religious significance, the type has lost much of its political character. The author of the epistle, as it seems to us, abides by the prediction of Daniel, and leaves the personality of Antichrist indefinite, precisely because this personality did not as yet present a distinct form to his eyes.

Thus the *parousia* of Antichrist is to precede and prepare for the *parousia* of the Lord. The latter will be a splendid and decisive triumph over the adversary. At a signal given by God, Christ will

---

What he asserts at the time of his writing is the existence of a wide and powerful leaven of evil, which will afterward have its incarnation in an individual, according to the terms of Daniel's prophecy, but which at present works in an impersonal form. Hence the general expression, τὸ μυστήριον ἐνεργεῖται τῆς ἀνομίας (ver. 7).

The point which it seems essential for us to maintain is that the author, in any case, clearly distinguishes the Roman Empire and Emperor from the personality of the Antichrist and the part which he plays. Indeed the Emperor is regarded as the κατέχων, and the Empire as τὸ κατέχον (*neuter*); *i.e.*, as the power of order and justice which as yet checks the outbreak of evil, and delays the disclosure of the mystery of iniquity in the personality of Antichrist and in the world-wide apostasy.

At a later time this distinction between the Roman Emperor and Empire on the one hand, and Antichrist on the other, disappeared; and not only that, but Rome itself became the mystery of iniquity, and the Emperor in person figures as the Beast in the Apocalypse (Rev. xiii., xvii.; comp. 1 Pet. v. 13). This identification of the powers that we here find contrasted, took place after the year 64 and in the person of Nero. But in the second letter to the Christians of Thessalonica, the Empire and Emperor are still regarded as the beneficent and protecting powers of social order. Indeed, Paul here entertains exactly the same views and opinions on this subject to which he gives expression in the epistle to the Romans, chap. xiii. 1-6: ὥστε ὁ ἀντιτασσόμενος τῇ ἐξουσίᾳ, τῇ τοῦ Θεοῦ διαταγῇ ἀνθέστηκεν . . . οἱ γὰρ ἄρχοντες οὐκ εἰσὶ φόβος τῷ ἀγαθῷ ἔργῳ, ἀλλὰ τῷ κακῷ . . . οὐ γὰρ εἰκῆ τὴν μάχαιραν φορεῖ· Θεοῦ γὰρ διάκονός ἐστιν, ἔκδικος εἰς ὀργὴν τῷ τὸ κακὸν πράσσοντι.

To our mind this correspondence is a decisive proof that this much-disputed second epistle to the Thessalonians was written before the year 64, and is consequently of Pauline origin.—*Note written by the author for this edition.*

descend from heaven with His mighty angels, as He has Himself announced. The day of the Parousia is uncertain and unknown; but as Jesus had apparently said that it would come before the generation then present had passed away, and that men should watch for it constantly, Paul, like the other apostles and all the early Christians, hopes to be still living at the time (1 Thess. iv. 15-17). We may observe, n passing, that this declaration would be very strange if these two epistles to the Thessalonians had been composed after the apostle's death; since the forgery would have credited Paul, gratuitously, with a hope that was obviously falsified.

The Christians who have died will rise first, and join those who are still alive; together they will be caught up in the clouds to meet the Lord descending from heaven, and will be for ever with the Lord. But this day of the Lord is at the same time the day of judgment. The destruction of Antichrist is nothing less than the first act of this judgment, which will also bring about the eternal ruin ($\check{o}\lambda\epsilon\theta\rho o\varsigma$ $a\mathit{i}\acute{\omega}\nu\iota o\varsigma$, 2 Thess. i. 8-10) of all the ungodly.

We meet with this eschatological doctrine once more in the first epistle to the Corinthians, wanting only the figure of the Antichrist. But it is already in course of transformation under the influence of the principle of the Pauline gospel, which as it unfolded itself, could not possibly remain confined within the very narrow lines of the Jewish Apocalypse. The description of 1 Corinthians xv. 15-52, which by its very phraseology so plainly recalls 1 Thessalonians iv. 16, is, however, sufficient proof that the eschatological hopes which we have just set forth were an essential feature in the earlier phase of the Pauline doctrine.

Such then, for the present, is this early type of Paulinism,—still closely allied in its general conception to the preaching of the other apostles, but bearing within it already the new and bold ideas to which subsequently it gave birth. It is admirably calculated to serve as a transition, and means of organic connexion, between the apostolic preaching with which Paul set out and the independent conception of the Gospel to which he afterwards attained. We shall now see the true Paulinism take shape, under the double pressure of the inner logic of its own principles and of the external opposition of the Judaizing party, which proved a still more effectual stimulus.

CHAPTER III.

FIRST CONFLICTS WITH THE JUDAIZING CHRISTIANS.—THE TIME OF CRISIS AND TRANSITION (Acts xv.; Galatians ii.).

IN order to understand the struggle which is about to begin, we must revert to the apostle's conversion, and note carefully the new course into which it directed his mind and his life.

The conversion of Paul had been, in point of fact, a radical negation of the Jewish principle. His apostleship to the Gentiles was its logical consequence; and this mission, pursued with equal boldness and success, was the practical realization of the kingdom of God beyond the sacred limits of the Jewish people. If during this first missionary period Paul does not attack the authority of the law in theory, he completely ignores it in fact, and carries on his work without the least reference to it. The very name of the law is not to be found in the two epistles to the Thessalonians. Through the unexpected progress of his work, the contradiction of Judaism implied in the apostle's faith passed from this inner sphere into the general life of the Church; it expressed itself in actual facts, previously to its being dogmatically formulated.

Meanwhile the Jewish principle on its part, conquered and negatived as it was in the soul of the apostle to the Gentiles and in his ministry, revived in the Jewish Churches of Palestine in a vigorous and obstinate form. It was not to be expected that the old principle would yield to the new without conflict. The astonishing success of the mission to the Gentiles caused, no doubt, more embarrassment than pleasure at Jerusalem. The old Judaism felt that its venerable claims were in jeopardy; and it could not maintain and defend them without endeavouring to enforce them on others.

Let us define clearly the great question which now arises. It is not as to whether Gentiles shall be admitted into the kingdom of God: on that point every one was agreed. The question was, *On what terms* were they to be admitted? Was it necessary to become a Jew in order to be a Christian? Must one pass through Judaism to reach the Gospel? This was the point at issue. Those who upheld the eternal claims of the old religion would, of necessity, impose circumcision on the Gentiles; for it was only through circumcision that they could be materially incorporated with the elect people, and become members of the family, of Abraham. Accordingly, it was over circumcision that the great battle came to be fought.

No wonder that it was long and fierce. Christianity and Judaism were now contending for their existence. If the Gentiles enter the Church directly, and there obtain through faith alone the same rank and privileges as the Jews, what becomes of the rights of Israel? what advantage has the elect people over other nations? Is not this utterly to deny the absolute validity of Judaism? On the other hand, if circumcision be imposed on the Gentile converts, is not that in itself a declaration that faith in Christ is insufficient for salvation? Does it not reduce the Gospel to the position of a mere accessory to Mosaism? Is not this to deny the absolute validity of the work of Jesus Christ?

Such was the fundamental question that Paul's missionary successes raised amongst the Judæan Churches. It could not fail to create a profound division of opinion. Up to this time Christianity and Judaism had marched hand in hand. But now a choice must be made. The Christian Jews, who belonged more to Moses than to Jesus (and there were many such), were prepared without hesitation to stand forward as the ardent champions of threatened Judaism. Paul, on the other hand, naturally became the apostle of Christian freedom. To defend the independence of the Gospel was to defend his own work, his apostleship, his faith, his conversion. This great cause became his personal cause. Betwixt the two parties, the Twelve are eclipsed. They appear full of anxiety and hesitation, seeking for a reconciliation between the two hostile principles, which could not be other than precarious.

The first conflict seems to have taken place upon Paul's return from his first missionary journey. Certain Pharisaic Christians, who had come down from Judæa to Antioch, sought to impose circumcision on the Gentile converts. "If you do not submit to circumcision," they said, "you cannot be saved" (Acts xv. 1). They alleged the authority of the Twelve in support of their claims. Great was the disturbance they excited, and violent the dispute. Paul did not underestimate the gravity of the struggle then beginning. The triumph of these new missionaries compromised his whole work; and he was keenly distressed. He could not tell what were, at the bottom, the real sentiments of the apostles at Jerusalem. He feared that a scandalous rupture would be caused. The right course to pursue was made plain to him by a revelation,—by a decisive illumination, an inspiration full of assurance and strength, following an interval of hesitation and inner conflict (Gal. ii. 2). He will go up to Jerusalem with Barnabas, and set forth his gospel to those who are accounted pillars in the Church; he will rehearse the triumphs that have been won, and the hopes that are entertained. And he will find means, if it prove necessary, to persuade or win them over to support him. They will be compelled to endorse his work, and protect it from the attacks of the *intruders*. In any case, he will deprive them of that authority from the apostles from which they draw their credit and strength (Gal. ii. 1-3).

In these hopes Paul was not deceived. The essential end he sought was gained. The revelation he had received, and upon which he acted, had not misled him. The Twelve in no wise supported the pretensions of the false brethren. Titus was not compelled to be circumcised. The authorities of the Church gave Paul's gospel their unreserved approval, and did not propose to add anything to it. They acknowledged the legitimacy of his apostleship, and gave him the right hand of fellowship; so that they might labour together in the work of God, the one party among the Gentiles and the other among the Jews. They even requested Paul and Barnabas to bear in mind the poor of Jerusalem, and to interest the new Gentile Christian Churches on their behalf.

At the same time, the Twelve could not share either in the boldness or confidence of Paul. They had other hopes, and judged things from a totally different standpoint. The Gospel might, indeed, have a partial, and more or less brilliant success among the Gentiles; but, in their eyes, this was quite a secondary matter. The main and chiefly important work was the conversion of the Jewish people, who were to be the first to enter, as a nation, into the new covenant; then the turn of the Gentiles would come. Therefore they must not scandalize the Jews, nor break with Judaism. The part played by the apostles in these keen debates was, and could only be, that of conciliation. All their efforts were directed to bring about through these deliberations such a compromise as would preserve unity among all divisions in the Church, without placing the new evangelical principle in peril. Hence the equivocal position in which they were found throughout, and the minor part they played in the history of these great struggles.[1]

The Acts of the Apostles has preserved for us the material result of these conferences in the form of a letter addressed by the Church at Jerusalem to the new Gentile Christian Churches, for the purpose of re-assuring and pacifying them. Their freedom is recognised. The letter is no more than a recommendation of observances such as Paul himself enjoined and the Churches already practised; *viz.* abstinence from meat sacrificed to idols, from blood,

---

[1] See an excellent estimate of the part taken by the Twelve in *L'Histoire de la théologie apostolique* of M. Reuss, vol. i., pp. 306–329 [Eng. trans., i., 263–283]; de Pressensé, *Histoire des trois premiers siècles*, vol. i., pp. 457–474 [Eng. trans., *The Apostolic Age*, pp. 125–141].

from things strangled,—and lastly, from fornication. In other words, they were to continue within those general limits under which the Jews received proselytes into social communion with themselves. These restrictions occur again in Paul's epistles to the Corinthians, and in the Apocalypse. While it is certain that the two parties at Jerusalem came at last to an understanding, it is equally certain that this agreement could not have been arrived at in any other way or upon any other basis.

This solution, it must however be said, was really no solution at all. It might have some effect in the sphere of practical life; but it left the question of principle untouched. The truth is, that from this time it was no longer possible to arrest the conflict between the Christian and the Jewish principle. The apostles at Jerusalem showed their tact and wisdom, as well as their moderation, in not entering upon it. Time alone could bring it to an issue. It was the dawn of a religious revolution, whose course it was useless to resist. So far from preventing it, the debates and resolutions of the council at Jerusalem served only to precipitate the struggle. The compromise then agreed upon became the starting point and occasion of still fiercer and more serious contest. The two hostile parties might each, indeed, regard it as a first victory. It was an obvious inference for Paul to conclude from it that the Gospel has abolished the Law for Jews as well as Gentiles. But on the other hand, his adversaries gained an equal advantage. It was well understood that the decision of the council only affected the Gentiles; and that the Law remained obligatory for the Jews who continued to form the nucleus of the Church, the Messianic community. In relation to the Jewish Church, therefore, Gentile Christians held an inferior position. They purchased their liberty at the cost of their privileges. They became the *proselytes of the gate* of Christianity; they remained, in fact, at the door of the kingdom. Thus the Judaizers had, seemingly, an equal right to claim the settlement made at Jerusalem as a first success. It furnished them with an excellent vantage ground for a new campaign. They were inevitably tempted to turn these proselytes of the gate into *proselytes of righteousness*. This persistent antagonism soon declared itself in the event.

A second contest, still more serious than that at Jerusalem, broke out at Antioch (Gal. ii. 13, ff.). This event, as we have seen [pp. 10, 11], finds its proper occasion on Paul's return from his second journey, at the end of the first and the beginning of the second period of our history.

In the vigorous discourse addressed to the Judaizers and summed up in the epistle to the Galatians, the full-grown Paul for the first time displays himself, with his great thesis of justification by faith, his radical negation of the law, and the irresistible logic of his polemics. The crisis now reaches its height.

Peter on coming to Antioch had eaten with Gentile Christians, without regard to the precepts of the law, which were in danger of being cast aside by the Jewish Christians themselves. But just then certain emissaries of James arrived, who protested against this apostasy and asserted the authority of the law. Peter was unable to withstand their influence. After having sanctioned Christian liberty by his example, he seemed to condemn it. He withdrew, and separated himself from the Gentile Christians in order to make common cause with those of the circumcision. Many other Christians, and Barnabas himself, were drawn into this act of hypocrisy; and there was a temporary revival of zeal for Judaism. Paul remained firm and faithful. "Seeing," he says, "that they walked not with straight foot according to the truth of the Gospel, I said to Peter before them all, If thou, being a Jew, livest like a Gentile, why dost thou compel the Gentiles to Judaize?" The inconsistency of Peter's double conduct could not be better shown. But Paul does not stop there; his argument goes to the root of the matter. This flagrant inconsistency of behaviour arose from an inner, though perhaps unconscious inconsistency, which was at the bottom of the doctrine of the Judaizing Christians, and which Paul's pitiless logic lays bare in the discourse which follows this apostrophe. All equivocation is cut short. This is the overwhelming dilemma to which Peter is shut up: Either faith in Christ is sufficient in itself —in that case, why ask anything more from the Gentiles, why glory in anything besides?—or else it is not sufficient; but if not, it is not really necessary,— and we Jews were mistaken in despairing of salvation through the law and in having recourse to faith and the death of Christ. In this case, His death was superfluous and useless! The whole discourse centres in this dilemma.

Paul, from the first, puts himself in the position of the Jewish Christians ($\dot{\eta}\mu\epsilon\hat{\iota}\varsigma$ $\phi\acute{\upsilon}\sigma\epsilon\iota$ $\text{'}Iov\delta a\hat{\iota}o\iota$); he aims at showing the radical contradiction existing, unawares to them, between their professed faith in Christ and the Jewish claims that they seek to impose on others. "We, who are Jews by origin and not Gentile sinners ($\dot{a}\mu a\rho\tau\omega\lambda o\acute{\iota}$), being convinced that man cannot be justified by the law, if he continue a stranger to faith in Christ,—we, I say, have also believed in Jesus Christ, that we might be justified by faith, and not by the works of the law. What does this mean, if not that our conversion to Christ is with us Jews an undoubted proof that the essential means of justification lies not in the law, but in faith? For we have only believed in Christ, after despairing of the law. It is true then to affirm that in our view also no flesh can be justified before God by the law." It is thus that Paul was led, in conflict with the Judaistic opposition, to the full development and definition of the grand thesis of his theology,—viz. *justification by faith*; and to apply it to Jews and Gentiles alike, without making any distinction. He asserts and logically deduces the consequences of the fundamental principle he has now arrived at. "In the work of our justification, faith in Christ is therefore substituted for the works of the law. In seeking to be justified through Christ, we acknowledge, by that very act, that the law is ineffectual to this end. Faith in Christ, therefore, implies the negation of the law for all."

In the seventeenth verse the objection is raised, which Paul's teaching has ever since continued to provoke. The suppression of the law will reduce the Jews to the rank of the ἁμαρτωλοὶ, the Gentiles. Sin will no longer be restrained; and if Jesus abolishes the law, He becomes the servant, the minister of sin (comp. Rom. vi. 1). Paul is not content to reject this conclusion, as he does, by an energetic μὴ γένοιτο. "So far from that," he exclaims, "it results, on the contrary, that if I build up again the law which I removed in coming to Christ, I am not only inconsistent with myself, but I lose what I have gained; in face of the law thus restored, I find, and indeed constitute myself, a transgressor! Of necessity, transgression is revived along with the law; and the death of Christ is rendered vain. But on the contrary, where there is no law, there is also no transgression. The truth is, that through the law I died to the law. I have been crucified and condemned by the law with Christ; I am therefore freed from the law. It is no longer I that live, it is Christ who lives in me; and that life which I still live in the flesh, I live not under the law, but by faith in the Son of God, who has loved me and given Himself for me." Finally, gathering up this profound and powerful argument into a single sentence, he declares, "If righteousness comes to us by any kind of law, Christ died for nothing!"

Thus understood, the discourse which Paul has condensed in this brief abstract is really the complete programme developed in the great epistles. It not only contains all the essential ideas of the Pauline theology, but they are presented already in the same logical order in which we shall find them in the epistle to the Romans: the inability of born Jews and of sinners among the Gentiles alike to justify themselves by their works; the necessity, identical for both parties, of believing in Christ; the opposition between justification by faith and justification by law; the abolishment of the law through faith; the conception of redemption as a death to the law and a resurrection with Christ, resulting in the glorious liberty of the children of God—all the links in this golden chain are found here in their organic connexion. The principle implanted in Paul's mind on his conversion at last yields its full result. The germ has become a mighty tree. We have passed through the first period of Paul's life; and we enter forthwith on the great conflicts of the second.

BOOK III.

SECOND PERIOD; OR, THE PERIOD OF THE GREAT CONFLICTS.

From 53 to 58 A.D.

THE discussion which took place at Antioch seems to have been a regular declaration of war. From this hour the struggle became general, and was carried out on both sides without truce or restraint. The Judaizing opposition, originating in Palestine, extends and breaks out everywhere; we find it disturbing Galatia, Ephesus, and the Church at Corinth by turns; and outrunning the apostle of the Gentiles himself, it gets to Rome before him. The Judaizing party had its missionaries, who followed in Paul's track, and in every place strove with embittered zeal to undermine his authority, to seduce his disciples, and to destroy his work under the pretence of rectifying it. It was a counter-mission systematically organized. The delegates arrived with letters of recommendation, and gave themselves out as representatives of the Twelve, denying Paul's apostleship and sowing distrust and suspicion of him everywhere by their odious calumnies.

With the apostle this was a time of bitter experiences and keen distress. His letters show us how greatly he suffered from this intestine struggle, from the treachery of some of his friends and the fickleness of his most beloved Churches. But, we hasten to add, without these great troubles we should never have known Paul at his greatest, nor guessed how tender his heart was, how heroic his faith, how vigorous his mind, how infinite the resources of his strong and supple genius. He was indeed born for conflict, and in it his spiritual nature acquired its full maturity and developed all its powers.

Attacked almost simultaneously at every point of his work, Paul does not shrink from the contest; he redoubles his energies, and makes himself almost ubiquitous, everywhere confronting his adversaries and never for one moment doubting of victory. For four or five years this great controversy absorbed his whole thought and energy; it was the leading fact which dominated and distinguished this second period. Our great epistles are the issue of these truly tragic circumstances, and can only be thoroughly understood in their light. These epistles are not theological treatises, so much as pamphlets; they are the crushing and terrible blows with which the mighty combatant openly answered the covert intrigues of his enemies. The contest is in reality a drama, which grows larger and more complicated as it advances from Galatia to Rome. The letters to the Galatians, the Corinthians, and the Romans, which are its principal acts, mark also its successive phases. They are in close connexion with each other, and enable us to establish a twofold progress, both in external events and in the mind of the apostle, which we shall now proceed to demonstrate.

CHAPTER I.

THE EPISTLE TO THE GALATIANS.

THE epistle to the Galatians, the earliest of the four, enables us to witness the first outbreak of this prolonged struggle. With its opening words, we are in the midst of the fray; and from beginning to end it is simply the apostle's vehement answer to the unlooked-for attack of his enemies. It would be hopeless, therefore, even to attempt to understand it, without first having a clear perception of the character of these Judaizing teachers, the nature of their contention, and the strength of their arguments. Upon these points, fortunately, the letter itself supplies us with all necessary information.

The Galatians had received Paul's earliest preaching with an enthusiasm and gratitude which had touched and charmed him (Gal. iv. 14). Their cordiality had been maintained throughout the apostle's sojourn with them; and he had carried away from Galatia the most pleasing impressions and the brightest hopes. When therefore he heard of such a speedy defection, his astonishment was only equalled by his distress (Gal. i. 6).

What is it that had happened? After Paul's departure, there had arrived in Galatia certain men whom he only chooses to designate by the somewhat scornful term τινές, *quidam* (i. 7). The new missionaries brought to these young societies not, as they would have it, another gospel, but those very Judaic claims for which they had already pleaded at Jerusalem, and obtained a momentary triumph at Antioch. They supported them by the name and example of the Twelve, and by the authority of the mother Church in Jerusalem. The apostles whom Christ has ordained, who lived with Him and received His directions and teaching, live and preach differently from Paul. Above all, it is not true, as Paul teaches, that the old covenant has been abolished by the death of Christ. God cannot be unfaithful and depart from His promise; nor take back what He has once given. Now, He made an *eternal* covenant with Abraham, and promised salvation to the children of Abraham only. The word of God remains. So far from having abolished this covenant, the death of Christ only has its full effect and actual virtue within the covenant, and for those who have entered into it. Into this covenant you must enter, if you wish to belong to the true Messianic people. Unless you are circumcised, and thus become children of Abraham, you cannot be saved. So they reasoned.

Paul's doctrine and that of the Judaizers may be summed up in two assertions. He declared: "The law and its ceremonies are nothing without the cross of Christ, and nothing to the believer in Christ."— "The death of Christ, and faith in Christ," they replied, "are nothing apart from circumcision and legal observance." At first sight, the difference between these phrases may not appear great; at the bottom it is enormous. The first proposition is the negation of Judaism; the second is the destruction of the Gospel.

But Paul's adversaries would seem powerful indeed

when they pointed out that his teaching ran counter to the entire Old Testament, and to the most solemn promises of Jehovah. Nor were they less so in quoting against him the example and teaching of the apostles at Jerusalem, the only true heirs of the word of Christ. Finally, they must have succeeded in shaking the apostle's firmest friends, when they urged that the abolition of the law compromised the holiness of God, and encouraged sin by removing the barriers against it; and when they showed that this so-called Christian liberty degenerated into a license that no longer had either law or limit. The doctrine of Paul, they concluded, is the subversion at once of all authority, all truth, and all morality.

But this radical negation of Paul's gospel involved the negation of his apostleship. The discussion of his views resolved itself inevitably into a violent personal attack. Who is this newcomer, that he should set himself up against the first apostles, and against the word of God itself? What is his authority? He has not seen Christ; he has not been made an apostle. What little he knows of the Gospel, has been learned from the Lord's real disciples; and now he revolts against them! Why does he separate himself from them? Why does he not reproduce their preaching in its full and proper form? His mission is purely extemporized; and he has constituted himself an apostle on his own authority, and out of his mere fancy. He claims, no doubt, to have received revelations, and to have had visions vouchsafed to him; but what proof have we that his assertions are true? Must we believe it on the strength of his word? Besides, how can these mere personal revelations that he alleges hold good against the traditional teaching of men who lived so long with Jesus, who saw His face and heard His words? Is not this tradition the standard by which we must test every private vision, in order to ascertain whether it comes from God or from the Devil? The surest proof that the *new* apostle's visions are nothing but falsehood is that they contradict and subvert the true doctrine of Jesus Christ. His assumed independence is nothing but culpable audacity; his gospel is a mutilated gospel; his apostleship, a usurpation; and his attack on the law, a sacrilege. The Galatians must beware of him as an enemy; they must hasten to enter into communion with the true Church of the Messiah by submitting themselves to the Divine ordinances.

What an impression this skilful and sweeping attack must have made on the fickle minds of these Galatian tribes! The new teachers, apparently, had the facts on their side—the external tradition of Christ and the apostles, and of the Old Testament. The gospel of Paul rested on his personal testimony alone. How could this authority counterbalance that of the traditions of Jerusalem?

Is it surprising that the Galatians, ready, it would seem, for all novelties, should have been seized with distrust of the apostle, and have eagerly accepted the *new* gospel?

But Paul was not the man to abandon the struggle. His defence rose to the height of the danger. So far from weakening the force of his opponents' argumentation, I conceive that his logical mind has strengthened it, and given it a sequence and inner cohesion that it probably lacked in their own representation. It may be reduced to these three essential points:

1. They deny the Divine origin of his gospel, and the independence of his apostleship: whatever he knows of the Gospel, he received, they say, from the other apostles, and his authority must consequently be subordinated to theirs. His adversaries may even have added that in the presence of the *pillars* of the Church at Jerusalem he had taken care not to assert his empty claims (Gal. ii. 11 ff.).

2. This gospel of human origin is, in addition, false in substance; for it destroys the law, and is in flagrant contradiction to the Old Testament.

3. This gospel, human in origin and false in principle, is further disastrous in its practical results. By doing away with the law it removes the barrier between the elect and sinners (ἁμαρτωλοί).[1]

This triple attack gives us the actual plan of the epistle to the Galatians, and enables us to see the strength of its structure. Paul proceeds to take up and refute these accusations. He has to maintain the independence and authority of his apostleship, and the intrinsic truth of his gospel; and moreover to explain the moral consequences *which, logically and in point of fact, result from it.* Hence the three main divisions of his letter, which has been somewhat inadequately divided into an historical (chaps. i., ii.), a dogmatical (chaps. iii., iv.), and moral section (chaps. v., vi.). These three parts follow each other in logical succession. They are, in fact, the three essential branches of the same demonstration. Perhaps no other of Paul's letters has such a powerful inner cohesion, or so much unity of character. Its one idea, from first to

---

[1] See Holsten, op. cit., *Inhalt und Gedankengang des Briefes an die Galater*, p. 241.

last, is *the Gospel of faith*, whose *origin, principle*, and *consequences* are explained in turn and in progressive order. The refutation of the Judaizers' arguments becomes, thanks to the apostle's dialectics, the luminous and triumphant exposition of his own views.

The general forms of thought which met the requirements of the apostle's missionary preaching, manifestly could no longer suffice for this controversy; and they disappeared. Paul's belief, in all its distinctness, at last finds trenchant and decisive utterance. Its whole import is contained in the following antithesis, which from this time becomes its characteristic: *Justification by faith*, and *justification through the law*; *things new*, and *things old*; *the flesh*, and *the spirit*; *the time of bondage*, and *the time of liberty*. Paulinism has reached its transforming crisis.

I. PAUL'S APOSTOLIC COMMISSION.

When writing to the Thessalonians, Paul did not in his superscription give himself any title. The superscription of the epistle to the Galatians, on the contrary, is exceptionally solemn. This circumstance by itself shows, from the outset, the change that had taken place in the apostle's position. He now asserts, and with remarkable emphasis, at once the Divine origin of his apostleship (ἀπόστολος οὐκ ἀπ' ἀνθρώπων οὐδὲ δι' ἀνθρώπου, ἀλλὰ διὰ Ἰησοῦ Χριστοῦ καὶ Θεοῦ πατρὸς), and the essential principle of that *Gospel* which it is his business to preach, and to defend against all opponents: "Jesus, delivered unto death for our sins, according to the will of God our Father" (chap. i. 4).

Full of indignation and astonishment, Paul flings himself eagerly into the question at issue. Verses

6-10 lay down the thesis to be demonstrated in the epistle: "I marvel that you should have allowed yourselves to be so quickly turned aside from Him who called you in the grace of Christ, to another gospel. —Another gospel? There is none. The fact is, there are certain mischief-makers who wish to pervert the gospel of Christ. But if any one, were it ourselves or an angel from heaven, came to declare a different gospel, let him be anathema! I have said, and I repeat, If any one preach a different gospel, let him be anathema! Am I seeking to commend myself to men, or to God? Or am I seeking to please men? If I were still trying to please men, I should not be a minister of Christ."[1]

After this exordium *ex abrupto*, the first part of the epistle immediately begins, and extends to the end of the second chapter. Paul first asserts the Divine origin of his gospel under its negative form: *The gospel that I have declared, is not according to man. I have not received, neither learned it from any man;* —then, under its positive form: *I hold it by a direct revelation from Jesus Christ* (chap. i. 11, 12). He proves this absolute independence of his gospel by a threefold series of arguments, which fortify each other and form a powerful gradation.

1. Paul insists on the absolutely miraculous nature of the event which made him a Christian, and an

---

[1] These last words, taken along with another passage in the epistle (v. 11), can only be understood as alluding to a time when Paul adopted a conciliatory policy toward certain men (the Judaizers), and made certain concessions in order to avoid giving offence. But the time for concession is now passed. The apostle may not suffer himself to be checked by any regard for persons, under pain of becoming himself unfaithful to Christ.

apostle. It was in the midst of his zeal for Judaism and his persecuting fury that the grace of God (εὐδόκησεν διὰ τῆς χάριτος αὐτοῦ), which had set him apart from his mother's womb, took possession of him. No man intervened between his conscience and the Divine call. It was God Himself who revealed His Son in his soul, and at the same time commissioned him to go and preach Him among the heathen. This work, begun without man's agency, was also completed without man's participation (οὐ προσανεθέμην σαρκὶ καὶ αἵματι). The purpose of vers. 16–24 is to insist on the isolation in which Paul lived: he emphatically declares that he did not see Peter and James until three years after his conversion, and then only for a few days. By virtue of this call, which was solely of God, he has laboured and preached as an apostle to the Gentiles for fourteen years; and with so much success that the Churches of Judæa, to whom he was unknown, glorified God nevertheless, because His grace had turned a persecutor into so mighty an instrument for the extension of His kingdom.

2. But this is not all. Not only did he carry on his labours as an apostle for a long period in absolute independence, but also the mission entrusted to him by God, and which, to be sure, needs no confirmation from men (however great and influential their position), has been *officially* recognised by the apostles at Jerusalem,—by those who pass for pillars of the Church, Peter, James, and John. They gave him the right hand of fellowship, and acknowledged that while Peter had received the apostleship of the Jews, he, Paul, was equally entitled to the apostleship of the Gentiles (chap. ii. 1–10).

3. Furthermore, his apostleship is so entirely in-

dependent of that of the other disciples of Jesus, that on one occasion he was enabled, in virtue of this Divine vocation and the authority it conferred upon him, to reprove Peter and recall him to the right path, from which he had attempted to depart. This was at Antioch. He went so far as to condemn Peter, because he was to be blamed; he made him feel both the duplicity of his conduct and the inconsistency of his views; he succeeded in making the Gospel of Jesus Christ triumph over all the fears and scruples of the one party, and the opposition of the other. He solemnly declared on that occasion the truth that he preaches—*viz.* that no flesh is justified by the law, but every believer is justified solely by his faith in Christ. For, he insisted, the choice must be made: either Christ saves us, and in that case the law does not; or else it is the law that saves, and in that case Christ died in vain. In this manner, Paul naturally passes from the subject of the origin of his gospel to its exposition and the demonstration of its contents. So the first leads to the second part of his letter.

II. THE DOCTRINE OF THE GOSPEL.

This threefold demonstration of the Divine origin of his gospel has wrought upon the apostle's own feelings. The truth at this point seems to him so plain, that he cannot possibly understand the defection of the Galatians: "O foolish Galatians, who then has bewitched you?" With this vigorous apostrophe the second part of the epistle opens. His object is now to show the intrinsic truth of his gospel, and its profound harmony with the Old Testament.

Without doubt, the saying of the new teachers which had done most to shake the Galatians' faith was that ancient, ever powerful phrase : "We are the children of Abraham" (comp. Matt. iii. 9). Salvation belongs to the elect race alone. Now, God has given in circumcision a sign by which the children of Abraham are to be known. Those who are without it do not belong to the people of God, and can have no share in their privileges. This is the reasoning that the apostle had to overthrow. For this theocratic and narrow Messianism, Paul will substitute the great universal scheme, the spiritual history of the kingdom of God and of its revelation upon earth. To the carnal descent from Abraham, he will oppose the spiritual and only true filiation—that of faith. He will appeal, in his turn, to the promise made to the father of the faithful ; he will show in what manner salvation is connected with it, and how the law is related to it. He will thus reconstruct the genuine tradition of Israel ; and it will be seen whether he or his enemies are its true representatives.

We can now understand why the faith of Abraham plays such an important part in Pauline theology. It was not arbitrarily that the apostle chose this example, rather than another. The promise made to the patriarch was the common basis of argument, both for Paul and the Judaizers; and upon this promise and its accompanying conditions a keen debate was sure to arise, for this was the crucial question. The whole discussion turns upon this first point. If the Law qualifies and limits the Promise, it is plain that it will continue to be the eternal condition of salvation. In the epistle to the Romans we shall find Paul returning to this example of Abraham, intent on showing that faith, without the observance of the law, is the sole condition implied in the promise.

He appeals here at the outset to the actual fact of the conversion of the Galatians—a fact which was undeniable, and, in his view, sufficient of itself to overthrow the Judaizers' vain pretensions. "You have been converted; you have received the Spirit, the earnest of life eternal, the pledge of your adoption. Well, I ask you, was it in consequence of the works of the law, or through the preaching of faith, that you experienced all that? Or is it all to be in vain? —See how inconsistent you are: you began in the Spirit, and you would finish in the flesh! God has wrought in you, and produced through His Spirit all the fruits of the new life: do you not see then that the promise made to Abraham is fulfilled in you through faith, and that the true sons of Abraham are those who are so by faith? Through faith the promise was given; through faith, and not by the law, it is fulfilled."

Paul now comes to the formulation of his great distinction between the law and the promise, which, in the first instance, he contrasts with each other. So far from the promise being fulfilled in and by the law, they produce a diametrically opposite effect. The end of the promise is *blessing* (εὐλογία); and the inevitable effect of the law is *the curse* (κατάρα). All those who place themselves under the law are under the curse (ὑπὸ κατάραν εἰσίν). Christ placed Himself under the law and became a curse for us, in order to redeem us from the curse. Wherefore it is in Jesus Christ, and not in the law, that it is possible for the Gentiles to obtain the blessing of Abraham (chap. iii. 9–14).

This reasoning seems unanswerable. But Paul further urges and illustrates it by a comparison drawn from human relationships (κατὰ ἄνθρωπον λέγω). When a man has made a testament, nothing can nullify his fixed decree; nothing can be added to it. Now a testament was made in favour of Abraham's heir (τῷ σπέρματι αὐτοῦ). The promise was made to his seed,—that is, to Christ. The law which came in 430 years later could neither abolish nor change it. So that it is not the law which gives us our title as heirs, but the promise, the free gift of the grace of God.

Hitherto Paul has been contrasting the promise and the law; he has shown that the law brought about a state diametrically opposed to that contemplated by the promise, whose realization it was bound to seek. But it was not enough to set aside the law thus absolutely by a mere negation; its positive value must also be understood and explained. If the law is contrary to the promise, of what use is it? What part was assigned to it in the Divine plan? Why was it given? This is the question which inevitably meets us here (τί οὖν ὁ νόμος; chap. iii. 19). The apostle, in answering it, completes his demonstration. The following verses, which contain this answer, are the most important and the most difficult in the epistle to the Galatians. They furnish the key to the Pauline theory of the progress of Divine revelation. But they are concise to an extent compared with which the style of Tacitus is prolixity itself. At every point thought defeats expression.

For what purpose is the law, it has been asked? It was superadded (προσετέθη) as something external, in a provisional, temporary sense (ἄχρις οὗ); and that for the sake of transgressions,—which is to say, in order to produce and multiply transgressions (τῶν παραβάσεων χάριν προσετέθη = ὁ νόμος παρεισῆλθεν ἵνα πλεονάσῃ τὸ παράπτωμα, Rom. v. 20). Thus transgression, the actual realization of sin, is the primary end of the law. It is an essential, but transitory factor in the development of the plan of salvation. The law was designed to carry sin to the height of its power and its extreme consequences; it had this function to fulfil, up till the time of the coming of the seed of Abraham—*viz.* Christ—to whom the promise had been made. The much disputed words which follow (διαταγεὶς δι' ἀγγέλων ἐν χειρὶ μεσίτου) are still part of Paul's answer to the question propounded. From the form and manner in which the law was given, Paul infers its character. The apostle, as Holsten rightly perceived, did not intend by these words either to disparage or glorify the law, but to bring out its intermediate and subordinate character.

Nothing shows better than these accessory circumstances that the law was not an end in itself, not the final goal, but simply a *means*. As the angels are ministers working after the Divine plan, so the law is a minister, working towards the fulfilment of the promise; given by the hand of a mediator, it still continues to be a mediator,—a middle term between the promise made to Abraham and its fulfilment in Christ, designed to fill up the interval that elapsed between Abraham and his heir.

But what is the meaning of the yet more obscure twentieth verse, ὁ μεσίτης ἑνὸς οὐκ ἔστιν, ὁ δὲ Θεὸς εἷς ἐστίν? In form the verse is a syllogism. The mediator is not of one alone; but God is one, therefore the mediator is not of God. What does this mean, if not that the mediation to be accomplished by the law has nothing to do with God? God being ever in absolute unity, has no need in Himself of any mediation. But every mediation at least implies a duality. It is in history, and in humanity, that this mediation has to be accomplished ; where, in fact, a duality does exist between the *Jews* and *Gentiles*, which has occupied the whole period intervening between the time of the promise and its accomplishment. The law, which multiplies transgressions, places Jews under sin as well as Gentiles ; it constitutes them sinners like the Gentiles ; and this is its function, till the Redeemer's coming. The law, therefore, is not contrary to the promise ; for in reality it is intended to bring about its fulfilment. Neither is the reign of the law a simple interregnum, or parenthesis, but a necessary factor in the evolution of Divine grace. The law is an active agent which labours, and with full success, to make men realize sin and to bring them all under the curse. It is a tutor, a pedagogue, who keeps them in this state against the coming of faith (ἐφρουρούμεθα συγκεκλεισμένοι).

This 23rd verse has often been misunderstood ; the words ἐφρουρούμεθα, παιδαγωγός, etc., have led some to believe that the law was given to check sin, and so to lead man by an actual progress up to Christ. This idea is not at all Pauline, but the very reverse of the apostle's real doctrine. The law has only one aim : to multiply sin by realizing it ; to constitute all men sinners, and like a gaoler to guard them, shut up under sin. Thus the law brings about the unity of all men after a negative fashion, by placing them all equally under the curse. Christ, on the contrary, realizes this unity in a positive manner, by making all men alike children of God. " In Christ there is no longer Greek nor Jew, nor slave nor free, nor man nor woman, for you are all united in Him. And if you are of Christ, you are of the seed of Abraham, and therefore heirs according to the promise." Such is the apostle's conclusion (chap. iii. 29).

To sum up, the law is neither absolutely identical with the promise, nor absolutely opposed to it. It is not the negation of the promise; but it is distinct from it, and subordinate to it. Its final purpose lies in the promise itself. It is an essential, but transitional element in the historical development of humanity. It must needs disappear on attaining its goal. Christ is *the end* of the law.

Thus Paul, in opposition to the theocratic and national Messianism of the Judaizers, succeeds in constructing a new economy of salvation, a history of redemption, broad, profound, and singularly spiritual. It attains its realization in three stages—*the Promise, the Law*, and *Christ*. The first and last terms are identical; the law is the intermediary through which the promise reaches its final realization.

A further comparison suffices to set the apostle's idea in its full light. Humanity is a child, who passes first of all through a period of minority. Man under the law is a minor in tutelage, a child with a pedagogue who simply forbids and commands. There is no difference between this condition and that of the slave. But this state of minority cannot last for ever. At the appointed time Christ came, to proclaim that the human race had attained its *majority*. Man henceforward is freed from tutelage; he is the heir put in possession of his patrimony. It is as reasonable a thing to seek to reduce the child of God again under the law, as it would be to make the mature man return to the rudiments, to those elementary things ($\sigma\tau o\iota\chi\epsilon\hat{\iota}a$)

which served to guide his youth. Between the religion of the letter and that of the spirit there is all the distance that lies between childhood and maturity. Such was the Divine adoption, the liberty and spiritual manhood which the apostle came to declare to the Galatians, and which they had received with so much enthusiasm and gratitude. Is all this to be rendered vain?

To make his victory complete, Paul sums up his exposition once more in his admirable allegory of Sarah the free-woman and Hagar the bond-woman. The children of the free-woman are free as she is; the children of the bond-woman are slaves like their mother. The true heir is not Ishmael, the purely carnal son; it is Isaac, the spiritual son, the child of faith.

III. THE GOSPEL IN ITS PRACTICAL EFFECT.

This allegory, while summing up the second part of the epistle to the Galatians, is also the transition which leads us to the third part. The goal of the apostle's powerful demonstration is the idea of Christian liberty, so that this last section is no less essential to the structure of the epistle than the other two. It is its completion and necessary conclusion. The Gospel of faith becomes the Gospel of freedom.

Paul's whole discourse centres in two ideas:

1. Christian liberty is a privilege of which the Galatians must not suffer themselves to be robbed. They must vindicate it against the attempts of the new teachers, who would re-impose the yoke from which Christ had freed them. "I Paul declare to you, that if you are circumcised, Christ will no longer avail you anything" (chap. v. 1-12).

2. But this liberty must not be used as a starting point or occasion for fleshly lusts; it asserts itself only that it may in turn submit to the law of love. "Free by faith, make yourselves slaves by love." Love is only another name for liberty; and liberty, so far from overthrowing the law, is on the contrary the sole means of its fulfilment. For the law is fulfilled by love (vers. 13–15).

Paul does not stop there. He wishes to show the actual consequences of his doctrine. To admit the principle of faith, and live in sin, is a logical impossibility. Here we have the first outlines of the moral psychology which is developed in the epistle to the Romans. The apostle points out to the Galatians the conflict existing in every man between the flesh and the spirit, one in which the law of good is always conquered by the power of sin. But, he adds, the flesh was crucified with Christ, so that the believer is, with Christ, dead to sin; if he lives henceforward, he lives by the new Spirit of Christ. By a necessary consequence, he must no longer walk according to the flesh which is dead, but according to the Spirit of holiness which raised Christ from the dead (chap. v. 16–26).

Such is the epistle to the Galatians, now lying before us complete in its three divisions,—the first, perhaps the most admirable, manifestation of the apostle's genius. There is nothing in ancient or modern literature to be compared with it. All the powers of Paul's soul shine forth in these few pages. Broad and luminous views, keen logic, biting irony —everything that is most forcible in argument, vehement in indignation, ardent and tender in affection.

is found here combined and poured forth in a single stream, forming a work of irresistible power. Its style is no less original than the matter of its ideas, and has in truth been perfected in the same conflict which matured the apostle's thought. Although Paul's manner is discernible in the two epistles to the Thessalonians, there is nevertheless a wide distinction in character between those two letters and the epistle to the Galatians. Here the true Pauline type reveals itself, in its bold and full originality. The celebrated maxim, The style is the man, was never better verified.

Paul's language is his living image. There is the same striking contrast between his thought and its expression as was presented by his feeble constitution and ardent spirit. It is an inferior style,—poor in its external form, its phraseology rude and incorrect, its accent barbarous. As the apostle's body, a "vessel of clay," yields under the weight of his ministry, so the words and form of his diction bend and break beneath the weight of his thought. But from this contrast spring the most marvellous effects. What power in weakness! What wealth in poverty! What a fiery soul in this frail body! The style does not sustain the thought, it is that which sustains the style, giving to it its force, its life and beauty. Thought presses on—overcharged, breathless and hurried—dragging the words after it!—It is a veritable torrent, which channels its own deep bed and rushes onward, overthrowing all barriers in its way. Unfinished phrases, daring omissions, parentheses which leave us out of sight and out of breath, rabbinical subtleties, audacious paradoxes, vehement apostrophes pour on like surging billows. Mere words, in their ordinary meaning, are insufficient to sustain this overwhelming plenitude of thought and feeling. Every phrase is obliged, so to speak, to bear a double and triple burden. In a single proposition, or in a couple of words strung together, Paul has lodged a whole world of ideas. It is this which makes the exegesis of his epistles so difficult, and their translation absolutely impossible.

From a dogmatic point of view, however, the epistle to the Galatians is after all no more than a programme. All the essential ideas of the Pauline system are indicated in it, but they are not worked out. It is indeed a masterly sketch; the epistle to the Romans turns the sketch into a picture.

CHAPTER II.

THE FIRST EPISTLE TO THE CORINTHIANS.

BETWEEN the epistle to the Galatians and the epistle to the Romans come in chronological order the two letters to the Corinthians.

The conflict raging in Galatia was of a simple and open character. It was the flagrant opposition of two contending principles. At Corinth the struggle was complicated by a multitude of special difficulties. It is less dogmatic, and more personal. Paul's enemies have renounced, or at least concealed their pretensions. They do not raise the question either of circumcision or of the law. But their animosity is none the less fierce for being more secret. It raises up a crowd of practical difficulties in the apostle's way, and forces upon him questions of the most grave and the most delicate nature, through which his authority is covertly assailed. Hence the changed character of Paul's polemics. In this complex situation the condensed and solid argumentation of the epistle to the Galatians would be inappropriate. He has not now to give a formal refutation of error, but to solve a variety of practical problems,—to quell disputes, repress disorders, and disconcert his opponents' schemes. For this task he needed tact equally with logic, adroitness as well as firmness. Paul's doctrine, so concentrated in the epistle to the Galatians, is here expanded in a multitude of varied applications. The stream hitherto pent in spreads itself into a thousand channels; but it flows in the same direction, and while dividing becomes enriched. We shall see in the epistle to the Romans, how at a later period all its streams meet again and resume their broad and mighty course.

The Church of Corinth was one of the apostle's noblest creations. It was, as he says himself, the child that he had begotten amid many sorrows (1 Cor. iv. 9-15), and had nourished and reared with tenderest love. But this child was of Greek birth, and retained the tendencies and temperament of its race. The quarrelsome spirit native to the Greek city re-appeared in the Christian Church. The new faith, with its hopes and mysteries, seems to have stimulated the hereditary disposition to curiosity and subtle disputations. In this town of Corinth, with its mixed population, so wealthy and so corrupt, the quest for pleasure and sensual enjoyment was combined with intellectual refinement. At that period, to lead a disorderly life was called *to Corinthianize*. On reading the descriptions of the moral condition of this great city given by pagan writers, we are no longer surprised that the little Christian congregation in its midst, formed probably out of its most impure elements, was tainted in some degree with the general corruption. These circumstances account for the situation of the Church, as it appears in Paul's first letter to the Corinthians.

Some of its members were leading disorderly lives. One of them was actually living with his father's wife, and had not been excommunicated. There were heated discussions about divorce, about the respective advantages of celibacy and marriage, about sacrificial meats. The celebration of the Agapæ gave rise to scandals. The assemblies were stormy ; every one was eager to parade, in season and out of season, the spiritual gifts that he claimed to possess. Pride and jealousies flourished. A few, more refined than the rest, did not believe in the resurrection of the body. Lastly—and this perhaps was the most serious symptom of all—the Church was split into factions, each taking for its flag the name of some preacher of the Gospel, as formerly in the Greek republics the citizens were wont to rally round one or other of the popular orators. One said, I am for *Apollos*; another, I am for *Paul*; another, I am for *Cephas*; another again, I am for *Christ* (1 Cor. i. 10-12).

What is the real import of these disputes ? Were there four parties, each with a definite and settled constitution ? Certainly not. From a dogmatic point of view, such sects could have had no *raison d'être*; and those who try to discover one are obliged to reduce them to two factions—that of Paul, and of Cephas. But it will be observed that in this first letter Paul nowhere combats a dogmatic tendency opposed to his own. In the earlier chapters especially, his condemnation bears on the mere fact of the disputes ; and indeed he throws blame on his own partisans and those of Apollos, rather than on the adherents of Cephas (chaps. iii. 4-9 ; iv. 6). Finally, he places Cephas, Paul, and Apollos on the same level, as so many servants of Christ belonging to the Corinthians, but to whom the Corinthians in their turn do not belong : " Whether Paul, Apollos, or Cephas— all are yours ; you are Christ's, and Christ is God's." Here is order ; and here is unity. If Paul had been encountering a party division, or a conflict similar to that in Galatia, how could such a mode of procedure on his part be explained? It is a vain attempt to seek to trace out these four parties, especially the Christ party, either in the remainder of this epistle or in the second.[1]

In fact, the language of chap. i. 12 does not describe a general and permanent state of affairs, but a momentary situation which very soon altered. It is the beginning of a fermentation in which all the elements are still mingled and contending together; the Church was seized with the fever of Greek democracy. In such rivalries persons play a more important part than principles. But the agitation wonderfully served to facilitate the attempts of Paul's antagonists. The latter, arriving with letters of recommendation, brought with them a new leaven; they laboured secretly to effect a profound schism. Paul's letter, the arrival of the Judaizing teachers (2 Cor. iii. 1), the logic of principles, and above all, as we shall see, the affair of the incestuous person, led to the separation of the contending elements; and from this general agitation there were evolved two parties radically opposed,— one adhering to Paul, the other to the Judaizers.

---

[1] *Paulus*, vol. i.; pp. 287 ff. [Eng. trans., i., 269 ff.]. The error of Baur's exegesis of 1 Cor. i. 10–12, to my mind, arises from the mistaken idea with which he starts, that the first and second epistles to the Corinthians imply an identical situation in the Church. But it is obvious that in the interval the situation had materially changed, and that for the worse. The four earlier parties had speedily disappeared, and given birth to two that were dogmatic and essentially different,—the Pauline and the Judaizing party. It is this progress of the contest at Corinth that we have endeavoured to make evident.

Such is the situation afterwards disclosed by the second epistle to the Corinthians. But the agitation is at present somewhat complicated and undefined. Beneath the actual disputes Paul's insight detects unmistakably a greater danger; he divines a secret hostility to his gospel; indeed he throws out already a few words here and there in the nature of a defence (chaps. iv., ix.), but always in a veiled and indirect manner. It is the interests of the Church for which he is here concerned, and in a general way. Farther on, when the Judaizing party is unmasked, we shall find him resuming the controversy in a style more ironical, more keen and penetrating than ever. Such, it seems to us, was the course of affairs, and the progress of the struggle in the midst of the Church at Corinth.

It was impossible that this epistle, addressed to so complex a situation and such varied needs, should assume the systematic and logical construction of the letter to the Galatians. The apostle, however, has managed to group into a few great divisions the numerous questions presented to him, and has imparted some degree of method to his long reply.

His letter seems to fall naturally into three main divisions:

1. The first includes the general questions (chaps. i.–vi.). Paul reviews the state of the Church, setting it in a decidedly gloomy aspect. He first of all protests against the internal divisions which are rending it asunder (chaps. i.–iv.); against the scandals which disgrace it, especially the crime of the incestuous person (chap. v.); and, lastly, against the habit which the believers have formed of carrying their law-suits before heathen tribunals (chap. vi.).

2. In a second group of questions the apostle distributes the inquiries that the Corinthians themselves had proposed to him in writing, περὶ δὲ ὧν ἐγράψατε (chaps. vii.–x.). He discusses in succession marriage, celibacy, widowhood, divorce, and meats sacrificed to idols. The solution of all these difficulties is deduced from a general principle, which Paul has always accepted as his own rule throughout his apostleship (chaps. ix. and x.), and which he lays down in the following terms: *All things are lawful, but all things edify not.*

3. Lastly, after disposing of these general questions, Paul enters more fully into the interior life of the Church, and corrects its defects and errors, proceeding by a well-marked gradation from the lighter to the more serious. He deals in succession with the position and deportment of women in the assemblies (chap. xi. 1–16); with the disorders which disturb the Agapæ (vers. 17–34); with spiritual gifts, their diversity and unity, and the charity which excels them all (chaps. xii., xiii.); with the gift of tongues (chap. xiv.); and, finally, with the resurrection of the body (chap. xv.). He adds some advice with respect to the collection for the saints at Jerusalem, which he was organizing in all the Churches; and sums up all his exhortations in the words so full of vigour: "Watch, stand fast in the faith, be manly and strong. Let love inspire all that you do" (chap. xvi. 13, 14).

Such is the order of this first epistle. In spite of the variety of questions touched upon, a profound unity prevails throughout it. Paul's dialectical mind, instead of stopping short at the surface of these particular questions and losing itself in the details of a finely drawn casuistry, always ascends from facts to principles, and thus sheds a fuller light on all the difficulties presented to it by the way. After he has carried the mind of his readers up to the serene heights of Christian thought, he sweeps down from this elevation with irresistible force; and each solution that he suggests is simply a new application of the permanent and general principles of the Gospel. This epistle exhibits, as one might say, the expansion of the Christian principle, as it spreads into the sphere of practical affairs. In it the new life created by the spirit of Jesus becomes conscious of itself, and asserts its unique and independent character,—distinguished on the one hand from the Jewish life with its servitude, and on the other from the pagan life with its license. Our modern Christian civilization, with its liberty and solidarity, its constant demand for reform its impulses towards progress, its delicate charity and scrupulousness, its inner vigour, and its ever enlarging ideal, is all here in the germ. A great revolution is commencing. Already accomplished in individual souls, it begins to manifest itself outwardly in social and domestic relationships. A new humanity is to issue from this new religion.

Such is the import of the first Corinthian epistle. While the letter to the Galatians was the foundation of *Christian dogma*, the two letters to the Corinthians, signalizing as they do the emancipation of the regenerate conscience, are the beginning of *Christian ethics*.

Paul has clearly formulated the essential principle of this new consciousness; it is the Spirit of God Himself immanent therein (1 Cor. ii. 10-16). This does not imply a mere illumination, or a sanctifying influence; but, if I may so call it, a transformation in the substance of our being. The Spirit becomes *us*, and we become essentially *spirit*. This Spirit of God, itself the creative power, makes of us a new creation (1 Cor. ii. 12). To the two classes of men thus formed there correspond *two kinds of wisdom*, the wisdom of the world and the wisdom of God, as contrary to each other as flesh and spirit, reason and folly. The carnal man cannot understand spiritual things (μωρία γὰρ αὐτῷ ἐστίν). The wisdom of God becomes *the folly of the cross*, even as carnal wisdom is nothing but *folly before God* (chap. i. 21-25).

The work of the Spirit within us is twofold. It is first of all negative, setting us free from all external dependence. "Where the Spirit of the Lord is, there is liberty" (2 Cor. iii. 17). "The spiritual man judges all things, and he himself is judged by nothing" (1 Cor. ii. 15). But this liberty is at the same time a positive virtue. For the Spirit is love, as essentially as He is liberty. This absolute independence becomes an absolute bondage; for it is an independence which enslaves itself through love, and which sacrificing itself unremittingly, by each sacrifice finds itself enlarged. "Free from all things," cries the apostle, "I submit myself to all, in order to gain more souls for Christ" (chap. ix. 19). The liberty of faith is found in the bondage of love.

From these principles results that great practical, eternal rule, which cuts short all casuistry, and which Paul is constantly applying: *All things are lawful for me, but not all things are expedient* (chap. vi. 12). It enables the apostle to make the logic of his principles everywhere triumphant without any wound to charity, and to resolve all moral questions in a manner in the highest degree both bold and delicate.

On one point only the apostle's judgment appears

to be still narrow,—I mean that of celibacy (chap. vii.). This narrowness, for which he has been so greatly blamed, does not arise from a dualistic asceticism. There is no dualism to be found in Paul's doctrine; and it is obvious that there would be a strange contradiction between the asceticism of practice supposed, and the broad moral principles which we have just expounded. It is his eschatological views which, in this instance, check and trammel the apostle's reasoning (chap. vii. 29). The *parousia* is imminent; the time is short; all other interests fade before this immediate future. But a further progress of thought on this subject was soon to take place in Paul's mind. Before long it finally shook off the narrow bonds of Jewish eschatology. In the epistles of the Captivity we shall find that he has arrived at a wider and more just appreciation[1] of marriage and domestic life.

[[1] From what has been said it is clear that at the juncture marked by 1 Corinthians this "wider and more just appreciation" would have been out of place. But one is reluctant to think that Paul himself, with his sympathetic nature and Jewish training, had still to arrive at a just appreciation of marriage and domestic life. At the same time, we quite admit that his appreciation of marriage in its Christian bearings widened in later years.]

CHAPTER III.

THE SECOND EPISTLE TO THE CORINTHIANS.

NO other of Paul's letters is of equal importance to this second epistle in its bearing on the history of his inner consciousness. In none does his personality so prominently come into play or so spontaneously and fully reveal itself, as it does under the pressure of the bitter experiences and cruel griefs here recounted. It is easy to perceive that the second epistle bears no resemblance to the first, either in tone or contents. Manifestly, it arises out of an entirely new state of things, both in the Church of Corinth and in the apostle's mind. To define the relations of this letter to its predecessor, by reconstructing the history of the troubles at Corinth, which had now issued in open revolt; to set forth the contents of the epistle; and to describe the evolution of Paul's religious ideas in this, the most critical period of his life—such is the threefold task which now devolves upon us.

I. STATE OF THE CORINTHIAN CHURCH.

The second epistle to the Corinthians affords further evidence of the keen anxiety which the Church of Corinth gave the apostle, and the feverish suspense which had made him long for the return of Titus, his latest messenger. At the time when he wrote, the storm was dispersing, and we only hear its final mutterings. But in the joy and gratitude with which Paul's soul overflows there linger the vibrations of his sorrow, his anger, and apprehension. A drama has evidently been enacted at Corinth, of which this letter is the *dénouement*. Can we retrace its course?

Unquestionably, this very serious crisis was connected with the affair of the incestuous person, whose excommunication Paul had demanded (1 Cor. v. 3). But the view of the subject generally taken is too narrow and isolated. This circumstance could not by itself have led to the far-reaching effects which are now apparent. It became a source of discord, only from the opportunity which it afforded Paul's adversaries for attacking the integrity of his character and the authority of his apostleship. We admit, indeed, that the individual referred to in 2 Corinthians ii. 5, 6, is identical with the incestuous person designated in the first epistle by the same general pronouns, ὁ τοιοῦτος, and τις. But he appears here in quite a different position. It is easy to see that there had been rebellion on his part, and that he had committed outrages against Paul (2 Cor. ii. 5 and 10). In his manner of recalling these injuries, we recognise the delicacy of the apostle's pen, and his disinterested spirit (εἰ δέ τις λελύπηκεν οὐκ ἐμὲ λελύπηκεν.—καὶ γὰρ ἐγὼ ὃ κεχάρισμαι, εἴ τι κεχάρισμαι δι' ὑμᾶς ἐν προσώπῳ Χριστοῦ). Nor is this all. Paul's directions had not been obeyed. Discussions had arisen on the mode of procedure proposed by the apostle, and the authority to which he laid claim. Instead of the unanimity in excommunicating the guilty person which he had expected from the Church, a majority and a minority had been formed; and when punishment did take place, it was only decreed by the majority (ἡ ἐπιτιμία ὑπὸ τῶν πλειόνων, chap. ii. 6).

A division like this, on a point of discipline so simple and obvious, is matter for astonishment. Is it conceivable that the minority hostile to Paul approved the conduct of the guilty person? We know that on the question of impurity the Jewish Christians were even stricter than the apostle's partisans. The cause of their opposition is to be found elsewhere.

In order to discover it, we must go back to chap. v. of the first epistle. "I, being absent in body, present in spirit, have resolved as if I were present, in the name of the Lord Jesus, you and my spirit being assembled, with the power of Jesus our Lord, to deliver such a man unto Satan, for the destruction of the flesh, and the salvation of the spirit at the day of the Lord." What did Paul mean by this demand? Evidently, he was thereby exercising his *apostolic authority* over the Church of Corinth. He was convoking a general assembly of the Church, over which he wished to preside spiritually. He was acting in the capacity of an apostle of Jesus Christ, on a level with the Twelve, assuming to himself the same rights and authority. But it was precisely these rights and this authority that his Judaizing adversaries at Corinth disputed. To obey his orders, under these circumstances, would be to acknowledge the very thing that they denied him. Now, it must not be forgotten how powerful the Judaizing tendency represented by the partisans of Cephas and Christ was in Corinth. The first epistle, without openly combating them, seems to suspect their hostility and secret menaces. Owing to the affair of the incestuous person and Paul's claims, that which in the first instance was only a discussion on the merits of different missionaries, had speedily become an ecclesiastical and dogmatic schism. The apostle's letter had helped to bring on the crisis, and to raise the main question. Furthermore, emissaries had arrived in the interval from Jerusalem or Palestine furnished with apostolic letters. The report of the violent debate between Paul and Peter at Antioch had got abroad, and the opposition to the apostle of the Gentiles had become strengthened and defined. How could his adversaries accept declarations such as that of 1 Corinthians ix. 1, where Paul asserts his apostleship and founds it on his vision of Christ; or those of chap. xv. 1-11, in which, while calling himself the last of the apostles, unworthy even to be called an apostle, he adds that by the grace of God he had laboured more than all the rest?

We see how a wider and more important question became involved in that of the incestuous person. Paul was accused of extravagant boasting. From a distance, said they, he speaks loudly and confidently; but he takes care not to come to Corinth, for his presence is ineffectual. Contrary to all reason and justice, he is usurping apostolic privileges. He is not competent for such an office, and has not been called to it ($ἱκανότης$, chaps. iii. and iv.). His wish is to lord it over Christ's heritage, in order to make his gain out of it (chap. xi. 7-12). He thinks only of vexing and destroying them (chap. xiii. 8-10). He is an intruder, a false brother among the Messianic people, one to be held in distrust (chap. xi. 21-23). We understand thus why it is that the whole discussion in this epistle, from first to last, turns on Paul's apostolic authority. He himself had raised this question in his first letter, by his mode of dealing with the case of the incestuous person.

That such was the course of events is highly probable on logical and intrinsic grounds; and it is further apparent from all that occurred between the two existing letters, and from the satisfactory way in which the obscure allusions, so numerous in the second, are thus explained. For a long time we refused to admit the existence of a lost letter written between the first and second epistle. A new study of the text has modified our previous opinion, and we consider that there was a letter written before the second epistle, just as there was another one before the first; so that the apostle must have written at least four epistles to the Church of Corinth, of which the second and fourth alone remain to us.

The loss of the third is the more to be regretted, because it went to the very root of the conflict at Corinth. Paul wrote it in a spirit of profound grief and indignation, that dictated stern language. He had written with tears, and in great distress of mind; and when the letter had gone, he went so far as to regret some expressions which were, possibly, extreme[1] (chap. vii. 5–12). What effect would it produce at Corinth? For some time this anxiety seems to have left him no rest. It was on this account that he sent Titus immediately after, or perhaps at the same time, to watch the events that might occur, and to re-establish harmony and confidence between himself and the Church. He awaited his return with impatience, and not finding him at Troas, went to meet him in Macedonia. It is evident that the character-

---

[1] May not the exaggerated character of this letter, and the kind of regret which Paul has expressed, explain why it has not been preserved?

istics of the letter to which Paul so often refers in our second epistle, do not properly belong to the first, which is highly pacific in tone and calm in its tenor, and, on the whole, kindly in feeling towards the Corinthians.

In the first epistle, moreover, Paul commended Timothy, his earlier messenger, to the Corinthians (1 Cor. iv. 17 ; xvi. 10, 11). Timothy, who was still very young, had not sufficient authority to allay the storm ; he was overmatched by the revolt, and returned to tell Paul of the fresh complications that had arisen. At the beginning of the second epistle, we find him with the apostle ; but it would be strange, unless some letters were written in the interval, that Paul says nothing of his return, or of the anxious tidings he had brought. It is Titus, on the contrary, who is now mentioned ; indeed Paul speaks of him only to the Corinthians. We cannot, therefore, question the existence of the lost letter, to which he refers more than once (chap. ii. 1-3 and 9) What did it contain ? It would be a daring thing to attempt its reproduction. We do not consider that M. Hausrath, who thinks he has found it in the last four chapters of the second epistle, has been happy in this hypothesis.[1] But the vehement, the ironical and impassioned tone of these last pages represents very fairly, I believe, that of the lost letter.

We may add, in accordance with chap. ii. 9 and chap. vii. 7, 11, 13, that in this letter Paul gave express orders, and demanded satisfaction. Clearly, the crisis was a serious one; it was a sort of *ultimatum* that Paul had sent. We can understand the anxiety

---

[1] *Der Viercapital Brief des Paulus an die Corinther.*

with which he awaited the news that Titus was to bring him, and the joy and gratitude which it excited. The two first chapters of the epistle are like a sigh of relief, a cry of deliverance (chap. ii. 14). Titus, armed with the severe letter of Paul which had preceded him, has brought the rebels and disturbers to reason. The man who had grossly outraged Paul has been punished; and the apostle now declares himself satisfied, and wishes him to be forgiven. Though the Corinthians had been mortified by his remonstrances, their trouble led to repentance, and to the display of a more ardent affection. The victory, in short, remained with Paul.[1]

---

[1] I do not now feel quite satisfied with this historical reconstruction of the crisis which occurred in the Church of Corinth. That there was a letter, now missing, which came between the two existing epistles, still seems to me uncontestable; but there was something more. These passages, when studied more closely, compel us to admit further a visit made by Paul to Corinth during the interval that elapsed between the two canonical epistles. Three passages in the second letter to the Corinthians establish the fact of this visit: (1) In 2 Cor. xiii. 1 and 2, the words τρίτον τοῦτο ἔρχομαι, and especially the phrase ὡς παρὼν τὸ δεύτερον, further followed by ὅτι ἐὰν ἔλθω εἰς τὸ πάλιν, cannot be explained by a merely projected journey, but imply a second, which was actually accomplished. (2) The same conclusion is equally apparent from 2 Cor. xii. 14: Ἰδοὺ τρίτον τοῦτο ἑτοίμως ἔχω ἐλθεῖν πρὸς ὑμᾶς, καὶ οὐ καταναρκήσω. The assertion contained in this latter verb can only be explained on the supposition of a second sojourn of Paul at Corinth, before he wrote the present epistle. (3) Paul, in his first letter, promised the Corinthians a speedy visit (1 Cor. xvi. 7 and iv. 21), and asked the faithful themselves to decide whether he should come with a rod of chastisement, or with the spirit of gentleness and love to console them. (4) Lastly, the language of 2 Cor. ii. 1–3 proves that this visit had taken place, and had been full of

II. PAUL'S REMONSTRANCE.

It was in order to secure and strengthen this new situation, even more than to prepare for the collection on behalf of the poor at Jerusalem, that the apostle took up his pen once more. Rightly to understand the tenor of the second epistle, apparently so strange, we must form a clear conception of the circumstances which called it forth. The crisis which had occurred at Corinth had come to a relatively favourable issue;

---

sorrow. The words, τὸ μὴ πάλιν ἐν λύπῃ ἐλθεῖν πρὸς ὑμᾶς, cannot refer to the occasion when Paul was evangelizing Corinth for the first time. The Church had not then given him any disappointment; for it did not as yet exist. The reference here is to a second, and quite recent visit, of which he retained a very sorrowful recollection, including it among the most bitter trials of his apostolical career. It will be observed, in fact, that Paul speaks in the same tone of this visit as he does of the missing letter, written immediately afterwards, under the shock of distress which it occasioned.

What, then, had taken place at Corinth during this visit of Paul? There are two passages which throw some light upon this question: 2 Cor. ii. 5-11; vii. 11, and especially ver. 12. It appears from these statements that Paul had been personally and directly affronted. There is some one at Corinth who in his own presence, and before the whole Church, has done him serious injury. The words τοῦ ἀδικήσαντος and τοῦ ἀδικηθέντος of 2 Cor. vii. 12 are only naturally applicable to Paul and the man who had affronted him. They could not refer, in this context, to the incestuous person of 1 Cor. v. and his father, as is generally supposed. How could Paul, in that case, have had anything to forgive? See 2 Cor. ii. 10. How could he say in the same passage that he had been directly wounded: ἐμὲ λελύπηκεν, ἐν λύπῃ (chap. ii. 1-5)? And how, in the last place, if it were still a question of the man whom in his first letter he had delivered to Satan (1 Cor. v. 5), could he now write about him so considerately in 2 Cor. ii. 7, μή πως τῇ περισσοτέρᾳ λύπῃ καταποθῇ,—and yet more in ver. 11?

but it left the Church still greatly divided. The majority had returned to the apostle's side, with the liveliest tokens of regret and affection. But besides this majority, there still remained a minority, obstinate in its hatred and hostile in its intentions. The letter, like the position of affairs, has a twofold aspect. Paul could not have written it on any other plan. He first addresses himself to the faithful majority, and pours out the feelings which fill his soul towards them. He has never written anything more touching (chaps.

The affair of the incestuous person may indeed, as we explain above, have helped to raise in the Church the great question, now under discussion, of Paul's apostolic dignity and authority; but it was not this man who had insulted Paul; and the vague expression $\tau\iota s$, $\dot{o}$ $\tau o\iota o\hat{v}\tau o s$, which Paul always uses to designate his adversaries, and which occurs again and again in the same epistle (chaps. x. 7 and xi. 4), must be applied to some influential person in the Church of Corinth, probably one of the Judaizers come from Palestine with letters of recommendation (2 Cor. iii. 1), who specially claimed to be *of Christ* according to the flesh and to speak in His name (chap. x. 7). It was this same person who said that, though Paul's letters were strong and weighty, his presence was ineffectual. He it was who publicly affronted Paul ($\dot{a}\delta\iota\kappa\dot{\eta}\sigma a\nu\tau o s$, chap. vii. 12), and had occasioned him so much distress ($\epsilon\dot{\iota}$ $\delta\dot{\epsilon}$ $\tau\iota s$ $\lambda\epsilon\lambda\dot{v}\pi\eta\kappa\epsilon\nu$, chap. ii. 5).

We can therefore reconstruct, with some degree of probability, the drama which was enacted at Corinth during Paul's second visit. The apostle had hastened thither to counteract the manœuvres of the emissaries from Judæa or Syria, who were undermining his authority. Debate and conflict arose. The Church assembled; and both Paul and his adversaries were present. His words were of no avail; the Church yielded in part to the specious arguments and more facile eloquence of the Judaizers. One of them, doubtless their leader, denounced Paul openly; he accused him of falsehood, treated his visions as chimerical, and reproached him with living at the expense of the Churches. The confidence of the Corinthians was shaken.

i.–viii.). Then, after briefly arranging the matter of the collection (chap. ix.), he turns abruptly to the hostile minority, and mercilessly chastises it with the lash of his irony. Nothing more biting than these last pages has proceeded from his pen (chaps. x.–xiii.). This is the natural explanation of the two, most dissimilar portions of his letter. Nothing bridges the transition from one to the other, because there was nothing in the facts to furnish a point of connexion.

Heartbroken by this affront, and feeling utterly helpless, Paul left Corinth. But a few days later, pen in hand, the apostle regained his power, and wrote a crushing letter, the vehement tone of which he seems at first to regret (2 Cor. vii. 5–9). This letter, further supported by the oral mission of Titus, seems with the majority to have prevailed over the calumnies and intrigues of his adversaries. The insult had been public; it was publicly withdrawn; and the offender was so earnestly disowned and censured by the majority of the believers, that Paul is now the first to ask mercy on his behalf.

These events, taken fully into account, demand a slight modification in our chronology of the two epistles. At first we had only allowed for an interval of five or six months between them, reckoning from about the Passover of 57 to the autumn of the same year. This space of time is too short for the occurrence of all the facts that we have now come to recognise. We must place the first epistle a year earlier, which is easily done, and date it at the Passover of the year 56 A.D., leaving the second in the autumn of 57 (written in Macedonia). This gives an interval of eighteen months between them, which is amply sufficient.

Let us restate the chronological order and development of the inner history of the Church of Corinth during this period.

1. Towards the end of the year 55, and upon his arrival at Ephesus, Paul writes his first letter to the Corinthians, now lost, but referred to in 1 Cor. v. 9. The heterogeneous fragment of 2 Cor. vi. 14–vii. 1 is doubtless one of its pages, which survived through having strayed into the context where it is found at present.

Notwithstanding their marked difference of tone and manner, the two parts are none the less linked together by a large unity of thought and aim. It is the same adversary that Paul combats in both parts, the Judaic spirit which strove by its pretensions to extinguish the Christian spirit,—that bondage to the letter which still prevailed over the liberty of the Gospel. He resumes, therefore, the warfare begun by

---

2. In the winter of 55-56: the answer of the Corinthians to Paul (1 Cor. vii. 1), the visit made to Paul at Ephesus by the members of Chloë's household (1 Cor. i. 11) and by other Corinthian Christians (1 Cor. xvi. 17), and the discussion in the Church on the merits of the different preachers (1 Cor. i. 12-14).

3. About the passover of the year 56: Paul's second letter—*our first epistle to the Corinthians*, and the mission of Timothy to Corinth (1 Cor. xvi. 10).

4. Arrival of the Judaizing emissaries with letters of recommendation (2 Cor. iii. 1). Great disturbance in the Church.

5. In the autumn of the year 56, Timothy reports his failure to Paul, who sets out for Corinth and spends one or two months there.

6. The public conflict between Paul and his adversaries. Paul is worsted, and leaves heartbroken. The Church seems lost to him.

7. In the spring of the year 57: Paul's third letter to the Church of Corinth, now lost (2 Cor. ii. 4 and vii. 5-9).

8. About the same time, the mission of Titus.

9. In the spring of 57: the meeting of Titus and Paul in Macedonia (2 Cor. vii. 5).

10. Autumn of 57: Paul's fourth letter (from Macedonia), *our second epistle to the Corinthians*.

11. Winter of 57-58: Paul's third visit to Corinth, a happy and peaceful one; for it was then that he wrote his great letter to the Romans.

Thus reconstructed, this dramatic chapter of the apostle's life enables us, better than anything else, to understand what that life was really like,—*Note of the author written for this edition.*

the epistle to the Galatians, and carries it a stage further. The battle is no longer about circumcision, but concerns the ministry of the old, and that of the new covenant.

In the third and fourth chapters Paul addresses himself to this fundamental question. The two covenants are powerfully described (chap. iii. 6, 7)—one as the letter, dead in itself and imparting death; the other as the spirit, having life in itself and giving life; one resulting in condemnation, the other in salvation. If the first was glorious, notwithstanding its limited and transitory character, how much more so is the second, which is not only called to have its phase of glory, but to abide in it (τὸ καταργούμενον διὰ δόξης . . . τὸ μένον ἐν δόξῃ, chap. iii. 11).

To the two covenants there correspond two ministries (διακονία γράμματος, διακονία πνεύματος). The first was that of Moses, whose face was veiled before the children of Israel, that they might not see its glory pass away. But the ministry of the new covenant, radiant with permanent glory, is manifested before all eyes without veil or reservation, because its glory is progressive; for where the Spirit of the Lord is, there is entire confidence (παῤῥησία),—a perfect liberty, a continual glorification (chap. iii. 12-18).

Here Paul introduces the dramatic contrast occupying the fourth and fifth chapters, between the inner might and glory of his ministry, and the humiliations and outward infirmities, which while they seem to eclipse it, only serve to reveal its Divine power more adequately. "We have this treasure in an earthen vessel, that the exceeding power of its virtue may be ascribed to God, and not to us.

We are afflicted on all sides, but not overwhelmed; always in distress, yet never brought to despair; persecuted, but not conquered; tempest-tossed, but not submerged; always bearing in our body the dying and mortified image of the Lord Jesus, that in the death of our flesh might also shine forth the vigour of His life."

Not merely do trial and reproach fail to injure our ministry, they even commend it, and are the Divine seal by which it may be recognised. The Christ whom we serve is not Christ according to the flesh, but the Christ who died and rose again. Thus everything that is glorious or powerful according to the flesh disappears from our ministry, as with Christ Himself, that the new life, the life of the Spirit, may be more fully manifested. "Thus we commend ourselves as ministers of God, by great patience, by sufferings, by trials, by the wounds we have received; in prisons, in watchings, in weariness, in fastings; through glory and dishonour, through renown and calumny. Treated as deceivers, and yet faithful; mistaken by men, and yet known of God; ever dying, ever living; always tried, yet always joyous; poorest of the poor, yet enriching multitudes." These admirable pages close with this touching appeal to the Corinthians: "Our mouth is open unto you, O Corinthians; our heart is enlarged. You are not straitened in our affections; recompense us in kind. Enlarge your hearts in turn" (chap. vi. 11).[1]

---

[1] It is impossible to discover the slightest connexion between the 13th verse of chap. vi. and the totally different line of thought beginning in ver. 14. The same breach of continuity recurs between the first and second verses of the 7th chapter. If, on the contrary, this section (chap. vi. 14–vii. 1) be removed,

Chapters vii.-ix. revert to some details which had been too briefly explained at first, and to the collection which had to be completed before Paul's return. The controversy with the Judaizers, which in the first letter was indirect and incidental, occupies, as we see, the whole of the second, and becomes keener and more urgent as the apostle proceeds. Now that he has disposed of the question of principle, Paul faces the accusations and calumnies directed against his own person by his adversaries. His long-repressed indignation bursts forth in a sudden explosion (chap. x. 1). "I Paul myself exhort you once more with all gentleness, and with the patience of Christ,—I, so lowly and humble among you, so bold when absent! God grant that when I come, I may not have to put forth my strength to bring to subjection those who represent me as walking according to the flesh."

After refuting the assertions of his enemies, he in his turn attacks them. He draws a parallel between their ministry and his own, in which the most lashing irony and the bitterest indignation are mingled with a most delicate reserve. "Well, though at the risk of appearing foolish, I too wish to boast a little: you will easily endure it. I am about to speak not after the Lord, but as a fool: no matter! since others sing their own praises, I too will sing mine. You who are so wise, can easily bear with fools! Whether one bring you into bondage, or devour you, or glorify himself, or strike you on the face, you bear it with admirable

---

there is a most natural connexion between chap. vi. 13 and vii. 2. The exegetes are therefore quite right in regarding the paragraph which so untowardly interrupts the thread of the discourse as an interpolated gloss, or a fragment of one of Paul's lost letters inserted in the midst of the second epistle.

patience. What would you have? I say it to my shame—but I also have my weaknesses. Of what do they boast?—I am a fool, but I too boast of the same. Are they Hebrews? so am I. Are they Israelites? so am I. Are they servants of Christ? (here my foolishness has no bounds) I am more so than they; in weariness, imprisonment, and wounds—in the endurance of suffering, I surpass them! I have five times received from the Jews forty stripes save one. I have thrice been beaten with rods, and once stoned. Thrice have I been shipwrecked. I was a night and a day in the jaws of the deep. Wearying journeys, perils on the rivers, dangers of every kind—from robbers, from my fellow countrymen, from the heathen, in cities and deserts, on the sea, and among false brethren—labour, sorrows, vigils, hunger, thirst, cold, nakedness,—I have braved everything, endured everything. . . . But enough! If I must needs glory, let me glory in my infirmities!" As in the epistle to the Galatians, so here Paul yields none of his rights. He does not fear to place himself on a level not only with those false apostles who came to trouble the Churches (ψευδαπόστολοι, ἐργάται δόλιοι, μετασχηματιζόμενοι εἰς ἀποστόλους Χριστοῦ, chap. xi. 13), but with those whose authority these others so much exalt, and whom he calls οἱ ὑπερλίαν ἀπόστολοι, the *arch-apostles* (chap. xi. 5). This expression of Paul's corresponds very well with those in the epistle to the Galatians,—στῦλοι, δοκοῦντες.

III. THE CRISIS IN PAUL'S SOUL.

While there was occurring at Corinth that profound schism which alone can explain both the form and substance of the second epistle, an equally momentous crisis had supervened in the great apostle's own soul. No external changes can account for all that we find in this letter; it gives evidence of other occurrences no less momentous, which took place in the author's inner life.

It is very remarkable that Paul's eschatological notions, which, as we have seen, are maintained to the end of the first epistle to the Corinthians, disappear —or, at least, are transformed—from the second onwards. From this time he no longer hopes to witness the coming of the Lord within his lifetime. This glorious *parousia*, which formed the horizon of his vision of the future, has been indefinitely postponed, and makes room for a darker and more sorrowful perspective. Instead of the appearance of Jesus, the apostle henceforward has the prospect of death and martyrdom before him; and beyond this painful stage, the hope of being finally reunited to the Lord (2 Cor. v. 1-10; Acts xx. 22-25; Phil. i. 20, 21).

This marked change in the Pauline eschatology took place in the interval between the two letters to the Corinthians. What has happened meanwhile? The beginning of our second epistle shows us. The last months of Paul's stay at Ephesus and in Asia seem to have been the darkest and most difficult of his life. For the moment, his hopes and his spirit flagged. Everything seemed to conspire against him. After the defection of the Galatians, he had just heard of the troubles in the Church at Corinth. He finds the same adversaries confronting him at Ephesus and furiously persecuting him. The care of all the Churches consumes him (2 Cor. xi. 28). He has no rest in his flesh; he is afflicted on every side (ἔξωθεν μάχαι, ἔσωθεν φόβοι, 2 Cor. vii. 5).

Nor is this all. He has just incurred a mysterious danger in Asia, of exceptional gravity (2 Cor. i. 8). This trial, which the apostle does not explain more definitely, but which could not have been the riot of Demetrius and his workmen at Ephesus (Acts xix. 30-41), surpassed all bounds, and exceeded his power of endurance (ὅτι καθ' ὑπερβολὴν ἐβαρήθημεν ὑπὲρ δύναμιν). He despaired of life. He carried within his soul a sentence of death. And now his unhoped for deliverance seems like an actual resurrection (chap. i. 8-10).

The hero's indomitable courage, shaken for the moment by this terrible crisis, was soon re-established. But there was one thing which was not restored: the hope of seeing with his own eyes the triumph of the Gospel, the establishment of the Messianic kingdom, and the immediate *parousia* of the Lord. In this crisis his faith at length freed itself from the last bonds of traditional Judaism; and Christian eschatology escaped from the narrow limits of the eschatology of the Pharisees. The spirit completes its triumph over the letter.

Paul sees new prospects opening before him. He can no longer reckon on the intervention of the archangel and the celestial trumpet for the founding of God's kingdom. It will be established by the weakness, by the devotion and the sufferings of its messengers. The image of death, with which the apostle had not hitherto concerned himself, enters for the first time within the scope of his doctrine.

In this season of anguish and distress, he seems to have had a clear vision of martyrdom. He was to seal his preaching of the Gospel with his blood. The disciple, like the Master, can only triumph through humiliation and suffering. But Paul's resolution is fixed. Henceforth he passionately devotes himself to this vision of the dying Jesus; he experiences a new and indescribable pride, a joy blended with anguish, in renewing in his own body the martyrdom of his Master, in carrying it forwards by his personal sufferings and completing it by his death (τὴν νέκρωσιν τοῦ Ἰησοῦ ἐν τῷ σώματι περιφέροντες, 2 Cor. iv. 10; comp. Col. i. 24; Phil. i. 20; ii. 17; 2 Tim. iv. 6). Thus the apostle's momentary defeat is changed into a higher, and, this time, a decisive victory.

From henceforth he is happy and contented; his mind has discovered its true bent, and he now feels that the various elements of his faith are brought into full and perfect harmony. If the earthly future is darkened, shrinking and closing up before his gaze, in the heavenly future there is revealed to his soul a new, wide, and luminous prospect. The mournful conception of *Sheol* vanishes from his mind; and with it the Messianic framework of the Jewish apocalypse gives way. Instead of the unconscious sleep of souls in the bosom of the earth, there emerges triumphant the Christian hope of the immediate reunion of the elect with the Saviour (2 Cor. v. 1-10). True, the struggle between the power of the Gospel and that of sin here on earth will be prolonged. Paul has no doubt that it will issue at last in the full triumph of Christ and His glorious advent; but he no longer attempts to estimate the length, or foresee the phases of this great drama. Like Jesus, and with the same filial submission, he leaves in the hands of God the Father the destiny of His kingdom. The spiritual principle of Christianity everywhere prevails. Death henceforth is completely vanquished and overcome by the Christian consciousness.

We know with what a crushing effect this idea of death weighed upon the Jewish, as well as the heathen mind. In spite of the doctrine of the resurrection, fairly established in the popular belief as it appears from the time of the production of the book of Daniel, Hades, or Sheol, retained its shadows, and death its terrors. The soul of Jesus had shuddered on approaching it. But the darkness speedily disappeared before the radiance of His faith; and He had entirely triumphed over death, by His sense of perfect and indissoluble union with the Father. To die was, for Jesus, to return to His Father and His God (John xx. 17). But neither the first Christians, nor the first apostles, had appropriated to themselves this victory of the Master. Death was not less fearful to them than to the Jews. The Messianic reign that they were expecting was only to be realized upon earth; they knew no other sphere of life. They were expecting the coming of the Lord; and when their friends died, they were deeply distressed on their account. This explains the anxiety of the Thessalonians about their dead—an anxiety which Paul endeavoured to soothe. In what manner? He could only at that time direct their expectation and faith to the impending event of the coming of Jesus, and assure them that the dead will then rise first of all, and, with the living, share His triumph. Death still retained its appalling mystery; it was only conquered in hope, and as regards the future.[1]

[[1] But see 1 Thess. v. 10: "Jesus died and rose again, that, whether we be waking or sleeping, we may *live together with Him*." Here is already a sense of indissoluble union with

In the second letter to the Corinthians already Paul comforts himself in a manner quite different from this, and more effectual. While the outer man succumbs to death, the inner man, whose principle of life is the Spirit of God Himself, is delivered from it. The trials which destroy the former only strengthen and glorify the latter. In proportion as the one decays, the other is renewed and reinvigorated (2 Cor. iv. 16). We sigh for the time when, above our mortal flesh condemned to die, we shall put on the celestial and spiritual body ($\dot{\epsilon}\pi\epsilon\nu\delta\dot{\upsilon}\sigma\alpha\sigma\theta\alpha\iota$). Though our earthly body be destroyed by death, we have yet in the heavens a spiritual body awaiting us; so that, when disrobed of our earthly covering, we shall not be found naked, any more than those living at the resurrection day (2 Cor. v. 3). So far, therefore, from fearing death, we should rather desire it. For while we are in the body, we are absent from the Lord: but out of the body, we are with the Lord. Death only despoils us of a perishable covering, to clothe us with an immortal body. For the Christian, therefore, death is truly conquered; it belies itself; it is nothing more than a point of transition, the final crisis which accomplishes our eternal glorification (2 Cor. iv. 17).

Thus regarded from the double standpoint of the conflict with Judaism and the development of the Pauline doctrine, we perceive how important in all respects is the place which is occupied in Paul's history by the second letter to the Corinthians.

Jesus, corresponding to that "sense of indissoluble union with the Father" by which Jesus triumphed over death. Comp. 1 Cor. xv. 55, 56 ("God . . . *giveth* us the victory"); also John vi. 50, 51; viii. 51; xi. 25, 26.]

CHAPTER IV.

THE EPISTLE TO THE ROMANS.

THE epistle to the Romans completes and crowns the progress achieved by the apostle's mind during this stormy period. The ideas briefly sketched in the epistle to the Galatians, or merely thrown out incidentally in the two letters to the Corinthians, here present themselves firmly bound together and brought to a powerful unity; they are dialectically established, and organized into a complete system.

The struggle in which Paul was engaged enters upon a new phase, and for himself at any rate, approaches its issue. The tranquillity which seems to be attained in his mind and thoughts imparts a breadth and calmness to this last letter which the others did not possess. It is no longer a question of circumcision, or of the attacks made upon Paul's person or apostleship. Personal feelings and private quarrels are forgotten; the question of principle about which the two parties were contending can now be seen in its full import. Fundamentally, indeed, the controversy is still the same; but the apostle's doctrine, disentangled from external incidents, is raised to a higher level and attains a freer and fuller development. Escaping from the violent antithesis by which it was hitherto dominated, it tends towards a general and culminating synthesis. Paul at last brings Judaism and Paganism within the scope of his contemplation. He is not content to contrast them with the Gospel, and to condemn them purely and simply; he endeavours to understand them in their historical functions and actual value, to assign them their due place as transitional but essential stages in the Divine plan of redemption. In this manner the new circle of Pauline thought is enlarged and completed. Having taken possession of the sphere of the conscience, it conquers the domain of history. The epistle to the Romans is the first attempt at what we should call, in modern phrase, a philosophy of the religious history of mankind.

Such appears to us to be the drift and character of this great letter. It is not a formal treatise of abstract theology, as our ancient theologians supposed; neither is it an expressly controversial writing like the epistle to the Galatians, or the second letter to the Corinthians. The apostle, while designing to combat the same tendency and achieve its final overthrow, directs against it a more general and less passionate style of argument. He places the question on the ground of principle, and is not so anxious to get the better of his old opponents as to do full justice to the truth. The epistle to the Romans marks the exact point at which controversy resolves itself naturally into dogma.

But we cannot hope to gain either a just appreciation or a full comprehension of this letter, unless we take exact account of the occasion which gave rise to it, and the aim by which it is inspired. Although Paul's doctrine is presented here in a more general and dialectical form, it would be a great mistake to look upon his letter as the work of a professed theologian, dictated by a purely speculative interest. Only the historical circumstances which produced the epistle will enable us to understand it.

I. THE CHURCH OF ROME.

Having arrived at Corinth shortly after his second letter to the Christians of that city, Paul stayed there some time,—about three months, according to the narrative of the Acts of the Apostles (xx. 2, 3). Doubtless his presence finally calmed the minds of the Corinthians, and confirmed his authority amongst them. At that time new and mighty projects were germinating in his soul.

This last sojourn at Corinth marks the brilliant climax of Paul's apostolic career. The epistle to the Romans, which was written then, seems on the one hand to conclude and crown the first stage of his life and work, and on the other to prepare for and inaugurate the second. The great missionary who had undertaken to carry the Gospel to the ends of the earth here pauses a moment, mid-way in his career. Taking a double survey, he looks back along the road he has traversed and forward to that which he intends to follow. Already from Jerusalem to Illyria there stretched the numerous succession of Churches which seemed to mark the halting places in his long journeys. From Corinth at the eastern extremity, he now sees opened before him an equally wide field of activity towards the west. Before pushing into these new regions, he wishes to go up to Jerusalem once more, and take to the mother Church the offerings of the Gentile Churches, that by this means the distrust of the Christians in Palestine may be finally overcome and banished; possibly also, desiring thus to make amends to some extent for the evil that he had formerly done to it. Then, leaving Syria, Asia, and Greece behind him, he intends to penetrate to the limits of the West, perhaps never more to return (Rom. xv. 22-29).[1]

With such a project in view, Rome of necessity was the object which in the first instance attracted and engaged the apostle's thoughts. The Church of this city afforded the most promising and convenient vantage ground for his new mission. In the centre of Italy, equally distant from Germany, Gaul, Spain, and Western Africa, Rome had the further advantage of being in direct line with the course which the apostle had hitherto pursued, thus linking the work he was about to undertake with that which he had already accomplished; so that, in Paul's view, the Church of Rome was destined to become a mother Church, and to be for the West what the great cities of Antioch, Ephesus, and Corinth had been by turn for the East, alike the goal and starting point of his new missionary enterprises (Rom. xv. 24).

The epistle to the Romans is nothing else but the first step in the execution of these vast designs. In announcing his impending arrival at the capital of the Empire, the apostle seeks to prepare his field of action, and to pave his way thither. A Christian Church had been in existence in Rome for some years, and it was of the first importance to secure its sympathy and support. This is the primary aim of the epistle to the Romans. Inasmuch as Paul

---

[1] Reuss, *Geschichte der Heiligen Schriften des N.T.*, § 105 [*History of the Sacred Scriptures of the N.T.*, p. 96.]

was bound to direct all his efforts towards this purpose, and made it his business to meet the feelings and special requirements of his readers, it is evident that his letter can only properly be explained by the position of the Church at Rome. There, and nowhere else, is the key to this epistle to be found.

Unfortunately, opinion is far from being unanimous upon this capital point. Critics and expositors have long been divided into two hostile camps. Some insist that the Church of Rome was essentially Gentile-Christian, and quote in support of their assertion Romans i. 6 and xi. 17–24—passages whose bearing and significance they perhaps exaggerate. Others, on the contrary, with Baur at their head, assert that it was essentially a Jewish-Christian Church, and openly hostile to Paulinism. From these two opposite conclusions there logically result two contradictory conceptions of the epistle.

Those who look upon the Church of Rome as Gentile-Christian, can only regard Paul's letter as a strictly dogmatic exposition of his gospel, made with the object of elevating and confirming the faith of the Romans; or, at most, of forearming them against the intrigues of the Judaizing teachers (chap. xvi. 17). According to this view, the dialectic exposition of the doctrine of Justification by Faith, which occupies the first eight chapters, forms the essential part of the apostle's letter. The ninth, tenth, and eleventh chapters are a mere historical corollary, having no direct connexion with the previous section, whose tenor and whose presence, from this point of view, it is impossible to explain.

On the opposite theory, the relation of these two component parts of the letter are exactly reversed.

Those who regard the epistle of the Romans as polemical, and addressed to an unknown or hostile Church, make these last three chapters, which, according to the first hypothesis, are disconnected with the rest, the central part and the essential basis of the letter. There only, according to these critics, is disclosed the apostle's true intention, the object which in reality occupies his mind. His object is to justify the substitution of the Gentiles for the Jewish nation; and the first eight chapters are therefore simply an introduction, preparatory to the burning question of the destiny of Israel.[1]

In point of fact, these two conceptions of the epistle to the Romans appear equally defective. They cut the epistle into two parts, whose connexion and unity are then entirely lost. It is very difficult, on the one hand, to regard the ninth, tenth, and eleventh chapters, charged with emotions so vivid, as being a mere appendix, foreign to the main body of the letter and unconnected with the state of opinion at Rome; on the other hand, it is no less difficult to treat the first eight chapters as a preliminary intro-

---

[1] The first opinion, which was that of the greater number of ancient interpreters, was taken up and maintained not long ago with great skill by M. Th. Schott : *Der Römerbrief, seinem Endzweck und Gedankengang nach ausgelegt.* (Erlangen, 1858.) This work of Schott provoked a still more remarkable study by M. Mangold, Professor at Marburg : *Der Römerbrief und die Anfänge der römischen Gemeinde.* (Marburg, 1866.) The latter adopts Baur's thesis, but with such corrections as to transform it. He seems to me to have proved decisively that the majority of the Christians at Rome were of Jewish origin. M. Godet, however, in his recent Commentary, has returned to the old opinion; and has even exaggerated it, to an extent that makes it wholly untenable.

duction. With so slender a body and so enormous a head, there would be something truly monstrous in the structure of the epistle. On the contrary, one of its great beauties is precisely the logical architecture which distinguishes it. A harmonious agreement prevails throughout its various parts and details. True, we seek in vain for any obvious transition between the two sections referred to; but have we not noticed a breach of continuity, at least as great, existing between the ninth and tenth chapters of 2 Corinthians? Paul's mind often takes these abrupt and violent turns, to the surprise and discomfiture of the superficial reader; but we may rest assured that even then, so far from departing from the right path, it is pursuing its end more directly and eagerly than ever.

Is it not obvious, for example, that the two halves of the epistle to the Romans are intimately connected at the bottom, and that the second without the first would have no foundation, while the first without the second would have no culmination? Is it not the case that these three later chapters, treating of Jews and Gentiles under the state of grace, correspond with, and form a pendant to the first three, in which the apostle exhibited them both in a state of sin? In view of this, how can it be doubted that the two portions of the epistle form an organic whole? We must therefore endeavour to discover some method of understanding the letter to the Romans which will preserve its internal unity, and determine its precise bearing.

To return to the Church at Rome. Its members were both of Jewish and Gentile extraction: this is a certain fact. Everything leads us to believe that the former constituted the great majority, and that in this sense the Church might be called Jewish-Christian. But does it follow from this that it was *Judaizing*,—distinctly hostile to Paul's gospel, and maintaining salvation through the rites of the law in opposition to salvation by faith? We answer decidedly, *No*; and Baur's error consisted in drawing this second inference from the former.

If, as we shall see presently, the Church of Rome did not belong to Paulinism, certainly it was just as free from the bias of the teachers of Galatia or Corinth. Paul does not regard it as hostile, or even alien to himself. On the contrary, he considers this Church to be included in the field of action assigned to him (ἔθνεσιν, ἐν οἷς ἐστὲ καὶ ὑμεῖς, chap. i. 6). He regards himself as its debtor, and declares himself ready to impart his gospel to it (chap. i. 14, 15). He applies to its members all the titles that he gave to his Churches in Asia (κλητοὶ Ἰησοῦ Χριστοῦ, ἀγαπητοὶ Θεοῦ, ἅγιοι). He not only praises their faith, but gives thanks to God on their behalf, just as for the faith of the Thessalonians and Corinthians; and as he had not done in writing to the Galatians. To view these words as a mere insinuating exordium, a sort of *captatio benevolentiæ*, is an injustice to Paul's character. To say that he has modified his way of looking at things and softened his views, is contradictory to the essential tenor of the epistle itself. We must recognise the fact that we have here a Church of Christians who cannot be placed in the same category with the Judaizers of Galatia or Corinth. The rest of the epistle accords with its beginning. The apostle's line of argument does not imply a declared hostility among his readers. There is no direct polemic. His design is to instruct, rather than refute; to expound his gospel, to dispel or anticipate misconceptions, rather than to repel particular attacks. The stern warning given to the Gentile Christians (chap. xi. 17-24) does not, indeed, prove that these were in the majority; but is it conceivable that Paul would address such words to a few friends of his own, lost in the mass of Jewish Christians openly hostile to them? Neither are the *weak* ($\dot{a}\sigma\theta\epsilon\nuo\hat{u}\nu\tau\epsilon\varsigma$) in the fourteenth and fifteenth chapters Judaizers of the same class as those of Corinth. But it is none the less true that Paul's appeal to the rest of the Church for tolerance and charity on their behalf, implies in it a considerable breadth of view. Any one, in short, who reads the fifteenth chapter attentively, will have difficulty in persuading himself that words like those could have been written to a Church which was confessedly hostile, and had made common cause with Paul's adversaries: "I exhort you by the Lord Jesus," he says in concluding, "to strive with me in your prayers to God, that I may be delivered from the rebels in Judæa,—that the offering I am taking to Jerusalem may be favourably received by the saints, and that I may come to you in joy and find refreshment and rest." Finally, if the fragment contained in chap. xvi. 17-20 belongs to this epistle, it would prove that the adversaries against whom Paul had formerly been compelled to defend himself, had not yet reached Rome; he hoped in his letter to be beforehand with them, and to anticipate their wonted attacks.

Are we to conclude from this that the Church at Rome was a Pauline Church? That would be going far beyond the meaning of the passages just examined, to another extreme even less warrantable than the former. If the Romans had attained the spiritual elevation of Paul, where would have been their need of such a long explanation and careful justification of his gospel? Those who adopt this hypothesis are obliged to regard the epistle to the Romans as a dogmatic treatise, written with a purely speculative end. But besides the fact that Paul has never composed anything of that kind, it would be impossible then to establish any connexion between the epistle and the Church to which it is addressed, and to explain why this dogmatic treatise was sent to Rome rather than elsewhere. The explanation of Paul's attempt must be found in the state of the Church at Rome. Now the apostle himself tells us what he wishes to impart to the Romans, and consequently what in his view was still lacking to them: "I earnestly desire to see you, that I may impart unto you *some spiritual gift*, that you may be established" (ἵνα τι μεταδῶ χάρισμα ὑμῖν πνευματικὸν εἰς τὸ στηριχθῆναι ὑμᾶς, chap. i. 11). What are we to understand by this χάρισμα πνευματικόν, this *donum spirituale?* If we reflect that in 1 Corinthians ii. 10-14 Paul has given the πνεῦμα as the vital principle of the Christian consciousness, the source of his own liberty of faith and of his spiritual conception of the Gospel; if we remember that in the above context he has distinguished between the πνευματικοὶ, judges of all things and free with respect to all, and the σαρκικοὶ still in bondage,—and that, lastly, he designates the Gospel as he understands it by the neuter πνευματικά, there can be no doubt that he must have intended by those two words a wider and more spiritual conception of the Gospel of Jesus and a clearer understanding of the intimate relation of the believing soul with the Spirit of God, which will make their faith stronger and more joyful and give it greater liberty. Does not the whole epistle reveal a persistent effort to raise the Christian faith of the Romans from a lower to a higher level? Written to a distinctly Pauline Church, it would cease to be comprehensible; the long disquisitions on the law, and the care with which Paul anticipates Judaistic objections are inexplicable. Still more perplexing would be the justification which Paul feels it necessary to offer of his mission to the Gentiles and their entrance into the kingdom of God. The nature of the questions raised, the precautions taken, the general tone—everything in the letter implies not a hostile Judaizing Church, but one of Jewish parentage, in which however the great questions were not yet raised which for some years past had agitated the Christianity of the East.

This peculiar and most remarkable position of the Church at Rome is accounted for by the history of its origin, and also by the comparative isolation in which it had existed until the arrival of Paul's letter. We have no reliable documents relating to the introduction of Christianity into Rome. But we may safely assume that here, as elsewhere, the Church had its rise in the Synagogue, and was only separated from it by a violent rupture. It is probable that the allusion of Suetonius (*Vit. Claud.*, § 25), *Claudius Judæos impulsore Chresto assidue tumultuantes expulit*, refers to the inevitable disturbances that broke out on this occasion in the Roman Jewry. This edict of Claudius was imperfectly or only temporarily carried into effect; while the Christian community suffered from it, it was not thereby destroyed.. It continued to recruit itself from among the Jews and the numerous proselytes, without renouncing Jewish ideas and customs. It was in the same position as that of the Churches of Syria, before the dissensions brought on by the great success of the Gentile mission. No apostolic teacher seems to have visited it, or to have given it any special and exclusive bias. It had been the spontaneous creation of the Gospel. Paul now encountered it in the field of labour which had fallen to his lot. Aquila and Priscilla had doubtless drawn the apostle's attention to this already flourishing community, and encouraged him to write to it, acquainting him with the kindly simplicity of its disposition, and the deficiencies of its faith.

We have followed the progress of the Judaistic agitation step by step from Jerusalem to Antioch, from Antioch to Galatia, from Galatia to Ephesus, and from Ephesus to Corinth. The Judaizing teachers only seem to have reached this last town, the limit of their progress westwards, in the year 57, during the interval between the two epistles to the Corinthians. They cannot therefore have arrived at Rome, where, moreover, there was no Paulinism to combat. This Church had remained in the simple and un-theological faith of the primitive days. It was virgin, and therefore *neutral* soil, which might easily be claimed by the first occupant. It was most important to Paul that he should take possession of it, and not allow himself to be anticipated. He will therefore himself expound his gospel to the Church at Rome, before his adversaries come to present it in caricature. He will endeavour to raise the Romans to the level of his own faith, and win them to the cause of the Gentile mission; or, at any rate, if that is too much success to hope from his letter, he will try by its means to secure a favourable reception for his gospel and his apostleship. Addressed to a Church like this, with this object in view, the epistle is its own explanation. Paul is not engaged in a controversy, for he is writing to brethren, not enemies; he is attempting to justify his gospel and apostleship before a community which, reared as it was in Judaism, might find both difficult for it to accept.[1]

The crisis now in progress throughout the Christian Churches, by which the Jewish and Christian spirit, so united at the first, were growing more and more distinct and coming into violent collision, could not but occur at Rome. But the epistle to the Romans was not subsequent to this crisis; on the contrary, it preceded and provoked it. It raised in that Church, for the first time, the great question of the abrogation of the law, and thereby marked a decisive epoch in its history. The Judaic spirit was to show itself here, as everywhere else, obstinate and implacable. Paul gained a few partizans, and made many adversaries. The Church became divided. The epistle to the Philippians, written three or four years later, shows us the breach accomplished (Phil. i. 12-18). Two (apparently authentic) passages in the second epistle to Timothy give us the saddest impression of Paul's position a few days before his death. He is alone,

---

[1] These considerations, I believe, afford sufficient refutation of the conjecture of M. Renan, who regards the epistle to the Romans as an encyclical letter addressed by the apostle to several Churches, but not more required by that of Rome than by any of the others. It might, indeed, only have been sent to the Roman community by way of exception! (See his *Saint Paul*, Introduction, p. 72.)

in prison, betrayed by some, deserted by the rest (2 Tim. i. 15-18; iv. 9-18). Nevertheless, this victory of the Judaizing party did not destroy Paul's influence at Rome. In the letter of Clement of Rome it appears again, still vigorous and profound. But it is time to return to the epistle itself.

II. THE PLAN OF THE EPISTLE.

To this Church, such as we have just described it, Paul had to explain two very important facts, and secure acceptance for them: the substitution in the new religious economy of the Gospel for the Law, and of the Gentiles for the people of Israel—the one *the defence of his teaching*, the other *the justification of his apostleship*. The essential contents of the dogmatic portion of the epistle are summed up in these two theses. The first eight chapters are the demonstration of the former; chapters ix.-xi. are the demonstration of the latter. From this general disposition of the subject matter, it is very evident that the two parts are equally essential to the structure of the epistle to the Romans, and equally important. The one is the logical consequence of the other.

Paul has formulated the fundamental thesis of his gospel in the 16th and 17th verses of the first chapter. He introduces it by the words οὐ γὰρ ἐπαισχύνομαι τὸ εὐαγγέλιον, which express the apostle's courage and boldness not only in face of the contempt of the Greek and Roman world, but most of all when confronting the hostility and scorn of the Judaizing party. The Gospel which he proclaims before all, he well defines as a δύναμις Θεοῦ, realizing the δικαιοσύνη Θεοῦ for the *salvation* (εἰς σωτηρίαν) of *every believer*,—of the *Jew* first, and also of the *pagan*.

This salvation is universal, just because it depends on faith alone—as it is written, *The just shall live by faith.* Whilst thus vigorously formulating the universal character of his doctrine, Paul carefully from the first avoids wounding the Jewish sentiment; he accords priority to the Jew (Ἰουδαίῳ πρῶτον). This is no concession; it is the recognition of the simple fact that the Jew, as the heir of the promises, was in the course of history called before the Gentile to enter the kingdom of God.

Paul establishes this great thesis by an admirable demonstration, in which we note four essential stages:

1. Chapter i. 18–iii. 31. Entering upon a survey of the moral and religious condition of humanity, the apostle shows that there is no salvation for it apart from Christ. He sketches in broad outlines the corruption of the heathen world, in which the just wrath of God is revealed, punishing sin through sin itself, unrighteousness by idolatry, and the latter by moral depravity (chap. i. 18-32). He then turns to the Jew, who has a better knowledge of the Divine law, but in practice keeps it still less; who condemns himself in condemning the Gentile, forgetting that external circumcision is nothing if the heart remain uncircumcised (chap. ii. 1-29).

At this point, Paul might already consider the basis of his doctrine as established; but he is anxious to remove, or to anticipate an objection which will infallibly be made. Does it not seem like denying the privileges of the Jews, to put them on the same level as the Gentiles? Hence the question with which the third chapter opens: What advantage, then, has the Jew? Paul recognises his historical privileges. The Jew received the oracles of God; and God is faithful, even towards men who are not so. But what is there in this belief to encourage such men, and to justify their unfaithfulness? Would any one draw the impious deduction that unfaithfulness, if serving to glorify the will of God, ought not to be punished? Would not this amount to saying, Let us do evil that good may come? The sin of the Jew remains, therefore, as much as that of the Gentile. To make his demonstration still more impressive, Paul sums it up in terms which are all borrowed from the Old Testament. Jews and pagans, alike impeached by the Divine justice, have equal need of salvation of God (chap. iii. 9-20). Here the apostle resumes the thesis in which he summed up his gospel, and develops it in a more complete and exact manner (chap. iii. 21-26). All are deprived of the glory of God, but the *righteousness* of God has been manifested apart from the law. We are justified by a gratuitous act of grace, by means of the redemption that is in Jesus Christ—through faith in His blood—in order to manifest the righteousness of God. This is no longer revealed in mere *punishment*, as was the case under the law, but *in justifying him that believes*. Vers. 27-31 deduce the consequences of this first demonstration of Paul's thesis.

2. Chapter iv. The apostle could not stop short at this point. His opponents would still have adduced against his syllogisms the authority of the Old Testament. He therefore changes the direction of his argument, and in the fourth chapter endeavours to prove that the doctrine of justification by faith is at the very root of the old covenant, and has the evidence of Scripture in its favour ($\mu\alpha\rho\tau\upsilon\rho\upsilon\mu\acute{\epsilon}\nu\eta$ $\dot{\upsilon}\pi\grave{o}$ $\tau\upsilon\hat{\upsilon}$ $\nu\acute{o}\mu\upsilon\upsilon$ $\kappa\alpha\grave{\iota}$

τῶν προφητῶν). Neither Abraham nor David was justified by works (chap. iv. 1-9). Abraham's faith was imputed to him for righteousness before he had received circumcision, which rite, so far from dispenssing with faith, has from the first merely been its confirmation (vers. 10-12). Lastly, it was to *faith* that the *promise* was given, and through faith also it is realized. Abraham believed in God, who raises the dead, and addresses the things that are not as things actually existing; for the word of God is, in fact, creative, and realizes by its own virtue all that it declares. In the same way we believe in God, who delivered Jesus to death for our sins and has raised Him again for our justification (vers. 13-25).

3. Chapter v. With the fifth chapter begins a new development of the subject. In order to complete the demonstration of this principle of faith, Paul allows it to explain and justify itself by its spiritual fruits (vers. 1-11). It gives a new life, of which the believer is intensely conscious, manifesting itself in the peace which he enjoys before God, in patient endurance of tribulation, in the love filling his heart, and in the firm hope that sustains him, of which the outpouring of the Holy Spirit is the sure pledge. Then, reviewing the whole history of humanity and summing up all that he has just set forth, the apostle goes on to show the power of sin entering the world through Adam's transgression, developing there by degrees as an organic force, and bringing in its train the death which comes to all men, because all are sinners. But beneath this progress of humanity in sin and towards death, he points out a new progress proceeding from Christ, the second Adam, which fulfils itself in holiness and tends to life. "Where sin abounded, grace super-

abounded; that as sin reigned by death, grace might reign through righteousness unto eternal life, through Jesus Christ our Lord" (vers. 12–21). Thus Paul has demonstrated his thesis, first by dialectic reasoning, then by Scriptural authority, and then by the conclusive evidence of experience and history.

4. Chapters vi.–viii. Arrived at the culminating point of his demonstration, Paul again encounters the perpetual objection made to his gospel, the same that had been raised at Antioch and in Galatia, and which his last words could not fail to arouse. Is not this doctrine of an absolute grace, abounding over the sin of men in order to cover it, the ruin of all morality? Will it not afford occasion and excuse for saying, Let us sin, that grace may abound? This objection brings the apostle to the very core of his doctrine, and suggests the admirable exposition of the seventh and eighth chapters, the profoundest pages which he has ever written. He there defines with wonderful clearness the relation of the three terms, ἁμαρτία, νόμος, χάρις. This common objection does not touch the Christian; for in his quality as a sinner he has been crucified with Christ. He left his sin in the grave of Jesus; and has risen with Him to a new life, which belongs wholly to God (chap. vi. 1–11). Instead of being the slave of sin, he is now the slave of righteousness (vers. 12–23).

But at the same time that he died to sin, he died also to the law; he escapes by death from this second power, as from the first, for it only had dominion over him so long as he lived. But *now* he has died! and if he is raised again, it is to obey not the old letter, but the new power of the Spirit of God to which henceforward he belongs (chap. vii.

1–6). Does that mean that the law is *sin?* Far from it. But the law gives life to sin by making it known as sin, and actualizing it in the form of transgression. The function of the law is to awaken within us this painful consciousness of sin, and intensify it to the point of despair. Thus the law, owing to our flesh in which the power of sin resides, brings us death (chap. vii. 7–24).

But at the very point where the law makes shipwreck and we founder on death, there triumphs the almighty grace of God, manifest in Jesus Christ. Paul here explains, more fully than he did in the fifth chapter, the wonderful effects of this grace: absolute freedom from all condemnation (chap. viii. 1–4); efficient sanctification by the Holy Spirit (vers. 5–11); filial adoption by God (vers. 12–27); the triumph of faith amidst even the severest trials, through the firm hope of the glory which shall be revealed in us (vers. 18–39). Thus triumphantly ends the demonstration of Paul's first thesis.

From this point, whither the logic of his doctrine and the impulse of his emotion have led him, he could not descend to the second thesis of his letter by any natural transition. It is useless, therefore, to look in the eighth chapter for anything which announces, or prepares for the developments to follow. The transition does not lie in the words. It takes place in Paul's feelings, in the painful contrast which forced itself upon him. In the midst of the joy with which his heart has just overflowed, he is seized with the thought that his people remain strangers to this covenant of grace. His joy changes suddenly to bitter sorrow, and it is with a heartfelt cry of distress (chap. ix. 1–5) that he begins the defence of his apostleship. In these three last chapters Paul is bent on one thing only —to make plain the agency of God in the religious revolution which has taken place, the issue of a plan which may seem unjust, but which increasingly vindicates itself as it is further unfolded. God is not bound to the Jewish people. If He rejects them now, in order to call the Gentiles, it is by a free decree of His sovereign grace. The Jews, moreover, have no right to complain; they have only themselves to blame for their unbelief. But this rejection is neither absolute nor final; if it brings about the conversion of the Gentiles, that in its turn will lead to the salvation of Israel. Such, in its historical sequence, is the universal plan of redemption. Where the Jews see nothing but painful contradictions, an insoluble enigma and dense darkness, the profounder insight of the apostle perceives and points out the glorious issue of the Divine plans. Hence the three essential stages in his argumentation—*the absolute freedom of the grace of God*, which justifies from the standpoint of the Divine will Paul's work among the Gentiles (chap. ix.); *the unbelief of the Jews,* justifying to their own understanding the decree of God which abandons them (chap. x.); *the final solution of this existing antithesis* between Israel and the Gentiles, in the complete redemption of both (chap. xi.).

1. Chapter ix. 6–29. Paul does not touch directly upon the question of the future of the Gentiles. His main point is to explain and reconcile his readers to the sorrowful fate of the people of Israel, who, with all their great privileges, continue strangers to the new covenant. The apostle starts with the principle that carnal descent from Abraham does not constitute a right to inherit the promise, but that this right

depends solely upon the free, sovereign grace of God. Just as in the family of Abraham, Isaac was chosen and not Ishmael; and in the family of Isaac, Jacob and not Esau; so now from among the people of Israel this grace calls some to salvation, and leaves the rest to destruction (vers. 6-13). It is true that a grave objection is here raised. In punishing him whom He has hardened, is not God unjust? Several passages in Scripture itself seem to confirm this accusation (vers. 14-18). Paul is content to repel it by absolutely refusing to man the right of contending with God, or of controlling His will (vers. 20, 21). God is free to create vessels of wrath to manifest the greatness of His judgments, and vessels of mercy to manifest the infinite riches of His love. These vessels of mercy may be taken from any quarter, from amongst the Gentiles as well as the Jews. God may, according to the word of Hosea, call those His people who were not His people,—and according to that of Isaiah, reduce to a feeble remnant, to a small number of elect, the great multitude of Israel (vers. 24-29).

2. Chapter ix. 30-x. 21. Hitherto Paul has only considered these dispensations from the absolute standpoint of the Divine sovereignty. But they have another aspect; and from vers. 30-33 a new point of view is disclosed, in which human responsibility regains all its importance. Why, after all, should the Jewish people complain? Is the judgment of God arbitrary? Is not the persistent unbelief of Israel its immediate and historical cause? Because the people obstinately sought righteousness by the works of the law, and despised that which comes by faith, therefore it is now rejected (chap. x. 1-11). The Jew had the same opportunity as the Gentile. The mercy of God is the

same toward all who call upon Him. But the difference lies in this, that the Gentiles have believed the Gospel, while the Jews have always proved rebellious (vers. 11–21).

3. Chapter xi. 1–32. Paul does not stop here. He will not leave his readers in a state of mournful resignation, dictated solely by a sense of the inevitable necessity of things. Beyond the darkness of the present, he desires to show them in the future the absolute triumph of the work of God. This is the design of the eleventh chapter. The apostle reminds them that the word of God is immutable, and that He cannot absolutely and finally reject His people. He saves even now a part of it. If the mass indeed is rejected, it is not that it may be eternally lost. This fall is in God's design a mode of bringing about the salvation of the Gentiles. But the salvation of the Gentiles, in turn, is intended to accomplish the full and perfect realization of the salvation of the Jews (vers. 1–12).

With this conviction, and in fulfilment of this Divine idea, the apostle labours with indefatigable zeal for the conversion of the Gentiles. As things are, it is the best thing he can do for his nation itself. He strives to excite it to jealousy, for he knows surely that it cannot perish. The Gentiles, indeed, should never forget that this people whose branches are now cut off, are none the less the holy root, the true olive-tree, on the trunk of which they are engrafted; and that while its fall led to their adoption, this in its turn will yet more certainly lead to its restoration. Thus the ways of God justify themselves; and thus the temporary oppositions and painful contradictions of the present are effaced, and disappear in the final unity and consummation of the redemption: "God has shut up all men in sin, that He might have mercy upon all!" Is it surprising that the apostle, stirred by such lofty thoughts and so grand a vision, suffers his enthusiasm to burst forth at the last in a hymn of adoration in praise of the unsearchable wisdom of God? (vers. 33–36.) The second victory won by Paul's dialectic is as great and final as the first. Not only has he justified his apostleship, by referring it to the Divine decree; not only has he proved that he derogates nothing from the Jews, who are called to faith equally with the Gentiles; but he has further shown that in reality he is indirectly serving, and effectively preparing for, the fulfilment of the destinies of the people of Israel.

There is no need that we should analyse the hortatory portion of this epistle, the precepts and moral exhortations of which are the practical issue of the principles that Paul has just developed. We may say, however, that nothing in chaps. xv. and xvi. gives any ground for the doubts raised by Baur respecting their authenticity. Only, these later pages of the letter are in great disorder. The manuscripts entirely disagree with each other, and present strange phenomena. The epistle to the Romans, as now constituted, has four, or even five terminations: chap. xiv. 23, where we sometimes find intercalated the doxology of chap. xvi. 25–27; then chap. xv. 33; chap. xvi. 20; xvi. 24; and the actual termination, chap. xvi. 25–27. Of all the hypotheses which have been assumed to explain these details, that of M. Renan still seems to me the best. According to this, several copies of the letter were made and sent to the different Churches, with appropriate additions from Paul himself; one, in particular, to Ephesus, to which may have been added the special note preserved in chap. xvi. 1–20.

This rapid analysis exhibits the new features of the epistle to the Romans and the theological progress accomplished since the letters to the Galatians and Corinthians. The Pauline doctrine has at last attained its unity. The apostle is no longer satisfied with contrasting the Gospel and the Law ; whilst rejecting the yoke of the latter, he goes further, and finds the Law fulfilled in the Gospel. In the same way, though he shows how the Gentiles take the place in the kingdom of God which the unbelieving Jews left vacant, he does not stop short at this contrast ; he feels the necessity of explaining to himself, as well as of justifying to others, this mystery in the plan of God. The necessary consequence of the Jews' rejection is to bring the Gospel out of the narrow circle of Judaism and spread it to the ends of the earth. But in this general conversion of the Gentiles, Paul only sees a new method by which God designs to bring back the people of Israel in their turn into the covenant of grace. Here again, reviewing the conflicts of history, his doctrine attains a final reconciliation. In this unity it finds repose. From this culminating point it surveys the progressive evolution of the plan of redemption, and of the destinies of humanity.

God has shut up all men into disobedience, that He might have mercy upon all. This great saying, which closes and crowns our epistle, is the keystone of the arch in the apostle's structure. Oneness and equality in sin, oneness and equality in redemption : these words sum up both the leading idea and the entire plan of this great work. From this historical point of view, the two portions of the epistle, which usually have been merely placed in juxtaposition, are blended together and recover their profound unity. While the first shows us the fall of humanity and its virtual uplifting in Jesus Christ, the second, still on the same lines, exhibits the progressive realization of the Kingdom of God in history, up to the point where it embraces all humanity. The religious philosophy broadly sketched in the epistle to the Galatians, is here defined and completed.

Viewed in the light of this final unity, all the intermediate stages through which the Divine conception passes in its fulfilment, in the very nature of things appear but transitory. We understand them alike in their historical necessity and their subordination, —in their essential *relativity*. Only the short-sighted could suffer themselves to be arrested or driven to despair by the inevitable antagonisms and conflicts. The true believer foresees the final reconciliation, and knows that all these struggles really serve to fulfil God's design. The apostle had to win acceptance, in minds still fettered by Judaism, for two facts equally revolting and equally painful—the abrogation of the Law by the Gospel, and the substitution of the Gentiles for the Jews in the Kingdom of God. How could he succeed better than by directly referring these two facts to the Divine will, and showing them to be essential stages in God's eternal plan?

We may say, therefore, that Paul's letter is preeminently a work of synthesis and reconciliation. We must not, however, go too far; we will not, with some theologians, speak of concessions, of advances made by the apostle towards his adversaries, of a Paulinism which is not so strict as that of the epistle to the

Galatians. Such an opinion could only be held by superficial readers, who judge from first impressions and do not attempt to analyse the epistle. None of Paul's letters sets forth with greater profundity or with more rigorous logic his most cherished ideas. His doctrine is rounded and completed, but not modified. It reduces to unity the two terms of that problem which had long disturbed it. Though we speak of reconciliation and of synthesis, it is of that logical reconciliation of his various ideas that must be sought by every earnest thinker, and of the final synthesis in which alone the mind can find repose.

Hence the admirable harmony, the calm sense of power which distinguish this epistle above all the others. A perfect equilibrium prevails in it from beginning to end. The balance is always justly held between Jew and Gentile. If the Gentile is corrupt, the Jew is no less guilty. By different routes they arrive inevitably at the same condemnation (οὐ γάρ ἐστιν διαστολή, chap. iii. 22). United in sin, they continue united in their redemption. Is God the God of the Jews only, is He not also the God of the pagans? (chap. iii. 27–30.) There are only two humanities— the one sinful, descended from Adam, to which all belong; the other redeemed and sanctified, the issue of Christ, the second Adam, to which all ought to belong. This equilibrium is still more striking in chaps. ix., x., and xi. Paul not only proves that the advantages of the one party are not acquired to the detriment of the other, but that neither obtains any grace which will not in the end redound to the benefit of all. If the Jews received the promises, it was that they might preserve them and transmit them to the Gentiles; and if the Gentiles enter into the new covenant, their conversion is to lead to that of the Jews. In the same way the apostle entreats the weak to respect the strong, and exhorts the strong to support the weak (chaps. xii., xiv., xv.). For blind rivalries he substitutes everywhere fraternal solidarity, and for intestine conflicts organic unity.

This is the culminating point which the Pauline theology has now attained. From the psychological sphere, where it discovered and established its fundamental principle, it has risen to the wide sphere of history, and there attains its full expansion. It pauses a moment to contemplate and admire the onward progress o the plan and the revelations of God. But at this height it has already reached its critical point, where the philosophy of history changes of necessity into speculative theory. As yet it does not pass this limit; but remains within the horizon of time. It even declares the wisdom of God unfathomable, and the secret of His ways impenetrable! But may it not attempt to gain some glimpse of them? Shall it refrain from seeking to unveil at last the metaphysical principles implied in its previous developments? May it not crown the edifice so laboriously constructed?

The inherent logic, the natural bias of the apostle's mind, was to lead him to climb this last summit. The new events and the important changes about to take place in his own history, and in that of his Churches in Asia, will soon furnish the occasion for this. In the epistles of the Captivity Paul's indefatigable intellect attains its final goal.

BOOK IV.

*THIRD PERIOD: THE PAULINISM OF
LATER TIMES.*

From 58 A.D. to —(?)

WITH the apostle's captivity begins the last epoch of his life. The letters usually referred to this period present us with a new type of doctrine as distinct from that of the great epistles as the latter was from primitive Paulinism. The striking antithesis between the Law and the Gospel formulated during the struggles of the preceding period is found here in a qualified and more general form, though it has not wholly disappeared (Phil. iii. 2, 3; i. 12-18). The Judaistic opposition seems relegated to the background. Errors of another, but no less dangerous character, threaten the apostle's work in Asia, and evoke a third and broader development of his doctrine.

Before entering upon the exposition of this last phase of Paul's teaching it is necessary, therefore, to define clearly the entirely new circumstances in which the apostle is now placed.

CHAPTER I.

THE ADDRESS AT MILETUS.—APPEARANCE OF THE GNOSTIC ASCETICISM. — NEW EVOLUTION IN PAUL'S THEOLOGICAL DOCTRINE.

THE farewell address delivered by the apostle at Miletus to the elders of the Church at Ephesus, forms the natural transition from the second period of his life to the third (Acts xx. 13-35).

Paul left Corinth a few days after the despatch of his letter to the Church at Rome (Rom. xv. 25; comp. Acts xx. 3). He was going up to Jerusalem. His journey through Macedonia and along the shores of Asia Minor was simply a long series of farewells. Paul accomplished it in great anxiety of mind and under the most gloomy forebodings. Vainly did his friends, who shared his fears, endeavour to shake his resolution. He obeyed the inward call of God; he was bound in conscience (Acts xx. 22). His hour had come. This journey reminds us of the last journey of Jesus to Jerusalem. At the end of his career the disciple, like the Master, was to undergo *his passion*. The tenderness of his heart, his serene faith in the midst of sorrow, his submissive and firm obedience, are strikingly exhibited in his pathetic farewell to the pastors of Ephesus.

The address at Miletus has a still greater historical

significance. The apostle was affected not only by the crisis about to take place in his own life, but by the changes which he already foresaw in the destiny of his Churches. The Judaistic opposition had spent its first fury, and no longer seemed very formidable. A new crisis was developing. *I know*, said the apostle, *that after my departure rapacious wolves will attack you, and will not spare the flock; from the midst of you will men arise uttering perverse things* (λαλοῦντες διεστραμμένα) *to draw the disciples after them* (Acts xx. 29, 30). It is very evident that these rapacious wolves, these false teachers coming actually from the midst of the Gentile Christian Churches, are no longer the Judaizing teachers with whom we have become familiar. What can their distorted talk be, but an unnatural perversion of the Gospel itself, tortured from it by their false wisdom? There is an obvious allusion here to the modes of interpretation familiar to *Gnosticism*. Some critics, it is true, have only brought forward this allusion as an argument against the authenticity of the Address itself, or at least against the fidelity of the narrator. The argument would be very strong, if this indication of the concealed presence of the Gnostic leaven and its hitherto secret working were an isolated fact. But there are other considerations, more explicit and less disputable than this, which serve to confirm and justify these predictions as coming from Paul's mouth.

Let us return to the epistle to the Romans. Let us ask ourselves who were the *weak members* of this Church, whom Paul describes in chapter xiv., and towards whom he preaches charity and tolerance? No doubt they were connected, more or less closely, with Judaism. It was from Judaism, and not from the Pythagorean philosophy, that their scruples and asceticism were derived. But they must not be confounded with the Judaizing Christians of Galatia and Corinth, or even identified with the Judaizers of Rome as a body. These Christian *ascetics* who insist, not on circumcision and Pharisaic observances, but on certain abstinences, are a new development, radically different from primitive Judæo-Christianity. They neither eat meat nor drink wine, living only on vegetables. Where shall we find the origin of this asceticism? Ritschl, not without some show of reason, regards it as a result of Essenism, the spirit of which was already creeping into the Church. Be that as it may, this practical asceticism had its basis either in a philosophical dualism, or in an interpretation of Scripture analogous to that employed by the Ebionites to justify the same abstinences.[1] But at Rome this ascetic morality seems to have propagated itself without the dogmas which justified it. Practice had anticipated theory. That is why the apostle, while condemning the principle of action adopted by these *weak members* (πέπεισμαι ἐν Κυρίῳ 'Ιησοῦ ὅτι οὐδὲν κοινὸν δι' ἑαυτοῦ), does not trouble himself to contend with them, and shows them the indulgence which is due to every scrupulous conscience. Later on, at Colossæ, the two elements of theory and practice are found in combination.[2] The tendency,

---

[1] See Epiphanius, *Hæres.*, 30. 15.
[2] Perhaps the language of Rom. xvi. 17-19 should be applied to Gnostic teachers elsewhere than at Rome. It would be more appropriate to such teachers, it seems to us, than to the early Judaizers. It is a new indication to add to those which we are now pointing out, of the early appearance of Gnosticism in the apostolic Churches.

hitherto vague and floating, presents itself to us here in a more decided and clearly marked shape.

The false teachers whom Paul attacks in his epistle to the Colossians, are distinguished in fact by these two characteristics: a very rigorous asceticism, and a very daring boldness of speculation. They seem indeed to have endeavoured, in concert with the Judaizers, to impose circumcision upon the Gentile Christians (Col. ii. 11), but their originality does not lie in this. It consists in that *voluntary* asceticism which spares not the flesh, which credits itself with something specially meritorious just because it goes beyond the commandments of God, and which Paul so aptly characterizes in the word ἐθελοθρησκεία (chap. ii. 22, 23). They not only observe the Sabbaths and the new moons, but they further command abstinence from certain kinds of food and drink: *touch not; taste not*. With this system of abstinence is joined the worship of angels, among whom, no doubt, Jesus Christ was reckoned.

This worship of angels implied something that went far beyond a mere popular superstition. It was a subject of speculation and transcendental science. These celestial beings were divided into classes and ranged in an elaborate hierarchy, which was intended to explain the relations of God and the world, the origin and nature of evil, the course of the world's history, and its final issue.[1] This system was destined to become transformed and perfected in the great Gnostic schools of the beginning of the second cen-

---

[1] It is well known that the worship of angels and a speculative philosophy of the celestial hierarchies formed an essential part of the Essenian theology.

tury. But it is already sketched out here. The vocabulary of Gnosticism is created. Its terms still preserve, it is true, the religious colouring, the positive character due to their origin; but they have already begun to merge both these in the metaphysical and abstract signification which constantly grows upon them. The æons are enumerated: θρόνοι, κυριότητες, ἀρχαί, αἰῶνες. Their totality is expressed by the Divine πλήρωμα. Between the lowest of the æons and the supreme God there is an ascending scale through which all these beings must rise, to re-enter by degrees the Divinity whence they issued.

Such was the fantastic world that the teachers of Colossæ were absorbed in contemplating. These are the far-fetched speculations, alike baseless and irrational, with which the apostle upbraids them in denouncing their religion of angels (ἃ μὴ ἑώρακεν ἐμβατεύων, chap. ii. 18). The more ingenious their theories, the prouder they were of them (εἰκῆ φυσιούμενος). They claimed to have found the true wisdom, and to possess all its treasures (chap. ii. 3, 4); they had sounded the depths of being; they *knew*, where others only *believed*. So they opposed their *gnosis* to the simple faith of humble Christians. Such is Judaistic Gnosticism, as it appears in the epistles to the Colossians and Ephesians.

Its image becomes still more definite and complete in the three *pastoral* epistles (so called). There we have the same asceticism, the same fantastic speculations, the same dreams of the imagination (1 Tim. iv. 1-7). The fundamental dualism of this philosophy is still more marked (chap. iv. 3, 4). The system acquires a more articulate and consistent form; it is a profane mythology (μῦθοι βέβηλοι καὶ γραώδεις) around whose figures metaphysics weaves stories of the strangest and most daring character. There are endless genealogies (γενεαλογίαι ἀπέραντοι), passionate and fruitless discussions, gratifying morbid curiosity. Finally, this philosophy already bears its historical title,—that of *gnosis* (1 Tim. vi. 20).[1]

There can be no doubt of the nature of this primitive Gnosticism. It was evidently a speculation which arose in Jewish circles, and which remained Judaistic. Its teachers not only counselled circumcision, the observance of the Sabbath, and the new moons (Col. ii. 11–18); they claimed moreover to be the true teachers of the law (νομοδιδάσκαλοι, 1 Tim. i. 7). Doubtless they started with the Old Testament, and by the mode of exegesis common at that time discovered in it all their dreams. The epistles call their fables μῦθοι Ἰουδαϊκοί (Tit. i. 14); either because these myths were originated by Jews, or —what is more probable—because they consisted in Jewish legends or narratives from the Old Testament, transformed into philosophical myths in the spirit and direction of Philonism.

But these new tendencies, which must from the beginning have assumed a variety of forms, were none the less fundamentally distinct from the Judæo-Christianity of the primitive days. The latter resembled a continuation of Pharisaism in the Christian Church; the former, as Ritschl and Mangold have well observed, has the appearance of a development of Essenism. We are unwilling to enter in this place upon the difficult question of the origin of Gnosticism.

---

[1] See Mangold, *Die Irrlehrer der Pastoralbriefe.* Marburg, 1856.

It probably took its rise spontaneously, in different places at the same time. It was not in fact a special philosophy, but a general impulse of the human mind, which made itself felt at that period in all schools and creeds alike, striving to transform the elements of tradition, to dissolve and absorb them by a laborious process of speculative reason. Thus neo-Platonism and Neo-pythagoreanism are nothing else but a philosophical Gnosticism; just as the speculations of Basilides or Valentinian are a Christian Gnosticism, and the Alexandrianism of Philo a Jewish Gnosticism. These systems are the result of the same spiritualizing processes, differently applied in different places and by different minds. They aim at the same goal, and pursue it by the same method, seeking not only discursive knowledge, but direct intuition, the possession and enjoyment of absolute truth. Finally, one permanent feature of all these schools is the union of speculative mysticism with practical asceticism.

If we consider the abundant development of this Gnosticism at the beginning of the second century, and recollect that it was then the dominating philosophy throughout the East, we can scarcely doubt that its origin lay as far back as the middle of the first century. It cannot, in short, be supposed that the systems which prevailed about 120 or 130 A.D., blossomed out all at once in the scholarly and finished form which then distinguished them. Gnosticism only arrived at this point of development by a somewhat lengthy process of elaboration. By this time it had its ancestors, its history, and traditions; it loved to connect itself directly with the apostles.[1]

---

[1] It is well known that Basilides, Valentinian, and Marcion

Its chronology, no doubt, is still very uncertain. But the Gnostic terms scattered through Paul's later epistles, especially in the epistle to the Colossians, can no longer be brought forward as proofs against their authenticity. They only show that the origin of Gnosticism is much earlier than has long been supposed. Can we wonder to see such a tendency breaking out thus early, in the very midst of the Christian Church? In explanation of this fact it is not necessary to refer to the eclectic methods of the time, or to the general fermentation of thought in the great cities of Asia Minor, which was then engendering so many strange phenomena. It is enough to observe the remarkable affinity of Gnosticism with the Gospel. Gnosticism had the same end in view—the union of man with God, the redemption of fallen beings ; and in practical life its asceticism might only seem a rigorous application of Jewish or Christian morality. But we can also understand what dangers the apostolic teaching incurred from this association. In becoming a metaphysical speculation, the Gospel was losing its moral character. The concrete facts and positive tradition on which it was based, and which constituted its strength, were dissolving, evaporating, changing into symbols of abstract ideas. The Gospel was becoming a mythology. The Christian redemption, which always implies human liberty, and which involves struggles of conscience and conversion, was no longer anything more than the theory of the

---

claimed to have collected secret traditions, which had been transmitted to them from the immediate disciples of the apostles. Thus Basilides was said to hold his doctrine from a certain Glaucias, an interpreter of Peter, and Valentinian from Theodas, a disciple of Paul.

gradual return to God of every being who had issued from Him. Finally, the person of Christ was on the point of being merged and lost amongst a crowd of intermediate beings, in the hierarchy of æons with whom His work and His glory were shared.[1]

Such was the new situation opening in Asia Minor, the dangers of which Paul was eager to avert. The apostle's penetrating mind, so swift to discern principles and to seize at the first glance both their nature and consequences, could not be mistaken as to the gravity of this movement. Still, as M. Reuss admirably remarks, "if the contact of Christianity with the leaven then working in men's minds had been purely hostile, it might perhaps have been possible to run the risk of leaving it alone to exhaust itself. But what made it specially dangerous was the incapacity of many minds to distinguish the radical difference between the two currents of ideas, and the predilections of so many Greeks who were attracted to the Church chiefly by the desire of knowledge and by philosophical aspirations, and who naturally turned to the quarter from which these aspirations seemed to receive the most ample satisfaction. There came a time, therefore, when the old reactionary party of the Judaizers seemed less dangerous than the advanced party,—that of the new philosophers."[2] In this way all the essential features in the Paulinism of later times are sufficiently explained.

1. Paulinism, hitherto of such a bold, I had almost said revolutionary character, was of necessity about to assume a more *conservative* form. Resistance

---

[1] See Reuss, *Histoire de la théologie apostolique*, vol. i., pp. 366–377. [Eng. trans., i., pp. 316–325.]
[2] See Reuss, vol. i., p. 378. [Eng. trans., i., p. 326.]

must succeed attack. The apostle seeks to recall men's minds to the old doctrine, the primitive traditions (Eph. iii. 2-5; ii. 20; Phil. iii. 1; Col. ii. 2-5).

2. The Pauline teaching, in face of this opposition, takes a more speculative form. In the first epistle to the Corinthians the apostle had already described his Gospel as *perfect wisdom* (σοφίαν ἐν τοῖς τελείοις, 1 Cor. ii. 6). But there he still preferred to contrast the *foolishness* of the cross with the wisdom of the world. Henceforward, without robbing the Gospel in any way of this Divine foolishness, or allowing the Christian to forget the sphere of the inner and sanctified life, he seeks to expound this perfect wisdom, and exhibits in his teaching the most exalted philosophy. Besides, his own instincts led him in this direction; and he must have found a certain delight in opposing to these daring speculations the true Christian knowledge, and thus crowning the labour of his whole system (Col. i. 9, 10; ii. 2; Eph. iii. 10: οἱ θησαυροὶ τῆς σοφίας καὶ τῆς γνώσεως ἐν Χριστῷ ἀπόκρυφοι, Col. ii. 3).

3. From this new point of view there inevitably issued a fresh result,—the concentration, or, I would say, the absorption, of the whole Christian system of dogma in *Christology*. The doctrines of justification by faith and universal salvation are summed up in the later epistles with equal vigour, precision, and fulness. But that is not the main design of these letters. These great ideas no longer seem in peril. It was, as we have already said, the supreme royalty of Jesus Christ which was in danger of being eclipsed amid the crowd of intermediate beings. Accordingly, it is with triumphant pride that Paul overthrows and lays prostrate at the feet of the Son of God all these

powers, thrones, and æons, that dispute with Him the honour of the work of redemption. The declaration of the transcendental worth of the person and work of Jesus follows as a matter of course.

4. Lastly, a final and no less important change was at the same time taking place in Paul's ethics. The letters to the Corinthians seemed to counsel some degree of asceticism, especially with regard to marriage. This asceticism, as we have said, was not deduced from the personal doctrine of the apostle; but the expectation of Christ's immediate coming, and the fear of the great tribulations which were to precede it, had led him to urge, somewhat too strongly, the precept of abstinence. Though marriage is good, he had said, celibacy is still better (1 Cor. vii. 1, 7, 28-31, 38). Already, in the epistle to the Romans, whatever exclusiveness and narrowness might be found in these sayings had disappeared (Rom. xiv.). A wider view of the matter is revealed. Evidently the apostle's horizon had extended in the direction of the future; the final catastrophe no longer seems imminent; family and social life, with their duties, resume henceforth their value and importance in his eyes. Indeed, it is above all in this sphere that the Christian life ought to unfold itself. Nowhere has the apostle insisted on social and domestic duties so much as in his later letters (Eph. v. 15-vi. 9; Col. iii. 17-iv. 6; Phil. iv. 8, 9). Asceticism is radically condemned, both in its principle and its precepts (1 Tim. iv. 1-5). On seeing it preached by such doubtful teachers, the apostle became more sensible of its danger.

It is time to study more closely the character of each of these epistles.

CHAPTER II.

THE EPISTLES TO PHILEMON, TO THE COLOSSIANS, AND TO THE EPHESIANS.

THESE three letters form a distinct group among the epistles of the Captivity, and must not be separated. Written at the same time, very probably from the prison at Cæsarea, and carried to Asia Minor by the same messengers, they preserve striking traces of this close connexion in their origin (Philem. 10 —comp. Col. iv. 9; Philem. 23, 24—comp. Col. iv. 10, 12, 14; Philem. 2—comp. Col. iv. 17; Col. iv. 7— comp. Eph. vi. 21). These epistles, in fact, mutually imply each other; and it soon becomes evident that they had one and the same author.

I. The Epistle to Philemon.

If they are not Paul's, it must be acknowledged that there existed a writer possessed of sufficient skill and information to invent a complete and happily conceived historical situation, and to insert in the apostle's life without violation of history a most reasonable and charming romance. To admit such a fiction will, perhaps, scarcely seem easier than to accept the apostolic origin of these three letters.

Onesimus, one of Paul's messengers, was a fugitive slave. He had been converted by the imprisoned apostle, had attached himself to his person, and lavished his services upon him. He belonged to a Christian master in the neighbourhood of Colossæ, named Philemon, a personal friend of Paul. The apostle sends him back in charge of Tychicus, and restores him to his master, giving him a brief note written in his own hand, designed to secure his favourable reception by Philemon.

The letter only contains a few friendly lines; but they are so full of grace and wit, of earnest, trustful affection, that this short epistle shines among the rich treasures of the New Testament as a pearl of exquisite fineness. Never has there been a better fulfilment of the precept given by Paul himself at the close of his letter to the Colossians: ὁ λόγος ὑμῶν πάντοτε ἐν χάριτι, ἅλατι ἠρτυμένος, εἰδέναι πῶς δεῖ ὑμᾶς ἑνὶ ἑκάστῳ ἀποκρίνεσθαι (chap. iv. 6). Baur sacrifices it to the logic of his system somewhat unwillingly. "This letter," he says, "is distinguished by the private nature of its contents; it has nothing of those commonplaces, those general doctrines void of originality, those repetitions of familiar things, which are so frequent in the supposed writings of the apostle. It deals with a concrete fact, a practical detail of ordinary life. . . . What objection can criticism make to these pleasant and charming lines, inspired by the purest Christian feeling, and against which suspicion has never been breathed?"[1] Alas! all these graces render the victim more interesting, but they do not save it! Beneath its innocent and candid appearance this epistle conceals what astonishing subtleties, what a treacherous aim! Baur has discovered a mysterious design, an ambitious dogmatic purpose underlying it;

---

[1] See Baur's *Paulus*, vol. ii., p. 82 [Eng. trans., ii., p. 80].

and the poor epistle is ruthlessly condemned! This impeachment of Baur's, however, reminds us a little of that of the wolf against the lamb. "If the Pauline origin of the other epistles of the Captivity, especially that of the Pastorals," says he, "gives rise to so many objections and is involved in so many difficulties, if therefore it is in the highest degree doubtful whether we have any letter belonging to this period of the apostle's life, how could this little friendly note, dealing with a matter of detail and private life, be allowed to make an exception?" Obviously, this is the wolf's final argument: If it was not thou, it was thy brother! The little note may be innocent in itself, but it has the fault and the misfortune to be too much akin to the other epistles, with their very suspicious character.

The complaint, doubtless, admits of no reply. But we may ask whether this argument would not be of equal force if we attempted to reverse it? Would it be less logical to say: The epistle to Philemon affords no ground for critical suspicion; and since it is inseparably connected with the epistles to the Colossians and Ephesians, its existence constitutes a very strong argument in favour of the two latter? In fact, this short letter to Philemon is so intensely original, so entirely innocent of dogmatic preoccupation, and Paul's mind has left its impress so clearly and indelibly upon it, that it can only be set aside by an act of sheer violence. Linked from the first with the two epistles to which we have just referred, it is virtually Paul's own signature appended as their guarantee, to accompany them through the centuries.

It is needless to say that we have not succeeded in perceiving the profound and ambitious design which Baur has detected in the letter to Philemon. We take it simply for what it is,—that is to say, a petition to a Christian friend on behalf of his slave. We delight to meet with it on our toilsome road, and to rest awhile with Paul from his great controversies and fatiguing labours in this refreshing oasis which Christian friendship offered to him. We are accustomed to conceive of the apostle as always armed for warfare, sheathed in logic and bristling with arguments. It is delightful to find him at his ease, and for a moment able to unbend, engaged in this friendly intercourse so full of freedom and even playfulness (vers. 11, 19, 20).

Paul has often been blamed for sending Onesimus back to his master. His conduct has been regarded as giving sanction to slavery. This accusation does not seem to me at all worthy of regard. The mighty force of the Gospel, which in regenerating the heart elevated all men, and created a new society without disturbing existing social institutions, is perhaps nowhere better exhibited than in these few lines. Where, I ask, could we find, not merely a more radical condemnation of the causes and results of slavery, but a more complete emancipation of the debased slave? Have we not here the practical realization of the beautiful Christian idea which merges all social distinctions in Christ, and restores to each man in his neighbour his brother, his other self, uniting them as members of the same family for all eternity? "I do not wish," writes the apostle to Philemon, " to decree anything authoritatively. It is the aged Paul who from his prison, and in the name of our mutual affection, entreats thee on behalf of his son—that son whom I have begotten in my chains—Onesimus, the once lost and useless slave, who now returns to thee, so dear and precious both to thee and me. . . . Thou didst lose him for a time; thou regainest him for eternity. Receive him no longer as a slave, but as a brother in the flesh, and in the Lord. If thou holdest me for a friend, receive him as thou wouldst myself." This epistle is not merely a revelation of the apostle's heart, it becomes further, through its moral significance, an invaluable document of the Pauline ethics.

II. Colossians and Ephesians.

The epistles to the Colossians and the Ephesians demand more extended consideration. Their mutual relations and obviously close connexion present to criticism the most difficult of problems. De Wette first of all expressed grave doubts of the apostolic origin of the epistle to the Ephesians; in the end, he absolutely rejected it. A strict comparison with the letter to the Colossians was decidedly unfavourable to it. It seemed to be nothing more than an oratorical and at times verbose amplification of the other; and, though not deficient in merit, it was at least wanting in originality.

But de Wette's investigations, although so accurate, were incomplete. The question wears another aspect, which has escaped his observation. Everything has not been said, when the dependence of the epistle to the Ephesians on that to the Colossians is once established. He should have asked whether this relation is not mutual, and whether the epistle to the Colossians, though apparently more original, is not in its turn inseparably connected with Ephesians. It is not surprising that the question, when approached from this side, has received an opposite solution.

Mayerhoff and Schneckenburger have maintained, not without some show of reason, that the epistle to the Ephesians was the original and primitive letter. The former, indeed, has not hesitated to bring the same accusation of plagiarism against Colossians that de Wette brought against Ephesians.

It becomes apparent from these conflicting arguments that the dependence of the two letters is mutual, and that they cannot really be separated. On that point Baur was not mistaken. Starting with the assumption that Ephesians is not authentic—a fact which he considered demonstrated by de Wette, he had no difficulty in exhibiting clearly the inner solidarity of the two epistles; and he insisted with logical force that the fall of the one necessarily involves that of the other. In his view, the identity of their aim, method, and dogmatic contents, and of the designation of their messenger, sufficiently attest their common authorship. It will perhaps be observed that in the end, and by this roundabout means, Baur's criticism almost annihilates those observations of de Wette which in the first instance were its support and starting-point. After reaching this conclusion, what are we to make of these exegetical and literary details which betray the imitator's hand? If there is plagiarism, it is in this case the author copying himself! Baur only departs from the original tradition on one point: he refers to the year 110 or 120 the literary phenomenon which has usually been placed about 60 A.D.; and he assumes as very probable in one of Paul's disciples a procedure which he considers absolutely impossible in the case of Paul himself.

In this way modern criticism brings us back to its own starting-point. We must, in fact, complete de

Wette's examination, if we do not wish to be misled at the outset by appearances. We have not here the simple relation of a copy to its original. The question is more complex and delicate. The coincidences of the two epistles are not merely external. Their unity of inspiration is even more striking than their resemblance in style. In both there is the same theological standpoint, and the same errors are controverted. There is between them, if I may so speak, an intimate and mutual interpenetration. The same matter is digested twice over; but the relation between the two treatises is such that, notwithstanding their constant resemblance, there is never on the one hand absolute originality, nor on the other servile imitation. And we have no more ground for regarding the epistle to the Ephesians as a secondary amplification of the epistle to the Colossians than for viewing the latter as a mere summary of the former.

The double relationship of the two epistles being once thoroughly apprehended, there can no longer be any doubt of their common origin. Conceived at the same time, in the same spirit, and produced under the same circumstances, carried to neighbouring Churches by the same messenger Tychicus, they seem to us like twin sisters, that suffer from separation, each of them complete only when the other is beside her. They are in secret compact, and each makes allusion to her sister in ways more or less direct or obscure, but nevertheless conclusive.

In the first place, it is evident that the epistle to the Ephesians corresponds with the epistle to the Colossians; it recalls and implies it. It reproduces its main ideas and characteristic phrases, and develops the same theme. At one point this tacit relation is conspicuous, and is revealed in a manner so incidental that the connexion becomes obvious without there being any possibility of regarding it as the *intentional* and studied work of a forger. Ephesians vi. 21 contains a manifest allusion to Colossians iv. 7. The author did not write the former passage without thinking of the latter: "Ἵνα εἰδῆτε καὶ ὑμεῖς τὰ κατ' ἐμέ. This conjunction καί, contained in all the manuscripts, would be inexplicable without the parallel passage in Colossians. Now can we imagine that an imitator, after having composed the epistle to the Ephesians, and conceiving the idea of connecting it with the epistle to the Colossians, would have confined himself in carrrying out his project to this simple conjunction? Such a proceeding requires a skill and delicacy beyond belief.

The epistle to the Colossians, in its turn, corresponds with that to the Ephesians; it assumes it and refers us to it. To be convinced of this, we must first of all abandon the common notion that the latter is an epistle addressed specially to the Church at Ephesus. It is well known that the words ἐν Ἐφέσῳ, of the superscription, are wanting in the most ancient manuscripts, and that Marcion read, on the contrary, ἐν Λαοδικείᾳ. What is still more decisive, is the fact that the so called letter to the Ephesians was addressed to readers whom Paul had never seen, and who had never seen him (Eph. i. 15-19; iii. 1-4; iv. 17-22). Who then were these readers? It is plain that they must be sought for not far from Colossæ, since the same messenger is charged with both letters.

A passage in the letter to the Colossians, hitherto overlooked by critics, seems to me to indicate them clearly enough: θέλω γὰρ ὑμᾶς εἰδέναι ἡλίκον ἀγῶνα ἔχω περὶ ὑμῶν καὶ τῶν ἐν Λαοδικείᾳ καὶ ὅσοι οὐχ ἑωράκαν τὸ πρόσωπόν μου ἐν σαρκί (Col. ii. 1). This passage proves that the author of Colossians had, when writing, several groups of readers in view—two at any rate—that of the Church of Colossæ, and that of the Church of Laodicea and other Churches who were unacquainted with the apostle. Does not this latter expression admirably describe the readers of the epistle to the Ephesians? Moreover, the author of the epistle to the Colossians wrote two letters—one to the Church of Colossæ, and another which he describes as intended to be sent on to Colossæ from Laodicea (Col. iv. 16). Can this be any other than the letter to the Ephesians? Whoever has duly appreciated the intimate connexion of the two epistles will not for a moment doubt that the author to the Colossians refers in this passage to the letter that we now possess, and which bears the address of Ephesus.

Does it follow that Marcion was right in reading ἐν Λαοδικείᾳ for ἐν Ἐφέσῳ? Certainly not. Marcion only made a conjecture, on the strength of the gap in the manuscripts, and one which arose naturally from this very passage (Col. iv. 16). Marcion's testimony at least proves that no other letter to the Laodiceans was known to early Christian antiquity. But we hasten to add that Marcion, and after him all critics who adopted his suggestion, both misread and still more misinterpreted the passage in Colossians on which they relied. The text, in fact, does not indicate a special letter sent from Paul to the Laodiceans. The existing epistle cannot have been addressed to Laodicea in particular, any more than to Ephesus. If Paul had addressed his letter to the Christians of Laodicea, how could he have sent greeting to them and their pastor Nymphas through those of Colossæ, instead of appending his salutations to the letter he was sending directly to themselves? But, in point of fact, we do not read in Colossians iv. 16 τὴν εἰς Λαοδικείαν, but τὴν ἐκ Λαοδικείας; that is, *the letter which will reach you from Laodicea*, and not the letter which I have addressed to Laodicea. The epistle must have been addressed to a circle of Churches in the neighbourhood which had never seen Paul.

We will not pursue the discussion further. The mutual affinity and solidarity of the two letters must be seen to be sufficiently established. Baur's demonstration on this head is irrefragable. The two letters come to us from one and the same author, who while writing one had the other planned in his mind, and in composing the second did not forget the first. Every attempt to separate them is doomed to failure. They will always stand or fall together. In these later days criticism seems to have better understood the complexity of this literary problem, and has invented another hypothesis for its solution. An attempt has been made to discover in the epistle to the Colossians an authentic nucleus, by the help of which a later writer might first of all have drawn up the epistle to the Ephesians, returning afterwards to Paul's own letter and amplifying it freely, in order to make it more conformable with his own work, hoping thus to conceal his device. History, and still more a candid exegesis, condemn this strange solution, which finds its impracticability so little of an embarrassment.

III. Progress of Paul's Doctrine.

The apostle, in these two epistles, does not resume the dialectical exposition of his doctrine of justification by faith. But it is easy to discover and trace in them the anthropological and soteriological basis of Paulinism (Eph. ii. 8-10; Col. ii. 12-14; Phil. iii. 3-10; Eph. i. 13, 14; Col. iii. 1-3). The union and perfect equality of Jews and Gentiles in Christ, so keenly contested in the preceding period, are here set forth as accomplished facts; this victory is won (Col. iii. 11). The lofty standpoint reached by the apostle in the epistle to the Romans is firmly maintained and powerfully vindicated (Eph. ii. 11-19; Col. i. 20-23). But all these preceding conquests are only the basis and starting point of a new development.

It is here, in fact, that the epistle to the Ephesians takes up the doctrinal work of the apostle, to continue it in a new sphere. We now pass the boundaries of history and time, and plunge into the realm of metaphysics; for it is really an essay in Christian metaphysics that Paul is about to make. The Person of Christ will of course be the corner-stone of this edifice.[1] Passing by the earlier conditions and historical stages through which the Divine plan has been accomplished, Paul apprehends the redemption as an eternal thought of God. This Divine conception becomes the generative principle of all future evolution. It is the cause and end of the entire creation; it explains everything, because it produced everything. The Gospel, hitherto conceived of merely as a means of salvation, is thus raised through the apostle's persistent study to the height of a universal

---

[1] The thought of the author of the Fourth Gospel pursued a kindred development. The Pauline theosophy and the Johannine mysticism, whilst diverse in origin, are united in their end.

principle. We must, however, hasten to add that while thus opening new vistas to Christian doctrine, by making the Gospel the subject of lofty contemplation, Paul is careful not to change the living realities of faith into barren abstractions or transform the moral drama of the redemption into a law of necessary development. His doctrine is enlarged and elevated, without losing any of its moral fulness and quality. But it had to create new forms for its new matter; and some of his expressions, such as πλήρωμα and αἰῶνες, while retaining their historical meaning (Eph. i. 10; ii. 7), acquire a metaphysical significance which they did not possess in the previous epistles.

Does this imply, as Baur supposed, that the writer has borrowed from the Gnostic systems of the early part of the second century? It seems to us that the change in Paul's vocabulary has a simpler explanation, that it is in fact a necessary consequence of the advance of his doctrine. If there has been any borrowing, it is rather on the side of Basilides and Valentinian, who most certainly formed their dialect on the religious phraseology of the New Testament.[1] Indeed, it is easy to see that in our epistles this terminology as yet is vague, and wavers between the popular and Gnostic meaning, and that no strict and settled order in the hierarchy of celestial beings is here imagined. In the second century, on the contrary, all this was arranged and determined with mathematical accuracy. It will always be difficult to believe that a Gnosticism of quite undeveloped form is posterior to that which had attained its full perfection. Certainly, Paul follows the daring speculation

---

[1] See Tertullian, *De præscriptione hæreticorum*, chap. xxxvii.

of the new teachers into the transcendental regions of the invisible world. He also sees fit to make, on his own account, a cursory enumeration of the spiritual powers (Eph. i. 21; Col. i. 16); for he has the spirit of the age, and reasons in the same manner. But he shows no interest, no curiosity about the subject. His sole purpose is to make Jesus Christ sovereign in heaven, as well as upon and beneath the earth (Eph. i. 10, 21, 22; Col. ii. 15).

It is in the epistle to the Ephesians that the apostle unfolds and sets forth the eternal plan of redemption, as it embraces not only the course of the ages, but the whole universe. This conception, which forms the basis of the epistle, gives it its original and distinctive character. Having in his letter to the Colossians disposed of the controversial question and of all incidental and personal matters, the apostle is here absorbed in this great idea, which he delights to set forth in all its fulness.

The basis of redemption is the *grace* of God (chap. ii. 6, 7). This unconditional grace, the absolute and eternal act of the Divine will, is the source of the predestination already indicated in Romans viii. 29; and it is developed with great affluence of expression in the first chapter of Ephesians: "Blessed be God our Father, who elected us before the creation of the world to be holy and without spot before Him; having beforehand decreed our adoption in Jesus Christ, in whom we have the pardon of our sins according to the riches of His grace. Thus He has made known to us the mystery of His will, which according to His good pleasure he had purposed in Himself." This plan of redemption remained uncomprehended and unrevealed until the time of its full realization. Paul calls it a *mystery* (chap. i. 9; comp. 1 Cor. ii. 7). As this mystery was revealed in Christ, and Christ is its essential content, it is also the mystery of Christ, or the mystery of the Gospel (chaps. iii. 4; vi. 19; comp. Rom. xvi. 25). That which had not become matter of history existed in this way beforehand in the mind of God. Salvation was actual, though not manifested. In this sense it is also regarded as a heritage reserved for the faithful, of which the Holy Spirit shed abroad in our hearts is already the certain guarantee (chap. i. 13, 14, 18; comp. Rom. viii. 16 and 2 Cor. i. 22).

This plan of salvation, the eternal conception of God, is a *Divine economy of the times and the worlds* (chap. i. 10). This economy, this plan of the ages (πρόθεσις τῶν αἰώνων), is a work of *wisdom*. Through it is revealed and made known in its wealth of variety the Divine wisdom, so fertile in its resources and rich in its means (ἡ πολυποίκιλος σοφία τοῦ Θεοῦ, chap. iii. 10). Thus, in the general economy, is ordained the succession of special *economies*, which simply mark stages in the progress of the work of universal redemption. This salvation, conceived in eternity and prepared in preceding ages, is revealed in its own time, which is the very fulness of the times (Gal. iv. 4; Eph. i. 10). But any one who has thoroughly apprehended the nature of the Pauline doctrine must know that it is pre-eminently realistic and matter of fact. It never represents the revelation of God as the exhibition of an abstract idea, but as the unfolding of a Divine operation. The consummation of revelation is therefore, at the same time, the consummation of God's creative work; and the *pleroma* of things corresponds of necessity with the *pleroma* of times. The word πλήρωμα thus passes naturally from its original to its metaphysical signification.

The starting point of this idea—a leading characteristic of these epistles—is in 1 Corinthians xv. 28. According to this passage, the supreme design of God, carried out in the whole creation throughout the entire succession of ages, is to permeate and *fill all things*, to become all in all. The apostle's doctrine, developing in this direction, conceived of the Divine action as pouring all its riches into the Person of Christ, who thus actually becomes the *pleroma of Divinity*. Christ in His turn constantly pours out and communicates all His riches upon and to His Church, which becomes the *pleroma of Christ*, the complete realization of His virtue, His actual body, precisely as Christ was the *corporeal manifestation* (σωματικῶς) of the Divine plenitude. Thus God fills Christ; Christ fills the Church; and the Church, extending to the limits of all things, fills the universe (chaps. iii. 19; i. 23).

The crisis of this Divine action is the appearance of Jesus upon earth; and in that appearance, His death upon the cross. The centre of gravity of Christ's work has not been removed. The historical cause of redemption is still the Saviour's expiatory death (chaps. i. 7; ii. 13, 16; Col. ii. 14, 15). The circumference is enlarged; the centre remains the same. It is from this standpoint that Paul contemplates the progressive realization of the plan of God, advancing towards its final goal, the reconciliation of all oppositions, and the consummation in Christ of the unity of the world. Thus has the barrier been overthrown already between Jews and Gentiles (τὸ μεσότοιχον τοῦ φραγμοῦ), now brought near and united in one and the same body by the virtue of the cross (σύσσωμα, chap. ii. 13–16). This work of reconciliation is to extend, not only to the utmost limits of the human race, but to the whole universe: "For it has pleased God to reconcile all things in Him, having made peace by the blood of His cross, whether on earth or in heaven" (Col. i. 19, 20).

This infinite extension of Christ's work implies of necessity a parallel exaltation of His Person. Since it is in and through Him that God realizes His eternal thought, Christ becomes by that very fact the actual medium of the Divine revelation and working. His Person now assumes in the transcendental region of metaphysics the supreme and kingly place that it already possesses in the Christian consciousness. To it must be referred the work of creation, as well as that of redemption. In it is attained the final unity of all things. The centre of the Gospel becomes the centre of the universe. The moral principle of the Christian life is also the metaphysical principle of the creation.

IV. THE CHRISTOLOGY OF COLOSSIANS.

This transcendental Christology, implied throughout the epistle to the Ephesians, constitutes the special object of the letter to the Colossians. The apostle remains at the same standpoint, and the same horizon stretches before him; but instead of considering, as before, the work of redemption as a whole, his attention is concentrated on the Person of Christ, in which moreover this work is summed up. The conception that he gives us of this Person rises almost to the height of the Johannine Christology. The name λόγος alone is wanting. But the actual name, which possibly Paul intentionally avoided, would scarcely modify in any way his conception (Col. i. 17; comp. John i. 3, 4).

In his previous epistles the apostle had not formulated any precise Christological doctrine. It would be indeed a vain attempt to try to discover in them all the ideas of the epistle to the Colossians. But, on the other hand, there is nothing in the earlier epistles to exclude by anticipation the development here assumed by the Pauline Christology. We may gather from them some indications which prepare us for it. The notion of the *ideal*, or *celestial man* (1 Cor. xv. 47; Rom. v. 15) does not exhaust the apostle's conception. The unique and sovereign place which he accorded Christ in his inner consciousness, the absolute dependence which he felt with regard to Him, the worship he rendered Him, in which he never separates Him from God, must inevitably have led him on, sooner or later, to loftier conclusions. Let us read over again 2 Corinthians xiii. 14; 1 Corinthians xii. 5–11. True, the doctrine of the Trinity is not formulated in these two passages; but whoever will compare them, and observe how Paul, in expressing the very foundation of his Christian convictions, spontaneously attributes to the Spirit, to the Lord, and to God an absolutely equal share in the work of redemption, will easily satisfy himself that there exists here the germ of an idea which will carry the writer much further. Nor are these isolated and singular texts. We will not dwell on Romans ix. 5, the interpretation of which is so much disputed. But let us consider 2 Corinthians iii. 17. Paul does not say, ὁ Κύριος πνεῦμά ἐστιν; but he says absolutely, ὁ Κύριος τὸ πνεῦμά ἐστιν. Is there not something here which goes beyond the idea of the "celestial man"? Once more,

16

let us look at 1 Corinthians viii. 6: εἷς Θεὸς ἐξ οὗ τὰ πάντα . . . εἷς κύριος Ἰησοῦς Χριστός, δι' οὗ[1] τὰ πάντα καὶ ἡμεῖς δι' αὐτοῦ. Baur limits this expression, δι' οὗ τὰ πάντα to the work of redemption. But is not this an arbitrary restriction? Are not the two propositions exactly parallel, and equally absolute? The context of the passage has a general bearing; it puts the contrast between the monotheistic and the polytheistic idea, stated in most general terms. God is said to be the absolute source of all things, and Christ His one Agent. Baur's explanation recalls those of the Socinians, who succeeded also in disposing of John's prologue and of the statements of the epistle to the Colossians, by restricting them to the Gospel economy. This passage, besides, should be compared with the one preceding it. Seeing that Christ is the Spirit, in an absolute sense, is it incredible that Paul should have seen in this Spirit the principal of the creation as well as of redemption? No doubt, there is not here all that we shall find in the epistle to the Colossians. But we have the germ out of which the Christology of later letters was developed. On this, as on all other points, we may assert that there was progress in the Pauline doctrine,—but progress with continuity.

To sum up the Christology of the epistle to the Colossians: Christ is the image of the invisible God; that is to say, the visible manifestation of God's invisible essence (chap. i. 15). He is, from the metaphysical point of view, the essential Mediator between

---

[1] The Codex Vaticanus has δι' ὃν instead of δι' οὗ. But there are no reasons, other than dogmatic, for preferring this reading to that of all the other manuscripts.

God and the world. It is through Him that God imparts Himself to the world, and that the world returns to God. No doubt the expression πρωτότοκος πάσης κτίσεως puts Christ in absolute subordination, and associates Him with creation, placing Him indeed at its head, but also in the rank of creatures.[1] On the other hand, in face of the creation, He is raised to the same level with God; for God has been pleased to pour into Him the plenitude of His divinity (Col. ii. 9). "In Him all things were created, in the heavens and on the earth, the visible and the invisible. He is before all things, and all things have the basis of their existence in Him" (τὰ πάντα ἐν αὐτῷ συνέστηκεν). He is the Divine πλήρωμα; *i.e.*, in Him is the plenitude, the totality of existence to be realized in the world (chap. i. 19). He is more particularly the Head of the Church, the First-born of the resurrection as of the creation, everywhere having the pre-eminence (ἐν πᾶσιν αὐτὸς πρωτεύων, chap. i. 18).

To comprehend these statements fully, we must admit the controversial aim which already begins to appear. The apostle seeks to give Christ supremacy in all things, so that His dignity shall not be diminished nor His glory eclipsed in the hierarchy of æons set up between God and the world. Christ is not a single æon, one of a crowd—not a part of things—but the πλήρωμα. From Him the whole series of celestial and terrestrial beings derive their life; to Him they must ever return, if they would not be separated from God. Paul knows but one Mediator in earth

---

[[1] On this phrase see Lightfoot, or Meyer *ad loc.* "First-born in respect of all *creation*" sets Christ in express contrast to the creatures. Comp. Heb. iii. 6: "Christ as *a Son over* His (God's) house."]

and heaven. The work of mediation and universal reconciliation is not a collective work; the apostle does not suffer it to be shared. Redemption is the work of the Crucified. In Him alone God reconciles all things. It is by the blood of His cross that peace has been made in the visible and invisible universe (εἰρηνοποιήσας διὰ τοῦ αἵματος τοῦ σταυροῦ αὐτοῦ).

From this point of view is obviously and naturally explained the passage in Colossians ii. 15, which has been so tortured by commentators: ἀπεκδυσάμενος τὰς ἀρχὰς καὶ τὰς ἐξουσίας, ἐδειγμάτισεν ἐν παρρησίᾳ, θριαμβεύσας αὐτοὺς ἐν αὐτῷ? What are these ἀρχαὶ and ἐξουσίαι? The majority of commentators, including de Wette and Meyer, regard them as demons, powers of sin and hell, and refer for proof to Eph. vi. 12. But the two passages are neither similar nor parallel. We might ask, moreover, what the triumph of God and Christ over the diabolical powers has to do with this passage of Colossians? Considering that the apostle has spoken already in Col. i. 16 of the ἀρχαὶ and ἐξουσίαι, and still continues within the same circle of ideas, there is absolutely no authority for seeing in the second passage any powers other than those mentioned in the first. Now in Colossians i. 16, there is no question at all of infernal powers, but of those intermediate beings that theory had multiplied between the world and God, and amongst whom speculation distributed the work and the honour of universal redemption. Of this honour Christ has deprived them; of this undeserved glory He despoiled them by His death on the cross. God has made Him Lord of all these powers, which now only serve in their vanquishment to adorn His triumphal chariot. This passage, which was useless in its traditional interpretation, and counted for nothing in the apostle's argument, is thus seen to be a decisive blow directed against the radical principle of the Gnostic speculation.

Paul does no more than rapidly traverse these lofty regions of the transcendental world; he confines himself to dispelling the clouds which might veil from our eyes the greatness of the Person and the work of Jesus. Only this purpose detains him there. He speaks of this invisible world with admirable sobriety; and hastens to descend into the sphere of practical life, of which he has never lost sight. But he returns bringing to it new wealth of thought. Upon the heights he has reached, he apprehends the relation of Christ to the Church from a new point of view.

Already, in Romans xii. 5 and 1 Corinthians xii. 12-27, the Church had been regarded as an organic and substantial reality, a body whose members are individuals, and which manifests in its permanent unity the wealth lying hidden in its principle of life. It has been already designated the body of Christ (ὑμεῖς δέ ἐστε σῶμα Χριστοῦ, 1 Cor. xii. 27),—that is to say, a body having the root of its existence and its principle of unity in the Person of the Saviour. This appellation, *the body of Christ*, is something more than a metaphor. The Church is not conceived of apart from Christ, nor Christ apart from the body of the Church; but Christ continues present in the Church as its immanent principle of life. Finally, the apostle treated the Church as the virgin affianced to Christ (2 Cor. xi. 2); he suggested the same relation in 1 Corinthians xi. 3, where Christ is called *head* (κεφαλή) of the man, as the man is head of the woman.

The speculative reflections to which the apostle

rises in the epistles of the Captivity give these ideas a new significance. The title of σῶμα acquires a transcendental import which it did not formerly possess; Paul no longer says σῶμα Χριστοῦ, but, in an absolute sense, τὸ σῶμα τοῦ Χριστοῦ. In the former idiom Χριστοῦ is an *objective genitive*; in the latter it becomes a *subjective genitive*. In the first instance, the Church depends on Christ for its existence; in the second, Christ Himself has need of the Church to manifest all the plenitude of the life within Him. Not that Paul has adopted a new mode of thought; but evidently he has changed his point of view. Formerly, he ascended from the Church to Christ; now, starting with the idea of the transcendental Christ, he contemplates the progressive manifestation and realization in the Church of the possibilities latent in Him. The Person of Christ is already the Church potentially (*in potentia*); and the Church is Christ Himself manifested (*in actu*).

It would be easy by abuse of logic to push this spiritual unity of Christ and the Church to the point of metaphysical identification. Paul himself, let us say at once, did not go to this length; his doctrine is entirely distinct from all pantheistic speculations on the subject. He holds, indeed, that the Church exists only in Christ; but he does not assert that Christ exists only in the Church. The Person of Christ is rooted in God Himself. We have not to deal here with a series of abstractions equivalent to each other; but with a *processus* of life, an organism consisting of living beings, who are distinct without being separated, and organically united without losing their identity.

The term σῶμα obviously gains its full meaning

only by combination with πλήρωμα, which at the bottom expresses the same idea under another form (ἥτις ἐστὶ τὸ σῶμα αὐτοῦ, τὸ πλήρωμα τοῦ τὰ πάντα ἐν πᾶσι πληρουμένου, Eph. i. 23). This passage is the summary of all the ideas developed in the two epistles. From the standpoint we have reached, it is its own interpretation. Just as Christ is the plenitude, the actual manifestation—we might almost say the σῶμα—of God (σωματικῶς κατοικεῖ πᾶν τὸ πλήρωμα τῆς θεότητος), so the Church is the *pleroma* of Christ, the body in which all the plenitude of the life within Him is realized. But as, after all, Christ communicates nothing which does not come from God, the Church, from the ideal point of view, may be justly called the actualized *pleroma* of God, who fills all in all. Thus the Church and Christ are related to each other as soul and body. The soul animates the body; and the body makes manifest the virtues of the soul. Thus it was that Paul could assert that the sufferings of the Christian are the filling up of the sufferings of Christ Himself (Col. i. 24); for the Church is simply the prolonging of Christ's life, present and immanent in her, as the vivifying principle from which comes her growth and strength. This new conception is admirably expressed in several passages, the fulness and vigour of which cannot be rendered in any translation (Col. ii. 19; Eph. iv. 15, 16; ii. 21).

Finally, the relations of Christ and the Church find perfect expression in the image of the intimate union established between the man and woman by marriage (Eph. v. 22-25). This analogy furnishes the apostle in return with an admirable conception of marriage, far superior to that which he had given in 1 Corinthians. The man and the woman form an indissoluble organic unity. Neither of the two attains full existence without the other. While the man is the head of the woman (κεφαλὴ τῆς γυναικός), the woman on her part is called the *body* of the man (σώματα τῶν ἄνδρων, chap. v. 28), in the same sense as the Church is the body of Christ. Thus each belongs to and finds itself in the other; and the bond of this living unity is love (chap. v. 28).

We can now admire the energy and force of logic with which Paul has guarded his Christian theory from the approaches of the Gnostic dualism that threatened to corrupt Christianity, alike in its dogmatic principle and its ethical practice, and the unfaltering consistency with which he has carried out his belief. From the Pauline theory there is deduced a morality which is indeed the very reverse of the Gnostic ethics. The profound connexion which exists between the hortatory and dogmatic portions of the two epistles has not always been fully apprehended. The apostle dwells solely on the natural and ordinary duties of man: those of marriage, of the education of children, of the master towards his slave, of the slave towards his master, and, in short, on social and domestic duties in general. On the other hand, he vigorously attacks the dualistic morality of the false teachers of Colossæ, which bordered on a barren asceticism. Nothing was more important from the first than to warn the Church against this fatal tendency, and to prevent it from falling into this well-worn groove. It is within the circle of life's ordinary duties that all the sanctifying freedom of the evangelical principle should be exhibited. Christian morality does not create or impose any other duties than those arising from the natural relations of men to each other; what it aims at and labours for, is to transform these relations, to purify and restore them to their ideal.

Natural duty fulfilled by the aid of Christ—that is the essence of religious duty. The Church is not to be a private society; it is human society regenerated by the spirit of the Saviour, a new *humanity*. Paul preaches above all things purity of heart, of conduct, and of speech. He sanctifies marriage by presenting for its type the union of Christ and the Church, and education by placing it under the oversight of God. He brings down the master to the level of the slave by charity; he raises the slave to the level of the master in appealing to his conscience. In a word, he opens to Christian humanity every path of progress. "For the rest, my brethren," he writes to the Philippians shortly after these two letters, "let everything that is true, that is pure, that is just, that is sound, lovable, and of good report, be the subject of your thoughts. Make every kind of virtue and of praise your aim" (Phil. iv. 8).

CHAPTER III.

THE EPISTLE TO THE PHILIPPIANS.

PAUL'S dogmatics are finally resolved and absorbed into a lofty Christology. This Christology in its turn attains its last and crowning expression in the famous passage, Philippians ii. 6-11, which may be regarded as the keystone of the apostle's theological edifice. But before discussing this text, it is absolutely necessary to make some reference to the epistle in which it is found.

This last letter, written from the Prætorium at Rome, closes the historical life of Paul as related in the Acts. If the apostle had expected by appealing to Cæsar to shorten the long imprisonment antecedent to his trial, his hope had been bitterly deceived. There was scarcely any more notice taken of him at Rome than at Cæsarea. He had patiently to resume the work of his apostleship, and to carry it on *in chains*. His earnest words won many souls among the military population of the Prætorium, and even among the members of Nero's household. But at the same time his courage and example, by giving a fresh impulse to all missionary work, occasioned a sharper division, and a more violent contention in the Church between the friends of his gospel and the Judaizing party. The old Jewish spirit, conquered in Greece, seemed to find in the genius and customs of the Roman race a more favourable soil, where it was to take deep root and speedily flourish anew.

Paul, therefore, had to pass through heavy trials and endure painful conflicts. Many Christians who should have comforted him disowned and rejected him. He suffered from prolonged isolation, and possibly from the denunciations of his brethren. When, however, he wrote his epistle to the Philippians, there seemed a break in the sky that had so long been overcast. Timothy was with him. Epaphroditus had come to bring him the precious token of the faithful affection of his spiritual children in Macedonia. He foresees at length a speedy issue to his trial, and awaits it, not without emotion, but in perfect resignation. Even his apprehensions cannot disturb or restrain the joy which overflows his heart. This long and wearisome imprisonment—a thing so fatal to feeble souls—had as little power to vanquish the old hero as the storms and struggles of his public life. He shows himself at this critical moment as indomitable and fervent as ever. Hear him cry, in those triumphant tones which he can always command in speaking of the cause of Christ: "And now, happen what may, Christ shall always be glorified in my flesh, whether by my life, or my death!" (chap. i. 20.)

In this short letter we must not look for any dogmatic controversy or design. Though the apostle occasionally refers to the Judaizing agitation, whether at Rome or at Philippi (chaps. i. 17 ; iii. 2, 18), it is only in passing, and by way of a pastoral warning. In like manner, the Christological passage (chap. ii. 6–11) forms an integral part of an entirely practical exhortation to self-renunciation and devotion. Neither of these points therefore can be regarded as indicating the aim of the epistle, or as constituting its direct object. We must abandon the attempt to discover a purpose in the letter, or else simply accept that which the author himself reveals. Paul wishes to thank the Philippians for their generous bounty, to give tidings of himself and hope of his speedy return (chap. ii. 24). This is just an intimate and familiar letter, in which he pours out with delight the fulness of his heart. He speaks to them of themselves, and of himself; and these two subjects, after alternating throughout the epistle, are in the end blended and lost in each other (comp. chaps. i. 1-12 and i. 12-26; i. 27 and ii. 17-30; chaps. iii. and iv.). That is the whole plan and order of the epistle. This explains the abrupt transitions and unexpected changes of tone, which have led some critics to suppose that we have here two, or even three, of Paul's letters combined in one.

They forget that Paul was a man, and an apostle, before he was a theologian; and are actually surprised at his not giving to this familiar letter the methodical order of a treatise. But we have only to read these few pages consecutively to apprehend, in the absence of the logical unity for which we have no right to look, their profound unity of inspiration and moral tendency. The logic of feeling differs from that of thought; it is perceived by the heart. Here the sentiments prompt and answer to each other, in the most natural and harmonious manner. These pages were written from a single inspiration. We may add, that they do not so much exhibit the apostle's theological creed, as the feelings of his heart and the maturity of his religious life. There is here a wealth of Christian experience, a fulness of faith, a strength and delicacy of affection, which remind us of the finest chapters in the second letter to the Corinthians. There is the same overflowing inner life ; only, prolonged trial and meditation have *deepened*, calmed, and matured it. The apostle does sometimes speak with his former severity (chap. iii. 2), but there is more gentleness and resignation (chap. iv. 18). Equally prepared either to live or die, his spirit is altogether less passionate and more tender, less susceptible and more detached from earth. It excites us less ; but it touches us more. A subtle note of melancholy pervades it. Paul is already crowned with the martyr's halo, and with the reflection of immortality.

Its practical character notwithstanding, the epistle none the less raises us to those lofty and luminous summits of Christian spirituality to which the apostle's doctrine finally attained, and whereon it rested. This spirituality is especially remarkable in its eschatological doctrine. Paul still expects, as he always had done, the great day of the Lord (ἡμέρα Χριστοῦ, chap. i. 10). The resurrection of the dead still seems to him the final goal of the development of the new humanity upon the earth (chap. iii. 11). The return of Jesus, coming to change this body of humiliation into the likeness of His glorified body, continues to be the object of his hope. But there is no longer any feverishness, or impatience, or distress in this glorious expectation. It is with an absolutely disinterested and submissive faith that Paul contemplates and traces out in history the slow yet constant unfolding of the Father's will. He entirely relinquishes the attempt to question a future whose secret is with God. Through this very renunciation he rises to the serene heights of the ideal of Jesus, the thought of the inner and progressive transformation of all humanity under the continuous organic action of the Gospel leaven. Let no one say that this spiritualized expectation of the consummation of the Kingdom is a remainder of Jewish superstition. It is of the very essence of the Christian faith; it belonged to the faith of Jesus; it will continue to be that of the Church. The Gospel, in truth, not only aims at the individual salvation of the soul after death; it has also, above all things, a social and universal import, and in the aim of its Founder had this from the first. It entered into the history of humanity as the decisive factor in its destinies. If human history is a drama, it is Christ who controls it and brings about its *dénouement*. The Day of Christ will be its consummation, which will consist in the final glorification of His Person and His work. Such is the inevitable conclusion of the Christian philosophy of history. If this conception of the destiny of the human race is mistaken, if the Gospel of Christ does not contain the last word of all our debates, it is plain that there is no salvation in Him. If Jesus ceases to be the Saviour of the world, He also ceases to be the Saviour of the individual.

It was its social aim that constituted the strength and greatness of Jewish Messianism. There was in this an element of profound truth, which Paul, following Jesus, extracted from it and preserved. The philosophy of history derived from this source, and which the apostle has gradually sketched out on the largest scale, is the chief glory of his doctrine. He has shaken off everything that was narrow, national, materialistic, or vulgarly supernatural in the Jewish conception. He sets aside its ingenious calculations, its "signs of the times," and fantastic visions. He courageously addresses himself to the practical tasks of everyday life, pointing out the way of progress, and walking in it himself without either discouragement or impatience, forgetting what has been already done that he may think only of what remains to be accomplished (ἐν δέ, τὰ μὲν ὀπίσω ἐπιλανθανόμενος, τοῖς δὲ ἔμπροσθεν ἐπεκτεινόμενος, chap. iii. 14).

But while the short-lived hopes of the popular Messianism have faded, others nobler and dearer have dawned on the Christian consciousness.

Paul felt himself too thoroughly united to Christ ever to admit the thought of separation from Him. " In life, and in death," he had written in the epistle to the Romans, "we are the Lord's" (ἐάν τε ζῶμεν ἐάν τε ἀποθνήσκωμεν, τοῦ Κυρίου ἐσμέν); and elsewhere: " I am persuaded that neither *death* nor *life*, nor anything else can separate us from the love of God in Jesus Christ our Lord" (Rom. xiv. 8 ; viii. 38). For a long time Paul had now lived in the presence of death ; and in death itself he had learned to find his Saviour, and his life. *Death had been swallowed up by life.* This spiritual triumph over death, which we have already noticed in the second letter to the Corinthians, we find consummated in the epistle to the Philippians. The continuance of this present existence, or its cessation, is an external accident which scarcely affects the apostle ; in either case it leaves his communion with Christ intact and uninterrupted. " For my part, to live—that is Christ ; and to die is my gain!" Death in itself seems to him desirable ; for his faith can only see in this last crisis a renewal of his being, and a decided advance which brings him nearer still to the Lord Jesus. " I am in a strait between two things ; my desire is to remove to be with Christ, which would be far the best for me." One can imagine the absolute independence that this faith gave to his soul. "I know how to be content with what I have. I have learned how to be in want, and in abundance. I have been initiated into every condition. I know how to endure hunger, and enjoy plenty ; to sustain wealth, and rejoice in poverty. I can do everything through Christ who strengthens me!" (chap. iv. 11–13.) Paul had now reached the close of his life ; and the fruit of his faith was ripe.

It is by keeping in view the practical character of the epistle to the Philippians, and its entire freedom from dogmatic pretension, that we arrive at a just appreciation of the passage in chap. ii. 6–11, which now remains for our consideration. Paul, in fact, only refers to Jesus in this place in order to exhibit in His conduct the ideal type that the Christian should strive to imitate and reproduce. It is the law of moral development, that glory is won through the cross. The connexion existing between sufferings willingly accepted, sacrifice joyfully fulfilled, and the Divine reward of future glory, was an essential and inseparable element of Paul's conception of the Christian life in general (2 Cor. i. 5–7 ; iv. 11–17 ; Rom. vi. 5 and xiv. 7). The Pauline Christology, in becoming transcendental, did not lose the ethical character belonging to it from the first. The cross is still the centre of gravity of the whole structure. We are not confronted here with a metaphysical abstraction, developed by a logical and inevitable *processus* ; but with a moral Being, who rises far above us it is true, but who nevertheless stands on our level, and who, of His own free will fulfilled His destiny, as we have to fulfil ours.

It is only from this essentially ethical point of view that we can grasp Paul's real conception.

After this, I hardly think it necessary to refute the interpretation of the text which Baur has given. The author, according to him, might have copied this admirable story of Jesus from that of some æon of Valentinian Gnosticism—which, in aiming to make itself equal with the supreme God, lapsed by a deserved fall from the πλήρωμα into a lower condition, that of the κένωμα, and finally rose by degrees and through long expiation to the highest place! These two conceptions are separated by a whole abyss; they belong to two different worlds which have nothing in common; and I seek in vain for the slightest connection between them. Baur quotes certain expressions in the passage that appear to favour Docetism. But, as M. Reuss has justly observed, the idea of Docetism is not present in the term μορφή, since it is used to designate the Divine essence; nor in ὁμοίωμα, which may be found in Romans viii. 3 (comp. chap. i. 23); nor in the words σχῆμα and εὑρεθείς, which always indicate an objective reality (comp. 1 Cor. vii. 31 and iv. 2; 2 Cor. v. 3; Gal. ii. 17). Furthermore, a Docetic interpretation of this passage would run directly counter to the author's express design. How could he found the glory of Christ upon a humiliation, obedience, and death, which were only apparent? The apostle is thinking, not of some celestial being, but of the historical Christ; and it is His earthly life that he so admirably sums up in the idea of renunciation and obedience.[1]

---

[1] See de Wette, *Exegetisches Handbuch*, second edition, on this passage in Philippians.

As for the idea of κένωσις itself, there is no need to look for it in the Valentinian Gnosticism. Its germ had long existed in the apostle's mind. It was the conclusion which he was bound inevitably to reach; and it enabled him to reconcile the historical standpoint from which he vigorously maintained the essential humanity of Jesus, with the metaphysical standpoint which led him to assert His Divine origin and condition. This passage in Philippians is the synthesis of the Christology of the great epistles with that of Colossians.

It was, in fact, essential to the logic of Paul's doctrine that he should conceive of the earthly condition of Jesus Christ as one of voluntary humiliation, and sum up His whole life in the idea of sacrifice (Gal. iv. 4; Rom. viii. 32). The words of 2 Corinthians viii. 9 should be called to mind: δι' ὑμᾶς ἐπτώχευσεν, πλούσιος ὤν. The exact bearing of this latter passage has often been misunderstood. The word ἐπτώχευσεν is not, indeed, the equivalent of ἐκένωσεν ἑαυτόν. The verb πτωχεύειν rather signifies to live in poverty, *paupertatem gerere*; but the aorist most certainly indicates the time when this condition began, when Christ *became* poor.[1] The impartial commentator will be compelled to see at the basis of this passage the idea of self-renunciation and relinquishment, which moreover alone gives force to the

---

[1] Neuter verbs in -ευω, -υω, -εω, etc., in the present tense express a condition, and in the aorist a *becoming*—*i.e.* the point at which the condition begins. Thus βασιλεύω signifies *I reign*, and ἐβασίλευσα *I became king*; πιστεύω signifies *I believe*, and ἐπίστευσα *I became a believer*. In the same way, ἔζησεν, in Rom. xiv. 9, signifies *He became alive*. See Holsten, *Paulus und Petrus*, p. 437.

apostle's reasoning in the context. Hence this passage of the epistle to the Philippians is simply the natural development of the idea indicated in the earlier text.

Having thus placed the text in its true light and referred it to its real historical origin, it will not be difficult to expound its content. The subject of the whole paragraph is the historical Christ, rising to glory through humiliation. But that this humiliation should take place, that there indeed should be room for renunciation, it was certainly necessary that Christ should have been already, in Himself and by nature, of a higher condition. This original state the apostle indicates in the words ἐν μορφῇ Θεοῦ ὑπάρχων, which form the most exalted metaphysical definition ever given by Paul to the Person of Christ. They express a substantial relation to God, a relation that the expressions εἰκὼν καὶ δόξα τοῦ Θεοῦ (2 Cor. iv. 6), which are sometimes adduced as a parallel, do not involve. Paul has said of man in his present condition that he is the *image and glory* of God (1 Cor. xi. 7); he would never have said of us, as of Christ, ἐν μορφῇ Θεοῦ ὑπάρχοντες. But on the other hand, the expression μορφὴ Θεοῦ does not mean absolute Divinity; there is still beyond it that which Paul calls equality with God, εἶναι ἴσα Θεῷ—a higher position which Christ might have thought of seizing, but which He did not usurp. Christ is of the Divine nature. But there is this difference between Him and God: that which He will be in the end, He has yet to become; and He becomes this *actually*, by the full development of His moral being. Thus the definitive condition to which Christ attains—and which Paul describes in the tenth verse—is not a mere return to the point of departure, to the original condition indicated in ver. 6. Between these two points there is for Christ Himself a progress, a real development of His being. On the other hand, Christ is no more able than we are to go beyond Himself, to exceed the limits of His nature. His development only makes manifest what was inherent in Him in principle, and the goal, which is the *Divine state*, implies for a starting point a Divine *nature and virtue*. These two phases of development are related to each other very much as *potentiality* is to *action*. Christ was *potentially* from the first, that which He finally became *in actuality*. Thus the child, being by its very nature ἐν μορφῇ ἀνθρώπου, finally attains full humanity. The μορφὴ Θεοῦ, therefore, indicates the general form of Christ's being; but is, if I may so speak, an empty form which has to be filled—that is to say, spiritually realized. There was in Him the *capacity* to receive and contain all the plenitude of the Divine life (πλήρωμα θεότητος).

This development of the Person of Christ is accomplished through a series of different periods or stages, which the apostle specifies and analyses in the text. The first, wholly negative, lies in the fact that He did not seek through egotism and pride to place Himself on a level with God, to usurp prematurely the Divine equality (οὐχ ἁρπαγμὸν ἡγήσατο τὸ εἶναι ἴσα Θεῷ). He resisted this first temptation to aggrandise and elevate Himself by a violent self-assertion, —called by Paul an *act of robbery*. Possibly this phrase alludes to Genesis iii. 5 and Matthew iv. 3.

The second stage—one that is, on the contrary, essentially positive—is denoted by the words ἐκένωσεν ἑαυτόν, which have been well translated, and without exaggeration, *He annihilated Himself.* We must not here conceive of the Johannine *Logos* in the bosom of the Father, already possessed of His full existence and Divine glory, as sacrificing His essence and destroying Himself in order to be born again and to attain full development. There is something inconceivable in the notion of a being who should transform and metamorphose himself in this way; it lies quite outside that sphere of moral life within which Paul always confined himself. The pre-existence of nature that he attributes to Christ is within the Godhead. Christ, who was by the order of His being (*genere essendi*) of Divine nature, renounces the Divine form of His essence, and annihilates His personal will in the presence of the Father's will. In a word, He sacrifices Himself. This annihilation is not a *metaphysical transubstantiation*, which is an impossible conception; it is a *moral act*, analogous to that which every spiritual being is called upon to perform, in order that he may become truly himself and fulfil his destiny. The words ἐκένωσεν ἑαυτὸν are explained by the three participles which follow, in well-marked gradation: μορφὴν δούλου λαβὼν—Christ who was by nature ἐν μορφῇ Κυρίου, took upon Him the μορφὴν δούλου, that He might develop Himself in this lower condition; He sacrificed His dignity, He became like men; and, finally, was found as a mere man. The two remaining clauses, ἐν ὁμοιώματι ἀνθρώπων γενόμενος, εὑρεθεὶς ὡς ἄνθρωπος, are only the explanation, the objective realization of the μορφὴ δούλου.

The third stage, rising upon and above the other two, is the *obedience* (γενόμενος ὑπήκοος)—an obedience which found its goal and consummation in the death on the cross. This development therefore is simply an ever deepening humiliation. But this humiliation is at the same time an exaltation; and it is here that the great law of the moral life is manifested. In His constant self-renunciation Christ actualized the virtualities of His nature. Every sacrifice left Him ennobled and enriched. Reaching the lowest depth of His humiliation, in His death on the cross, He attained the very height of His glory. Thus Jesus fulfilled His original destiny, and arrived at last at a condition of complete and actual Divine royalty. "Therefore," as Paul has so finely said, "God has supremely exalted Him, and given Him a name above every name : that at the name of Jesus every knee should bend, in heaven, upon earth, and under the earth ; and that every tongue should confess that Jesus Christ is Lord, to the glory of God the Father."

This is the final summit reached by Paul's doctrine. It had but to take one step more to attain the idea of the $\Lambda \acute{o} \gamma o s$. This conception cannot have been unknown to him. If he has never applied this name to his Master, it was certainly from a fixed determination. Nor must we be surprised. His conception of Christology is radically different from that of the Fourth Gospel, which is a Christology formed from the Divine standpoint. Hence, as it appears to us, *the Word made flesh* of St. John never comes to be fully and simply man. Paul's Christology, on the contrary, was framed from the human standpoint. It has an anthropological origin, and retains something of this essentially human character even in its metaphysical form. This is doubtless the reason why the Christ of Paul never comes to be simply and absolutely God. In His full Godhead He still retains the features of His glorified humanity.

CHAPTER IV.

THE THREE PASTORAL EPISTLES.

IT now only remains to consider the three *Pastoral* epistles. It is somewhat unfortunate for them, to begin with, that they do not belong to the organic whole formed by Paul's other letters, and are related to it less as an integral part than as an appendix, adding nothing of essential moment to the results already obtained.

It is impossible, in fact, to speak here of a new advance of Paulinism. True, it is presented to us in a different phase; but instead of growing richer, it seems impoverished. With the epistle to the Philippians the *living progress* ceases; with the Pastoral letters the *conservative tradition* begins. Paul's doctrine is there; but the soul which sustained and vivified it appears already to have left it. The powerful assimilation and fruitful activity of life is at an end; the body, still recognisable, seems stiffened and chilled; the dialectical articulations of the system are no longer perceptible. In any case, we have reached a point of arrest. This statement, incontrovertible under any hypothesis, is not intended to decide the critical problem raised by the origin of the three letters. They present a series of enigmas which, in the utter absence of historical information about the latter period of the apostle's life, will long remain insoluble.

We humbly confess that, after a long, critical study of the subject, we remain completely undecided.[1] The defenders of the epistles do indeed succeed in making us question their apocryphal origin, but not in convincing us of their authenticity. Their adversaries easily throw doubt upon the authenticity of these writings, but without enabling us to understand their later origin. We do not wish to enter upon the discussion here; but there is one point which we consider beyond all question and which we shall proceed to establish,—*viz.* that these three letters are posterior to all the others, and cannot be included in the scheme of Paul's life given in the Acts of the Apostles. If they are authentic, they belong to a later period of his life, of which we are wholly ignorant.

Let us notice, to begin with, a preliminary fact of decisive importance, and one fully established by the studies of de Wette and Baur; namely, the intimate connexion of the three epistles, and their perfect resemblance to each other. This resemblance not only obliges us to admit all the three as authentic or to reject them together as apocryphal, but absolutely prevents our ascribing them to separate periods of Paul's life. The style, the basis of thought, the heresies combated, the ecclesiastical situation pourtrayed, the practical counsels laid down—in a word,

---

[1] During the last twenty years we have more than once taken up this very obscure problem. We must confess that the reasons against the authenticity of the three letters, which perhaps were drawn up with the help of a few of Paul's notes, and by his disciples, seem to us to carry the day. See *Encyclopédie des sciences religieuses:* art. " Pastorales."

everything about the letters is similar, not to say identical. In some instances, we are tempted to think, they repeat and copy each other (comp. 1 Tim. iv. 1, 7 ; 2 Tim. ii. 23 ; and Tit. iii. 9, i. 14 : 1 Tim. iii. 2, and Tit. i. 7 : 1 Tim. iv. 1 ff., and 2 Tim. iii. 1 : 1 Tim. ii. 7, and 2 Tim. i. 11). Finally, besides this mutual resemblance, we must further note that they are all distinguished from the other epistles by their common cast of doctrine ; and in these essential differences they share alike.

This incontestable and uncontested fact at once condemns, beyond appeal, any hypothesis dating the letters in question at intervals of four or five years from each other, or which puts any one of Paul's other epistles between them. There is, in fact, only one supposition which adequately explains their fundamental resemblance—*viz.* that they were written within a very short space of time, and a long while after all the rest, at a period when the circumstances surrounding the apostle had changed, and when perhaps the burden of age and his prolonged trials had left their traces on his genius. The Pastoral epistles certainly seem to betray, here and there, a sort of weariness and enfeeblement.

Of all the attempts made to find a likely place for these epistles in the historical framework of Paul's life, the most ingenious is unquestionably the hypothesis of M. Reuss.[1] This theologian assuming that the apostle, during his three years' sojourn at Ephesus, made a circular tour to Crete, Corinth, Macedonia, and Epirus, formed for the epistle to Titus and the

---

[1] *History of the Sacred Scriptures of the New Testament*, §§ 87–92. He has since abandoned this hypothesis.

first to Timothy a ring fairly natural and sufficient to link them with this period of Paul's life. The second epistle to Timothy might have been written later, at Rome, before the epistle to the Philippians. Thus two of the Pastoral epistles would be placed between the epistle to the Galatians and the first epistle to the Corinthians. But such an idea is wholly inadmissible, and to our thinking incomprehensible. How, we repeat with M. Renan, could Paul have penned these mild effusions just after the epistle to the Galatians, and on the eve of writing those to the Corinthians? He must have abandoned his usual style on leaving Ephesus, and resumed it upon his return, except when he reverted a few years later to the diction employed during this supposed journey, in writing to Timothy a second time.[1] An interval of at least four years would separate this second letter to Timothy from the other two; and what is a still greater difficulty than the number of years, is that during this interval the apostle must have written the epistles to the Ephesians, the Colossians, and Philemon. Will any one suppose that Paul in writing to a friend, after this space of time, can have made extracts for the purpose from some of his old letters? The thing is inconceivable.

Besides, this literary difficulty is by no means the most serious one. The character of the heresies controverted, and the ecclesiastical situation these letters present, constitute others which are in themselves decisive. We might further discuss the sort of heretics to whom the Pastoral epistles refer. But it is absolutely certain that they are not the Judaizing

---

[1] Renan: *Saint Paul*, Introd., p. 31.

teachers of Galatia and Corinth, and do not in any wise resemble them It would be more easy to find a connecting link between them and the false teachers of Colossæ. There is the same arbitrary asceticism, resting on a similar dualism of principles (1 Tim. iv. 1–5), and accompanied by fantastic speculations, as senseless as they were useless. Their dualistic doctrines, however, belong to a far more highly developed and more dangerous form of Gnosticism than that to which the epistles to the Ephesians and Colossians refer. In these latter we find no more than a tendency to these notions: here, they have already taken shape and are distinctly formulated; they are sharply distinguished from the evangelical teaching, and openly oppose themselves to it.

Any one who still wishes to separate the three letters by placing an interval of four or five years between them, is logically compelled to admit that these heresies existed before the composition of the epistles to the Corinthians, and were even at that period threatening the Church's existence. But is it conceivable that such a danger had arisen at Ephesus at the time when Paul had stayed but a year in this city, and when the Christian community was only beginning to establish itself? If the danger did exist, why do we find no indication of it in the two epistles to the Corinthians, or in the epistle to the Romans? Besides, if two of the Pastorals are contemporary with Galatians and Corinthians, how is it that they bear no trace of the strenuous conflict with the Judaizers, which at this time most certainly engrossed the apostle's thought and life? The epistles must of necessity be subsequent to the address at Miletus. To place them earlier is an utter moral impossibility.

In one particular this impossibility becomes, indeed, matter of positive fact: I refer to the heresy of Hymenæus, Alexander, and Philetus, against which the epistles to Timothy are both directed (1 Tim. i. 20; comp. 2 Tim. ii. 17). It is sufficient to compare these two passages to feel certain that the letters could not have been separated by a long interval. One might even think that the passage in the second letter was written before that in the first. Hymenæus, who in the latter is excommunicated, does not seem to be so as yet at the date of the other epistle.

The general ecclesiastical situation implied in the three letters can only have occurred somewhat later. One year after Paul's first preaching at Ephesus, we cannot understand the possibility either of the development that these heresies had already assumed, or of the moral disorders that the apostle points out; or his counsels respecting widows, bishops, and deacons; or, in short, the ecclesiastical code that we find in these epistles. Let any one who wishes to realize the difference in the condition of the times, compare the picture drawn of Church life in the Corinthian community (1 Cor. xii.–xiv.) with the situation apparent in the Pastoral letters. The period of tumultuous spontaneity has been succeeded by that of prudent and orderly administration.

Without pausing to discuss more fully the individual details of this hypothesis, details which raise many other difficulties of a geographical and historical nature,[1] let us boldly conclude that the three epistles

---

[1] 1 Tim. i. 3, in particular, is a stumbling block to any hypothesis which intercalates the letter to Titus and the first to Timothy in Paul's supposed circular tour.

in question belong to one period of Paul's life and constitute a cycle of their own, of later date in the history of his doctrine. Either Paul's career did not end at the point where the Acts leaves off, or else the Pastoral letters are not authentic. Such is the dilemma in which we are landed; and I do not think there is any possibility of escape from it. This dilemma, unfortunately, at the same time creates a circle within which the action of criticism is confined. Historical information of any certainty on the latter period of Paul's life is entirely wanting. While the epistles require this unknown period, and a second captivity, as a basis for their apostolic origin,—on the other hand, the hypothesis of a second captivity scarcely finds any real foundation except in the three Pastoral letters.

It is enough for our purpose to have proved that the three epistles actually represent the latest stage of Paulinism. We may leave undecided the question whether this last transformation took place in the apostle's lifetime, or only after his death. In whatever way it is settled, it cannot be denied that the letters belong to the history of the Pauline system. They are not unworthy of the great apostle, either in form or substance.[1] The idea of the evangelical ministry which they unfold is unmistakably his. We meet here and there with the profound mysticism of his former letters (2 Tim. i. 9, 10; ii. 9–11). The controversial argumentations of Galatians and Romans have disappeared; but the doctrine that underlies those epistles is expressed in all its energy and pro-

---

[1] See the excellent defence of them made by M. Reuss, *History of the Sacred Scriptures of the N.T.*, §§ 88–92.

fundity (Tit. iii. 5-7). It is justifiable therefore, and even necessary, before concluding, to pourtray the dogmatic character of these three letters.

A very serious difficulty, under the hypothesis of their unauthenticity, is to determine the dogmatic design and end that the author had in view when inventing them. What strikes us most of all in these letters is their practical bearing. It is easy enough, from this point of view, to connect them with Paul's other epistles, and to explain their special physiognomy. The epistle to the Philippians proves the practical turn that Paul's doctrine took in the latter years of his life, and the simplification and *condensation* thus effected in his ideas. The dialectic apparatus which had served to formulate and defend them was gradually disappearing, and the results obtained were summed up in short and simple affirmations.

Also the conservative character of the epistles may very well be connected with a traditional element which is not wanting in any of the earlier letters, and which at all times was an essential feature of the apostle's teaching (1 Cor. xv. 1-11 ; 2 Thess. ii. 15 ; Eph. iv. 3 ; Phil. iii. 1 ; Col. ii. 6; Rom. xvi. 17). We must never weary of repeating, because it is continually forgotten, that Paul was an apostle before he was a theologian. To him the need of conservation was more urgent than that of innovation. His gospel was, above everything else, a message that he had received, and that he had to deliver and defend. He preaches not only with authority, but *by authority*; and the greatest misfortune which can befall those who have received his message is to betray the trust, or to allow it to be perverted (Gal. i. 6-9).

In this way the character of these epistles can

easily be understood. They are summed up in one thought: *Guard the good deposit* (2 Tim. i. 14). This good deposit, which must not be allowed to be lost or corrupted, naturally becomes, in contrast with the errors of all kinds arising in the Churches, *the right way*, *the sound doctrine* (λόγος ὑγιής, ὑγιαίνοντες λόγοι). With this idea of *orthodoxy* arose of necessity the correlative conception of *heresy*. Beside this perseverance in the received faith, the author dwells no less forcibly upon the necessity of purity of life, and launches out into most vigorous practical exhortations. But this is not done without involving some degree of separation between dogma and practical life, a separation which is not to be found in the earlier epistles. Here Christianity evidently tends to resolve itself into *a doctrine*, and *a morality*. The organic bond between faith and life, which in Paul's great letters was so close, is loosened, if not already broken. In that consists the real inferiority of these later epistles.

The author, whoever he may be, does not limit himself to abstract exhortations to maintain faithfully the received tradition. He carefully indicates how this deposit can and ought to be preserved, entrusted as it was to the Church at large, which lives by it and is responsible for it. The Church is "the pillar and stay of the truth" (1 Tim. iii. 15). But that is not enough; it is necessary to commit this charge into individual hands. As Paul himself delivered the good deposit to his disciples, they in their turn must confide it to sure hands. Hence the repeated directions about the choice of bishops, deacons, and of elders in general,—directions which occupy so much space in the letters, and are thus connected directly with their general and leading idea.

By all the features we have described—the separation of dogma and morality, the conception of the Church, of tradition and apostolical succession—these epistles furnish the transition from Paulinism to the Catholicism of the second century, which was in fact a synthesis of the various tendencies of the apostolic age.—The creative epoch has come to an end.

The close of the apostle's life is involved in impenetrable obscurity. The practical welfare of the Church of Christ, which had been his first care, was doubtless also his last thought. It was not his anxiety so much to complete and crown his system worthily, as to finish before his death the work that the Master had given him to do. This great work is now accomplished. The heroic combatant may at last enjoy the repose that in his lifetime neither his will, nor conscience, nor intellect ever knew.

Paul was only a disciple. This, from first to last, was his *rôle* and his ambition. But his life certainly presents to our eyes the most heroic effort humanity has made to apprehend and appropriate the Divine teaching and life of the Master. Among all His disciples, Jesus has had no greater.

BOOK V.

ORGANIC FORM OF PAUL'S THEOLOGICAL SYSTEM.

WE have followed the progressive course of Paul's doctrine throughout his epistles. We have left it, in some sort, to disclose itself in its succeeding manifestations. It now remains for us to apprehend and set it forth as an organic whole. We wish to trace out the strong and delicate articulation of the structure that we have watched as it rose slowly upon our view.

Ancient theology never seems to have suspected that the apostle's doctrine had an organism of its own, which ought to be valued as an essential element in its truth. The epistles served it simply as a collection of *dicta probantia*. The general scheme of dogma being officially prescribed, it only remained to distribute these passages according to the traditional rubrics: Theology, Christology, Pneumatology, Anthropology, etc. Did the dogmatic teachers arrive at the Pauline theology by this violent procedure? Certainly not. They had cut it to pieces. Nothing was left of it but scattered and lifeless fragments—*membra disjecta*.

Usteri, whose labours we have already noticed,

was the first to perceive that, in order to have Paul's doctrine in its life and entirety, we must apprehend and unfold it in its own organic character, and make its inner cohesion and logical unity apparent. He therefore devoted all his efforts to reconstructing the Pauline system; and his work is an early and noteworthy attempt at a sound historical interpretation. Usteri indeed was not sufficiently independent of the prevailing ideas of his time; he viewed Paul's system too much through that of Schleiermacher. Nevertheless his attempt opened up a new path, and led men's minds to a truer understanding of this great system of doctrine. He divided the Pauline system into two parts, corresponding with two historical periods: the epoch previous to Christianity ($\chi\rho o\nu o\iota$ $\tau\hat{\eta}s$ $\dot{a}\gamma\nu o\acute{\iota}as$), and the epoch of Christianity itself ($\pi\lambda\acute{\eta}\rho\omega\mu a$ $\tau\hat{\omega}\nu$ $\chi\rho\acute{o}\nu\omega\nu$). The first period embraces the development of Paganism and Judaism, both being comprehended under the dogmatic conception of *sin*. The reign of sin and death over humanity, the relation between sin and the law, the powerlessness of the latter to justify man, and the ardent longing for redemption that was the outcome of this long preparatory period,—these are the topics naturally included within it.

In the second part, Usteri penetrates to the heart of the Pauline theology. He studies in succession the work of redemption in the individual; the development of this work in the Christian society, or Church; and, lastly, its consummation in the final realization of the kingdom of God upon earth.

We cannot but recognise the inherent sequence of this exposition. But it is also very easy to indicate its serious defect. The theory of man's justification, with its negative and positive aspect and its essential antithesis between the law and faith, is maimed and disjointed; in order to reconstruct it, its scattered elements have to be sought in all directions. Thus Paul's closely woven system is torn asunder; and the rent proceeds from its very centre, with a most disastrous effect on the entire construction. The exposition of the Pauline theology has become that of the historical scheme of Divine revelation. No doubt this idea supplied an essential factor in the apostle's conception; but it is not the only one, nor the most important. Paul did not conceive this idea of the historical scheme of redemption *à priori*, and from the outset. He only arrived at it, as we have seen, by a long and laborious progress. The anthropological evidently preceded the historical point of view. Justification by faith without the law is, both in experience and theory, the logical antecedent of the other question. It was from this subjective side that Paul's doctrine received its first impulse; and with that we must of necessity begin. Now this individual point of view, this anthropological factor, is completely sacrificed in Usteri's scheme. Hence it has no substantial basis; and though it may have fascinated one's mind for a time, it has not secured final acceptance.

Next to this work of Usteri, the most remarkable exposition of Paulinism is undeniably that of Baur.[1]

---

[1] We refer now to the exposition of Paul's doctrine contained in the *Paulus* of Baur. We still prefer it, notwithstanding its omissions, to that which the learned Professor afterwards gave in his *Neutestamentliche Theologie*, published in 1864, after the death of the author.

It shows a decided advance upon the former. It is open to correction, and completion in its details; but it lays down the true method of reconstruction, and fixes the right point of departure. Baur was very sensible of the radical defect of Usteri's exposition, and fully succeeded in rectifying it. He has thoroughly apprehended and demonstrated the psychological origin of Paulinism. He bases his reconstruction on the great idea of justification by faith, preserving its characteristic antithetical form and dialectic movement. He then proceeds to trace the development of this idea in social life and the sphere of history, and shows how from these premises was logically deduced that great philosophy of history which defined the relation of Judaism and Paganism respectively to the Gospel. At this point Baur stopped short. The critical deductions from which he set out scarcely admitted of his further advance. We may however, and indeed we must, charge him with having misconceived and slighted the metaphysical principles of Paulinism. He has briefly touched upon them in a short chapter entitled "Secondary Questions" (*Nebenfragen*). But is it permissible to call the Pauline conceptions of God, of the Person of Christ, of predestination and revelation, secondary questions? Are they not, on the contrary, so many essential keystones, that preserve the harmony and solidity of the entire structure? While Usteri's exposition appeared to want foundation, this of Baur may be said to want its topstone.

The exposition presented by M. Reuss, in his turn, is the most scrupulous and exact in detail that has ever been given. But on the special point which we are now considering, *viz.* the logical structure of the system, it can hardly be said to show any real advance on the preceding theories. M. Reuss has correctly indicated the general character of Paul's theology; he has pointed out its primary origin in the apostle's moral and religious experience; and he has even sketched its main outlines with precision and certainty. But the psychological and historical aspects of the subject run into each other, and are so blended together that neither of them is brought out with sufficient emphasis nor developed with logical completeness. The rich philosophy of history, so powerfully wrought out in Paul's mind, fades and disappears. Neither is the order of the individual doctrines as they pass under review, nor their connexion with the generative idea of the system, always thoroughly apprehended. In short, in this very lucid and facile exposition of Paul's doctrine there is more art than logic.

Obviously, it is no easy undertaking to attempt to reproduce, without distortion or injury, the internal organization of the apostle's system of thought. We should even draw back from the task, were retreat permissible. But it is too late. From the historical exposition that we have just given is logically and spontaneously evolved an organic system which it behoves us to expound. We have not created it *à priori*; history itself has given it us, and in the name of history alone we finally proceed to set it forth. Our sketch of the Pauline system will, in effect, furnish a brief summary of the history whose course we have followed up to this point.

Paul's theology has its roots in the fact of his conversion. Each of his ideas may be said to have been a fact of inward experience, a feeling, before it was formulated by the understanding. We must not be misled by its external dress, by the scholastic forms which moulded the apostle's doctrine; for at the bottom there was nothing at all abstract or formal about it. Deduction is not its favourite process. On the contrary, it always advances from the concrete to the abstract, and rises from experience to principles. Paul's is not a speculative theology, logically deduced from an abstract conception; it is unmistakably positive, having its starting point in the internal reality of faith. It would be impossible to find anything more vigorous and active in growth than Paul's doctrine. It is, when properly understood, simply the direct transcription of his experience, the pure outflow of his moral and religious life, which ascending from the depths of his soul into the sphere of the intellect, there finally expands into its theoretical form. That is why pious souls have read and ever will read with profit these letters, apparently so difficult. Behind their scholastic apparatus, the consciousness of the humble Christian perceives and responds to that of the great apostle. A corresponding inward experience establishes between them by anticipation a mysterious harmony, a secret understanding; and it very often happens that these simple souls comprehend the mind of Paul better than professed scholars. He who has never in any degree experienced the inward change which transformed Saul of Tarsus will never fully understand his writings; there is a hidden depth in them to which he cannot penetrate.

Paul's theology being of this character, it is no wonder that it was not at once completed. His doctrine always followed the course of his religious experience; and never once outran it. Originated in the sphere of personal life, it advanced by a process of generalization to the spheres of social life and history; until, striving continually after unity and ultimate principles, it finally attained its full expansion in the sphere of metaphysics. It is through this upward progress and constant enlargement that we must comprehend it. We shall thus follow the actual course that its history has marked out for us.

The three different zones traversed by Paul's thought, correspond in fact to the three great periods of his life. The first was that of personal faith and confession; here the subjective aspect predominated in his theology. The conflicts of the second stage compelled the apostle to bring himself into harmony with the past, and thus led him to the historical standpoint which prevails in the major epistles. Paul now came to survey the whole destiny of humanity, from the first to the second Adam, and from Christ to the end of time. Finally, in his later letters, his mind passes the bounds which separate history from metaphysics; he endeavours to find in God Himself the first and final cause, the beginning and the end of the great drama enacted through the course of time.

We must not make a forced separation between these three parts of Paul's system, and the three periods of his life. Their logical connexion is very close. The apostle's historical views arise from his anthropology, his speculative ideas from his scheme of history; and all these developments were alike contained in his early faith, just as the plant lies hid in the germ which produces it.

Involved at the outset in the violent antithesis of

the law and faith, Paul's doctrine in its development instinctively tended to rise above it. In the end it succeeded. It is in the psychological sphere, in fact, that we find the fundamental opposition between works and grace, flesh and spirit, bondage and liberty, most strongly marked. In the sphere of social life and history, the antithesis assumes a wider and different character; it reappears in the contrast between the old and new Covenants, between Adam and Christ, between the period of tutelage and of independence. But as early as the epistle to the Romans, this opposition has diminished; Judaism and Paganism become subordinate to the Gospel; and the antithesis gives way to the higher conception of an evolution in the Divine plan. Finally, in the sphere of metaphysics, all dualism terminates. In the supreme conception of God, all contradictions are reconciled and all differences disappear. The final word of the Pauline theology is this: *God is all in all.*

Thus Paul's doctrine originated and grew up, like a magnificent tree, rooted deeply in the soil of the Christian consciousness and towering to the heavens.

SYNOPTICAL TABLE OF THE PAULINE SYSTEM.

Generative principle.—The Person of Christ, the principle of the Christian consciousness.

I.

THE CHRISTIAN PRINCIPLE IN THE SPHERE OF PSYCHOLOGY.

Anthropology.

1. Impossibility of attaining justification by the

law.—ἁμαρτία, σάρξ.—ὁ νόμος, ὁ θάνατος.—*Negative development.*

2. Justification by faith.—ἡ δικαιοσύνη Θεοῦ.—ὁ λόγος τοῦ σταυροῦ.—ἡ πίστις.—ἡ ζωή.—*Positive development.*

II.

THE CHRISTIAN PRINCIPLE IN THE SPHERE OF SOCIAL LIFE AND HISTORY.

Religious Philosophy of History.

1. Christ and the Church,—σῶμα Χριστοῦ.
2. The old and the new Covenant: ἡ ἐπαγγελία, ὁ νόμος, ἡ πίστις.
3. Adam and Christ; or, the ages of humanity.
4. Eschatology,—τὸ τέλος.
5. Faith, hope, love.

III.

THE CHRISTIAN PRINCIPLE IN THE SPHERE OF METAPHYSICS.

Theology.

1. Grace and Predestination: ἡ χάρις, ἡ πρόθεσις τοῦ Θεοῦ.
2. Christology,—ὁ Χριστός.
3. The Father, the Lord, the Holy Spirit: ὁ Πατήρ, ὁ Κύριος, τὸ ἅγιον Πνεῦμα.
4. The conception of God: Θεὸς τὰ πάντα ἐν πᾶσιν.

CHAPTER I.

THE PERSON OF CHRIST, THE PRINCIPLE OF THE CHRISTIAN CONSCIOUSNESS.

IN Paul's view, the only principle of the Christian consciousness is the Person of Jesus Christ, which characterizes, defines, and constitutes it. It is important to state clearly the intimate and peculiar relation existing between the apostle's regenerate consciousness and the actual Person of Jesus.

Paul was never a disciple of the crucified One, in the sense in which he was formerly a disciple of Gamaliel. It was not his business to be eternally repeating the Master's words, or even commenting on them as the rabbi explained or recited the precepts of the law. To Paul, this reproduction of a traditional text, this knowledge learned by rote, could only have been a dead and death-giving letter (διακονία γράμματος, διακονία θανάτου ἐν γράμματι, 2 Cor. iii. 6, 7). He never regarded Jesus in the light of a Teacher of wisdom, whose smallest words one must be careful to treasure up. In an external tradition of this kind he would have only seen a carnal and unfruitful knowledge.

Beyond this inferior stage, this wisdom of the schools, there is a deeper and more vital method of learning. It lies in the disciple's devoted effort to assimilate his master's method and spirit, and to reproduce them in his own life and thought. Thus Plato, taking his inspiration from Socrates, continued and completed the Socratic philosophy. The master in this case is not merely an initiator, he is still more an ideal which men contemplate and strive to reproduce. Undoubtedly Paul contemplated and admired in this fashion that ideal life of Jesus, in which he delighted to perceive and display the perfect standard of man's spiritual development ($\mu\acute{\epsilon}\tau\rho o\nu$ $\dot{\eta}\lambda\iota\kappa\acute{\iota}as$, Eph. iv. 13). With his attention concentrated on this Divine type, he endeavoured to realize it more and more fully in himself.

And yet this relationship, intimate as it was, does not fully explain the new consciousness of the apostle. To him Christ was more than a great ideal. Expressions like the following, which occur so often in Paul's writings—*Christ is my life*: *As for myself, I live no longer; it is Christ who lives in me*—evidently go further, and reveal a unique and peculiar relation between his consciousness and the Person of Jesus, such as could not possibly exist between one man and another.

In every man, however great he may be, there is, in truth, a material element which cannot and ought not to enter into ourselves, an element which the mind cannot *assimilate*. The most enthusiastic and faithful disciple has always to make a distinction between the mind of his master and its outward form, the husk that contains and limits it. In other words, there is in every human personality a negative element, a residuum which our admiration sets aside and ignores. This limitation separates and always will separate the adherence of the disciple from the faith of the believer; it distinguishes enthusiasm from adoration. There is but one Being in whom God is all, and who can become all in us. Because Jesus was able to say, "He that hath seen Me hath seen the Father," therefore He could give His own Person as the object of the soul's faith and love, as its veritable sustenance. His personality is so perfectly holy, so entirely spiritual, that in accepting it we receive it as a whole, without making any distinction or division. Jesus was, like no other, *the spiritual Man.* As a quickening spirit ($\pi\nu\epsilon\hat{v}\mu\alpha$ $\zeta\omega$-$\pi o\iota o\hat{v}\nu$, 1 Cor. xv. 45), He becomes a principle of life for other spirits. Paul even goes further: he declares that the Lord is actually *the Spirit* (2 Cor. iii. 17). Hence His office, and His power. That which is merely metaphor, when we speak of a philosopher as living again in his disciples, is a spiritual reality when applied to Jesus in relation to Christians. Christ was not only the Founder of the Church; He is still its principle of life, the inner soul which causes its constant growth and makes its death impossible.

Paul, then, was not merely the disciple or the imitator of Jesus. Nor did he regard himself as a new incarnation of the same spirit, which would imply that the first had only a relative and temporary value. He became a *member* of Christ; he was possessed by Him. He had the invincible assurance that Christ was not only the cause, but the ever active Creator of his spiritual life and thought. No one must represent Paul as having a religious genius of the nature of that possessed by Jesus of Nazareth! Jesus is the Master; Paul is the *slave*. This daring genius bears the yoke; and the independence of which he boasts, and which has sometimes been so much misunderstood, is in reality nothing but an *absolute* dependence upon Christ. His freedom sprang from his faith, and would have disappeared with it. In short, that which Jehovah was to the consciousness of the Old Testament prophets, Jesus became to the consciousness of His apostle. He speaks in the name of Jesus, as they spoke in the name of the LORD.

But the Lord being actually the Spirit, His entrance into our hearts is at the same time the outpouring of the Holy Spirit within us. Accordingly, Paul distinctly calls this Spirit the *Spirit of Christ.* The Spirit thenceforward forms the new *essence* of the regenerate consciousness. By virtue of it we are transformed and become, like Jesus Christ, *spiritual men*, πνευματικοί. This constant renewal is a *spiritualization*, a permanent glorification of our whole being, physical and moral at once. We put off the bonds of the flesh and rise to liberty, to perfect and eternal communion with God. Christianity being a religion of the Spirit, thus becomes the absolute religion. It completely realizes the highest aspiration of every religious consciousness,—union with God. In it all barriers are overthrown, and the final veil rent asunder. We may now at last behold God face to face.

CHAPTER II.

THE CHRISTIAN PRINCIPLE IN THE SPHERE OF PSYCHOLOGY (ANTHROPOLOGY).

THE prime necessity of Paul's consciousness was righteousness. This idea of *righteousness*, derived by him from the Old Testament, linked together the two periods of his life, the Jewish and the Christian. It sways the whole of his teaching, as it engrossed his whole existence.

Righteousness is the expression of the normal relation between the will of man and the will of God. It is the supreme end of every human life. In that alone can we find rest and happiness. But as soon as man attempts to realize it, he immediately finds a contrary principle rising up within him—viz. *sin*, which is the very negation of righteousness. From the conflict between these two opposing principles the entire Pauline theology was engendered.

Just as Paul's life was divided by his conversion into two parts, one of which was the radical negation of the other, so also his Christian belief was formulated in a sweeping antithesis: justification impossible under the law; justification obtained by faith. The apostle always developed its two terms on parallel lines, because each is defined and explained by the other. As Baur justly perceived, this opposition is the double aspect of one and the same theory, which is completely summed up in these two contradictory propositions:

I. ἐξ ἔργων νόμου οὐ δικαιωθήσεται πᾶσα σὰρξ ἐνώπιον Θεοῦ (Rom. iii. 20).

II. ὁ ἄνθρωπος δικαιοῦται πίστει (Rom. iii. 28).

I. LEGAL JUSTIFICATION IMPOSSIBLE.

Man will never be justified before God by the works of the Law.—In the first three chapters of his letter to the Romans Paul establishes this first thesis, by means of the testimony of moral and religious experience. The fact of sin, denounced by the individual conscience, was indeed the starting point of his religious thought. But it does not stop at this first stage. In that which every one experiences in his own life, the apostle recognises and points out a general and universal law of the history of humanity. All men without distinction, both Jews and Gentiles, are the slaves of sin. A fact so general must have its explanation in human nature. Sin is universal, —because it is inevitable. The apostle, by a very obvious dialectical course, advances from the universality of sin to the idea of its moral necessity. This admirable demonstration of his first thesis brings us to the heart of the Pauline anthropology. In its final analysis, it is based upon the ideas of *sin*, of *the flesh*, and of *the law*, which we must endeavour to define.

1. Ἁμαρτία, σάρξ. *Sin, and the Flesh.*

An insurmountable obstacle rises up between man and righteousness; it is sin. In Paul's phraseology, this word not only designates a particular sinful action, but a principle immanent in human nature, of which individual sins are simply the external manifestation (Rom. vii. 8). This principle is not a pure abstraction, but an objective and positive power (δύναμις), governing humanity and enslaving the individual will. Nowhere is this objective character of the power of sin more strikingly exhibited than in Romans v. 12. Paul there depicts it as a new force entering into the development of the world, and constituting the whole human race sinners. He expressly says that it brings death upon all men, both upon those who, like Adam, transgressed a positive law, and on those who lived without it, like the generations between Adam and Moses. The words ἐφ' ᾧ πάντες ἥμαρτον, which are employed to justify the universality of death, do not indicate a subjective and active guilt in the individual, but an objective and passive state of sin. Sin having come into the world by the transgression of one man, entered (εἰσῆλθεν) like leaven into the general life of humanity and extended its power to every individual (εἰς πάντας διῆλθεν), constituting men sinners by nature, even before the manifestation of their individual will. This power takes growing possession of the world and of humanity, permeating and transforming them till they become instruments, or rather *incarnations* of sin.

How does this development of evil accomplish itself and reach its climax? We cannot answer this question, nor advance further, without explaining the relation of this power of sin to that which Paul calls the *flesh*. This is the most delicate and difficult point to elucidate in his whole system.

Paul's doctrine is equally remote from the Gnostic dualism and from Pelagianism.

The apostle expressly says that the flesh is the seat of sin (οἰκοῦσα ἐν ἐμοί . . . τοῦτ' ἔστιν ἐν τῇ σαρκί μου, Rom. vii. 17, 18; comp. ver. 23). Did he see in the flesh the essential principle of sin, and was his theory, after all, based on a metaphysical dualism? Did he on this point depart from Hebrew tradition and Jewish modes of thought, which excluded all dualism, and adopt in preference the ancient conception of heathen philosophy? M. Holsten has vigorously advanced this view, and has perseveringly ransacked the Pauline theology for evidence of this pretended dualism. Hardly anywhere, to our thinking, has he grasped more than a fleeting shadow. The relation of sin to the flesh is not purely *immanent*, but also *transcendent*. It is not that the physical law of the flesh constitutes sin; but on the contrary, the law of sin has become, and continues to be, the law of the flesh. From the time that it was subjugated by the power of evil, the flesh became *weak*, subjected to *vanity* and the *bondage of corruption* (ματαιότητι, τῇ δουλείᾳ τῆς φθορᾶς, chap. viii. 20, 21). In other words, the relation of sin to the flesh is, in Paul's view, identical with that which the Πνεῦμα (the Divine Spirit) sustains to the soul of the believer. In both cases there is an actual immanence, but an immanence which presupposes an objective transcendence. This transcendence of the power of sin is strikingly prominent in the passage we have just analysed (Rom. v. 12). Sin entered the world not at the time of man's creation, but through the transgression (παράπτωμα) of the first Adam. So, too, in attributing to Christ a flesh like ours, the apostle does not mean to attribute sin to Him, and most jealously maintains His absolute purity (2 Cor. v. 21). In the third place, how could he, from the dualistic point of view, speak of a *redemption of the body*, and represent this as the final accomplishment of salvation (Rom. viii. 23)? Our salvation, in that case, would have been complete as soon as our souls were freed from material bonds.[1]

To escape this dualism, we need not, on the other

---

[1] Paul nowhere expressly speaks of the origin of evil; perhaps he never even considered this metaphysical question. If his ideas about sin are logically worked out, we find that they divide and flow in two opposing currents. At first sight, there s the traditional theological explanation of evil as a metaphysical and transcendent force introduced into the world by the Devil-serpent (Rom. v. 12; comp. 2 Cor. xi. 3). This is the opinion which Paul received from the schools, and which he did not reject. But his own reflection and psychological analysis took another direction. According to Rom. vii. 7-21 and 1 Cor. xv. 46 man appears at the first as *psychical*,—or carnal; from this inferior condition the spiritual man has to be developed. The transition is effected by the revelation of the law, which comes to disturb the unity and peace of man in his childish, animal condition, bringing division and inward conflict. Without the law, sin was dead. It came into life and existence through the law; so that the latter inevitably led to the fall. In the first moral action, therefore, there are two things: the appearance of *the law*, which implies an advance, for the law is holy, just, and good; and of *transgression*, which is a fall. But the two elements are inseparable. The latter theory is the only one which accords with the logical organization of Paul's system.

[The author resumes this question in his essay entitled *L'origine du péché dans le système théologique de Paul* (Paris, 1887). He here develops with brilliant logic the "psychological" solution of this problem; and boldly subordinates the interpretation of Rom. v. 12-14 to that of vii. 7-21, seeing in Paul's inner conflict a rehearsal and a mirror of that which took place in Adam. But this explanation ignores the factor of *heredity*; and here, it seems to us, lies its fatal defect. Paul is not where Adam was; for he is a *son of Adam*.]

hand, like some expositors, go the length of making Paul's doctrine meaningless and robbing it of originality, by separating sin and the flesh to such an extent that it becomes impossible to understand why the apostle always associates them so closely. True, the word σὰρξ is sometimes applied to the whole man; but even then it does not entirely lose its original meaning; the fundamental idea is still that of the material organization. The term *flesh* when applied to human nature in general, designates it in so far as it is governed by the laws of material existence. Hence the apostle speaks of the *mind*, *will* and even *spirit* of the flesh (φρόνημα τῆς σαρκός, Rom. viii. 6; θέλημα τῆς σαρκός, Eph. ii. 3; νοῦς τῆς σαρκός, Col. ii. 18). The flesh already governed by sin, in its turn gives the mind, the will, and the entire nature of man its bias towards sin. To persist in considering the subjective determination of the individual will as the origin of sin would prevent our having the least understanding of Paul's doctrine. Sin within us is pre-existent to the will. It has its seat in our material organization; and as this organization takes the lead in our development, sin grows with it, and takes possession of us even before we acquire self-consciousness.

How did our flesh become sinful? This Paul never explains. He contents himself with establishing the fact that man's physical organization and his spiritual nature are in conflict, and that in this conflict the spirit has been vanquished and swallowed up in the flesh. The spirit should have glorified and spiritualized the body; but the body has humiliated and materialized the spirit. The man has become *carnal*; and in this fact the triumph of sin consists. It has so possessed itself of the flesh, as to become incarnate there. Through this instrument it now reigns, and holds all men captive (Rom. vi. 19). Thus there is a radical dualism between the flesh and the spirit asserted in Paul's doctrine; but it does not possess the metaphysical character M. Holsten imputes to it. Though reaching beyond the moral sphere, the dualism established by the apostle is nevertheless essentially ethical; and this gives it its tragical and distressing character. The spirit, which is still the organ of the mind, and the flesh now become the instrument of sin (σὰρξ ἁμαρτίας, σῶμα τῆς ἁμαρτίας, Rom. viii. 3; vi. 6), are constantly brought into collision by their conflicting desires (ταῦτα δὲ ἀλλήλοις ἀντίκειται, Gal. v. 17). This contest can only be ended by the utter annihilation of the flesh. Sin must be destroyed in it and with it (Rom. vi. 10; viii. 13; 1 Cor. xv. 50).

We may now gain some idea of man's real state. He is no longer free; he is *sold* to sin (ἐγὼ δὲ σαρκινὸς, πεπραμένος ὑπὸ τὴν ἁμαρτίαν, Rom. vii. 14). Nevertheless, he is not altogether evil; he still makes a distinction in himself, the distinction between his real nature and the power of evil which prevails over him. There is in him what Paul calls *the inward man* (chap. vii. 22), which delights in the law of God. He continues to possess the νοῦς, which desires and perceives the good. But this knowledge is only theoretical, having no decisive influence on the will; it is an empty form without spiritual power, wanting the πνεῦμα which alone can give it efficacy.[1] Man thence-

---

[1] Setting aside the ψυχὴ, elsewhere included in the flesh, of which indeed it is the vital principle (ψυχικός = σαρκινός, 1 Cor. ii. 14; iii. 1), we may say that the Pauline psychology distinguishes

forward feels himself divided between the impotent wish to do good and the irresistible impulses of the flesh. In this unhappy condition his life is protracted for a brief space, only to be extinguished in the end; for the power of sin is essentially destructive. It has stirred up the flesh against the spirit, to destroy the spiritual life. But the flesh, in its turn, when separated from the spirit, finds the vital force departing by which it had been sustained; it grows weak; it is doomed to corruption. A struggle breaks out between its various inclinations; and its life becomes simply a rapid progress towards death. Thus Paul calls the flesh when sold to sin *a body of death*, or *the body of this death* (τὸ σῶμα τοῦ θανάτου τούτου, Rom. vii. 24).

Such is the development of human life towards

---

in man four elements: σῶμα, σάρξ, νοῦς, πνεῦμα. Two of them fall under the general category of *substance*,—σάρξ, πνεῦμα: the first being the substance of the body, the other the substance of his inner being. The two others fall under the general category of *form*: the σῶμα is the individual form of the σάρξ; the νοῦς is the human form of the πνεῦμα. That which constitutes the weakness of man's spiritual nature is his loss of the substantial force of the πνεῦμα. This spiritual force has been replaced in the νοῦς by that of the σάρξ. The νοῦς has thus become a νοῦς σαρκός, its thought a φρόνημα τῆς σαρκός, and its will a θέλημα τῆς σαρκός. Hence, in the Pauline theology, man's redemption is of necessity a *new spiritual creation*. To the question, Does Paul recognise the existence of πνεῦμα in the natural man? we must therefore reply in the negative. In every passage where he speaks of the πνεῦμα of the sinful man, this word no longer has the specific meaning that we have just defined, but the general sense of our word *mind*. Finally, that which Paul calls the heart (καρδία), is not the region of feeling alone; it is the centre where all the elements constituting human nature are blended into one organic whole.

death, which the apostle constantly sets forth as carried on organically through the working of sin. But at this point a new power intervenes to accelerate this fatal issue and render it yet more tragic. This power is *the law*.

2. Ὁ νόμος. *The Law.*

The law, being the perfect expression of the will of God, is holy, just, and good (Rom. vii. 12). The cause of its want of power does not lie in itself, but entirely in the flesh (Rom. viii. 3). The law is spiritual—man is carnal; and hence a mutual and irreconcilable contradiction (ὁ νόμος πνευματικὸς—ἐγὼ δὲ σαρκινός, Rom. vii. 14).

God did not give the law, therefore, to bring about the justification of sinners. In order to be saved, man must be restored to life; but it is not within the power of a law to give him life (εἰ γὰρ ἐδόθη νόμος ὁ δυνάμενος ζωοποιῆσαι, ὄντως ἐκ νόμου ἂν ἦν ἡ δικαιοσύνη, Gal. iii. 21). The law shows man what righteousness is, but does not impart it to him: it is unattainable by the flesh. For it was promulgated not to effect righteousness, but to realize and multiply sin (Rom. v. 20; vii. 7-11; Gal. iii. 19).

In truth, sin, before it can be pardoned and destroyed, must realize all its *potentialities* and attain its complete development. The very function of the law is to bring sin to this full maturity. The law, in this sense, is actually the power of sin (ἡ δύναμις τῆς ἁμαρτίας ὁ νόμος, 1 Cor. xv. 56). It is that which gives to it subjective reality,—which, in short, makes sin *sinful*. It pushes sin onward from its virtual condition to that of positive transgression (Rom. vii. 8, 9; iv. 15).

With no less penetration than vigour, Paul describes this inevitable development of sin under the irresistible impulse of the law. We do not know sin except by the law (τὴν ἁμαρτίαν οὐκ ἔγνων, εἰ μὴ διὰ νόμου, Rom. vii. 7). Setting itself up before me as the sovereign rule of my actions, the law at the same time makes me conscious of their moral imperfection. It is the law, for instance, which reveals to me the sin of covetousness by saying to me: Thou shalt not covet. (Διὰ νόμου ἐπίγνωσις ἁμαρτίας, Rom. iii. 20.) It does still more. Previously to the coming of the law, sin indeed was within me; but I had not the slightest consciousness of it; it was there as a latent, unawakened force,—as Paul puts it, it was dead (ἁμαρτία νεκρά, chap. vii. 8). The law awakens and re-animates it. Without law, there is no transgression. More than this, not only does transgression become possible under the commandment; but the prohibition inevitably gives birth in me to the desire for the thing forbidden (Rom. vii. 11). *Nitimur in vetitum semper.* Thus sin becomes transgression, and brings itself under the curse. The law passes the sentence of death against me; instead of giving me life, it slays me. Such is the revolution inevitably effected by it in my nature. Formerly, without the law, I was alive. My life flourished unimpeded; nothing disturbed its unity. Now the law has come; sin has revived in me; and I myself am dead!

The consciousness of sin, the realization of sin through transgression, the sentence of death passed upon the sinner,—these are the three stages of the development of evil brought about by the law. But this penalty of death, the wages of sin, is not only passed by the law against the sinner from without, in the form of a judicial sentence; it is also realized within, exciting in human nature that unhappy conflict between the law of the members and the law of the understanding, in which the life of the individual is consumed. The apostle, at the close of the seventh chapter of Romans, sets before us this inward struggle and progress towards dissolution, which inevitably terminates in death. The holier the law and the more clearly it shows me what I ought to be, so much the more does it overwhelm me with the sense of what I am. The spiritual height of the command only helps me the better to measure the depth of my corruption. Between what I desire and what I can do, between my understanding which apprehends the good, and my flesh which realizes the evil, between my aspirations and my tendencies, there is an ever-widening contrast. It seems as though I were only engaged in my own destruction, desiring good but practising evil, and condemning myself for doing so. It is an intestine war, in which my understanding attacks and scorns my flesh, and my flesh revenges itself by crushing the vain desires of my understanding. I no longer know what I am about; for I fail to do what I would, and I do just that which I hate. In vain do I strive to put an end to the conflict; in vain do I redouble my efforts to observe the law and overcome the flesh. In this struggle, in which I am my own adversary, I am invariably defeated. I shall never escape from it, till I am dead. My life cannot last in this agony; I sink in that despair which is the beginning and the foretaste of death!

Paul brings the demonstration of his first thesis to a close with an energy that is truly terrible. Not only does man fail to obtain justification by means of the law, but it logically conducts him to a diametrically opposite result. The law is holy and spiritual, it is true; but as man can only fulfil it by means of the flesh, it comes to pass that the works of the law (ἔργα νόμου) are, in reality, mere works of the flesh (ἔργα σαρκός). It is useless to multiply these external works; he only multiplies the causes of his condemnation and aggravates his guilt. We see that the abyss is really bottomless; and every effort which the man makes to extricate himself, only plunges him further in its depths. But at the very point where he despairs of himself, the grace of God takes hold of him and saves him.

II. Man Justified by Faith in Christ.

This development of the power of sin, under the impetus given by the law, is met in the apostle's doctrine by a corresponding development of holiness, the essential principle of which is God's *righteousness*; its means, *faith* in Jesus Christ—its end, *life*.

What Paul intended by his use of the expression δικαιοσύνη Θεοῦ has not always been fully apprehended. This genitive case has often been considered equivalent to ἐνώπιον Θεοῦ, and has been translated the righteousness *that avails before God* (Rom. iii. 20). Righteousness, it is said, was the end in view; and Paul only wished to ascertain whether it could be obtained by the law or by faith. On that view, the passage would express a general notion, resolved into two subordinate ideas—negative and positive respectively; and the Pauline theory might be interpreted thus:

ἡ δικαιοσύνη τοῦ Θεοῦ.

ἡ ἐκ νόμου δικαιοσύνη.   ἡ ἐκ πίστεως δικαιοσύνη.[1]

There is, however, a grave error here, which touches the very essence of the apostle's doctrine, and misrepresents it from the outset. In every passage where this expression recurs, the δικαιοσύνη Θεοῦ is directly opposed to justification by the law, as an absolutely contrary idea; it is represented as being itself the source of justification by faith (Rom. i. 17; iii. 21). If the righteousness obtained by faith is in opposition to justification by the fulfilment of the law, the δικαιοσύνη Θεοῦ must be opposed to the ἰδία δικαιοσύνη (Rom. x. 3). Instead of the foregoing triad, we have a double antithesis:

ἡ ἰδία δικαιοσύνη—ἡ δικαιοσύνη τοῦ Θεοῦ :
ἡ ἐκ νόμου δικαιοσύνη—ἡ ἐκ πίστεως δικαιοσύνη.

The δικαιοσύνη Θεοῦ is the righteousness of which God is the Author, and which He gives freely, in contrast to the righteousness which man seeks by his own efforts (ἰδία δικαιοσύνη). This righteousness exists already in God as an attribute and active force; it is transferred to man, and realized in him by the action of Divine grace (δικαιούμενοι δωρεὰν τῇ αὐτοῦ χάριτι, Rom. iii. 24). Paul himself has explained his doctrine very fully in Romans iii. 25, 26. In this latter passage the words πρὸς τὴν ἔνδειξιν τῆς δικαιοσύνης αὐτοῦ are fully defined by those that follow: εἰς τὸ εἶναι αὐτὸν δίκαιον, καὶ δικαιοῦντα τὸν ἐκ πίστεως. Thus δικαιοσύνη Θεοῦ = Θεὸς δίκαιος καὶ δικαιῶν. The idea is that of a positive righteousness immanent in

---

[1] See Baur, *Paulus*, vol. ii., p. 147 [Eng. trans., ii., 136]. He seems to have abandoned this view in his *Neutestamentliche Theologie* (1864), p. 134.

God, and manifesting itself outwardly in the sinner's justification. This conception is surprising to us, accustomed as we are, by our very use of language, to give the word righteousness a merely negative meaning. We are so thoroughly prepossessed with this judicial and inferior notion, that it is difficult for us to rise to this far higher and finer idea of a righteousness which is imparted, and which tends everywhere to substitute good for evil and life for death. No contradiction must be asserted, therefore, between the *righteousness of God*, in the apostle's sense of this word, and the grace of God. While the word χάρις indicates the act of love by which God saves man, the phrase δικαιοσύνη Θεοῦ simply defines the nature and moral quality of this Divine act.

The δικαιοσύνη Θεοῦ, thus understood, is more than a simple acquittal of the guilty; it is an actual power (δύναμις Θεοῦ), which enters into the world and is organically developed there,—like the power of sin, but in opposition to it. We have observed how the latter passed from its virtual (ἁμαρτία) to its actual state, and became realized in transgression (παράβασις), thus arriving at its final condition of παράπτωμα. The *righteousness of God* follows a dialectical course exactly parallel to this. The δικαιοσύνη Θεοῦ, itself a transcendent principle, finds expression in the δικαίωσις, the act of justification; and reaches its end in the δικαίωμα, which is righteousness realized. The first process results of necessity in death; the latter, with equal necessity, results in life. In each case there is a similar logical *processus*, accomplished both in the individual life and in history.

We can at once perceive how far removed was Paul's real belief from the theory of *forensic justi-*

fication elaborated by the scholasticism of the Middle Ages. According to this theory, the act of justification is a mere *verdict of nonsuit (ordonnance de non-lieu)* on the part of God,—a sentence alike inadequate and arbitrary. The whole case is reduced to that of an old *debt* paid to God by Jesus. On this assumption there ceases to be any organic connexion between justification and regeneration; at the most, there remains, as a mere external bond, the sentiment of gratitude due from the man who is set free to his liberator. Not only is the nerve of the apostle's reasoning thus destroyed, but we cannot, on this conception of the matter, even prove sufficiently the duty of gratitude.

Is it not obvious, indeed, that to insist on the necessity of this one duty is to return in the end, by a circuitous route, to the very principle to be avoided, *viz.* that of justification by works; and that this theory leaves us with an irreducible dualism set up in our soteriology?

Paul would not have found words severe enough to stigmatize such a flagrant misinterpretation of his doctrine. True, he has said that God in His mercy declares justification and deliverance for the sinner; but he does not know—and had he known, would never have admitted—that subtle distinction between *declaring righteous* and *making righteous, justum dicere* and *justum facere*, which has been the object of so much dispute. To him, the word of God is always *creative* and full of power; it always produces an actual effect. In declaring a man justified, therefore, it actually and directly creates within him a new beginning of righteousness. The δικαιοσύνη Θεοῦ from that moment enters as an active force into the heart and life of the believer, and there becomes the fruitful source of a permanent sanctification. Regeneration is simply the consequence of justification; and works are but the outcome of faith.

Such is the profound unity and organic sequence of the Pauline doctrine. We shall now endeavour to reproduce it by indicating its essential features.

3. Ὁ λόγος τοῦ σταυροῦ. *The Cross.*

In the death of Jesus the righteousness of God in its active force was historically realized and revealed to all men (πεφανέρωται). It there appears as a positive act of justification (δικαίωσις), seeking to realize itself finally through faith in the soul of the believer, where it becomes an actual state of righteousness (δικαίωμα, Rom. iii. 24; iv. 25; viii. 4).

Thus the death of Jesus comes to be the centre of the whole Pauline system. The apostle's Christianity is summed up in the Person of Christ; but this Person itself only acquires its proper redemptive significance when He dies on the cross. Hence we can quite understand the apostle's declaration that he wishes to know nothing but *Christ* and *Christ crucified* (1 Cor. ii. 2). With the death of Jesus, however, is necessarily associated the fact of His resurrection. Not only are these two logically connected in Paul's doctrine, but we might even consider them as one and the same act, since they set forth the two successive and essential stages of justification. With the first Paul connects the entire negative aspect of redemption—deliverance from *guilt*, and the destruction of the power of sin; to the second he refers its whole positive aspect—justification, and the creation of spiritual life (Rom. iv. 25; vi. 1-11).

The ecclesiastical theory of expiation, so far from interpreting the apostle's doctrine aright, amounts to its formal contradiction.[1] The idea of an external *satisfaction*, given to God in order to wrest the pardon of sinners from Him, is foreign to all the epistles. Paul nowhere says that God needed to be appeased. He starts from the contrary point of view. The pardon of sin is ever the spontaneous act of God's love. It is His sovereign and absolute grace which took, and still maintains the initiative in the work of redemption. The sacrifice of Christ, so far from being the cause of this love, is its effect. It was not accomplished outside the sphere of grace—outside, as one might say, of God Himself—in order to influence the Divine will; but *God Himself was in Christ, reconciling the world to Himself by Him* (2 Cor. v. 19).

As Paul does not admit the traditional dualism in God between love and righteousness, so neither does he make any separation between the forgiveness of sins and the destruction of sin itself. The idea of an external expiation was not enough for him. The standard passages upon which it has been founded (Rom. iii. 25 ; Gal. iii. 13) are far from giving us his whole teaching on the subject ; nor have they in the Pauline theory the capital importance attributed to them by scholastic theology. If we have any regard for the logical unity of the Pauline doctrine, we must

---

[[1] M. Sabatier is scarcely fair to the "ecclesiastical theory," which originated in a profound, though possibly one-sided, sense of the *guilt* of sin and the *anger* which it has provoked in the holy nature of God. On his side, such texts as Rom. i. 18 (in connexion with vers. 16, 17); v. 10; Gal. iii. 13, demand further elucidation. See Dorner's *System of Christian Doctrine*, vol. iii., pp. 120-132 ; iv., 99-107, 201.]

expound these texts in harmony with Romans vi. 1-11; viii. 3; and 2 Corinthians v. 21. Only by the aid of these latter passages can we gain an adequate view of the apostle's entire doctrine of Redemption. Now, these texts make the practical effect of the death of Jesus to consist not in the satisfaction which it rendered to God, but in the destruction of sin that it accomplished.

The more foreign is the idea of satisfaction to Pauline soteriology, the more essential, on the contrary, seems to be that of *substitution* (2 Cor. v. 14-16). The apostle's whole theory rests, in its final analysis, upon a mystical identification of Jesus with believers: Jesus becomes all that we were; and we, on our part, become all that Christ was. He is *sin* in us; we are *righteousness* in Him (τὸν μὴ γνόντα ἁμαρτίαν . . . ἁμαρτίαν ἐποίησεν, ἵνα ἡμεῖς γενώμεθα δικαιοσύνη Θεοῦ ἐν αὐτῷ, 2 Cor. v. 21). He made Himself poor with all our poverty, in order to enrich us with His whole wealth (2 Cor. viii. 9). Jesus, it seems, could not save humanity while apart from it. To realize in it the righteousness of God and begin for it a new organic development, He must of necessity appear within it as one of its members. Thus the entire burden of the work of redemption rests upon Christ's humanity,—not, as in Anselm's theory, upon His Divinity (δι' ἀνθρώπου, τοῦ ἑνὸς ἀνθρώπου Ἰησοῦ Χριστοῦ, 1 Cor. xv. 21; comp. xv. 45, and Rom. v. 15). Not only must the Redeemer belong to humanity, but He must subject Himself to all the powers which control it, to the objective power of sin, of the law and of death, that He may really vanquish them. In other words, summing up in Himself all humanity, He must allow the fatal issue of the life of sin already described to reproduce itself,—and as it were, to spend itself upon His person.

So it was with Jesus. When the time was fulfilled the Son of God appeared in the world as a mere man. He was born of a woman, and lived under the law (Gal. iv. 4); He died to redeem us from sin, to free us from the law and rescue us from death. Sin is destroyed in the death of Jesus, not only because it is openly condemned and actually punished, but also because it has at last produced its worst result. In attaining its full development, it exhausts and destroys itself. A new development may then begin. Thus Jesus only properly expiates sin by bringing it to its issue. His death is the consummation of the first period of the life of humanity; it terminates the life of the flesh.

We must note, further, the precise link by which this wonderful theory of redemption is connected with that which Paul has said concerning the flesh in its relation to sin. The power of evil which it was Christ's mission to destroy had taken possession of the flesh and even, as we said, become incarnate there. Sin, therefore, could not be absolutely conquered except by the destruction of the flesh. Hence that theological axiom on which the whole theory of the apostle rests: *He that is dead is freed from sin* (ὁ γὰρ ἀποθανὼν δεδικαίωται ἀπὸ τῆς ἁμαρτίας, Rom. vi. 7). Paul makes strict application of this axiom to the death of Jesus. He brings the Redeemer as near to sinful and carnal humanity as it is possible to do, without compromising His holiness. Such is the imperative logic of his doctrine, that he does not shrink from that most startling expression, " God made Him to be *sin*, who knew no sin." At last, in Romans viii. 3, he plainly says: "God sent His Son in *flesh entirely resembling our sinful flesh*, and thus condemned sin *in the flesh.*" The flesh of Christ, no less than all the rest of His Person, has therefore a representative value; it represents, in very deed, the sinful flesh of humanity, the organ and seat of sin. In the death of Christ sin is condemned, the flesh is crucified and destroyed, and redemption is objectively accomplished.

4. Ἡ πίστις. *Faith.*

By love Christ accomplishes His identification with humanity; by faith man attains his identification with Christ. Through it we so thoroughly participate with Jesus and become so entirely one with Him, that His death becomes our death, and His resurrection our own resurrection. With Him we die to sin, to the law and the flesh; with Him we triumph over death, and are born again to new life (Rom. vi. 1–11). Faith carries on and repeats in each individual life the decisive crisis, the revolution that the death of Jesus wrought in history. It is the destruction of sin within us, the inward creation of the Divine life. The justification and regeneration of the individual are only the continuation of the original redemption, which was accomplished in the Head of humanity and is realized in turn by each of its members. Faith does not save us by its own virtue; in itself it is a mere vain and empty form; but we are saved by its Divine object— by the δικαιοσύνη Θεοῦ realized in Jesus Christ, which becomes thenceforward an immanent, living principle in us. Through faith we are not only pardoned and set free; we are at the same time regenerated, enfranchised, and, in a word, restored to life.

5. Ἡ ζωή. *Life.*

Life is the natural fruit of righteousness, just as death was the consequence and wages of sin (Rom. vi. 22, 23). Though the flesh, which has the principle of sin still within it, is doomed to death, the believer possesses in Christ's own Spirit (πνεῦμα ζωοποιοῦν) a principle of immortal life, which permeates, raises, and transforms his entire nature. Formerly there was conflict in the carnal man, a conflict ending in the growing triumph of sin, and in death; there is still a struggle in the regenerate man between the old principle which is dying out, and the new which is gaining strength; but this struggle now results in a victory of life over death, more and more perfect and glorious. All that is mortal within us will in the end be absorbed in life. Righteousness will restore everything that sin had destroyed.

Through faith the Christian possesses by anticipation all the riches of this new life. He really "lives by his faith." His inner life is one of perfect liberty. He is not without law; for Christ has become law immanent in him (ἔννομος Χριστοῦ, 1 Cor. ix. 21). But this law is simply a principle of love, enabling him to fulfil the will of God with joyous ease. The life of love is nothing but the outcome of faith (Gal. v. 6). Thus Paul's great doctrine, having been perfectly established in the realm of theory, wins a yet more splendid triumph in the sphere of practical life. No wonder that for the past eighteen centuries it has inspired the great thinkers of Christianity in the world of intellect, and in the moral world created its great heroes.

CHAPTER III

THE CHRISTIAN PRINCIPLE IN THE SPHERE OF SOCIETY AND HISTORY.

The Religious Philosophy of History.

I. THE PERSON OF CHRIST, THE VITAL PRINCIPLE OF THE CHURCH.

HITHERTO the Christian principle has been confined within the sphere of the individual life. But it tends by its very nature towards a universal realization. All that Christ is for one member of humanity, He is and must become for all; and the result of this new development of the Christian principle is *the Church*. The unity of the Church rests upon the sense, common to all its members, of a living communion with Christ.

To set forth this essential unity of the Church, Paul several times compares it to the organization of the human body (1 Cor. xii. 12, ff.; Rom. xii. 4): "As in *one* body we have *many* members, which have not all the same office, so we are all one body in Christ; and we are towards each other what the members of one body are among themselves." This body is called σῶμα Χριστοῦ (1 Cor. xii. 27)—that is, a body having the principle of its being and the basis of its life in Christ. Christ is not only its Head, but its very soul; He manifests in and through it all His hidden virtues (Eph. iv. 16; Col. ii. 19). Thus regarded, the Church becomes *the body of Christ* (τὸ σῶμα τοῦ Χριστοῦ); it serves as the external and visible manifestation, the material realization of all that Christ Himself is invisibly. Into this body Christ pours His plenitude of life, so that the Church, filled with the virtues of its Head, becomes in turn the πλήρωμα τοῦ Χριστοῦ (Eph. i. 23).

The Church can only realize the full virtue of its vital principle through a laborious process of evolution. But all development implies variety; and hence the apostle perceives and acknowledges in the Church diverse offices, gifts, and ministries (διαιρέσεις χαρισμάτων εἰσίν, 1 Cor. xii. 4). To each of these separate gifts he allows free and full development; and through them the wealth of life in the Church is manifested. But on the other hand, these different *charisms* proceed from one and the same Spirit (ἐνεργεῖ τὸ ἓν καὶ τὸ αὐτὸ Πνεῦμα); and with love as their common inspiration, all tend to the same goal, the perfecting of the whole body of the Church. So the unity of the Church is, in the first instance, broken up and expanded into a rich variety; but this, in its turn, is absorbed into the supreme unity. Such is the organic and harmonious development of the life of the Church.

From this conception of the Church is derived the Pauline idea of *baptism*, and of the *Lord's supper*, which centres in that of the substantial union of the Christian with Christ. Baptism, the symbol of faith, obtains its significance from faith itself; it becomes the symbol of our death and resurrection with Christ. In baptism we are buried with Jesus in His death, and rise again with Him that we may walk in

newness of life (Rom. vi. 3, 4). In like manner, the
Lord's supper expresses the mystical union of the
members of the Church with Christ and with one
another; they are *one loaf, one body* (1 Cor. x. 17).
By its means they appropriate and assimilate the life
of Christ, the substance of His spiritual being. So the
Church grows both without and within, both in extent
and in spiritual power; for it is not only the creation
of the Spirit of Christ, but, if we may so speak, His
enlarged existence and continued life.

II. THE OLD COVENANT AND THE NEW.

Ἡ ἐπαγγελία, ὁ νόμος, ἡ πίστις.

The strong antithesis between the law and faith
established in the preceding chapter, tends to find
its solution, so soon as Paul examines it from the
historical standpoint. The apostle, indeed, could not
assume an entirely negative position towards Judaism.
Not only did he believe in the revelation of God in
the Old Testament, but he further admitted the
Divine origin of the law itself. It was therefore inevitable that he should formulate the relationship of
the Old and New Covenant in their positive aspect.

Judaism, so regarded, was at once reduced from
its position as the supreme religion to that of a preparatory revelation. The old covenant between God
and His people was indeed a reality; but not being
an end in itself, it could not be final (2 Cor. iii. 7, 11).
It came in as an essential but transitional stage in
the progress of the Divine plan, designed to prepare
for that final manifestation of the righteousness of
God in Christ to which it bears witness (Rom. iii. 21).

This preparation has its positive side in the primordial gift of *the promise*, while it has another, essentially negative, in the intervention and operation of *the law*. Between faith and the promise there exists, indeed, a full resemblance and identity; for they have the same object, *viz.*, the grace of God. The promise is the anticipation of faith; and faith is the realization of the promise. Hence Paul's strong assertion that no other justification was at any time possible to man before God, except justification by faith,—that this was the primary and original idea of Divine revelation, distinctly antecedent to the institution of the law itself. This idea he readily discovers contained in the promise made to the patriarch. Abraham believed in God; and this faith was imputed to him for righteousness. The beginning of salvation by faith may therefore be traced back to him (Gal. iii. 7). It was to faith alone, and to faith without circumcision, that the promise was made (Rom. iv. 10). Hence the capital importance that belongs to the person of Abraham, according to Paul's view, in the order of Divine revelation. Abraham's experience marks the point where the promise enters into history—the juncture at which the justifying grace of God was for the first time declared to the world. So the name of the patriarch stands at the head of one of the great epochs of religious history. This promise is a veritable *testament*, which from the first has secured the right of believers to the paternal inheritance,—a testament that no subsequent event could either modify or set aside (Gal. iii. 15).

While the promise and faith are thus identical in their origin, the law on the contrary represents an external element, radically different from both. It intervenes between the two, in order to bring about the fulfilment of the promise; but it has no direct connexion with it. Its ministry represents a great parenthesis in history ($\pi\alpha\rho\epsilon\iota\sigma\tilde{\eta}\lambda\theta\epsilon\nu$). Coming 430 years afterwards, it is not the continuation of the promise; for in that case we should have to admit that God had modified His first intention. But the word of God cannot be annulled. The law, therefore, has an object quite distinct from the promise. Its mission solely consists in realizing and multiplying sin (Gal. iii. 19; Rom v. 20); and to this end it intervened between the promise and its fulfilment, and served as a middle term and mediator, linking together these two stages of history. In what did this temporary mediation consist? In the fact that it placed all men under sin and the curse, keeping them under this double yoke until the coming of Christ. The realization of grace, in fact, could not have taken place before sin had been realized; and it was in accomplishing this end that the law worked effectually to prepare for the advent of grace. Such was its office,—that of a *pedagogue*, and temporary *mediator*.

Though justification does not come through the law, and although the law produces a wholly opposite result, still, it is not contrary either to the promise or to faith; it has, to be sure, its place and part in the Divine plan; it represents a stage of condemnation interposed between promise and faith, through which man has to pass before he attains the full consciousness of his reconciliation with God. Thus, at the close of the discussion, the apostle's doctrine recovers its unity of thought, for a time impaired; and the *rôle* of the Law is defined, alike in its essential difference from the Gospel, and in its historical relation to it.

The promise, the law, faith—Abraham, Moses, Christ—indicate the three successive stages in the Divine plan, as they are logically connected and logically necessary to each other.

This view differs fundamentally from the mode in which the Jews and Jewish Christians persisted in regarding the Old Testament. It is, indeed, so bold and original, that the Christian theology of following centuries could neither understand nor reproduce it. It preserves the letter of the old covenant, but interprets it by the spirit of the new. Paul was fully aware that the Jew could not of himself attain this spiritual standpoint. "A veil remains," he says, "upon the old covenant. It can be lifted by Christ alone. But to this day the Jews read Moses without understanding him." They did not perceive the subordinate character and the ephemeral glory of Moses' ministry. It was not without glory, for it was a manifestation of the will of God; but its glory was fleeting, because the ministry itself was not to be permanent. It fades and disappears before a glory that is surpassing and imperishable (2 Cor. iii. 6-15).

III. Adam and Christ; or the Two Ages of Humanity.

Paul's doctrine hitherto had not gone beyond the sacred limits of the Old Testament; but it evidently tended to embrace within its scope the whole historical development of humanity, completed and crowned by the Gospel of Christ.

The apostle delights to compare the life of the human race, as a whole, to the natural course of the individual life, and to trace in the first the various phases belonging to the second. Humanity itself begins with childhood, and is obliged to pass through a slow and painful period of education and minority. It is certainly an heir, but an heir under age, who has to remain in ward until the time of his full majority. The promise corresponds to the paternal testament; the guardian, severe and inflexible, is the law which fulfils its office until the time appointed by the father himself. The heir until then is treated as a slave. It is in Christ that man finally gains his rights of sonship, and attains his full majority ($\pi\lambda\eta\rho\omega\mu\alpha\ \tau o\hat{v}\ \chi\rho\acute{o}\nu o\nu$). At this point, the period of childhood and youth spent in subjection ends; and the second phase in human life begins, that of mature age, characterized by liberty and the right of self-control (Gal. iv. 1-7).

All the ideas, and all the Jewish and heathen institutions which had governed humanity before the coming of Christ, come under this general designation: $\dot{\alpha}\sigma\theta\epsilon\nu\hat{\eta}\ \kappa\alpha\grave{\iota}\ \pi\tau\omega\chi\grave{\alpha}\ \sigma\tau o\iota\chi\epsilon\hat{\iota}\alpha$—*things rudimentary, primitive elements*, by whose means the human race was formerly educated, but which are no longer suited to Christian humanity in its freedom and maturity (Gal. iv. 9). By this bold conception Paul has ranged Jewish and heathen traditions alike under the same category; and in some sort has blended them, by subordinating them both to the Gospel.

This lofty philosophy of history is still better expressed in the parallel between the *two Adams*, in which it reaches its climax (Rom. v. 12-21; 1 Cor. xv. 45-49). The importance of these two passages is not, in my judgment, fully apprehended by those who see in them a mere typological figure, a figure more remarkable perhaps than others, but still serving only to illustrate the apostle's discourse. Placed in the logical connexion in which we find it, this parallel is of capital importance in Paul's system, and expresses one of his finest ideas.

Adam and Christ represent the two great periods in the life of humanity. The flesh and sin, the law and death, reign over the first; the Spirit and faith, righteousness and life, are the powers that prevail in the second. The first Adam was earthly and carnal (χοϊκὸς and ψυχικός). All his descendants have been earthly and carnal, have lived his life and borne his image. With Adam's transgression, sin entered into the world; it has reigned over all the children of Adam, giving them over to death, the inevitable wages of sin. Such is the natural development of this period. Its organic bond of connexion with the second epoch, which is summed up in Christ, has not always been fully apprehended. This new period does not intervene abruptly, as though it were obtruded by an arbitrary act; it originates in the first, and is evolved from it. The carnal and psychic life has to precede the *pneumatic* life, giving scope for its due development (1 Cor. xv. 46). The second period does not begin, as it has been supposed, with the supernatural birth of Jesus; it may even be asked whether in Paul's theory there is any place for this supernatural birth.[1]

---

[1] Paul ascribes to Christ a unique Divine sonship and untainted holiness: at the same time, he asserts the heredity of sin, and the solidarity in transgression of the descendants of Adam. This flagrant contradiction does not in the least embarrass him. How could his logical mind have held together these contrary beliefs, unless there lay behind them a knowledge of the exceptional character of the birth of Jesus? That there was *reserve* upon this subject in the first generation was natural, especially while the virgin mother lived, "*keeping* all these things in her heart." See Weiss's *Life of Christ* vol. i., pp. 222-233.]

The position that this fact occupies in ecclesiastical theology, is filled in the apostle's system by that of the resurrection. The new epoch of history begins with the Saviour's resurrection, which was the first manifestation of the *spiritual* life on earth. The historical life of Jesus belongs, in reality, to the first period. Christ Himself was also a descendant of Adam,—*born of a woman*, coming under the law, with a flesh like ours, living in the realm of sin and death, so that under the same conditions He might develop and display the Divine life which animated Him.

From this point of view, everything turns upon the fact of Christ's actual humanity. The second Adam is from heaven, it is true; but He also comes forth from the bosom of humanity. He enters the human race as a living member thereof, and becomes for it the father of a new humanity. The *Spirit, righteousness, and life* are in Him not merely qualities, but powers, entering into history and unfolding there like the sin transmitted by descent from Adam. In fact, precisely as we by our origin are in *communion* with Adam's sin and participate in his death, so those who enter into communion with Christ are partakers of His life and righteousness. If there is a difference, it is entirely to the advantage of the second Adam: a single sin was the source of condemnation for the many; redemption, on the contrary, starts with the multitude of actual sins over which Christ triumphs, and in the midst of which He makes manifest, through His obedience, both righteousness and life (Rom. v. 15-17).

Christianity, though supernatural in its Divine cause, does not make any abrupt or violent entrance into history, so as to interrupt its course. It manifests itself in due time, issuing from the very midst of humanity, where God at the appointed hour causes the new life to appear. The idea of a fall of the human race as understood by Augustine, has no logical existence in Paul's system. Or, at any rate, if the apostle does admit a failure, a fall of the human race into sin, the idea is finally absorbed in the loftier one of constant progress. The second Adam not only repairs the fault of the first; He brings about actual progress, and marks out a higher order of life. The resurrection of Christ completes the creation of humanity.

IV. ESCHATOLOGY.

The struggles of history are summed up, according to Paul, in the constant antagonism of two opposing principles, *death* and *life*. This great drama is to have its *dénouement*. The power of death is virtually already broken by the resurrection of Jesus Christ; with this first triumph the Pauline eschatology begins. This doctrine signifies nothing else than the unfolding or progressive realization of all the individual, social, and cosmical consequences existing in germ in this *fundamental fact*. By no means does the apostle limit to humanity that radical transformation announced and commenced in the personal triumph of Jesus. It will extend to every celestial sphere, and throughout physical nature. The resurrection of Christ is a crisis in the development of universal life (Rom. viii. 18–24).

How will this transformation be effected? For the external mechanism of Jewish eschatology the apostle, as we have seen, endeavoured to substitute a moral force. It would, however, be a misconception of his doctrine to attribute to him the modern notion of the unlimited progress of history. He most certainly pictured the end as a dramatic finale, brought about by God at the moment foreseen in His designs. Though he may have relinquished the hope of being present in his life-time at the *parousia* of the Lord, he always expected this great event, and wished those who came after him to expect it (1 Cor. xv. 22 ; Phil. i. 10 ; iii. 20). There is no contradiction, though it has been asserted, between this ultimate expectation and the hope that Paul cherished of being united by death immediately to Christ and God (Phil. i. 21 ; 2 Cor. v. 8). Until the time of the external and historical manifestation of the Lord, all Christians, whether living or dead, have their glory and their life hidden in God, as the glory of Christ Himself is now hidden from the eyes of the world (Col. iii. 1–4).

The time of the Parousia will be that of the resurrection. Then the principle of the new life which is in Christ will reveal its full power, in raising up *our mortal bodies* and thus completing the work of redemption (Rom. viii. 23). On the other side, Paul is equally decided in excluding *flesh and blood* from this glorious resurrection (1 Cor. xv. 50). Evidently, on his principles, the flesh, the seat and organ of sin, must be destroyed. An essential distinction, therefore, must be made between the body and the flesh. The flesh is the material substance of the body. The body is the essential form of the human being. From the philosophical point of view, it may be asked how the form can subsist when the substance which filled it has disappeared? Paul did not concern himself with this question. He strove to make his own meaning clear; and in this he has succeeded admirably, by his comparison of the resurrection to the germination of a grain of corn. The new plant is not composed of the same matter; and yet the type remains, despite the change of substance. The new body develops organically from the germ which gives it birth. There is therefore a real connexion between the body which is sown in corruption, and the body which is raised in incorruption. It is the same, and yet a new body. The body, in fact, represents to Paul a Divine idea essential and necessary to the full development of the individual life; it is even the cause or principle of our individuality. This Divine type is successively realized in elements of a diverse character (ἄλλη σάρξ); like the soul itself, it rises by the crisis of death to a higher state of life. It becomes a spiritual body, inasmuch as the πνεῦμα will hereafter animate it, as the ψυχή does at present.

This resurrection will be the time of the Lord's full triumph. All power and authority will yield to Him. His enemies will fall beneath His feet (1 Cor. xv. 24-28). Must this final victory be regarded as an external triumph? Is it a question of the enforced submission of hostile powers, or of their transformation, conversion, and glorification? To some, perhaps, the first conception may seem the more probable; yet when Paul declares that death itself shall be abolished for ever, it seems to imply that evil will actually cease to exist. The apostle says nothing of the final fate reserved for the wicked, or the Devil. But the idea of an eternal damnation evidently lies outside the logic of his doctrine, which would rather require the absolute annihilation of wicked beings. It is particularly to be observed that Paul makes no reference to any resurrection of the wicked.¹ Not having the principle of life in themselves, they cannot live again. When this complete victory of good over evil and life over death is accomplished, Christ will then restore the kingdom to God His Father. His office will cease with His triumph; He will efface Himself in His turn; and God, consummating the eternal unity, will be all in all. Such is the final and glorious end of history.

V. Faith, Hope, Love.

Ἡ πίστις, ἡ ἐλπίς, ἡ ἀγάπη.

This historical development of the kingdom of God remains for the present concentrated and summed up in the Christian consciousness. The main stages in this progressive life are there represented objectively by *faith, hope, love.* "These three are," as Calvin has well said, "a brief summary of the whole of Christianity."

The first in order of time is faith. It is the creative fact, containing the germ of the other two. Faith looks back towards the Divine promise and the salvation accomplished by the death of Christ. There is its object and its foundation. But while faith cast its roots into the past, and lives in the present, neither

---

[¹ Then we must put out of court Acts xxiv. 15. Paul shared the belief of his people, and of Jesus Himself, in a *general* resurrection. Comp. Dan. xii. 2; Matt. xxv. 32; John v. 28, 29. And "the logic of his doctrine" requires it. How can the retribution of 2 Thess. i. 6-10, *e.g.*, be limited to the wicked who happen to be alive on earth at Christ's return? and how otherwise are we to understand Rom. ii. 5, 6, or 2 Cor. v. 10, 11 (*the things done through the body,—whether good or bad*)?]

present nor past can suffice it ; it takes possession of the future and becomes *hope*.

Faith bears hope within it, just as the past and present contain the future. Hope, in truth, is only the development of faith ; it is the side of the soul which looks toward life eternal. The profounder the discord, the more painful the contrast that exists between our spiritual calling as believers and our earthly condition, between our aspirations and our trials, by so much the more vivid and mighty is the energy with which hope springs out of faith. "In truth," says the apostle, "we are only saved by hope." Our existence here is one long affliction, a continual bondage (θλῖψις, στενοχωρία), in which the life of the spirit is repressed and fretted by the temptations, weaknesses, and sufferings of the flesh. "We walk by faith, not by sight." Hope is the prospect of faith.

But the essential and abiding disposition of the Christian consciousness, that wherein lies its eternal element, and which in this character enters into faith and hope alike, is *love*. The two former are but temporary phases of the spiritual life ; they are the virtues of travellers. The third expresses the inner essence, the abiding and unchangeable substance of Christian life. Love is the very life of God.—" Now remain these three virtues : faith, hope, and love ; but the greatest of them is love" (1 Cor. xiii. 13).

CHAPTER IV.

THE CHRISTIAN PRINCIPLE IN THE SPHERE OF METAPHYSICS.

Theology.

ALL human thought, like all life, has its source in God. It is impossible to follow out any idea for long, without tracing it to this first cause. There was no need for Paul to set himself to speculate, with a view to formulating the transcendental principles of his theology. His mind, exclusively religious as it was, rose spontaneously to God. God was the beginning and the end, the starting point and goal of his meditations. In Him is the first and ever-active source of that great unfolding of righteousness and life, in history and in the human understanding, which we have just surveyed. This cause is known as *grace*.

I. GRACE, PREDESTINATION.

Ἡ χάρις, ἡ πρόθεσις τοῦ Θεοῦ.

It is with a sort of jealousy that Paul claims for God alone the entire and *unconditional* initiative in the work of redemption. This initiative on the part of

God springs from His *infinite love* (Eph. i. 3, ff.; ii. 4-7; Rom. v. 8; 2 Cor. xiii. 14; 2 Thess. ii. 16).

The apostle, as we have already said, does not admit the existence in God of that antithesis between His *love* and His *righteousness* which ecclesiastical theology has so often asserted. God's righteousness is not legal, it is not a negative virtue such as could be satisfied by the punishment of evil. The Divine power which punishes evil is called in Paul's phraseology the *wrath of God* (ὀργὴ Θεοῦ, Rom. i. 18; ii. 8). The δικαιοσύνη Θεοῦ is a positive virtue which imparts and bestows itself, which loses itself in love. Righteousness, in this aspect, might be called the actual substance of God's love; and love the essential form of His righteousness (Rom. iii. 21-26).

The love of God, as exercised towards sinful men, receives the name of *mercy* (ἔλεος, Rom. ix. 15, 16, 23; Eph. ii. 4; 1 Tim. i. 2). It has a still more definite name in *grace* (ἡ χάρις). No other word occurs oftener in Paul's writings. It designates the love of God in action, as it intervenes definitely and directly in the destinies of humanity in order to raise it. Grace, therefore, is the primary source, the one absolute cause of man's salvation. Since Christ is the essential means by which the grace of God is realized, it is also called the *grace of Christ* (Gal. i. 6; 2 Cor. viii. 9; 2 Thess. i. 12; χάρις Χριστοῦ, or χάρις ἐν Χριστῷ). As it depends entirely upon God's good pleasure, it is further called εὐδοκία (Eph. i. 5; Gal. i. 15; 1 Cor. i. 21). It is God, in fact, who is our Saviour (1 Tim. i. 1; iv. 10; Tit. i. 3; 1 Cor. i. 21).

This act of love by which God saves men, is a decree of His will superior to time, an *eternal decree* (βουλὴ τοῦ θελήματος αὐτοῦ, Eph. i. 11). But while love inspires redemption, it is wisdom which conceives and ordains its plan (Eph. iii. 10, etc. ; Rom. xi. 33). This Divine plan, which is also the plan of history, is only fulfilled and revealed by degrees. It was unknown and concealed from human wisdom until the appearance of Christ, the perfect Revealer. Hence Paul calls it a *mystery* (μυστήριον τοῦ θελήματος αὐτοῦ, Eph. i. 9 ; σοφίαν ἐν μυστηρίῳ τὴν ἀποκεκρυμμένην, 1 Cor. ii. 7). This plan is simply the outflow of the eternal grace of God (ἵνα ἐνδείξηται ἐν τοῖς αἰῶσιν τὸ ὑπερβάλλον πλοῦτος τῆς χάριτος αὐτοῦ, Eph. ii. 7). Grace is the beginning, middle, and end of the redemptive work, always equally sovereign and equally absolute. But as soon as it comes to be applied practically to nations and to individuals, there arises the inevitable question of the relation between this absolute action on God's part and man's free-will; in other words, the terrible question of *predestination*.

Divine grace has to be accepted by faith ; it cannot be realized in any other way. Now faith depends upon man ; and Paul makes most earnest appeals to the responsibility and freedom of the individual. But, on the other hand, there is nothing good found in man which is not the work of the grace of God ; so that faith itself, to begin with, exists in us as the effect of this grace. The apostle was led to consider human action from this point of view, quite as much by his own experience as by the logic of his belief. He himself was the conquest of that higher Power which, from the moment that it mastered him at the gates of Damascus, led him through the world as its *slave*, fulfilling in and through him its work upon earth (2 Cor. ii. 14 ; v. 14 ; 1 Cor. ix. 16 ; xv. 10). His apostolic vocation was based on the sense that he was simply an instrument in the hands of Him whom he preached. He felt himself in absolute dependence upon God. This feeling, we may add, is essential to all deep piety. It is the characteristic of piety to renounce itself, to refer everything to God, to absorb the individual life in the Divine activity. Predestination, thus understood, is a normal product of religious faith ; and the consciousness of the former is never weakened without involving, and signalizing, an equal diminution of the latter.

It will not be surprising, therefore, to find this fundamental antinomy between human freedom and the Divine action in the teaching of Jesus (Matt. xi. 25; xiii. 11; xxii. 14); it pervades the New Testament writings (1 Pet. i. 2 ; John vi. 44, and *passim* ; Acts xiii. 48). Paul is not to be credited with having introduced this question, but only with having made it part of theology. The ninth and tenth chapters of Romans, as is well known, contain the fullest declaration of the apostle's views on the subject.

Expositors vainly endeavour to eliminate from the ninth chapter the idea of an absolute predestination. It is Paul's express object to impute nothing to man which can in any sense influence or determine the Divine will. The better to do this, he is not afraid of going to the length of denying all independent action on man's part as he stands before God. What we are and what we do has so little power to compel God, that we ever are and do it only by the will of God. He chooses Jacob and rejects Esau, without regard to their personal merit ; He hardens whom He will ; He shows mercy on whom it pleases Him. This thought has yet more outspoken expression in the illustration of the potter and the clay, by which superficial minds are too easily disturbed.[1] What is the meaning of this simile, but to express the idea of the sovereign independence of the Divine working, the *supreme causality* of that absolute Will which gives account to no man, and from which no man has the right to demand account—a philosophical idea so natural and inevitable, that every thoughtful mind apprehends it at the first glance, when it has once discarded the assumption of a *moralism* which is equally superficial and commonplace?

But the worst possible misconception of the apostle's doctrine would be to make it amount to a mechanical determinism, an arbitrary and *external decree*, controlling the actions and state of individuals by anticipation. He devotes as much energy in the tenth chapter to asserting man's moral responsibility as he has just shown in maintaining the absolute and unconditional character of the Divine working. We now find salvation and condemnation depending solely on the faith or unbelief of the individual. We must not suppose that Paul intended in this way to limit the application of what he had before asserted. No; he was absolute in his previous affirmations, and is equally so in these. Nor was he, as I think, in the slightest degree conscious of any self-contradiction.

He does not write these three chapters from a speculative point of view; nor is it the dogmatic question of predestination that he discusses. His standpoint is that of history; and his object is to

---

[1] Paul invented neither the comparison nor the argument. I am not sure whether both did not recur frequently in the rabbinical discussions of the time; but both are to be found in the Old Testament (comp. Isai. xlv. 9; xxix. 16; Jer. xviii. 2-6).

solve an historical question—*viz.* the rejection of the Jews and the coming in of the Gentiles. Why were the Jews rejected? Because they sought the righteousness of works, and had not faith. Why were the Gentiles received? Because they accepted the righteousness of faith. That is the first and *subjective* solution of the problem, amply satisfactory to the individual conscience. But what relation does the faith of the one and the unbelief of the other bear severally to the Divine plan? Paul answers unhesitatingly: it is fulfilled by both alike. The unbelief of the Jews exhibits the long-suffering of God, and His eternal righteousness; the faith of the Gentiles manifests the riches of His mercy. God is glorified in all; and man is silenced. This is the second and *objective* solution. Paul sees no contradiction between the two, because he will not conceive of one apart from the other, and because, in his view, it is precisely under the historical form of moral responsibility that Divine predestination is fulfilled, human freewill having no scope outside of God's plans. History is the outcome both of Divine and human action; it is the same reality, now considered from man's standpoint and now from that of God. The truth will be found not in separating these two aspects of the question, nor even in placing them side by side, but in blending them together at every point.

II. Christology.

Ὁ Χριστός.

The eternal plan of God centres in the Person of the Redeemer. It is in and through this Person that *grace* becomes an active power, entering into the world and manifested (πεφανέρωται, Rom. iii. 21). Paul's whole doctrine comes to a head in his *Christology*.

Pauline Christology does not consist either in a simple transfer of the Messianic attributes to the Person of Jesus, or in investing that Person with metaphysical ideas borrowed from the Alexandrian philosophy. It is an essentially original doctrine which takes its rise in the actual fact of salvation, and is the logical outcome of that doctrine of redemption wherein lies the very core of Paulinism.

The Redeemer must be really man, for He could only save humanity by partaking of its nature and becoming an actual organic member thereof. On the other hand, it is just as necessary for Him to be absolutely distinct from sinful humanity; for if He belonged to it simply as a part belongs to the whole, He Himself would have the same need of salvation, and could not bestow it on others. The *human sinlessness* of Jesus is, therefore, the primary basis of Pauline Christology. Not only does the apostle always, and in every place, take it for granted, but in a leading passage on redemption he declares that Christ *knew no sin* (2 Cor. v. 21).

It is true that after the words τὸν μὴ γνόντα ἁμαρτίαν the apostle adds ἁμαρτίαν ἐποίησεν. M. Holsten has connected this passage with that in Romans viii. 3, and has maintained that in these two passages Paul actually attributes sin to Christ, as being inherent in His flesh. This interpretation is the logical result of the metaphysical dualism between the flesh and the spirit which this theologian thinks he has found underlying Paulinism. The apostle, he says, could not actually invest Christ with a flesh like ours, without by that very means attributing sin to Him. He does so very definitely in the words of Romans. viii. 3 : ἐν ὁμοιώματι σαρκὸς ἁμαρτίας . . . κατέκρινεν τὴν ἁμαρτίαν ἐν τῇ σαρκί. If sin was destroyed and condemned in the flesh of Jesus, it must of course have been really there. This is the nerve of Paul's whole theory of redemption, and by cutting it you bring about a breach of continuity in the very basis of his doctrine: an incoherence which enfeebles, or even destroys it.

The reasoning just quoted is, no doubt, very specious. Let us, however, follow out M. Holsten's idea, and see whether it is true to the logic of the Pauline system throughout. Sin, he says, exists in Christ's flesh as an actual power. Did not this sin make Christ a sinner? No, answers M. Holsten ; for in Him the ἁμαρτία never became παράβασις ; this power of sin never brought forth transgression. Why not? we inquire further. Christ lived under the law ; and is it not, from the Pauline point of view, inevitable that the law, being the strength of sin, wherever sin is latent should rouse it into manifestation and activity? And at this point does not M. Holsten in his turn destroy the internal logic of Paul's doctrine? In short, either sin was not and could not be manifested in Jesus ; and in that case, what has M. Holsten discovered beyond that which the apostle, and the Church after him, call ὁμοίωμα σαρκὸς ἁμαρτίας? Or else, the sin inherent in the flesh of Christ was realized in His life, and constituted Him a sinner ; and then how could His death effect the redemption of his brethren? We are thus driven on either hand into a logical contradiction, far more serious than that which M. Holsten just now pointed out.

We gain, therefore, no further light upon the general

structure of the Pauline system, by interpreting the two passages quoted above as this theologian does; while, from the standpoint of simple grammatical exegesis, we involve ourselves in very serious difficulties. Without doubt the words of Romans viii. 3, ἐν ὁμοιώματι σαρκὸς ἁμαρτίας, tend to assimilate the flesh of Christ to our sinful flesh; but it is equally true that with this very assimilation the term ὁμοίωμα asserts an essential difference; or why should the apostle have used this expression, instead of simply saying ἐν σαρκὶ ἁμαρτίας? In every passage where this word recurs it designates an approximate identification, never an absolute material identity (comp. Rom. i. 23; vi. 5). It should be noticed, finally, in how general a manner the sentence in question ends. Paul does not say, κατέκρινεν τὴν ἁμαρτίαν ἐν σαρκὶ αὐτοῦ, *in His flesh*; but, in an abstract fashion, ἐν τῇ σαρκὶ, *in the flesh*. Christ's flesh, therefore, only represents in a general manner the flesh of humanity. The two ideas of the flesh and sin are always correlative, but still dogmatically distinct.

The analogous interpretation that M. Holsten gives of 2 Corinthians v. 21, is even less tenable. The words "God *made sin* Him who did not know sin," he understands in a material sense, as though Christ became sin by taking upon Him the flesh of sin. This obliges M. Holsten to refer the phrase ἐποίησεν ἁμαρτίαν to the mere incarnation of the Son of God, and the preceding words, τὸν μὴ γνόντα ἁμαρτίαν, to the pre-existent Christ—two things equally impossible. In short, it is evident, with absolute clearness, that this passage refers solely to the Christ of history, and that the words ἐποίησεν ἁμαρτίαν do not allude to the fact of the incarnation of the Son of God, but to the death of Jesus upon the cross. But how could Christ at that moment become sin, except by means of an ideal substitution, as indeed is plainly indicated in the words ὑπὲρ ἡμῶν? The fact of this substitution is the essential basis of the Pauline theory. And the very idea of substitution implies a distinction in the two terms, for otherwise it would have no meaning. Redemption consists precisely in this, that God sees in Christ that which is in us,—namely, sin; and in us that which is in Christ,—namely, righteousness. No doubt this is a logical contradiction; but it is the Divine contradiction of love. The logic of the heart triumphs over that of the intellect.

The personality of Christ, then, was without sin. But this definition is purely negative. Paul has given a more positive description of His Person at the beginning of the epistle to the Romans: γενομένου ἐκ σπέρματος Δαβὶδ κατὰ σάρκα, ὁρισθέντος υἱοῦ Θεοῦ ἐν δυνάμει κατὰ πνεῦμα ἁγιωσύνης ἐξ ἀναστάσεως νεκρῶν (i. 3, 4). There is no reference here to the miraculous conception of Jesus in the womb of the Virgin Mary by the special virtue of the Holy Spirit. Paul is neither combating nor confirming the narratives of Luke and Matthew; he simply ignores them. The apostle in this passage considers the Person of Jesus under a twofold aspect,—as regards His external material frame, and His inner and spiritual nature. Jesus owed His earthly being to the family of David. But by the side of this carnal descent Paul points out another, higher and more mysterious origin—a Divine descent after the Spirit. Just as the flesh formed the substance of His body, so the spirit of holiness formed the substance of His moral being. We must note again the words ἐν δυνάμει: they explain themselves, provided they have as their antithesis the other expression ἐν ἀσθενείᾳ. Jesus was the Son of God from the very first; but He was the Son of God in weakness during the whole of His earthly life (ἐξ ἀσθενείας ἐσταυρώθη, ἀλλὰ ζῇ ἐκ δυνάμεως, 2 Cor. xiii. 4). The spirit of holiness which constituted His being was restrained within the prison of feeble flesh. But when the flesh was destroyed on the cross, Christ was then manifested, and at His resurrection appeared in power as the Son of God (ὁρισθέντος . . . ἐν δυνάμει . . . ἐξ ἀναστάσεως νεκρῶν). Death as it broke all fleshly bonds and destroyed every material barrier, set free the spirit, the very essence of His nature. From that moment Christ became absolutely spiritual. He retains a body, it is true; but it is a spiritual one, which, so far from interfering with the action of the spirit, merely obeys and makes it manifest. The reign of the Redeemer does not actually begin until the resurrection. The risen Christ alone is the perfect Christ. Then, and not till then, He appears as the *second Adam*, the celestial man (1 Cor. xv. 22, 45-49).

But this new designation of Christ has not the importance nor the metaphysical significance which many theologians attach to it; it does not so much indicate the essential nature of Jesus, as His part in history as a member of humanity. The words ὁ δεύτερος ἄνθρωπος ἐξ οὐρανοῦ (ver. 47) do not in any wise imply pre-existence; and it would be a serious mistake to conclude that in the view of the apostle the pre-existence of Christ was that of the *ideal* or *typical man*. This latter idea belongs to Philonism, and is altogether foreign to the Pauline system. There is a radical difference between the two systems. Philo always takes a purely speculative view; Paul adheres to the historical one. The former would say that the ideal man is the first, and that the psychical man, the imperfect reproduction of the Divine type, comes afterwards; the latter, on the contrary, expressly says that the psychical man appears first, and then the spiritual man. The δεύτερος ἄνθρωπος of which the apostle here speaks, is not the pre-existent, but the *risen Christ*, as the whole context sufficiently proves. The antithesis asserted between the words ἐκ τῆς γῆς χοϊκὸς and ἐξ οὐρανοῦ ἐπουράνιος has no bearing on the idea of *priority*, but solely on that of *quality*; a fact so unmistakable, that in the same passage Christians themselves are called ἐπουράνιοι (comp. Phil. iii. 20). Paul's object is not to establish the fact of Christ's pre-existence to Adam, but of His essentially different nature.

Leaving, therefore, this conception of the heavenly man—which is wholly misleading—we will return to the far more fruitful idea of the *spirit of holiness*, the very essence of Christ. Paul has not only said that the Lord is a life-giving spirit (πνεῦμα ζωοποιοῦν), he goes further, and adds, "The Lord is the *spirit itself*" (ὁ δὲ Κύριος τὸ πνεῦμά ἐστιν, 2 Cor. iii. 17). It must not be asserted that in Paul's view the Lord is spirit because He has become a life-giving spirit in the soul of believers; He only became a principle of immanent life in them, because He is spirit in His very essence. Thus we reach this new definition. Christ is the Spirit Himself personified, the Divine Spirit in the form of human individuality.

Here we reach the very centre of the Pauline Christology. It is with this most original conception of the Divine essence of Jesus Christ that we must associate the fact of His pre-existence. Paul, as we have seen, does not assert the pre-existence of the heavenly man, the second Adam; but he does assert that of the Son of God (Gal. iv. 4; Rom. viii. 32; 1 Cor. viii. 6; 2 Cor. viii. 9). Christ was in God, antecedently to creation, the original form of His existence being Divine (ἐν μορφῇ Θεοῦ ὑπάρχων, Phil. ii. 6; Col. i. 15). This pre-existence, however, is not the Divine eternity, and we are still far from the Trinitarian formulæ of Nicæa. The phrase of Colossians, πρωτότοκος πάσης κτίσεως, even implies the opposite; while raising Jesus above creation, it still links Him closely to it. The Person of Christ is not the *absolute;* it is neither the supreme cause, nor the final end of the universe. His very existence, according to the apostle, seems to depend on that of the world of which it is the Divine type, the perfect *résumé* (ἀνακεφαλαιώσασθαι τὰ πάντα ἐν τῷ Χριστῷ,[1] Eph. i. 10). The pre-existent Christ, like the historical Christ, remains essentially *Mediator.* His Person, if we may so speak, is the metaphysical *locus* at which God and creation meet.

How did Paul represent to himself this pre-existence? What was its mode? Was it a personal, or simply an ideal existence? The apostle is not

[1 But this, as the entire context shows, is "the (historical) Christ," the centre and sum of the Divine plans for the world. Nothing is said here of the pre-existent Christ. Is not *eternity* involved in the μορφὴ Θεοῦ of Phil. ii. 6? If the existence of the historical Christ depends on that of the created world, the existence of the latter depends in turn, according to Paul's logic —and according to M. Sabatier's—on the pre-existence of the Divine Christ, whom Col. i. 15-17 "links" indeed "to creation," but with an infinite disparity of nature. Comp. note on p. 243.

very explicit on the point. We are disposed to think that his doctrine on this subject halted at a middle point, somewhat difficult to seize, between the two opinions, a position implying something less than the one theory and more than the other. The latter view is purely abstract; and the Hebraic genius neither favoured nor understood abstractions. The former might seem to lend itself to schemes of Divine and mythological genealogy; and might easily be pushed to Docetic consequences. Paul seems to have avoided both these snares. The pre-historical action of Christ is blended with that of the Divine Πνεῦμα. It was this Divine Spirit which appeared as a human person in Christ; and it is difficult, if not impossible, to conceive His separate pre-existence.

However that may be, the principle of the *Divine Sonship* of Christ is precisely that Divine Spirit which constitutes its essence. Paul does not call Jesus the Son of God because he has found in Him the Messiah. The term υἱὸς τοῦ Θεοῦ implies, to his thinking, something very different. Jesus is the Son of God, because, being the spirit of holiness, He proceeds in His essence from the Divine nature. This spirit forms an *essential* bond of relationship between the Father and the Son. Thus Paul calls Christ in a very special sense God's *own* Son (ἰδίου υἱοῦ, Rom. viii. 32). This is because Christ, when coming to dwell in our souls, brings thither His own substance, His Spirit, so that we also in our turn become in and through Him *sons* of God (υἱοὶ τοῦ Θεοῦ), co-heirs with Christ. The Spirit of Jesus is therefore called the Spirit of adoption (πνεῦμα υἱοθεσίας, Rom. viii. 15). We are thus raised to the same plane as Christ, and become in fact *His brethren* (εἰς τὸ εἶναι αὐτὸν πρωτότοκον ἐν πολλοῖς ἀδελφοῖς, Rom. viii. 29). This dignity, however, is with us purely a favour; but with Him a natural right. We have to rise; He had to stoop! Christ, in short, is God's own Son,—*essentially* His. We are, and shall always be so by adoption only.

Lastly, this same *virtue* of the Spirit which is in Christ, is the foundation of His sovereign dominion (Ἰησοῦς Κύριος, 1 Cor. xii. 3) over the historical development of humanity. This sovereignty is not limited to the work of redemption; or rather, His work itself is universal in scope, and links itself to creation as an essential stage in the evolution of the world. Hence the creation is nothing more than the beginning of redemption; and the latter is the completion of creation; so that in the end each alike finds its place within the sphere of Christ. In Him and by Him God created all things, just as in Him and by Him He reconciles all things to Himself.

The starting-point of this Christological theory is still the work of salvation. The cross is the centre of that vast circumference which includes the whole work of Christ. The sovereignty of the Lord coincides with His redemptive mission, and is only of the same duration. The former ceases with the consummation of the latter. Its constant tendency therefore, if I may venture to use the expression, is to render itself needless. So Paul in all his epistles maintains a strict distinction between the *Lord* (Κύριος) and the supreme God. Everything has to be subjected to Christ, except God; but when everything shall have been subjected to Him, the Son in His turn will submit himself to God (καὶ αὐτὸς ὁ υἱός). He will restore the kingdom to God His Father, in order that God may be all in all (1 Cor. xv. 28).

Christ's office will then terminate. But here a last question presents itself. At the close of this evolution, what will be the final and natural position of the Saviour? Will He re-enter humanity as the eldest among many brethren, or will He return to the bosom of God as an integral member of the Divinity? The second is the ecclesiastical opinion; the first, we believe, is Paul's; at least, it is that which the logic of his system seems to require. Paul, in fact, is not explicit on this point. Had the question been presented to him, he would probably have dismissed it as idle. It could not really occur, from the standpoint of the Pauline theology. As soon as we reach the final stage, the moment when God shall be *all* in all, it seems decidedly superfluous to discuss the categories of the Divine and human further, since from that time they are resolved into each other. On the other hand, this submission of Christ to God, this resignation into the Father's hands, cannot possibly be regarded as a downfall or abasement of the Son. On the contrary, will it not be the grandest moment of His triumph? He will remain united to humanity, not by stooping again to it, but by its elevation to Himself.

The Christological conception which best corresponds with Paul's ideas still seems to me that of the *God-man*. The human and Divine elements of His nature are firmly maintained to the end. How did Paul harmonize them? This question seems not to have perplexed him, or even crossed his mind. He carried out his various lines of thought boldly, starting with the great fact of redemption, without concerning himself with the metaphysical problem which they involved. The basis of Paul's system was soteriological and experimental. On this foundation he had slowly raised a most elaborate mental structure. The edifice was never completed; and the efforts since made by ecclesiastical theology to finish it have sufficiently proved the apostle's wisdom, and the impotence of speculation.

III. THE FATHER, THE LORD, THE SPIRIT.
Ὁ Πατήρ, ὁ Κύριος, τὸ ἅγιον Πνεῦμα.

Since we have not found the ecclesiastical Christology in Paul's epistles, neither must we expect to find there the doctrine of the Trinity.[1] The *triad* forming the title of this chapter is very different from that of the Nicene formulary. The apostle, who does not admit the equality of Christ and the Father, seems to have been equally without the notion of the personality of the Holy Spirit. To him the Spirit is evidently a Divine power and faculty, not yet a distinct Person. He does, however, make distinctions in the Divine working, which may be regarded as a starting point for subsequent speculation and for ecclesiastical metaphysics: *ἡ χάρις τοῦ Κυρίου Ἰησοῦ Χριστοῦ, καὶ ἡ ἀγάπη τοῦ Θεοῦ, καὶ ἡ κοινωνία τοῦ ἁγίου Πνεύματος* (2 Cor. xiii. 14; comp. 1 Cor. xii. 4–11). This formula simply expresses the unity and sequence of

---

[[1] Supposing Paul's Trinitarianism to be adequately represented here (and this will be disputed), we still remember that Paul was not the only, nor the last, exponent of New Testament doctrine. The theology of the Church has to take account of John as well as Paul. On the doctrine of the *essential tri-unity of God*, in its biblical and ecclesiastical developments, see the profound and well-balanced discussion of Dorner, *System of Christian Doctrine*, vol. i., pp. 344–412.]

the historical development of salvation, in its essential stages: the love of the Father which is its permanent cause, the *grace* of Jesus the Lord which makes it manifest, and the Holy Spirit who gives it reality within the soul. The very order of the apostle's words shows how far he was from any metaphysical design.

Not only did Paul's theology terminate otherwise than the traditional theology, not only does the dogma of the Trinity lie outside its scope, but it seems to me that, instead of seeking in such a dogma his final conclusion and the crown of his system, he has found both in the absolute idea of God.

IV. THE CONCEPTION OF GOD.
Ὁ Θεὸς τὰ πάντα ἐν πᾶσιν.

God is one (εἷς Θεὸς ὁ Πατήρ, 1 Cor. viii. 6). Of Him, by Him, and for Him are all things (ἐξ αὐτοῦ καὶ δι' αὐτοῦ καὶ εἰς αὐτὸν τὰ πάντα, Rom. xi. 36). He is the beginning, middle, and end of all existence. In Him every creature has its source, its life, and object. It was the constant aim of the apostle to assert this absolute and supreme causality of God in man, in history, and in the universe. This idea of the absoluteness of God is the real metaphysical basis of salvation by grace, justification by faith, and predestination: God does everything in redemption, as in creation. Again, it is the foundation of the universalism of the apostle of the Gentiles. The supreme, absolute God is the God of all. "Is God the God of the Jews? is He not also the God of the Gentiles?" (Rom. iii. 29.) Lastly, it is the basis of his religious philosophy of history, as sketched in the epistle to the Romans. This idea of the absolute unity of God, and of His universal and permanent activity, is just what constitutes the unity of human history and brings its every part and epoch into one plan, the plan of the Divine working.

This work of God assumes different forms; but it is neither intermittent nor external; it is continuous and immanent. The world and God are indeed essentially distinct, but not separate. God works upon, and in the world; He permeates and transforms it; He reveals Himself in it; "He manifests in the world His eternal power and His Divinity" (Rom. i. 20). God reveals Himself still more fully in the redemption, which is the consequence and completion of creation, the last stage of progress in the Divine activity. Christ is the medium of this revelation. In Him it is concentred. He conveys, and communicates it. God has poured His Godhead into Him; He becomes the *pleroma* of God, as the Church in its turn, embracing in its extended sphere the universe, is the *pleroma* of Christ (Eph. i. 23; Col. ii. 9). Everything comes from God; everything returns to Him. The perfect union of God and His creation—that is the glorious end of all things.

By pushing this view and these declarations of the apostle to their strict consequences in the way of formal and abstract logic, it would be easy to deduce from them a sort of dialectical pantheism. But let us remember once more, that Paul never indulged in pure speculation; his reasonings advanced from experience to principles, but were never wrought out by the method of abstract deduction. God does not become lost in the world; the world is transfigured into the Divine. The apostle's metaphysics are strictly theistic. While he does not distinguish a plurality of Persons in God, he maintains the existence in Him of an inner personal life—that of the Spirit which searches the depths of God (1 Cor. ii. 10). The Spirit, therefore, is in God Himself, as in us, the essential principle of consciousness, knowledge, and personality. The God of Paul is a *living* God (1 Thess. i. 9). His true name is that which Jesus gave Him : Θεὸς καὶ ὁ Πατήρ (1 Cor. viii. 6). This name of FATHER is the first word, and the last, in the gospel of the great apostle.

APPENDIX ON THE EPISTLES TO TIMOTHY AND TITUS.

By Geo. G. Findlay, B.A.

THE following essay on the Epistles of Paul to Timothy and Titus[1] is appended to this volume on the suggestion of the General Editor of the series, and with the consent, freely and courteously granted, of the distinguished author, M. A. Sabatier. Those who are responsible for the English translation of *L'apôtre Paul* regard the Pastoral Epistles as having a good right to bear St. Paul's name, and as therefore demanding a place in the history of his doctrine. Deprived of these documents, it appears to us that the representation of the apostle's work in teaching and founding the Church is incomplete. We are no longer able to trace the progress of his thoughts, and the unfolding of his plans and hopes for the future to their latest stage. The interpreters who reject or distrust these writings, and who believe that the closing verses of the Acts of the Apostles have said the last word of Paul's history, are compelled to see his sun set before its time; they terminate his career with a sudden and mysterious eclipse. The pensive hours of evening, the broken yet touching accents of old age, the final directions and warnings to his children of the father who knows that it is time to set his house in order and to resign his earthly charge, the dying testimony and the last farewell—these pathetic elements of the drama of life are wanting to the image of the great apostle, if the letters to Timothy and Titus are not truly his own. We do not say this by way of plea for their authenticity, nor in order to enlist a sentimental pre-judgment in their favour, but in

---

[1] This essay is in substance a reprint of the articles on "St. Paul and the Pastoral Epistles," and "Doctrine and Church in the Pastoral Epistles," that appeared in the *London Quarterly Review* for October, 1889 and 1890.

justification of our attempt, which possibly may seem invidious or presumptuous, to supplement the masterly work here presented to the English public. Convinced of the genuineness and the importance of the Pastoral Epistles, and regretting that our author is obliged to leave their place vacant in his admirable picture, we thought it right to endeavour, with however inferior art, to fill in the unoccupied space in the canvas. We desire, in effect, to add a fourth, completing section to the analysis of "Paul's theological system" given above (Book V.), under this title: *The Christian Principle in the Sphere of Ethics and Church Life* (*The Care of Souls*).

The Appendix necessarily assumes a polemical shape. We are compelled to vindicate, while we expound the Pastoral Epistles. But the writer has directed his apologetic to a practical and constructive aim. Indeed no defence of documents such as these can be satisfactory, or thoroughly valid, which does not disclose in them a lesson for all time, a message and doctrine worthy of the apostle of the Gentiles, basing itself by its intrinsic character and import upon his fundamental teaching and the mission of his life.

I. THE PASTORAL EPISTLES IN MODERN CRITICISM.

The Pastoral Epistles were the first of the writings bearing St. Paul's name to be denounced by modern historical scepticism. They are the last which it seems likely to release from its grasp. Schleiermacher, from whom the theology of the present century has received in so many directions its initiative, in the year 1807 definitely raised this critical problem. He attempted to show on internal grounds that the "so called" First Epistle of Paul to Timothy was in reality a compilation from 2 Timothy and Titus, worked over and adapted to post-apostolic times. Eichhorn, in his *Introduction*, and de Wette still more decidedly in his *Commentary*, extended the same doubts to all three epistles. These attacks, were, however, of a desultory and negative character, and left the origin of the documents unexplained. They proved to be the prelude to a far more dangerous assault, directed against the historical character and claims of the New Testament generally, which was commenced in the year 1835 by the epoch-making work of F. C. Baur, of Tübingen, on the "so called Pastoral Epistles of the apostle Paul." In this discussion Baur first developed his peculiar critical method, and laid down the principles on which the Tendency School has based its reconstruction of the history of the Primitive Church and the growth of the New Testament canon.

The preface of this manifesto contains the following pregnant sentences:

"I, at least, cannot see how the question [of authorship] is to be decided otherwise than in relation to the historical phenomena of the entire period in which these letters originated—that is to say, in the light of the history of the first two centuries. It is only after such inquiry that we shall be in a position to show where, in the course of these phenomena, the place of the writings in question is to be found."

The Tübingen master found in the Pastoral Epistles a product of second-century orthodoxy, written under cover of the apostle's name, as polemical tractates against the Gnosticism of the time, and in the interest of catholic Church union and ecclesiastical discipline. From the standpoint gained in this essay, Baur proceeded to attack the other Pauline writings, leaving at last only the four major epistles standing as authentic remains of the veritable Paul.

The defenders of the New Testament have by this time driven back the Tübingen assault along the whole line. Baur's successors in Germany have, in almost every instance, retreated from the extreme positions of their leader; and the genuineness of all the thirteen epistles, with the exception of the Pastorals and Ephesians, is admitted by one or other of the leading negative critics. With these writers we must range, on this particular question, other scholars of eminence, who are undoubtedly on the side of faith in Jesus and the Resurrection, such as Harnack [1] of Germany, and the lamented Dr. Edwin Hatch,[2] of Oxford, along with Professor Sabatier,[3] who decline to accept the letters to Timothy and Titus in their canonical form as genuine writings of the apostle Paul.

Those who hold by the Pauline authorship are therefore called upon to give some reason for their faith. And this is the more needful in view of the revived interest visible on many sides in questions of Church history and polity, which cannot fail to bring these documents into the front of the field of controversy. We want to be sure of the ground on which we stand. Of what practical use are these epistles to us, if it remain doubtful whether they are the genuine expression of St. Paul's mind ; or whether they have not been imposed on the Church by some clever ecclesiastic of the second century, and embody in reality the ideas and aims prevailing in the Church at that very different epoch? The question of the genuineness of the Pastorals is vital to our entire conception of the apostolic Church. It was essential to Baur's theory of early Christianity that their spuriousness should first of all be demonstrated. If they can be proved genuine, the whole Tübingen construction falls to the ground. On the other hand, let these epistles be struck out of the canon, and while the fundamental doctrines of the Gospel remain unimpaired, we should still feel ourselves greatly impoverished, missing not only some that we have counted amongst the most precious passages of inspired Scripture, but robbed of much that has helped (as we thought) to form our view of the life and growth, the difficulties and temptations of the early Church—of much, too, of precious import bearing on the history and inner mind of the great apostle.

---

[1] See the *Expositor*, 3rd series, v. 335, note 1.
[2] Article "Pastoral Epistles," in the *Encyclopædia Britannica*, ninth edition.
[3] See pp. 263-272 above; also article "Pastorales," in the *Encyclopédie des Sciences religieuses*.

Great as our loss would be, we must still submit to it, if the Church proves to have been deceived in these long treasured writings. "We can do nothing against the truth." To foreclose such questions and forbid inquiry into the authenticity and historical worth of canonical writings on dogmatic grounds or on the authority of ecclesiastical tradition, is a useless and, for Protestant Churches, a suicidal policy. The Bible has nothing to fear from honest criticism. In the case of these epistles, we are persuaded that it concerns historical truth even more than Christian orthodoxy, that they should be cleared from the suspicions cherished against them.

The interpretation of these books, it is to be regretted, has fallen behind that of the other epistles of St. Paul. A more complete and penetrating exegesis would, we imagine, set some controverted passages in a different light, and would reveal connexion of thought and historical relevance in what often seems pointless and obscure. Bishop Ellicott's grammatical method, admirable and indispensable within its limits, scarcely touches the crucial difficulties of the subject. Huther's industry and good sense are only a partial substitute for the exegetical genius of Meyer,[1] whose work unfortunately terminated with the epistles to Colossians and Philemon. English students miss still more in this obscure field the help of the broad and luminous scholarship and the fine literary tact of Bishop Lightfoot, —for whose guidance, alas! we must look no more.

Dr. Wace has supplied a powerful vindication of the Pastorals in his *Introduction* to the Speaker's Commentary, and Canon Farrar in the appendix to his *St. Paul*; Dr. Salmon in his masterly *Introduction to the New Testament*, and, finally, Dr. Plummer, in his excellent and most useful

---

[1] This great critic has ranged himself amongst the opponents of authenticity. His "remark" on the epistles to Timothy and Titus appended to sect. 1 of the "Introduction" to his Commentary on Romans, amounts, however, to little more than an *ipse dixit*.

commentary in the "Expositor's Bible," have carried on the defence very effectively. Dr. Samuel Davidson, on the other side, in the last edition of his *Introduction to the New Testament*, gives a complete and lucid summary of the negative arguments. In Germany, Wiesinger, the *collaborateur* of Olshausen, and Hofmann, amongst other defenders of the Pauline authenticity, have grappled with the subject in its modern aspects with conspicuous ability. Hofmann's exposition,[1] though marred by his caprice and super-subtlety, has materially advanced the study of these writings. Dr. Ernst Kühl has likewise put us under great obligations by his keen and judicial essay on the "Church Order of the Pastoral Epistles" (*Die Gemeinde-ordnung in den Pastoral-briefen*. Berlin, 1885).

Holtzmann's recent work on the subject[2] contains the most full and authoritative treatment which it has received from the opponents of authenticity. He maintains, following Baur, that the letters originated with the orthodox Church party in Rome about the year 140 of our Lord. Holtzmann, however, lays less emphasis on their anti-heretical and more upon their "catholicizing" tendency than did his predecessors, regarding it as the principal object of these writings to confirm Church authority and surround it with an apostolic halo. Connected with this purpose, in his view, was the endeavour of the unknown author to strike a blow at Gnostic heresy, in the form that it was assuming toward the middle of the second century. Pfleiderer, in his great critical work on the Chris-

---

[1] *Die heilige Schrift neuen Testamentes zusammenhängend untersucht. Sechster Theil* (*Timotheus u. Titus*). Nördlingen, 1874. Hofmann appears to unusual advantage in this volume, where he is free from the rivalry of Meyer.

[2] *Die Pastoralbriefe, kritisch und exegetisch behandelt*. Leipzig, 1880. The exegetical part of the book does not strike one as containing much that is original or valuable. The "critical behandling" has taken the life out of Holtzmann's exegesis. It reads like a *post mortem* inquiry. So soon as the epistles are detached from the personality of St. Paul, their living purpose and meaning are gone.

tian origins, *Das Urchristenthum*, returns to Baur's opinion as to the date of the epistles; in the *Paulinismus* he had referred them to a somewhat earlier period. The picture which the epistles give of Church organization and of heretical teaching—a confused representation, as Holtzmann regards it—he attributes to the attempt of the *falsarius* to combine the notions of his own day with what he imagined proper to St. Paul.

This theory, it will be seen, makes decided concessions to the defensive criticism. It admits a large element of Pauline verisimilitude previously denied.[1] And it ascribes to the supposed ecclesiastical romancer a conscious, and largely successful, reproduction of the social and mental conditions of a bygone age, as well as of the dialect and manner of the apostle—a kind of success, so far as we know, quite unexampled and foreign to the literary habits and attainments of early Christian writers.[2]

Holtzmann is a veteran critic, and master of many legions in the field of biblical scholarship. In this work he brings them all into the battle. In his five hundred closely printed pages of multifarious learning and keen analysis, the fruit

---

[1] Renan's account of the Pastorals (*L'église chrétienne*, pp. 95-106, and *Saint Paul*, pp. xxiii.-lii,) indicates a certain reaction against the extreme rigour of the Baurian hypothesis. M. Renan's literary conscience saves him from endorsing the charges of *feebleness* and *vapidity* which it suits the Tendency critics to make against these writings. "Some passages of these letters," he says, "are so beautiful, that we cannot help asking whether the forger had not in his hands some authentic notes of St. Paul, which he incorporated in his apocryphal composition." Again he writes, "What runs through the whole is admirable practical good sense. . . . The piety our author advocates is wholly spiritual. You can perceive the influence of St. Paul, . . . a sort of sobriety in mysticism, a great fund of rectitude and sincerity." This in a *forger*! In M. Renan paradox often verges upon jest. Renan dates the epistles about 100 A.D.

[2] Contrast this extraordinary skill of the supposed *falsarius* in mimicking the style, sentiment, and doctrine of Paul with the bungling failure of his attempt, on the "critical" hypothesis, to fit his compositions into the historical framework given him in the Acts of the Apostles. Who ever heard of a forger at once so clever and so stupid —so adroit and maladroit?

of immense industry, the subject is exhausted. Not a point is missed; not a single contribution to the study of the question, of any moment, seems to be overlooked. Everything is said that criticism can possibly say. It is well if our poor little letters are not crushed by the mere weight of the ponderous indictment! May we dare to say that we rise from a repeated perusal of this able and exhaustive book more convinced than ever that Paul, and no other, wrote the epistles to Timothy and Titus from the first page to the last? Holtzmann's work is admirable as a critical *tour de force*. If we might forget the conditions of historical and literary construction, and imagine ourselves in a world peopled by vocabularies and phrase-books, where sentences come together and works of literature are composed by some kind of elective affinity or fortuitous concourse of verbal atoms, then such theories would be plausible. Their condemnation is that, as M. Sabatier says (p. 234), they are so "little embarrassed by their impracticability." Try as we will, we cannot form any coherent mental image of such a writer as the Tendency School would have us imagine for these letters.

Indeed Holtzmann's hypothesis of the Pastorals, like some other of his critical reconstructions, is its own refutation. It breaks down by its very ingenuity. No fabricator of the second century was clever enough to need all this ado to find him out. It would have required a skill surpassing that of the detectives to contrive a plot that still seems to baffle them. The cunning interpolations and imitations, the deft touches of Pauline colouring, the veiled allusions and nicely calculated introduction of matter relevant to later times which the critics with incredible acuteness have discovered, the deceptive air of truthfulness and unstudied freshness which the pseudo-Paul has thrown over his work—all this belongs to the literary artifice of the nineteenth century. Baur and his disciples have projected their own subtlety and the accomplishments of their cultured professional circles into the Christian mind of the second century, to which such aptitudes were wholly wanting. At the same time they impute to that mind a readiness to deceive and to be deceived, which is contrary to what we know of its character. The early Church neither could invent such documents as these, nor would have entertained them, so invented, without grave questioning. For specimens of fictitious early Christian literature, we have the pseudo-Clementine books, the Apocryphal Gospels, and the Epistle to the Laodiceans; and who would say that these writings approach in any degree to the *vraisemblance* of our epistles—or to their success?

The *external* attestation of these epistles is met in an evasive and unsatisfactory way by the Tendency critics. They habitually minimize the force of patristic evidence. Holtzmann devotes to this branch of the subject but nine out of his 282 pages of criticism, reserving it for a concluding subsection of his argument (pp. 257-266). It would be impossible to express more decidedly than Holtzmann does in this way, one's contempt for the judgment of the great Church leaders who established the New Testament canon. Weiss's statement, that "the Pastoral epistles are as strongly attested as any writings of Paul," remains unshaken. Holtzmann himself admits it to be nearer the truth than the hardy assertion of Baur, to the effect that they are supported by "no testimony of any weight earlier than the end of the second century." How Holtzmann reconciles their acknowledged use in the epistles of Ignatius and Polycarp with the date he assigns to them, we are at a loss to understand. Marcion, with Tatian (in regard to 1 and 2 Timothy), and some other Gnostics, alone dissented from the Church of the second century in this matter; but Marcion must have ceased to be a Marcionite, if he had given a place in his Apostolicon to these writings. Now that it is demonstrated that Marcion's *Luke* - the only Gospel he accepted—was a mutilated edition of the canoni cal Third Gospel,[1] his name ceases to be of weight in questions of canonicity. Tertullian's reference to Marcion on this point implies that Marcion *knew* these books and *excluded* them from the list of Pauline epistles, where they already held a recognised place. If Tertullian is to be trusted, we can therefore trace as far back as the middle of the second century, not the *origin*, but the *general recognition and ecclesiastical use* of the Pastoral Epistles; and this involves their previous diffusion through the Church, and a considerable term of pre-existence. This is but one point out of several in which recent investigation has brought out more clearly the force and definiteness of the testimony to their early reception. "If the battle had to be fought on the ground of external evidence," Dr. Salmon justly says, "the Pastoral epistles would gain a complete victory."

But we must now betake ourselves to the field of *internal criticism*. Here, we hasten to admit, there are difficulties and obscurities which call for inquiry, such as in the modern critical mind were bound to awaken misgiving. Chief amongst these is the fact—now generally admitted, and against which apologists like Otto and Wieseler, and even Reuss in his earlier discussions, have contended in vain—that no place exists for the Pastorals in the scheme of Paul's life given us in the Acts of the Apostles. On the other hand, Luke's biography expressly leaves the apostle's story unfinished; and if there be evidence sufficient to prove these letters written by St. Paul, they become themselves a decisive proof that his life extended beyond the point reached in Acts xxviii. Against this supposition there is no counter-evidence of any positive worth. The testimony of tradition, such as it is,[2] inclines in its favour.

---

[1] See Sanday's *Gospels in the Second Century*, and the section on "Marcion's Gospel" in Salmon's *Introduction to the New Testament*.

[2] It is strange, indeed, that the Church preserved so shadowy a recollection of later apostolic times. With the last sentence of the Acts the curtain drops suddenly upon an unfinished scene, full of light and action, which we were watching with the most eager interest.

The record of the Acts, if it does not supply the historical basis of these epistles, at any rate leaves the ground clear for them. Granting, however, their fullest force to the embarrassments and uncertainties of the traditional view, it appears to us, on a candid re-examination, that the difficulties in the way of the contrary hypothesis are very considerably greater, and amount, in fact, to a literary and historical impossibility.

We proceed to examine, in support of this position, *the vocabulary and style* of the Pastoral Epistles; their *personal and circumstantial details;* their *doctrinal features;* and *the ecclesiastical situation* which they assume.

II. VOCABULARY AND STYLE.

In examining the vocabulary of the Pastorals every observer is struck by the number of their hapax-legomena. Holtzmann (pp. 86–95) enumerates seventy-four in the six chapters of 1 Timothy, forty-six in the four of 2 Timothy, and twenty-eight in the three of Titus; to these add twenty-three verbal peculiarities common to two or more of the letters, and we have a total of 171 out of 897, or *nearly a fifth* of the words of the Pastorals, which are found nowhere else in the New Testament. (The list given in the valuable appendices to the Grimm-Thayer New Testament Lexicon agrees closely with this estimate.) On the first blush of the matter, this looks suspicious. The epistle to the Hebrews, whose authorship we cannot claim for St. Paul, contains in its thirteen longer chapters a slightly smaller number of hapax-legomena. The epistle of James, the only extant work of its author, in five chapters has but seventy-three,

---

It seems, to change the figure, as though the glare of the fires of burning Rome and Jerusalem had thrown all contemporary events into the shade. Christian minds were so occupied and overwhelmed with the national convulsions taking place, which in view of the prophecies of Christ appeared to portend the end of the world, that personal incidents remained unrecorded or left but a faint impress on the memory.

one less than 1 Timothy with six; while the Apocalypse, with all its specialty of matter, has only 156 such words in its twenty-two chapters.

But let us compare the vocabulary of the Pastorals with that of other Pauline epistles, and the matter assumes a different aspect. The apostle Paul excelled his companion writers in the New Testament in versatility of expression, no less than in intellectual breadth and force. And we are able to trace a gradual advance in the freedom and variety of his dialect. In the two Thessalonian epistles, forming the first group of his writings, there is an average of *five* hapax-legomena to the chapter; in Romans, of the second group, the average number is nearly *seven*; in Ephesians and Colossians taken together, *eight*; in Philippians, a little later—although the subject-matter is of so general a purport—the figure reaches *ten*. It is not surprising, therefore, that the Pastorals furnish *thirteen* hapax-legomena to the chapter, especially when it is considered that this is the last group of the four, and that if later writings from the same hand had been extant, the list of its peculiarities would in all likelihood have been reduced. The regular progression of the above figures marks them as belonging to one and the same series. They show in St. Paul a writer whose mind, fixed as it was in its essential principles, yet never grew stereotyped nor encased itself in set phrases and formulæ, but to the last was active and sensitive, taking on new colours and modes of expression from its changing environment.

That this is the true interpretation of the statistics we have given is confirmed by the variety of language apparent in this single group. Only *a ninth* of their entire vocabulary is common to the three epistles, notwithstanding their close connexion of thought. This ninth of the whole forms *a third* of the words of Titus—evidently the middle letter of the group, as it is the least peculiar; somewhat less than *a fourth* of its verbiage occurs in neither of its comrades; and the remainder, *nearly a half*, it shares with one or other of the two, but not with both. Now an imitator, seeking to palm off his writings as St. Paul's, would presumably have followed the language of his exemplar more closely than the actual writer has done; he would infallibly have *repeated himself* more frequently, when he had once formed a dialect which he thought would pass for the apostle's.

On comparing Colossians with its neighbours, Ephesians and Philippians, we find it agreeing with both in a little less, and differing from both in somewhat more than *a third* of its vocabulary; in the remaining third it coincides with one or other of the two, with Ephesians, of course, in a greatly preponderating degree. Of the words of Galatians, *above two-thirds* recur in the kindred Romans. These results correspond very closely with that given by comparison of Titus with its fellows, allowance being made for the greater variety of matter in the earlier sets of letters. The author of the Pastoral Epistles has the same freedom and fertility of expression that distinguished the Paul of the accepted epistles. And after all, his language is substantially Pauline. Out of the 726 words common to the Pastorals with other New Testament books, while 133 occur elsewhere only in non-Pauline books (including Hebrews), in the remaining 593, or as nearly as possible *two-thirds* of their whole lexical content—the same proportion in which Galatians is identified with Romans—they associate themselves with the older epistles of the apostle.

The analysis of the 171 hapax-legomena yields interesting results. A number of them are merely variations of characteristic words of Paul, branches of the same word-stem—*e.g.*, ἀκαίρως, ἀνάλυσις,[1] ἑδραίωμα, σεμνότης, ὑπερπλεο-

---

[1] The first two of these belong to a small group of words, including also κέρδος, προκοπή, σεμνός, σπένδομαι, by which the Pastorals are connected with Philippians, probably the most recent of Paul's previous writings.

νάζω, ὑποτύπωσις, φρεναπάτης. In the earlier epistles one notes an increasing fondness[1] for *compound* words, sometimes of strange and original forms. This tendency is yet more noticeable in the Pastorals. Out of some 200 negative compounds (in ἀ- or ἀν-) in the Greek Testament Lexicon, 40 are peculiar to the other Pauline epistles, and no less than 15 to these books alone. In Paul and the Pastorals alone are found compounds of ἑτερο-, καλο-, κενο-, ὀρθο- ; ἱερο- appears but once (A. xix. 37) elsewhere. Compare, further, the peculiar derivatives of οἰκο-, φιλο-, ψευδο-, and of λόγος and φρήν (-φρον-) in the second member, with their parallels in other epistles. Such comparison, when extending to a large number of particulars, seems to us to supply a peculiarly delicate test of authorship. For while a forger may with some success reproduce in novel combinations the identical language of his original, to create fresh words on the same analogy, and even to carry on further, up to the date required, the growing verbal habits and hobbies (if we may so say) of the master, is a feat of literary personation beyond belief.

Subtracting from the Pastoral vocabulary that which is either contained in other Pauline letters or has its analogy and basis there, the residue is, for the most part, not difficult of explanation. The bulk of the really isolated and extraordinary expressions of these books are due to their subject-matter. *Faith unfeigned, sound speech uncondemned, the doctrine according to godliness, a spirit of discipline, a good degree; the deposit, the laying on of hands, the presbytery;* and, on the other hand, *fables and endless genealogies, questionings and logomachies, oppositions of falsely named knowledge; men diseased, puffed up, corrupted in mind and bereft of truth, vain talkers and deceivers, greedy of base gain,*

---

[1] Any one who will compare the hapax-legomena of Colossians or Philippians with those of any of the epistles of the earlier groups, as given in Thayer's *Appendix* to Grimm's Lexicon, will easily verify this statement.

making shipwreck of faith—these phrases are as distinctive of and proper to the Pastoral Epistles as *justification* and *adoption, bondage* and *works of law* to Romans and Galatians; or *the fulness of Christ, His body the Church, principalities and powers, wisdom* and *mystery* to Ephesians and Colossians. Provided there is nothing un-Pauline in their structure, the novelty of such words tells in no way against them. New circumstances, in a mind like St. Paul's, inevitably call forth new ideas and expressions. The question passes from the domain of language to that of history. And we shall have to consider whether it was possible and likely that before the apostle's death the condition of things had come about which the expressions we have quoted indicate and describe.

There is, it is curious to observe, a group of words connecting these letters with the epistle to the Hebrews and the writings of Luke (between which, as is well known, there are many resemblances of language). Out of the 133 words employed in these but not in other acknowledged letters of St. Paul, 17 belong to the epistle to the Hebrews, and 34 to the Third Gospel or the Acts.[1] Amongst these are a few so rare and distinctive, that they strongly suggest the existence of some bond of association connecting the several writers with each other. We note, as bearing on the same point, the predilection of our author for *medical* figures and phrases, of which there are dis-

---

[1] See *The Pauline Antilegomena*, a paper by the lamented W. H. Simcox, in the *Expositor*, 3rd series, viii. 180-192; also Holtzmann, pp. 95-97. A few words are special to the three in common. Amongst the distinctive expressions peculiar to the Pastorals and Hebrews are ἀνυπότακτος, ἀφιλάργυρος, βέβηλος, ἐκτρέπεσθαι, κοσμικός, ὀρέγεσθαι, πρόδηλος. Peculiar to Luke (Gospel or Acts) and the Pastorals in the N.T., are ἄνοια, ἀντιλαμβάνεσθαι, ἀντιλέγειν, ἀχάριστος, βυθίζειν, δυνάστης, ἐξαρτίζειν, ζωγρεῖν, ζωογονεῖν, νομοδιδάσκαλος, νοσφίζεσθαι, πειθαρχεῖν, περίεργος, προδότης, προπετής, σωφροσύνη, φιλανθρωπία. Peculiar to the three: δι' ἣν αἰτίαν (elsewhere διὸ in St. Paul), μεταλαμβάνειν, παραιτεῖσθαι, τυγχάνειν, χάριν ἔχειν (elsewhere the Pauline εὐχαριστῶ). In 1 Timothy and Hebrews alone Christ is called "mediator."

tinct but less numerous traces in earlier epistles.[1] These features of the dialect of the Pastorals are naturally explained by the intimate and prolonged companionship which "Luke, the beloved physician," enjoyed with the apostle in his declining years. The pathetic reference of 2 Timothy iv. 11, "Only Luke is with me," affords one of those undesigned coincidences which are of peculiar force in arguments of this kind. Hebrews xiii. 23, 24, supplies a link connecting the writer of this epistle with Timothy and Rome; and leads us to suppose that he was in touch with the little circle surrounding the apostle in his Roman prison.

Occasional *Latinisms*,[2] appearing now for the first time, may indicate the effect on Paul's speech of his prison-life in Italy and his travels in the West—probably as far as Spain (to "the limits of the West," *Clemens Romanus*). If there is still left, after all that has been said, a residuum of expressions that "defy all attempts at explanation" (Weiss), this will not surprise us when we remember how much of the circumstances of Paul's life in these latest years, and of his mental history, is unknown to us. Much the same might be said concerning the language of the undoubted epistles.

When we look at the larger features of style and composition, the conclusion drawn from our examination of the writer's vocabulary is confirmed. True, we miss here, as Holtzmann says, "the pervasive dialectical character," the organic unity and logical articulation of the major epistles; although, in some instances, this defect lies with the in-

---

[1] On *St. Luke and St. Paul, their mutual relations*, see the *Expositor* (Dean Plumptre), 1st series, iv. 134-160. E.g., *cancer, cauterized, diseased about questions, having itching ears*; and especially the frequent recurrence of *sound, wholesome*, and the opposite, applied to character and teaching. For other epistles, see Col. ii. 19, and Lightfoot's note in his *Commentary*.

[2] *E.g.*, ὃν τρόπον, οἵους διωγμοὺς (2 Tim. iii. 8, 11); ἀδηλότης, πρόκριμα (*præiudicium*), σεσωρευμένα ἁμαρτίαις. See Holtzmann, p. 109.

terpreter rather than the author, and we may fail to catch the logical thread which in reality runs through these detached warnings and instructions. We miss also notably the passion and glow, the incomparable verve of the earlier Paul. This is only to be expected. We are listening to "Paul the aged," as he called himself perhaps three years before this time (Philem. 9), a man broken by extreme mental strain and physical labour, by hardship and imprisonment. In the epistle to the Romans the apostle's thought and style were in their noontide of strength and fervour; in Ephesians we find their mellow afternoon; and in the Pastorals the time of evening has arrived, with its shaded light and slackened step. Neither the subjects on which he writes, nor the need of his correspondents call for the effort put forth in the letters to Corinth and Rome. But if these writings do not exhibit the *sustained* power of the great epistles, the *same* power manifests itself—the Pauline subtlety of reasoning, and wealth of theological conception, and intensity of personal feeling—coming out in single expressions and sentences that flash with the genius of the old master. Who but the apostle Paul could have penned such passages as 1 Timothy i. 8–11; ii. 5–7; 2 Timothy i. 8–12; iv. 6–8; Titus ii. 11–15; iii. 4–8? "E'en in our ashes live their wonted fires." The Church has not erred in discerning in these books the ring of Paul's voice and inspiration.

If the logical particles of the argumentative epistles are missing—if γάρ, for instance, recurs oftener in Galatians than in the three Pastorals together, and ἄρα, ἔπειτα, ἔτι, ὥσπερ never put in an appearance—this is in favour of authenticity rather than otherwise. Nothing would have been easier for a man steeped in Paulinism like our author, than to sprinkle his pages with catchwords of this kind. This objection applies with almost equal force to the letters of the first imprisonment, which form in several respects a middle term between the major epistles and the Pastorals.

It is true, again, that instances of *anacoluthon* and *parenthesis*, of the interrupted and varied periods so characteristic of Paul's style, are infrequent here; but the reason for this is obvious—namely, that the long-drawn argument and passionate feeling of the great epistles are also wanting. Broken periods, notwithstanding, do occur, as in 1 Timothy i. 3, ff. (comp. Rom. v. 12, ff.); 1 Timothy ii. 1, resumed in ver. 12 (comp. Eph. iii. 1–14); 1 Timothy iii. 15, f.; Titus i. 1–3; iii. 4–7. The tendency of Paul's sentences to grow out of shape, extending themselves indefinitely in a chain of prepositional, participial, or relative clauses, reaches an extreme in such passages as 1 Timothy i. 18–20 (comp., for the string of relatives, 1 Cor. ii. 7, 8; Col. i. 27–29); iv. 1–3; vi. 13–16; 2 Timothy i. 3–5, 8–12; Titus i. 1–4 (comp. Rom. i. 1–7); ii. 11–14. These periods reproduce the Pauline manner, without the least sign of artifice or imitation. In what other writer can we find such looseness of grammatical construction combined with such closeness and continuity of thought? "St. Paul's style," M. Renan says, "is the most personal that ever was—hardly a consecutive phrase in it; it is a rapid conversation stenographed, and reproduced without correction." This is precisely the impression which the reading of these epistles makes on the Greek Testament scholar.

Let the student compare, for example, 1 Timothy ii. with a practical section of the early epistles—say, Romans xiii. He will discover an identical method and movement of mind in both places—injunction guarded by careful distinction and explanation, supported by large general principles, and enforced by appeals to the presence of God or of Christ—all this poured out as a living stream of thought, in the most informal manner one can conceive. Or let him put 1 Timothy vi. 3–12 by the side of Colossians ii. 8—iii. 4, as a specimen of the apostle's later polemical style. In each case he sets out by stating the contradiction of the principles condemned to the doctrine of Christ, going on to indicate the character of their professors and the outcome of their teaching, and concludes by urging his readers to pursue the opposite path and showing them its glorious issue.

Among minor mannerisms in which this writer identifies himself with St. Paul, are the argumentative use of οἶδα in such phrases as *Knowing this, But we know*, etc.; the reference to opponents as τινές (*certain persons*); the frequent use of *if any, if anything else*, for *whosoever, whatever else*; the characteristic *in Christ* as a distinguishing adjunct of Christian acts and states; the intensive use of πᾶς to heighten qualities, as *all acceptation, all long-suffering*, etc.; the employment of πιστεύω in the *passive* (exclusively Pauline in the New Testament, found thrice here, five times elsewhere); of μάλιστα, *especially*, in qualifications (four times here, thrice in Paul elsewhere); the agreement of ὅστις with its predicate (1 Tim. iii. 15, six times in other epp.; Acts xvi. 12 is different); and the *accusative of apposition to a sentence*, an idiom confined to 1 Timothy ii. 6 and two earlier passages of St. Paul. Most remarkable of all, perhaps, is the order *Christ Jesus* (according to the critical texts) in which our Saviour's name is written wherever His official character or His present rule over His servants or relation to them is in the writer's mind. The distinction between *Jesus Christ* (historical) and *Christ Jesus* (official) has never been observed by any other Christian writer with the same instinctive care and delicacy as by St. Paul.[1]

Now, the appearance of new and disappearance of older forms of speech are accountable in the later compositions of a versatile writer. But the persistence in these epistles of so many Pauline idiosyncrasies, and these of so varied a

---

[1] See on this subject a valuable essay by the late revered Benjamin Hellier on "The Pauline Usage of the Names of Christ," in the *Theological Monthly* for February, April, and July, 1890. Mr. Hellier finds that this criterion tells decisively in favour of the Pauline authorship of the Pastorals, but against that of the epistle to the Hebrews.

character as we have shown them to be, sporadic in their occurrence and inwoven into the entire texture of thought and speech, is only consistent with one assumption—namely, that their titular is also their actual author, and that the word *Paul*, with which they each begin, is the honest truth.

III. PERSONAL DATA OF THE PASTORALS.

In the case of 2 Timothy the references to person and place are so multiplied (more numerous, in fact, than in any other epistle except Romans) and wear so genuine an aspect, that they have secured in its favour the verdict of many critics, including Schleiermacher, Bleek, Neander, Ritschl, and finally Reuss (formerly accepting all three), who reject one or both of its comrades. Others, such as Ewald, Renan, Hausrath, Hitzig, Pfleiderer, Sabatier, are inclined to see in these circumstantial notices (2 Tim. i. 15-18; iv. 9-21; also Tit. iii. 12-15) fragments of one or more lost letters of the apostle. Holtzmann, following Baur, declines all theories of partial authenticity (pp. 119-126); he regards these verses as *concocted* for the express purpose of giving a colour to documents wholly spurious and supposititious. This is, at least, consistent. The three epistles must stand or fall together, and in their integrity; they are of one piece and texture. If the genuineness of 2 Timothy is certified by circumstantial evidence, the reason is gone for impugning the rest; for their dialect, and the ecclesiastical situation they suppose, are already proved to be Pauline. Let us review these passages, and see if they do not commend themselves and the documents to which they belong.

The mention of the Asiatic party "of whom is Phygelus and Hermogenes" (2 Tim. i. 15), serves as a motive for Timothy to "guard the good deposit" (ver. 14; comp. chap. ii. 1, 2); and the desertion of these men in turn reminds Paul of the contrasted behaviour of Onesiphorus (vers. 16-18). This parenthesis (vers. 15-18) enforces the need for courage and faithfulness on Timothy's part, and for the choice of a succession of "faithful men" as teachers in the Church. It cannot be detached from the context.

The tidings and messages concluding the letter are the most miscellaneous of the kind in Paul's correspondence. They are thrown out with the unstudied freedom natural when the heart is full and there are many things to say, and perhaps little time to say them. Renan's phrase, "conversation stenographed," exactly describes 2 Timothy iv. 9-21. The repeated "Come quickly" of Paul's yearning heart (vers. 9, 21) is put down by Holtzmann (p. 62), as in Titus iii. 12, to the "tendency" of the writer, who is anxious that Timothy and Titus "should not seem too independent by the side of the apostle!"—a pitiful example of the Tübingen method.—The allusion to the despatch of "Titus to Dalmatia" in 2 Timothy iv. 10 agrees with the summons previously given him in Titus iii. 12 "to Nicopolis," lying in the same direction.—The apostle wishes to have *Mark* by his side, as well as Timothy himself (ver. 11); and this surely suggests his saying, "Tychicus have I sent[1] *to Ephesus*" (ver. 12); he is not forgetting that Timothy is there,[2] but intimates that *Ephesus* would not be left without oversight (comp. Tit. iii. 12). We know from Colossians iv. 10 that Mark had recovered St. Paul's esteem, forfeited by the conduct related in Acts xiii. 13, and was with him during the former imprisonment at Rome, where he had doubtless shown himself "useful for service"; and, moreover, that he was then about to set out for Asia—whence Paul now desires to recall him.—The "cloak" and "books" (ver. 13), we presume, were "left at Troas with Carpus" on St. Paul's last

---

[1] "Sent" probably with this very letter. Ἀπέστειλα we may take to be *epistolary aorist*, written from the reader's standpoint, as in Col. iv. 8.

[2] So we learn from ver. 19, if not from the general tenor of the letter, in its connexion with 1 Timothy.

journey to Macedonia (1 Tim. i. 3), which found an unexpected terminus in the prison at Rome. The Tendency critics are sadly at a loss to account for the manufacture by the pseudo-Paul of these articles. The thought of the coming "winter" (ver. 21) reminds the imprisoned man of his old cloak; and in his solitude he craves the companionship of books.—"Alexander the coppersmith" (vers. 14, 15) forms a link between the apostle's directions to Timothy (vers. 9-13), and the account of his own position he is about to give in vers. 16-18. This man had borne witness, directly or indirectly, against Paul at Rome, and this was not the first injury suffered from him: was it through his machinations that the apostle's renewed imprisonment had come about? Timothy, in starting for Rome, is warned against his plots.—The satisfaction St. Paul feels in having proclaimed his great message on the occasion of his defence before the Emperor's tribunal (ver. 17) is in keeping with what he intimates in Romans i. 8, 14-16 (comp. Acts xxiii. 11) touching the importance that, in his judgment, belonged to the imperial city as a centre for Gentile Christianity. This opportunity was, in truth, the climax of the apostle's mission to the heathen (Acts ix. 15; xxvii. 24). Ver. 18 signifies that his present deliverance is but a respite, perhaps for a few months (ver. 21), leaving no doubt in his mind as to the final issue; it is "into Christ's *heavenly* kingdom" that Paul now looks to be "saved."—Perhaps the salutation to "the house of Onesiphorus" (ver. 19; comp. chap. i. 16) recalls to the writer's mind "Erastus" and "Trophimus" (ver. 20), who had failed to render him the service expected from them. One is surprised, however, that Timothy should be told of what had occurred "at Miletus," but a few miles distant from Ephesus, months before this time. Possibly the apostle at this point is talking to *himself* rather than to Timothy; he drops into soliloquy. We have met before with Erastus and Trophimus in Timothy's company (Acts xix. 22; xx. 4: not the Erastus of Romans xvi. 23).

The names of those who greet Timothy from Rome bear the marks of authenticity. They are new to the epistles; two of them are Greek, two Latin names. "Linus" appears in the list of the first bishops of Rome.

Twenty-three members of the apostolic Church are mentioned in this letter; eleven of them for the first and last time in the New Testament. In the cases of the other twelve, there is nothing at variance with, nor anything repeated from, what we learn elsewhere about the persons referred to, but much that agrees with it, and in unexpected ways.

Towards Timothy and Titus, some of the critics say, Paul is made to assume a domineering attitude, lecturing and "scolding" Timothy, forsooth, as if he were "a raw catechumen"! This is grossly exaggerated. What we do see is the apostolic dignity, softened by a tender sympathy and blended in Timothy's case with apprehension, with which St. Paul, in the presence of the Church, charges his representatives placed in circumstances of grave responsibility and peril. He addresses Timothy, his helper for many years, as a *young* man (1 Tim. iv. 12; 2 Tim. ii. 22; comp. Tit. ii. 15); but when these letters were written Timothy had scarcely passed his thirtieth year, and he was set over the eldership of Ephesus. He was of a nature apt to retain its youth; and to old men those of the next generation always seem young.

On the whole, it does not appear that Timothy's character had matured in the way we might have hoped. He was not prepared to be thrown on his own resources. The youthful timidity hinted at in 1 Corinthians xvi. 10, 11 he had not sufficiently outgrown; the repeated exhortations to courage and endurance addressed to him in the second epistle imply some failure in this respect. With this was connected a want of firmness, a pliability and accessibility to private influences, against which he needed to be cautioned (1 Tim. v. 19, 22). We imagine there was something recluse and contemplative in his disposition, tending to abstract him from public and practical duties (1 Tim. iv. 11–16); and associated with this a touch of asceticism, which made him weaker to resist the very temptations he most shunned (1 Tim. v. 22, 23). And we suspect that Hofmann is right in inferring from 1 Timothy vi. 3–12, that the young minister was sometimes inclined in his weariness and despondency to envy the easy, gainful life which false teachers were pursuing under his eyes.

In fact, Timothy's was a fine, but not a robust nature; liable to suffer from an uncongenial atmosphere, and ill-framed for conflict and leadership, with more of the ivy in its composition than the oak. St. Paul found in him the complement of his own bold and active temperament, as Peter did in John, and Luther in Melanchthon. In the apostle's company Timothy had shown admirable devotion and steadfastness (Phil. ii. 19–23). But he drooped alone. Separated so long from his leader, amid surroundings trying in the last degree to his sensitive disposition and delicate frame, his faith and his character were severely strained. The "tears" with which he parted from the apostle (2 Tim. i. 4) and his reluctance to be left longer at Ephesus (1 Tim. i. 3) were due not merely to his love for his father in Christ, but to the peculiar difficulty to him of the work laid upon him. The portrait which these letters give us of young Timothy is consistent and life-like, and it harmonizes well with the slighter traits preserved in the other epistles and the Acts of the Apostles.

A plausible objection to 1 Timothy lies in the fact that when he wrote this letter, St. Paul, it appears, had very recently left Timothy behind at Ephesus, after himself paying a visit to the city (chap. i. 3). What need, then, for these detailed and reiterated advices, about matters, too, which, one would have thought, the apostle might have arranged himself when he was on the spot? Our answer is that, in all probability, *Paul had not been at Ephesus at this time.*

"The words of 1 Timothy i. 3 only say that Paul wished Timothy to stay at Ephesus where he then was, while he himself went on to Macedonia" (Hofmann). Προσμεῖναι means *to remain still, to stay on* (Acts xviii. 18), not *to remain behind*, which is ὑπομένειν (Acts xvii. 14) or might have been expressed as in Titus i. 5. And πορευόμενος may signify *on my way, in the course of my journey to Macedonia*, just as well as *setting out to Macedonia* (see Acts xxi. 6). The apostle was bound for Macedonia, and could not afford to turn aside to Ephesus;[1] for this very reason he desired Timothy to continue his sojourn there, in order to carry out instructions already given in brief, and which he now communicates at length. The incident of Acts xx. 17 ("from Miletus he sent to Ephesus and called the elders of the Church") seems to have repeated itself, perhaps at the same spot (comp. 2 Tim. iv. 20); only Paul is now travelling in the opposite direction (chap. iv. 13, 20),[2] and summons Timothy

---

[1] Another reason suggests itself for St. Paul's giving Ephesus the go-by. His first ministry there ended in a great popular tumult. He had made powerful and bitter enemies in the city, and left it shaken both in mind and body and in peril of his life (comp. 2 Cor. i. 8–10 with 1 Cor. xv. 32 and Acts xix.). It was "the Jews from Asia" who began the murderous assault upon him afterwards in Jerusalem (Acts xxi. 27); and "Alexander the coppersmith," in all likelihood the Jewish leader whom his countrymen put forward in the Ephesian riot (Acts xix 33), about this time did the apostle "much evil." Paul sought help from his friends "in Asia" (2 Tim. i. 15; comp. Acts xix. 30, 31)—probably rebutting evidence; and it was refused (through the influence of his opponents there?). All this goes to show that Ephesus was a most dangerous place for St. Paul, and that he had good reason for the sorrowful anticipation of Acts xx. 25. His relation to Ephesus was something like that to Thessalonica long before, when he "would fain have come once and again; but Satan hindered."

[2] It is evident that the three Pastoral Epistles were written in quick succession, and that the events connected with them marched rapidly. The course of Paul's movements, in our view, was something like this: He sailed from Crete (calling there, perhaps, on his way East from Spain), where he left Titus; then coasted along the Asiatic shore, calling at Miletus and Troas amongst other places; wrote to Timothy from Macedonia, shortly afterwards to Titus; then proceeded to Corinth, and was arrested and hurried to Rome during the summer, before he reached Nicopolis. The journey to the East proposed in Phil. ii. 24 and Philemon 22 was accomplished, we imagine, *before* the mission to Spain.

(not the body of the elders) from Ephesus for an interview,[1] at the end of which his young helper, tearful (chap. i. 4) and reluctant ("I exhorted thee"), returns to his station, and the apostle pursues his journey, promising to send Timothy a full letter of instructions based on the representations his assistant had made to him touching the condition of things in the Ephesian Church. Such a letter we have in the first epistle to Timothy. Since Paul and Timothy had met so recently, there would be no need for inserting anything in the shape of news or private messages. All that remained to be said was of an official character, and pertained to the public conduct of Timothy's ministry at Ephesus.

If our view of the order of things be correct, then St. Paul's presentiment of six or seven years ago, that the Ephesians would "see his face no more" (Acts xx. 25) was verified. He still "hopes to come" (1 Tim. iii. 14; iv. 13), but with no certainty ; and we gather from the silence of the second letter that he had failed to do so, and Timothy had still to remain month after month at his unwelcome post, without sight of his dear master and enduring the hope deferred which "maketh the heart sick." The service of Onesiphorus to the apostle "in Ephesus" (2 Tim. i. 18) may just as well have been rendered to him during his former long residence there. His repulse by "all those in Asia," and the "evil" done him by Alexander, related probably to his trial now in process at Rome, when unfavourable evidence was given by the latter and favourable evidence withheld by the former (chap. i. 15; iv. 14–16). The sentence against "Hymenæus and Alexander" (1 Tim. i. 20)—not the Alexander of 2 Timothy iv. 14—could have been pro-

---

[1] Hofmann does not suppose an interview necessary (pp. 66, 67). He thinks the "exhortation" of 1 Tim. i. 3 was made by letter ; and that the "tears" of 2 Tim. i. 4 were *wept by letter* in return (*brieflich geweint*) —a conceit by which he compromises an otherwise strong position. There is no need for the apostle in either epistle to refer further to the circumstances of his meeting with Timothy. A meeting *somewhere* there clearly had been

nounced from a distance, like that against the Corinthian offender (1 Cor. v. 3-5). None of these allusions compel us to suppose that Paul had himself been recently in Ephesus.

Against the authenticity of 2 Timothy it is contended that the exhortations of chap. ii. 1–iv. 6 are inconsistent with the "speedy" coming to Rome which Paul urges on his friend. But it will be observed that these directions are much less specific than those previously given in the first epistle, and bear on Timothy's own spirit and character rather than his administrative duties; also that his "*doing his diligence* to come before winter" does not exclude—it rather implies—uncertainty and causes of delay. Especially we must bear in mind that the apostle knew his end to be near, and feared that this might be his last message to his "dear child Timothy" (2 Tim. iv. 5, 6).

A similar objection is brought against the epistle to Titus, grounded on chap. iii. 12, and much the same reply may be made. In this case it will be noticed that Paul expressly provides for the continuance of Titus' mission by "Artemas, or Tychicus"; in which event, we may presume, Titus would hand over the instructions now received to the brother who relieved him.

We have finally to consider the light in which *Paul himself* appears in these epistles. Why, it is asked, should he write to his old assistants and familiars, his "true children" in the faith, with so much stiffness and formality and such an air of authority, so that the greeting to Titus, for example, is only surpassed by that of the epistle to the Romans in its solemnity and rhetorical fulness? The answer lies partly in the fact that these epistles, especially 1 Timothy and Titus, are "open," or quasi-public letters, written with the Churches of Ephesus and Crete in view, and such as it would be suitable to read, in part at least, at their assemblies. The case of Philemon is quite different. And the apostle writes, above all in 2 Timothy,

24

under the sense that "the time of his departure is at hand." His words have the grave and pathetic dignity of a valedictory address to his successors in the ministry of Christ.

The critics find something of exaggeration and "extreme rhetoric" in the allusions of 1 Timothy i. 12–17 to Paul's earlier life. But these references are in keeping with 1 Corinthians xv. 9 and Ephesians iii. 8. The ardent gratitude and profound self-abasement before the sovereignty of Divine grace which animated the apostle throughout his ministry naturally, come to their fullest expression in his closing years. We catch in these words the very beating of St. Paul's heart. *Nemo potest Paulinum pectus effingere* (Erasmus). To treat them as the cold and crafty invention of a forger is little short of sacrilege. It is said that there is an egotism in the letters, a fondness for reverting to his own history and making himself a model for others, unlike the genuine Paul. (See however, 1 Thess. ii. 1, 2; 1 Cor. ix.; iv. 1–6; x. 33–xi. 1; Gal. iv. 11–20, etc.) This feature of the Pastorals is, to our mind, one of the subtlest traits of reality. How naturally the old man's mind turns to the days of his youth! His memory lingers over the past. He delights to dwell on the great trust that God first committed to him, and which must so soon pass into the hands of others. It is truly affecting thus to see the old warrior "fight his battles o'er again," and to note the simple-hearted joy with which he draws from his own trials and triumphs encouragements for the fearful Timothy. His references to the family and childhood of Timothy further show how much the aged apostle's mind is living in the past (2 Tim. i. 5; iii. 14, 15).

The beauty of St. Paul's "swan-song," in 2 Timothy iv. 6–8, should have raised it for ever above critical mistrust. No passage in his epistles is more finely touched with the apostle's genius. It has the Hebraistic rhythm of all his more exalted utterances. It echoes earlier sayings, but without repetition. It is the cup of a deep spring filled to the brim with Paul's finest thought and tenderest feeling, expressed with a serenity which came to his strenuous nature only at rare moments, and speaks of a heart at ease within itself and that knows its labour ended and its storms gone by. These verses have an ideal fitness as the apostle's final record and pronouncement upon his own career. They put the seal of their faithful testimony on the earthly conflicts and toils of Christ's servant, crowned already with the earnest of the crown that awaits him from the hand of his Saviour and Judge. Nor has Christian faith since found any higher expression of its sense of victory in the presence of the last enemy.

The concluding line, in which the apostle claims this crown for "all," with himself, "who have loved the Lord's appearing," breathes the essence of the Pauline spirit. It was exactly like him to say this at the summit of his gladness and hope, whose life was a sacrifice to the Church of God and his glory and crown of rejoicing in the consummate salvation of his brethren in Christ. He invites us to share his own perfected fellowship in the joy of our Lord. We accept the token and hold it fast, *knowing from whom we have received it.*

We have now completed our examination of the language of the disputed epistles, and the circumstantial evidence for their origin which they themselves supply. However defective the inquiry, and open to objection in the details of interpretation, we venture to think that it furnishes sufficient proof that the canonical epistles to Timothy and Titus are the work of the apostle Paul, and that the early Church was justified in accepting these three letters in the name which they bore, and incorporating them with the other ten epistles upon the same footing of unquestioned authority. Neither in the style of the writings, nor in the tenor of their personal allusions, is there adequate ground, it seems to us, for the serious and long-sustained suspicions which exist against them. It is in the *subject-matter* of the epistles, in the nature of their theological and ecclesiastical contents, that these doubts have their motive and their real basis. Holtzmann is almost alone among his associates in seeking to ground his theory on a proper linguistic analysis of the documents. For the most part the Tendency critics take it as a thing self-evident and beyond the need of proof, that the heretics condemned in the Pastorals were Gnostics of the second century; and their interpretation proceeds on this assumption.

The closing sentences of Dr. Pfleiderer's account of the epistles, given in his *Urchristenthum*, exhibit very clearly the point of view from which the school he represents regard these writings, and the path by which they have arrived at their conclusions:—

"The Pastoral Epistles, especially the latest of them, the so-called *First to Timothy*—pave the way for that development of episcopacy in the Church which we find completed in the Ignatian Letters; and it is in this very purpose of helping to victory the idea of the episcopate as an apostolic institution, that we discover, side by side with the polemic against Gnostic heresy, the second main object of these epistles. In reality, these two objects are one and the same. . . . From the necessity that the Church should assert herself against the heretics there came about, on the one hand, the authentication of tradition in the form of *ecclesiastical dogma*, and on the other, the apostolic authorization of the episcopacy—*ecclesiastical hierarchy*: the latter being the practical embodiment of the former, the former the ideal ground of the latter.

"Now, in order to vindicate the doctrine and constitution of the Church effectually against heresy, they must above all things be based on apostolic tradition and authority; and the interests of the Church imperatively required that the advocate of the principle of authority should publish his warnings and injunctions in the name of that apostle who was held in chief—indeed, on this point, in sole esteem and deference,—that is to say, *in the name of Paul*. Strange indeed, and tragical, that the apostle of freedom has at last been enlisted as voucher for the principle of authority, and founder of the hierarchy! But if there is any one to blame for this perversion, it must be no other than

Marcion, who by his ultra-Paulinism forced the men of order and sound reason[1] into this awkward position!" (pp. 822, 823.)

With Pfleiderer at present, as with Baur fifty years ago, the deductions of this school against the authenticity of so many New Testament writings rest upon their *à priori* construction of the history of the primitive Church. That construction has been remodelled in Pfleiderer's hands; but in principle and method it remains the same as when first laid down by Baur.

No judgment, however, that we might form respecting the system of doctrine and Church organization indicated in these epistles, whether favourable or adverse to authenticity, ought to be regarded as in itself decisive upon this point. The data for such a judgment must be gathered from an unprejudiced examination of the documents; and they are themselves contingent on a multitude of questions of language and circumstantial detail, which need to be first carefully considered. The literary character of the epistles, and the personal and local references they contain, along with the external attestation to their origin, supply the *proof* of authorship in the first instance. It is enough if the ideas contained in the letters are in no way contradictory to the presumption already established. At the same time, our inquiry into their governing ideas and aims will, as we hope, serve more than a merely defensive and negative purpose. We shall strive to show, what is at least manifest to ourselves, that the teaching of the Pastoral epistles and the life of the Church as therein disclosed stand in an intimate, genetic connexion with that which the previous and acknowledged epistles of St. Paul present to us.

---

[1] This explanation, if it were true, throws a sad light on the character of "the men of order and sound reason" in the Church of the second century. It puts the Pastoral epistles on a level with the pseudo-Isidorian decretals. Any forger could plead as good an excuse.

IV. The Doctrinal Characteristics.

In reviewing the doctrine of the Pastorals, we take for our starting point the following sentence of Holtzmann (p. 159):

> "The general basis of ideas is unquestionably Pauline. It is no other doctrine than that of Paul which these writings profess and seek to expound. But the bare and impoverished form of this representation betrays its unauthenticity. Paul's doctrinal conceptions are weakened and brought down to the level of a later age. We have before us a diluted Paulinism, accommodated to the demands of an advanced stage of Church life, ecclesiastically modified and stereotyped, and which has come to terms with Jewish Christianity, the Paulinist and Legalist parties being at length compelled to join hands under the pressure of Gnostic and heretical assaults."

So far as this "impoverishment" of the true Paulinism is matter of expression, we have discussed it already (pp. 357, 358). As a description of the theological character of the epistles, there is a modicum of truth involved in Holtzmann's depreciatory estimate. St. Paul's characteristic doctrines do not here assume the commanding prominence given to them in the major epistles; they are not thrown into the same bold relief, nor developed with the same logical completeness. But then this observation applies equally to his earliest writings—the two epistles to the Thessalonians. When those former letters were written, the Legalist controversy, which occupied the central period of Paul's apostleship and called forth the mightiest efforts of his genius, had not yet arisen; by this time it had to a large extent subsided. The doctrines of salvation are quietly assumed, where before they were vehemently argued and defended. For they constitute, in the view alike of writer and readers, a conquest securely won, a foundation enduringly laid. But in this matter-of-fact assumption they lose nothing of their cardinal importance. The sentences in which they are affirmed serve to re-state, with axiomatic weight and precision, that Gospel which is to Paul and his sons in the faith a fundamental certainty (see 1 Tim. ii.

4–6; iii. 15, 16; 2 Tim. i. 9, 10). The Tendency critics are untrue to their own principle of evolution when they assume that the mind of Paul stood still, that he could write nothing but letters after the manner of Romans and Galatians, and when they insist upon our taking these great works as in style and proportion and theological purport the sole test of what is Pauline.

Most of all do the doctrinal passages of the epistle to Titus (i. 1–4; ii. 10–14; iii. 3–7) protest against the disparagement that the Pastorals contain a half-effaced and diluted Paulinism. These luminous *aperçus* of the method of redemption carry it backward to the Divine causation—"which God, who cannot lie, promised before times eternal"—and forward to its moral operation, and its issues in the life beyond; while they describe in full and glowing language the agency by which the work of man's renewal is brought about:

"We were senseless, disobedient, wandering, enslaved to manifold lusts and pleasures. But when the kindness and philanthropy of God our Saviour appeared—not by works done in righteousness, which we had wrought, but according to His mercy He saved us, through the washing of regeneration and the renewing of the Holy Spirit, which He poured on us richly through Jesus Christ our Saviour, that being justified by His grace, we might be made heirs according to the hope of eternal life."

There is no sign of poverty, or of laboured imitation, in a mind whose wealth runs over in this way. Here there is drawn for us, in a mere incidental passage, by a few rapid strokes of the pen, a picture of the whole Gospel in miniature. The sayings of the Pastoral Epistles bring the doctrines of grace to a rounded fulness and chastened ripeness of expression, that warrant us in seeing in them the authentic conclusion of the Pauline gospel of salvation in the mind which first conceived it.

It is impossible, within moderate limits, to discuss all the points in which Holtzmann detects a difference between the teaching of the Pastorals and that of the genuine epistles. We will deal with the most considerable of the alleged discrepancies, and those which alone raise any serious difficulty: (1) Amongst the chief is that touching *the nature of God*. The Divine character and agency are set forth under appellations new to us in St. Paul, and some of them unique. He is the "King of the ages, incorruptible, invisible, the only God"; "the blessed and only Potentate, the King of kings, and Lord of lords, who alone hath immortality, dwelling in light unapproachable, whom none of men hath seen, nor can see" (1 Tim. i. 17; vi. 15, 16); "the living God, who is Saviour of all men," and "gives life to all things" (1 Tim. iv. 10; vi. 13). Six times does the expression "God (our) Saviour" recur in these epistles, found but twice besides in the New Testament (Luke i. 47; Jude 26).

The emphasis thus laid on the Divine absoluteness has manifestly a polemical intention. But it is not necessary to go to the second century for its explanation. The clue lies nearer to our hand. We find it in the false dualism, current amongst Hellenistic Jews in St. Paul's time, which separated God from the world and treated the material creation as the work of inferior and intermediate beings. This system of theosophy, the daughter of Platonism and mother of Gnosticism, the apostle has already combated in his epistle to the Colossians, dealing with it there chiefly in its bearing on the Person and work of Christ. Philo of Alexandria, Paul's contemporary, was the chief exponent of this doctrine on Jewish ground. He represents what we may call the *Broad Church* of Judaism, whose influence inevitably made itself felt amongst Pauline Christians at a very early time. Indeed Gnosticism, as Dr. Jowett aptly says,[1] might be described as "the mental atmosphere of the Greek cities of Asia, a conducting medium between heathenism and Christianity"; perhaps we might say, a common solvent

---

[1] *Commentary* on 1 Thessalonians, second edition, p. 94.

of heathenism, Judaism, and Christianity. It limited the Divine prerogatives, confining the supreme God, under a false notion of reverence, to a purely spiritual and transcendental region. Hence God is here acknowledged as wielding in unshared dominion all creaturely and earthly powers, while in His own nature and blessedness He holds a realm of light inaccessible and life undecaying.

The dualism of the earliest Gnostics, or Gnosticizing Judaists, is reproved in its *ascetic* consequences in 1 Timothy iv. 3-5, where marriage and physical sustenance are vindicated as things of the Divine order—"sanctified by the word of God and prayer" (compare, and contrast Col. ii. 20-23). But the writer condemns the false spiritualism of the coming "latter times" in no other strain than we should expect from the Paul of 1 Corinthians, who had said, "To us there is but one God, the Father, of whom are all things and we for Him"—whose is "earth and its fulness"; and who again has written, "The woman is of the man, and the man through the woman; but all things of God."

The work of grace is placed with emphasis in the hands of *God*, in the interests of the Divine unity, and in tacit contradiction to those who "professing" above others "to know God," yet barred Him out from contact with human life, and so robbed Him of the honours of salvation. At the same time, the expression has an intrinsic fitness. The apostle's *theology* proper, his doctrine of God, resumes and absorbs his *soteriology*. His system of thought anticipates the goal marked out for the course of redemption—when "God shall be all in all" (1 Cor. xv. 28). See p. 338.

(2) "*The image of Christ* presented in the Pastorals is indeed composed of Pauline formulæ, but it is lacking in the Pauline spirit and feeling, in the mystic inwardness, the religious depth and moral force that live in the Christ of Paul." So says Schenkel, quoted by Holtzmann with approval (pp. 166, 167). Of the justice of this stricture every one will form his own estimate. It appeals not to

the critical expert, but to the feeling and discernment of the devout Christian reader. For ourselves, we find no defect, either of depth or force, in such a sentence as 1 Timothy ii. 5, 6, with its conception of the "one mediator between God and men, Christ Jesus, who is man; who gave Himself a ransom for all—the testimony to be borne in its own time;" which, moreover, is precisely *not* "composed of Pauline formulæ," for Christ is here called *mediator* for the first time (comp. Heb. viii. 6, etc). Nor are his mysticism and religious depth at all to seek in 1 Timothy iii. 15, 16 (the "mystery of godliness, He who was manifested in the flesh," etc.). The expression "in Christ Jesus," almost peculiar to Paul, and which carries with it all the inwardness and depth of his sense of the believer's relation to his Lord, is employed seven times in the two letters to Timothy in application to Christian acts and states.

It is said that the emphasis thrown upon the Divine "manifestation" and the "appearing" ($\epsilon\pi\iota\phi\alpha\nu\epsilon\iota\alpha$) of Christ (1 Tim. iii. 16; 2 Tim. i. 10; Tit. ii. 13; iii. 4) "is a sign of later Gnostic influence." But in 1 and 2 Thessalonians similar language is used of the second advent of Christ; and in 2 Corinthians iv. 4, 6, touching His first appearance. These expressions, in truth, reflect the glory of the Divine manifestation of Jesus made to Saul on the Damascus road. In a form of like splendour Paul pictures to himself the Saviour's reappearance. It is the Gnostics who have borrowed their language from our New Testament writings —not the latter from the former.

The Parousia forms a significant link between the earliest and latest of the apostle's letters. It is, in a sense, his Alpha and Omega. But a change has supervened in his view of the event. It is still to him, and more than ever, "that *blessed hope* and appearing of the glory of our great God and Saviour Jesus Christ" (Tit. ii. 13); but he no longer speaks of it in the terms of personal anticipation that we find in 1 Thessalonians and 1 Corinthians xv. For he has reconciled himself, as already in 2 Corinthians v., to the fact that he must pass away by death before the Lord's return. He rejoices to feel that "the time of his departure is come' (2 Tim. iv. 6). He has learnt increasingly to see in the inward victories of the Christian life and the "earnest of the Spirit in our hearts" (Rom. viii. 11–23; Eph. i. 13, 14) the pledge of the believer's final glorification. Though the Parousia ceases to occupy the immediate foreground of the apostle's outlook, it is no less certainly in prospect, and has become a vision yet more splendid to the eyes of his heart. Meanwhile, the intervening future grows more distinct, in its darker as well as its brighter aspects. "Evil men and impostors will wax worse and worse, deceiving and being deceived" (2 Tim. iii. 13) The second coming "furnishes the shining background for the gloomy picture of the troublous *last times*" (Holtzmann, p. 188; see 1 Tim. v. 1; 2 Tim. iii. 1; iv. 3, 4). In all directions the horizon is threatening, and the air thick with the sense of coming trouble. The predictions of these epistles only give greater distinctness to forebodings already expressed by Paul in Acts xx. 29–31, and elsewhere.

On the other hand, their representations of present or impending conflict differ, both in colouring and proportion, from any picture furnished by the age of Marcion and Justin Martyr. It is superfluous to discuss the identifications offered to us; for they contradict each other, and every new critic fixes on a type of Gnosticism different from the last. Holtzmann and Pfleiderer themselves so far fail in the attempt, that they are compelled to assume an artificial infusion into the supposed polemic against Marcionite heresy of elements drawn from St. Paul's time, such as would have made the attack confused and ineffective for the end for which they imagine it designed.

When "Christ Jesus" appears in 1 Timothy v. 21 (comp. 2 Tim. iv. 1) accompanied by "the elect angels," it is because He is thought of as in 2 Thessalonians i. 7 (comp

Luke ix. 26) as the future Judge of men. The connexion of thought resembles that of 2 Corinthians v. 10, 11, where the sense of his present "manifestation to God" carries the apostle's mind onward to the scene of his future appearance at "the tribunal of Christ."

In these latest epistles, the eschatology of the earliest reappears, viewed however through a longer perspective, and enriched by the deeper Christology of the intervening letters.

(3) In regard to the writer's attitude toward the great Pauline antithesis of *law and grace*, the crucial text is 1 Timothy i. 8-11 :—

"We know that the law is good, if one use it lawfully. . . . Law is not imposed for a righteous man, but for the lawless, etc., . . . and whatsoever else is contrary to the sound teaching, according to the gospel of the glory of the blessed God, with which I was entrusted."

This passage, as Holtzmann allows, belongs to "the writer's general standpoint," and cannot be dismissed as a mere polemical stroke against the Marcionites (p. 160). But the standpoint is that of Paul himself, the same which he asserted in Romans and Galatians. The "lawful use" of the law consists in its giving "the knowledge of sin," by "making the offence to abound" and so "working out wrath." It was added "for the sake of transgressions." Hence it is designed "for the lawless and unruly"—to mark and condemn them as such; while the truly "righteous man" is "not under law, but under grace." This is "according to the gospel" of Paul's great evangelical epistles; and "knowing" it, Timothy will know how to "use the law," not in Jewish fashion as a yoke for the saint, but as a whip for the sinner. This passage negatives at the outset Schleiermacher's assertion, that "the author of 1 Timothy silently passes over the chief position advanced by Paul against the Judaistic standpoint."

When we read in Titus ii. 14 of Christ's sacrifice as "ransoming us from all *lawlessness*," this complements instead of contradicting St. Paul's earlier watchword of redemption "from *the curse* of the law" (Gal. iii. 10-14); for lawlessness, if it does not actually constitute that curse, is its cause and concomitant. A redemption saving from sin's punishment, but not from sin, is obviously illusive. In fact, we are here carried forward, along the line of Romans vi., from the idea of justification as mere acquittal to its positive issue in the new law-keeping, but not law-subject, life of the believer. In the unique and Paul-like compound ἀντίλυτρον (*ransom-price*), of 1 Timothy ii. 6, the New Testament doctrine of the vicarious sacrifice culminates. This word alone is sufficient to make the first epistle to Timothy immortal. In vain does Holtzmann speak of the death and resurrection of Christ—"these two facts of central importance, in Paul's view, for the Christian consciousness"—as "receiving but cursory reference" (p. 170). The three epistles are steeped in their influence. As well argue that the author of Galatians thought little of the resurrection, because in that letter he happens only once, and in passing, to make verbal mention of it!

It is more to the purpose when our critic observes (p. 169) that in these writings *the Church* rather than the individual is the recipient of the blessings of salvation, and when he sees in this a link between the Pastorals and Ephesians[1] (comp. Tit. ii. 14 with Eph. v. 25-27). The writer's mind dwells mainly on the general and collective aspects of the Gospel. He is thinking not so much of Him "who loved *me* and gave Himself up *for me*," as of "the philanthropy of God our Saviour." And his repeated assertion of the universalism of the Gospel is opposed not, as in Romans iii. 29, 30, to Jewish exclusiveness of race, but to the Gnosticizing pride that reserved the knowledge of God to the initiated few. This narrow and vain intellectualism was just

---

[1] Holtzmann, and the school of Baur generally, continue to reject this latter with the former as Pauline epistles. Not so, however, M. Sabatier; see pp. 229-234 above.

now the greatest danger of the Church, sure to be the parent of a brood of errors and corruptions; it struck at what is most vital to Christianity, in God's universal grace to mankind; and the apostle's detection of the evil and his determined opposition to it were already manifest in the epistles of the second group (Col. i. 28; ii. 3, 8, 18, 19; Eph. i. 17, 18; iii. 9).

In this connexion we can better understand the principle laid down in 2 Timothy ii. 19–21, that whatever "vessel" in the "great house" is "purified from unrighteousness," is a "vessel unto honour," being "sanctified" and therefore "useful to the Master." For it is holiness of character, not mere "knowledge," often "falsely so called," that qualifies the vessels of the Lord. Holtzmann, however, can only see in this definition "a characteristic complement to Paul's notion of Predestination, supplying an ethical content to the *decretum absolutum*," which in Romans is matter of pure sovereignty (p. 172). Yet in Romans ix. 22 there is implied in the "vessels of wrath fitted for destruction" a like ethical content to that found in these "vessels of dishonour." It is not to the Pastorals that we have first to look in order to find St. Paul's doctrine of election balanced and safeguarded by the assertion of man's responsibility. Nor, on the other hand, is the absoluteness of the Divine initiative in the work of salvation at all sacrificed in our epistles. God's "purpose and grace" are held forth, in opposition to "our works," as the moving cause of redemption (2 Tim. i. 9; Tit. iii. 5) as strongly as in Romans or Ephesians, and with an unction and *empressement* entirely Pauline.

· (4) *A higher sacramental doctrine* than that of the genuine Paul is detected in Titus iii. 5 (Holtzmann, p. 172). We might agree with the critic on this point, if, with Ellicott and others, following the Vulgate, we construed "renewal of the Holy Spirit" in dependence upon "laver" (the Greek genitive is here ambiguous). But the alternative rendering of Bengel, Alford, and Hofmann is decidedly preferable. The *laver (washing*, A.V.) *of regeneration* and *renewal of the Holy Spirit* are two conjoint though distinct agencies. This text echoes our Lord's great dictum on the new birth "of water and of the Spirit" (John iii. 5), and makes the same distinction between the outward or symbolic and the inward and essential means of Divine renewal. So the passage brings to a focus what we have already learnt concerning Baptism from Romans vi. 1-6; Galatians iii. 27; Colossians ii. 12; Ephesians v. 26, where it represents and gives a name to that entire change in the Christian believer, of which it is the divinely appointed token.

There is one rite, however, which we meet here for the first time in the Pauline epistles—that of *the laying on of hands* (1 Tim. iv. 14; v. 22; 2 Tim. i. 6). It is the means of conveying special endowments of grace (*charismata*), bestowed on individual men to fit them for their special vocation in the Church. There is nothing new, or foreign to St. Paul, in the elements of this conception. The idea of the "charism" is perfectly familiar (see Rom. xii. 6, etc.). And the Acts of the Apostles shows (viii. 17-19, etc.) that this form of ordination—an ancient and expressive Jewish custom—belonged to the earliest times of the Church. That no magical efficacy is attributed to the rite is evident from the words of the epistles: "The charism that is in thee, . . . given thee through prophecy, with laying on of the presbytery's hands"; again, "the charism of God that is in thee, through the laying on of my hands." The essence of the matter does not lie in the particular official hands that ministered in Timothy's ordination; but the grace was God's immediate and inward bestowment, attested by the voice of His Spirit in the Church, then sealed and acknowledged on the Church's part in the appropriate form.

These writings are also said to teach a higher doctrine of *inspiration* than is found in the undisputed epistles. Baur discovered in 2 Timothy iii. 14-17 a covert attack on Marcion (who rejected the Old Testament), and an attempt to rehabilitate the Law in the face of second-century Gnosticism. "The sacred *writings*," it is said, "are silently contrasted with the oral *traditions* current in the Gnostic sects; and the phrase '*all* Scripture' protests against the arbitrary use made by heretics of certain parts of it." Granting the correctness of this interpretation, it is quite appropriate to the apostle's time. Theorists such as the false teachers of Colossæ were sure to neglect the practical and moral parts of Scripture. It is the vanity and uselessness of the teaching broached by the men whom Timothy and Titus are to oppose that the writer stigmatizes, rather than anything positively false or corrupting in it (see 1 Tim. i. 4, 6; vi. 3-5; 2 Tim. ii. 16, 23; Tit. i. 10-14). In this "vain jangling," however, he sees the germ and beginnings of the most fatal moral errors (1 Tim. iv. 1-3; 2 Tim. ii. 17, 18; iii. 1-9, 13; iv. 3), a mischief of unlimited potency, that "will wax worse and worse;" for this evil Scripture affords the true and sufficient remedy. The "fables and endless genealogies," "Jewish fables," etc., on which these letters pour contempt, were the stock-in-trade of men versed in the allegorical method, and who practised a puerile and speculative treatment of inspired Scripture. So the occasion has come to formulate the doctrine of inspiration implicit throughout St. Paul's teaching (see specially Rom. xv. 4, and 1 Cor. x. 11). That doctrine exhibits in the words "through faith that is in Christ Jesus" its specially Pauline stamp and character.

Baur and Holtzmann fail to convince us that the second saying of 1 Timothy v. 18 ("The workman is worthy of his hire.") is quoted as "Scripture," on a footing with the Old Testament, from a written Gospel. Indeed such quotation would be scarcely more probable in the middle of the second century than in the apostle Paul's own time.

(5) The critics note throughout these letters "a retreat of the one-sided religious interest of former Pauline epistles in favour of *a more ethical conception of the purpose of life*" (Holtzmann p. 172). This observation, apart from the colouring of censure conveyed in its terms, is true enough. Only what Holtzmann calls "a retreat" we should describe as an advance. Evangelical doctrine, now established and consolidated, is applied on all sides to the practical conduct of life. "The grace of God" which "appeared" in Christ, "bringing salvation to all men," has developed a new moral discipline (παιδεύουσα, Tit. ii. 12). The religious principle of Paulinism, instead of being "sacrificed" to moral objects, realizes in them its living effect, the "fruits" by which its truth and worth are evidenced. Such passages as Romans xii. 1; 2 Corinthians vii. 1; 2 Thessalonians i. 11, contain in germ all that is unfolded in the detailed ethical instruction of later epistles.[1]

"Righteousness," says Holtzmann (pp. 174, 175), appears in 1 Timothy vi. 11; 2 Timothy ii. 22; "as a virtue to be sought after," instead of being, in the specially Pauline sense, "a peculiar relation to God." But this is equally the case in Romans vi. 18, 20; 2 Corinthians ix. 10; on the other hand, gratuitous justification is unequivocally asserted in the Pastoral epistles (Tit. iii. 7, etc.). The bond connecting the religious and moral is never broken by the apostle in his employment of this cardinal term of his theology. The righteousness of imputation he always conceived as the basis of a new actual righteousness of life and behaviour (see Sabatier, p. 300). Holtzmann repeats this objection, which he regards as of decisive weight, when he declares (p. 175) that "there is no room for justification in the Pauline meaning, where salvation is made to depend, as in 1 Timothy iv. 6, 16, vi. 14; Titus i. 9, on the careful

---

[1] The "separation of dogma and morality" alleged by M. Sabatier (pp. 271, 272), we fail to recognise.

observance of traditional doctrine." In reply to this, it is enough to say that the stricture applies with equal force to such passages as 2 Thessalonians ii. 15; Romans vi. 17; or 1 Corinthians xv. 1, 2. In every case "doctrine" and "tradition" are the means of continued salvation, inasmuch as they supply the objective basis of a continued faith.

(6) But it is after all in the *religious* rather than the ethical effect of salvation that the interest of the Pastoral epistles centres. The Christian "profession" is, in one word, "godliness" (1 Tim. ii. 9, 10; θεοσέβεια "reverence for God"—one of the unique expressions of the Pastorals), of which "good works" are the "fitting ornament." Christianity is "the truth" or "the doctrine *according to godliness*." Fourteen times is the noun εὐσέβεια, or its congeners, employed in the three epistles, while it occurs not once (except in the *negative* in Romans) in any other writings of St. Paul. This remarkable fact is due to the cause that we noted at the outset. The apostle's teaching about *God* and about *godliness* come into like prominence. It was not so much the way of salvation, it was not so much the Person of Christ, nor even the moral practice of Christianity that was endangered by the pretended "knowledge" of the new Judaists, with their "fables" and "logomachies"; religion itself was at stake. The theories which separated God from nature and body from spirit were fatal to piety. They tended to dissolve the religious conception of life, to destroy godliness and virtue—"faith and a good conscience"—both at one stroke (see 1 Tim. iv. 1–5; vi. 3–5).

With such dangers present to his mind, and likely to grow in force and seductiveness in the future, the aged apostle bends all his efforts to guard and strengthen the spirit of religion. His exhortations to Timothy, and his injunctions to both his helpers touching their conduct of Church affairs, bear with concentrated urgency upon this one essential. The appeal, while it springs from the profound piety of St. Paul's own nature, is foreshadowed by such passages as Romans i. 18; v. 6, where sin is "ungodliness"; so Colossians ii. 18, 23, condemning false and superstitious notions of worship; and Ephesians iv. 24, which combines "righteousness and piety (coming) of the truth" as the leading dispositions of the "new man." Just as we found that Paul's doctrines of grace had enriched his views of the Divine nature, so they appear to have deepened and enlarged his conception of worship (1 Tim. ii. 1-8), and his sense of the part which reverence plays in sanctifying human life.

To the same causes, increased perhaps in their effect by the writer's advanced age, we may refer the stress that is laid in these letters on "sobriety" and decorum of behaviour. We note, too, in this connexion the admiration expressed for a "quiet and gentle life" (1 Tim. ii. 2). These preferences are by no means new features in St. Paul's character (see 1 Thess. iv. 11, 12; 1 Cor, xi. 2, 16; xiv. 33, 40); but they receive new emphasis.

In general, it is in "the other conditions, partly combined with and partly substituted for faith," that Holtzmann sees "the mediating and catholicizing character of these epistles, their smoothed and softened Paulinism, made most apparent" (p. 179). We should lose, in truth, some of the most precious lessons of the Pastorals if we did not observe this combination, if we failed to note the frequency of such expressions as *faith and love, faith and truth, faith and a good conscience; love, faith, and purity; godliness, faith, love*, etc. But the just induction from these varied combinations is not that "faith" has lost its supremacy and is merged in "other conditions," but that these are its accompaniments and the guarantees of its reality. On this point, 1 Timothy i. 5 is instructive: "faith unfeigned" is made the ultimate source of the "love" which is "the end of the charge"—that is to say, the goal of all practical Christian teaching. This is nothing else than the "faith working through love" of Galatians v. 6, in ampler phrase. In other places "faith" stands alone, as the basis of Christian experience and life (1 Tim. i. 2; iii. 13; 2 Tim. iii. 15; iv. 7). Weiss and Ellicott rightly refuse to recognise in these epistles the ecclesiastical notion of the *fides quam credimus*, the substitution of the content or object of faith for its subjective exercise. 2 Thessalonians ii. 12, 13 presents the same antithesis of "faith" and "truth" as subjective and objective counterparts, that we find in 1 Timothy ii. 7; iv. 3, 6. It is singular that faith is spoken of oftener, proportionately, in these than in any other of the epistles, except Galatians. Grace and Faith form the double seal by which the apostle stamps these writings as his own. No one could imitate his accent, or reproduce by artifice the vivid and delicate sensibility with which these master words of Paul's gospel are employed in the letters to Timothy and Titus.

(7) Once more let us listen to Dr. Holtzmann. "Practical piety," he says, "and *correct doctrine* form the two poles, equally dominant," of the Pastoral epistles (p. 183). The latter of these two dominant notes he connects with "the growing churchliness" of the second century, under whose influence Christianity comes to be called "doctrine" (Tit. ii. 10), and Christ assumes mainly the *rôle* of Teacher. The preaching of the Gospel takes a conventional form; and in its conflict with heretical theories the truth as it is in Jesus stiffens into a system of authoritative dogma. If orthodoxy is not yet known by name, the idea of it is there; and the ὀρθοτομεῖν of 2 Timothy ii. 15 comes next door to the word itself.

This contention, in substance, we admit. The question is, whether such a phenomenon was possible in the later apostolic age. To us it seems inevitable. The conservatism of "such an one as Paul the aged," if he lived until the middle of the seventh Christian decade, was sure to take this shape. Looking back on the pathway which his thought has trodden led by the Spirit of God, and on the completed teaching of his life, he puts his final seal upon it, in face of the denials and perversions to which it was already, and would be increasingly and on many sides exposed. Such a certification seems even necessary to the ideal completeness of St. Paul's theological work. From the first he has sought to give to his teaching a well-defined form; and from the first he has claimed for it unqualified authority. The "type of doctrine" into which the Roman believers had "been delivered," and which they had "obeyed from the heart" (Rom. vi. 17), was a definite and settled creed, like the "form of sound words," the "sound doctrine," the "faithful word according to the teaching," on which this writer expatiates; and it becomes "*sound* doctrine" because, and so soon as, in other quarters corruption and disease have taken hold of it. These expressions of the Pastorals only gather up and reaffirm the assertions made in regard to particular doctrines in St. Paul's previous controversial epistles. The "anathema" of Galatians i. 7–9 is a vehement affirmation of the dogmatic principle (comp. Rom. xvi. 17; 1 Cor. xiv. 37; xv. 1–11; Eph. iv. 14; Col. i. 6, 7; Phil. iii. 15, 16; 2 Thess. ii. 15).

Now that his teaching has become the recognised creed of a great community, it is natural that Paul should speak of himself as "apostle according to the faith of God's elect" (Tit. i. 1). Himself "ready to be offered up," with his battle fought and his course run, the apostle's chief remaining care is that he may see the great "deposit" committed into faithful and worthy hands. He desires to leave behind him in the Churches he has founded a community so well ordered and equipped, so rooted and built up in Christ and possessed by His Spirit, that it shall be for all time to come a "pillar and ground of the truth." In the epistle to the Ephesians, as Holtzmann points out (p. 187), the step had been completed by which Paulinism passed from the idea of the local to that of the œcumenical Church. To the Christian society thus fully constituted, is committed the "mystery of godliness" now fully revealed. There rises before the mind of the dying apostle the image of a universal Church, to which is entrusted for the salvation of all men the charge of that Gospel long ago imparted to himself by Christ Jesus his Lord. Such is the situation which the last group of the Pauline epistles exhibit. Does it not bear the marks of historical and psychological reality?

Thus we pass from the thought of the "great house," unfolded in the Ephesian letter, to that of the "vessels" of its service, their qualities and uses, and the solemn responsibilities which accrue to them. Their worth lies in the greatness of the Church they serve; and hers in the greatness of the truth she holds in trust for mankind.

V. THE CHURCH SYSTEM OF THE PASTORALS.

We are now, therefore, as we hope, in a position to appreciate the peculiar features of *the Church order and organization* set before us in the Pastoral epistles, and so to complete the task proposed in this inquiry.

To promote "godliness" and "sound doctrine" is the leading object of these letters. This purpose dictates the qualifications laid down in 1 Timothy iii. and Titus i. for ministerial office; and it accounts for the fact that these conditions are so nearly alike for bishops (or presbyters) and for deacons:

"The bishop must be without reproach, husband of one wife, sober, sensible, orderly, hospitable, apt to teach, . . . gentle, peaceable, ree from the love of money . . . Deacons *in like manner* must be grave . . . not double-tongued, not given to wine, nor seeking base gain, holding the mystery of faith in a pure conscience."

These instructions, on the face of them, are not intended as an exhaustive description of what the bishop and deacon should be. They scarcely look beyond the moral qualities of an ordinary, reputable Christian man. But it is just here, in their commonplace and unambitious character, that the point of the specifications lies. To the need of other, more shining gifts the Churches were sufficiently alive. What the apostle insists upon is that solid, moral qualities shall not be overlooked, nor taken for granted in any case without strict inquiry. The danger was lest talent and cleverness should carry the day, and the leadership of the Church fall into the hands of men deficient in the elements of a worthy Christian character. The enemy had sown his tares among the wheat of Christ's field. The discrepancy between the actual and ideal Church was already painfully manifest (2 Tim. ii. 19-21). Self-seeking teachers had insinuated themselves into the Christian societies, who knew how to impose on the credulous or unstable by their show of learning and asceticism (1 Tim. i. 6, 7; iv. 1-3; vi. 3-10). Entrance into the ministry must be barred to such candidates as these; and officers must be chosen whose character commanded the respect of the community, and who would be likely to exert a wholesome and steadying influence on the Church's life, at a time of transition and feverish unrest. Kühl very aptly says :

"The prescriptions of these epistles bear throughout an eminently practical stamp, and find their characteristic expression in the exhortation to Timothy: *Be thou a pattern of the believers.* The false intellectualism of the errorists is traced to their want of practical piety; and this εὐσέβεια, this open sense for the divine, has in turn its practical moral guarantee in a Christianly moral life. Such piety it is the aim of these writings, in their whole tenor, to quicken and renew."

If godliness was the chief desideratum for the Church at large, so much the more was it essential to the official ministry. This anxiety on the apostle's part is in profound accord with the sentiments that he always cherished concerning his own position as a minister of Christ.

"Our glorying is this, the testimony of our conscience that in holiness and sincerity of God we have had our conversation in the world. . . . . In all things commending ourselves as ministers of God : in pureness, in knowledge, in long-suffering, in kindness, in the Holy Spirit, in love unfeigned,—by the armour of righteousness on the right hand and on the left" (2 Cor. i. 12; vi. 4-7).

. So he wrote years ago to the captious Corinthians; and such a testimony, both from within and from without, he desires for his successors.

Along with the primary responsibility for character in the pastors of the Church, there devolves *the charge of doctrine* —not indeed committed solely, but specially and by way of guardianship, to the separated ministry. "Faithful men" they must be, able to "teach others," to whom above others the things "heard," says the apostle, "from me amongst many witnesses" are to be "committed" (2 Tim. ii. 2). There is then an *apostolical succession*; but it descends to the humblest preacher, duly qualified and appointed in a loyal Christian community. The chain of the succession lies in the believing transmission of the doctrine.

Besides provision for public teaching (Gal. vi. 6; Rom. xii. 7), there were administrative and disciplinary offices to be performed in the Christian societies. And it was for these purposes that local ministers were first required. The relation and adjustment of these several functions to each other in the early Church is a question of extreme difficulty. There are two distinctions which must be carefully borne in mind—distinctions complicated with each other in various ways: (1) That existing between the official and what we may call the *charismatic* ministry; *i.e.*, between the ministry of persons formally appointed to Church office, and that exercised in virtue of some extraordinary Divine endowment in the man, but not such as of itself qualified him to bear rule in the Church; or, in other words, between the ministry of *official status* and that of *personal gift*, the former in some measure implying the latter, but the latter not of necessity carrying with it the former (see 1 Cor. xii. 4-11; Rom. xii. 3-8). (2) Another distinction, of the greatest practical moment, is that which separated the *local and congregational* from the *itinerant* or *missionary ministry*. To the former of these classes "the bishops and deacons" of Philippians and of the Pastorals belonged; to the latter the "apostles" and "evangelists"; while "prophets" and "teachers" might labour in a single community (Acts xiii. 1), or might, and in post-apostolic times commonly did, extend their work over a wide area (see the *Teaching of the Apostles*, and the *Shepherd* of Hermas).

In the earliest times, public teaching in the Christian assemblies was free. Each member of the Church might speak, provided it were "in order" and "to edification" (see 1 Cor. xiv.). We must presume, however, that even at Corinth there were "presidents" of some sort to determine, in harmony with the sense of the assembly, *what* was in order and to edification (comp. 1 Thess. v. 12; Rom. xii. 8, and the "presiding elders" of 1 Tim. v. 17). Only the "women must keep silence in the assemblies" (1 Cor. xiv. 34, 35). When, now, it is said in 1 Timothy ii. 12, "*A woman* I do not permit to teach," we presume that the right of teaching was still reserved for all other competent Church members (comp. ver. 8, "I wish *the men* to pray in every place," obviously relating to the exercise of public prayer). But this license in no long time had come to be abused. Talkative and pretentious men found their advantage in it. The Church meetings were made a theatre of "discussions and logomachies, out of which envy and strife arose," tending to "questionings" rather than to promote "the dispensation of God which is in faith" (1 Tim. i. 4; vi. 3–5). While the writer does not for this reason forbid the established liberty of preaching and prophesying,[1] he is anxious that the bishops should be efficient

---

[1] The teaching office of the bishop is most emphasized in the epistle to Titus. He was organizing new Churches in Crete, where no pre-established license of teaching existed, to stand in the way of the full authority of the presbyter-bishops. We observe, moreover, that there is no mention of *deacons* here, who might not be required in small Churches, at least in the first stage of Church organization (comp. Acts xiv. 23). Nor is it prescribed that the bishop shall not be a "neophyte," as in the older Church of Ephesus (1 Tim. iii. 6); but he must have "believing children"—a condition necessary to mention in a new community, but that takes a different and stricter form in the directions addressed to Timothy at Ephesus (1 Tim. iii. 4, 5).

in this respect, competent to take a leading part in public instruction and to counteract the attempts of false and foolish teachers. The words of 1 Timothy v. 17 make it tolerably clear that while teaching was not, like ruling, an exclusive nor indispensable attribute of the official elders, still they frequently exercised this function, and the writer wishes to encourage them in doing so.

There is little evidence to be gleaned from other sources as to the connexion between ruling and teaching in the local ministry in apostolic times. Hebrews xiii. 7 indicates that, amongst Jewish Christians at least in the seventh decade, the two offices were commonly regarded as one. James iii. 1 belongs to an earlier time, when things were tending in that direction. . In the Gentile communities the liberty of teaching continued to a much later epoch; indeed, the tradition of it remains in the *Apostolic Constitutions* (viii. 32.), which in their present form are referred to the third or fourth century. In Ephesians iv. 11, however, "the pastors and teachers" form a single group, if not identical yet closely allied, and alike distinguished from the several orders of "apostles," "prophets," and "evangelists." It is just this tendency to unite the pastoral and teaching offices to which the Pastoral epistles give expression.

When we turn to the newly discovered *Teaching of the Apostles*, our most important witness for the development of Church organization in the post-apostolic period, we find that now "the bishops and deacons themselves discharge the ministry of prophets and teachers" (chap. xv.), while at the same time there are itinerant "prophets" and "teachers," who possess a preponderant influence, and may even supersede the local officers in the conduct of the Eucharist (chaps. x.–xiii.). The *Shepherd* of Hermas—dating from the early part of the second century, as the *Teaching* probably from the close of the first—gives evidence to the same effect. Now, it is noticeable that our epistles make no reference to these roving prophets and teachers, whose ascendency is the most conspicuous feature in the picture of Church life afforded by the *Teaching*. Their prominence belongs to the transitional period between the personal rule of the apostles and the official rule of the mon-episcopal hierarchy established in the second century. Instead of the *Teaching of the Apostles* forming, as Harnack says, "a mean term between 1 Corinthians xii. and the Pastorals," the truth is that the Pastorals and Ephesians together are the mean term between 1 Corinthians xii., with its fluid and unformed Church life, and the settled and formal order which the *Teaching* delineates.

Since Bishop Lightfoot's famous *Dissertation on the Christian Ministry*, the identity of "bishop" and "elder" in the New Testament may be regarded as an established fact.[1] The presiding congregational officers are *elders* in respect of rank and "honour" (1 Tim. v. 17), and *bishops* in respect of their "work" and responsibility (1 Tim. iii. 1; Tit. i. 7; Acts xx. 28). The late Dr. Hatch (whose removal by death we deeply deplore, in common with all Christian scholars) attempted in his Bampton Lectures to show that the two offices were of distinct and independent origin. He argued that the presbyterate was a *Jewish*, and purely magisterial and disciplinary order; while the episcopate was *Greek* in its derivation, financial and administrative in the first instance, but taking on in the Church a spiritual and charismatic character. This theory, we are persuaded, will not be sustained on mature examination.[2] According to

---

[1] Some able scholars maintain that elder is the wider term, denoting Church office generally, and embracing bishop and deacon alike; so Dr. Milligan in the *Expositor*, 3rd series, vi., 348 ff. This position cannot, we think, be sustained in face of Titus i. 5, 7, so precisely identifying "elders" and "the bishop"; nor does it accord with 1 Timothy iv. 14, v. 17,—texts which imply a *presidential* dignity, inappropriate to the name and calling of the "deacons." The deacons would more naturally come in the first instance from the ranks of the young men. "Young men" is a quasi-official term in Acts v. 6, 10.

[2] Kühl subjects Dr. Hatch's theory of the episcopate to a searching criticism, in pp. 87 ff. of his *Gemeindeordnung*; and Gore's recent

Hatch's hypothesis, it was only gradually, towards the end of the first century, that the two systems were amalgamated and presbyter and bishop shared the same functions, until the bishop was differentiated from the presbytery in a new way under the mon-episcopal *régime* of Ignatius. If Dr. Hatch is right, then the Pastoral and Ephesian epistles, the Acts of the Apostles, and the epistle of James, and 1 Peter must all be relegated, at the earliest, to the closing years of the first century. So Harnack [1] inferred with irresistible logic from Hatch's premises; and while Dr. Hatch did not draw these conclusions in the Bampton Lectures, his articles on *Paul* and *Pastoral Epistles* in the *Encyclopædia Britannica* (9th ed.) show that he had reached the same result in the case of Ephesians and the Pastorals, and inclined to it in regard to the Acts. This is a heavy price to pay for Dr. Hatch's attractive theory. So far as any case has been made out for St. Paul's authorship of these letters, it negatives the supposition that the presbyterate and episcopate were fundamentally different offices.

Very significant for the primitive meaning of *episcopus* is 1 Peter ii. 25, where Christ Himself is called "the shepherd and bishop of your souls"; and with the "bishop" of this passage the "presbyters" of chap. v. 1–4 are linked as those who "*shepherd* the flock" under the "Chief Shepherd," just as in Acts xx. 17–28 "the elders of the Church" at Ephesus are exhorted to "take heed to *the flock* over which the Holy Spirit made them overseers (bishops)";

---

and important work on *The Ministry of the Christian Church*, while less successful in its constructive argument, makes some effective criticisms on the *Hatch-Harnack* hypothesis. See also the discussion on the *Origin of the Christian Ministry* in the *Expositor*, 3rd series, vols. v., vi.; especially the contributions of Drs. Sanday and Salmon.

[1] In his notes to the German translation of Hatch's Lectures (*Die Gesellschaftsverfassung*, etc.), and *Analecten zu Hatch*. In the *Expositor*, 3rd series, vol. v. pp. 334, 335, Harnack says, "I regard the Pastoral Epistles as writings which, in their present form, were composed in the middle of the second century; but older documents were made use of in their composition."

similarly, "shepherds" is the designation for Church rulers in Ephesians iv. 11. The same conception of the bishop's work underlies the directions of the Pastorals; it comes out vividly in the question of 1 Timothy iii. 5: "If he knows not how to preside over his own house, how will he *care for* the Church of God?" (comp. John x. 13)—a higher care, surely, than that of the Church's money chest! These documents bear a common witness to the moral and spiritual character of the episcopal calling, and through it a mutual testimony to each other. They unite to express with fine simplicity, and without a trace of second century ecclesiasticism, the apostolical conception of the Christian ministry—viz., that of *spiritual shepherding*.

Still the question remains: If presbyter and bishop meant the same thing, *why the two names?* For answer, we are left to conjecture. We venture to think that the title *bishop*, first appearing in the speech and from the pen of St. Paul, is due to the apostle himself, original as he was in so many things. *Elder* preoccupied the field in a community of Jewish origin, and came into use as a matter of course, so soon as a board of managers was needed in the new society (Acts xi. 30; xiv. 23, etc.). But this designation had certain obvious defects. It was ambiguous (see 1 Tim. v. 1, 17; 1 Pet. v. 1, 5), and unexpressive. It was, moreover, in constant use among the Jews as a title of civil office—a circumstance liable to cause confusion, and perhaps distaste to Gentile Christians. The Old Testament suggested *episcopus*[1] to those casting about for a substitute; and this term commended itself by the fact that it indicated the peculiar nature of the office (overseership), and was kindred in meaning to *shepherd*, a figure hallowed and endeared by the lips of Christ (John x.; comp. 1 Pet. ii. 25).

---

[1] See Cremer's *Biblico-theological Lexicon*, s.v. 'Επίσκοπος; and Lightfoot's Note in his *Commentary on Philippians*, pp. 93 ff., also his *Dissertation on the Christian Ministry* in the same vol., which still remains the best elucidation of the subject.

If about the same time, in the older Pauline Churches, assistant officers came to be needed in the shape of *deacons*; after the model of Jerusalem (Acts vi.), it would be still more necessary to give the superior functionaries a name implying *superintendence*. We find, in fact, that "bishop" and "deacon" are correlative. It is possible that St. Paul's address at Miletus, reported in Acts xx., marks the juncture at which the new appellation was making its appearance, and that the remarkable words of ver. 28 were expressly chosen in order to recommend its use; when he writes to the Philippians a few years later (chap. i. 1), it is an accepted and familiar title. The "helps" and "governments" of 1 Corinthians xii. 28 contain in the abstract the antithesis of "deacon" and "bishop," present at this earlier time in the apostle's mind, although it had not yet at Corinth crystallized into formal expression. But whatever be the true explanation of the double name, it is surely past question that in the Acts and epistles elder and bishop are synonymous.

The long section devoted to *Church widows*, in 1 Timothy v. 3–16, is interesting on many grounds. It speaks for an early date for the epistle, that the claims of dependent widows had not hitherto been fully discussed and settled. The sixth chapter of the Acts, accepted on all hands as a genuine picture of primitive Church life, shows that the matter from the first received much attention. Our author is anxious, too, that the influence of the "aged women" generally should be utilized in the guidance of their sex (Tit. ii. 3–5). It is not the first time that St. Paul has shown his sense of the importance attaching to the position of women in Christian society (1 Cor. xi. 2–16); and the attempts of heretical teachers to win their adherence (2 Tim. iii. 6) made it the more necessary that the Church should be guarded upon this side. Holtzmann curiously argues (pp. 245, 246) that the recommendation of 1 Timothy v. 14, approving the re-marriage of "younger widows," came from the experience of "a later generation"; and he is surprised at the appearance, within the lifetime of the apostle Paul, of "widows grown grey in the service of the Church"! Grant ten years' existence to the Ephesian Church, and a moderate knowledge of human life to the apostle, and these critical difficulties are solved. In the young Cretan Churches the question of the widows has not yet arisen.

There is, no doubt, a difference between the Paul of 1 Corinthians vii. and of 1 Timothy in the tenor of their observations on marriage and "child-bearing." But the advices of the former passage were based on prudential and temporary considerations (vers. 28, 29). Now that the Church appears likely to continue on earth for a longer space, family life resumes its natural importance; and the epistles of the third group (Colossians and Ephesians) give to it the highest ethical and religious value.

It remains finally, and in distinction from the local officership of the Churches, to consider *the ecclesiastical status of Timothy and Titus.* Since the failure of Baur's attempt to identify the bishop of the Pastorals with the mon-episcopus[1] (or monarchical bishop) of the second century, his successors have turned the functions of Timothy and Titus to account in favour of the Tendency theory. They seek to show that the position of these apostolic commissioners is magnified in the interests of episcopal autocracy.

If so, the supposed episcopalian forger has shown himself both timid and blundering in the extreme; and the partisans of the Ignatian episcopate can have had little to thank him for. The epistles of Ignatius, unquestionably, make use of the Pastorals, but in no instance, so far as we can find, in the sense imputed to the latter by the Tübingen school. The "tendency" of the epistles to Timothy and Titus had not then been discovered! The only title the writer ventures to

---

[1] We owe this convenient term to Mr. Gore's *Ministry of the Christian Church.*

give to either of the delegates is that of "evangelist." They stand in no fixed relationship to the local Churches. The powers they exercise for the time in Ephesus or Crete, as formerly in Corinth or Thessalonica, are the powers of the living apostle exercised through them; and are of an expressly occasional and limited character. They are to choose and ordain Church officers in the apostle's absence, subject to the approval of the voice of the Church (implied throughout 1 Tim. iii. 1-13); and, in Timothy's case, to investigate complaints that might be made against "elders" already in office (1 Tim. v. 19-25; also Tit. i. 6-9). And this is all! There is nothing to show that they charged themselves with details of local administration, or with the discipline of lay members of the flock. Paul had himself excommunicated certain persons (1 Tim. i. 20); Timothy and Titus are bidden merely to "avoid" the mischief-makers. In this unique commission there is more that differs from than resembles the functions of the latter monarchical bishop. Holtzmann says, indeed, that Timothy and Titus, with their powers of visitation, were prototypes of the *archepiscopate* (p. 266). But who ever thought of archbishops in the second century?

After all, their relations with the Ephesian or Cretan presbyteries constituted only the incidental part of the life-work of these apostolic men. "The testimony of our Lord" was laid upon Timothy, through God's gift of grace solemnly attested and committed to him at the outset of his career (2 Tim. i. 6-14); and this it was his business everywhere to proclaim. It is his to "do the work of an evangelist," and to share with his master in the glorious toils and sufferings of a missionary preacher (2 Tim. i. 8; ii. 1-13). This mission required, beyond the repetition of the Gospel story and the announcement of God's message of peace to mankind (1 Tim. ii. 3-7), that the purpose of grace should be carried out to its practical issues in the moral life of believers—"the things which become the sound doctrine,

It is not a testimony only, but a *charge* that is entrusted to "my child Timothy," that he may "war the good warfare, holding faith and a good conscience" (1 Tim. i. 3-11, 18, 19; Tit. ii. 11, 12). This testimony and charge are of universal import; they belong to the ministry of Christ's servants and soldiers wherever exercised. And, in fact, the apostle dwells with greatest emphasis on Timothy's personal vocation in the second letter, when his commission at Ephesus is about to terminate, and he is in the act of summoning him to join himself at Rome.

It is no question, therefore, or ecclesiastical system or episcopal claims that weighs on the mind of the writer of these memorable letters. His supreme concern is for the maintenance of character and true doctrine in the Christian ministry, and through it, in the Church it serves. All that was local and of the occasion in the charge of the departing apostle to his children merges itself in that which belonged to their essential calling, as bearers of the message of the glory of the blessed God. The same call, conveyed through diversities of operation, is given to every true minister of Christ. Whatever human hands may take part in its bestowal, it is God's *charism*, His immediate and sovereign gift of grace. It is manifest, now as then, in the spirit of power and love and discipline. To all who bear it the great herald and apostle cries: *Preach the word. Guard the good deposit. Suffer hardship with me, as a good soldier of Christ Jesus.*

Paul's living utterance makes itself heard in these severe and lofty tones, not that of some actor on the ecclesiastical stage who has assumed his mask, some impostor hidden under the dead lion's skin. Words, thoughts, spirit in these letters alike speak for their great author—great in his latest work, wise and far-seeing in his care for the flock of Christ, skilful to fence its fold against the approaching wolves, as he had been mighty in word and doctrine in those wondrous years when he founded Gentile Christendom and built up the imperishable fabric of the New Testament theology. The second century never spoke as these epistles speak. By their voice we discover the apostle still alive, when all other clear record of him has perished amid the confusion of the latter years of Nero's rule. He has lived, happily, to send to the Church out of that time of fear and darkness a last watchword,—his message of farewell to the men he trusted most, and to us all through them. It is a word full of hope, and full of solemn warning,—a message of discipline, of courage, and of unchanging faith in Christ

ΠΙΣΤΟΣ Ο ΛΟΓΟΣ.

See index p. 280   355
See "Then shall son subject himself, that God all in all."

On Paul's appearance, on arriving at Lych
— "And he saw Paul coming, a man
small in size, handy-legged, bald headed,
well built, with eye brows meeting, rather
long nosed, full of grace. For sometimes he
looked like a man, and sometimes he had
the countenance of an angel."
                Acts of Paul & Thecla. Quoted in
            Robers Apostolic Age, page 133

www.ingramcontent.com/pod-product-compliance
Lightning Source LLC
Chambersburg PA
CBHW030552300426
44111CB00009B/952